GREGG TYPING FOR COLLEGES

COMPLETE COURSE

GREGG COLLEGE TYPING, SERIES FIVE

ALAN C. LLOYD, Ph.D.
Director of Career Advancement
The Olsten Corporation
Westbury, New York

ROBERT P. POLAND, Ph.D.
Professor, Business and
Distributive Education
Michigan State University
East Lansing, Michigan

ALBERT D. ROSSETTI, Ed.D.
Chairman, Department of
Business Education and
Office Systems Administration
Montclair State College
Montclair, New Jersey

FRED E. WINGER, Ed.D.
Former Professor, Office
Administration and
Business Education
Oregon State University
Corvallis, Oregon

ROBERT N. HANSON, Ed.D.
Dean, School of Business
and Management
Northern Michigan University
Marquette, Michigan

SCOT OBER, Ph.D
Chairperson, Department of
Administrative Services and
Business Teacher Education
Central Michigan University
Mount Pleasant, Michigan

JOHN L. ROWE, Ed.D.
Late Chairman, Business
and Vocational Education
University of North Dakota
Grand Forks, North Dakota

GREGG DIVISION/McGRAW-HILL BOOK COMPANY

NEW YORK • ATLANTA • DALLAS • ST. LOUIS
SAN FRANCISCO • AUCKLAND • BOGOTÁ
GUATEMALA • HAMBURG • LISBON
LONDON • MADRID • MEXICO
MONTREAL • NEW DELHI • PANAMA • PARIS
SAN JUAN • SÃO PAULO • SINGAPORE
SYDNEY • TOKYO • TORONTO

SPONSORING EDITOR: Audrey S. Rubin
EDITING SUPERVISORS: Matthew Fung, Gloria S. Lewis
DESIGN AND ART SUPERVISOR: Nancy Axelrod
COVER AND INTERIOR DESIGN: Nancy Axelrod
PRODUCTION SUPERVISOR: Laurence Charnow

COPY EDITOR: Susan Sobel
COVER AND INTERIOR PHOTOGRAPHER: Belott/Wolfson Photography, Inc.
TECHNICAL STUDIO: Burmar Technical Corporation

The equipment shown in the photographs on pages x and xii–xv was provided through the courtesy of IBM.

Library of Congress Cataloging in Publication Data
Main entry under title:

Gregg typing for colleges: complete course.

(Gregg college typing, series five)
Includes index.
1. Typewriting. I. Lloyd, Alan C. II. Series.
Z49.G832 1985   652.3'024   84-5675
ISBN 0-07-038320-0

GREGG COLLEGE TYPING, SERIES FIVE
GREGG TYPING FOR COLLEGES: Complete Course

Part of the text portion of this publication is published simultaneously as the work entitled *Gregg Typing for Colleges, Intensive Course.* Lessons 1–75 are also published simultaneously as part of the work entitled *Typing 75, Kit 1: Basic;* Lessons 76–150, as part of the work entitled *Typing 75, Kit 2: Intermediate;* and Lessons 151–225, as part of the work entitled *Typing 75, Kit 3: Expert.*

7890 J&HJ&H 891098

ISBN 0-07-038320-0

CONTENTS

PRODUCTION ASSIGNMENTS

INDEX

TIMED WRITINGS

3-Minute

Page	Words	Page	Words
41	81	60	87
44	81	63	87
47	81	65	90
48	84	69	90
52	84	72	90
55	84	74	90
57	87		

5-Minute

Page	Words	Page	Words
79	160	182	200
82	160	187	210
85	160	190	210
86	165	192	210
89	165	193	215
93	165	196	215
96	170	199	215
99	170	202	220
102	170	205	220
104	175	209	220
107	175	211	225
109	175	215	225
111	175	220	225
116	175	223	225
119	175	229	225
121	175	232	225
122	175	234	225
125	175	235	225
128	175	238	225
130	175	241	225
133	175	243	225
136	175	246	225
138	175	249	225
141	175	251	225
144	175	256	225
146	175	260	225
151	185	262	225
154	185	267	235
156	185	275	240
157	190	283	245
160	190	291	250
163	190	298	250
166	195	303	260
169	195	312	265
172	195	321	270
174	200	331	275
177	200	339	275
180	200		

Gregg College Typing, Series Five is a multicomponent instructional system designed to give the student and the instructor a high degree of flexibility and a high degree of success in meeting their respective goals. To facilitate the choice and use of materials, the core components of this teaching-learning system are available either in a kit format entitled Typing 75 or in a book format entitled Gregg Typing for Colleges.

TYPING 75 (The Kit Format)
Gregg College Typing, Series Five gives the student and the instructor the opportunity to obtain a complete kit of materials for each of the three semesters in the typing curriculum generally offered by colleges. Each of the Typing 75 kits, which are briefly described below, contains a softcover textbook, a pad of workbook materials, a cardboard easel for use as a copyholder, and a set of proofguides (self-check keys) to the practice and production exercises in the textbook.

The text in each kit contains instructional materials for 75 lessons. Each workbook—called a Workguide—provides learning guides, letterheads and other stationery for use in completing the production jobs, placement guides, and other materials. This new edition also contains a special section devoted to diagnostic typing, individualized skill building, and language arts.

TYPING 75, Kit 1: Basic. This kit provides the text, workguide, and proofguide materials for Lessons 1 through 75. Since this kit is designed for the beginning student, its major objectives are to develop touch control of the keyboard and proper typing techniques, build basic speed and accuracy skills, and provide practice in applying those basic skills to the production of letters, tables, reports, memorandums, forms, and other kinds of personal, personal-business, and business communications.

TYPING 75, Kit 2: Intermediate. This kit includes the text, workguide, and proofguide materials for Lessons 76 through 150. This second-semester course continues the development of basic typing skills and emphasizes the production of various kinds of business correspondence, tabulations, reports, and forms from unarranged and rough-draft copy sources.

TYPING 75, Kit 3: Expert. This kit, which covers Lessons 151 through 225, is designed for the third semester. After a brief review of basic production techniques, each unit in

this kit places the student in a different office situation where the emphasis is on such important modern office skills as editing, abstracting information, decision making, setting priorities, work flow, following directions, and working under pressure and with interruptions.

GREGG TYPING FOR COLLEGES (The Book Format)
For the convenience of those who wish to obtain the core instructional materials separately, the **Gregg College Typing, Series Five** system offers the following hardcover textbooks, workbooks, and self-check keys. In each instance, the content of the Gregg Typing for Colleges components is identical with that of the corresponding part or parts of the Typing 75 program.

Textbooks. Gregg Typing for Colleges, Intensive Course contains Lessons 1 through 150. The content and objectives of this two-semester hardcover text exactly match the content and objectives of the softcover texts in the Typing 75, Basic and Intermediate kits.

Gregg Typing for Colleges, Complete Course contains the text materials for Lessons 1 through 225. Thus it combines in one hardcover volume all the lessons contained in the three Typing 75 kits.

Workbooks. The Workguide for each semester's work is available separately for use with Gregg Typing for Colleges. These three workbooks are identical in content and purpose with those in the Typing 75 kits.

Self-Check Keys. The Proofguides packaged in the Typing 75 kits are also available separately for those who wish to use them with the Gregg Typing for Colleges textbooks.

GREGG TYPING, IPM (The Multimedia Format)
Gregg Typing, IPM is an audiovisual program designed to enable the student using Typing 75 or Gregg Typing for Colleges to complete all or any part of a two-semester course by the individual progress method (IPM). Each of the two major parts of the IPM program (Basic and Intermediate) includes a progress folder that guides and directs the student in using the text, workguide, and proofguide, as well as the slide and tape components of this multimedia teaching-learning system.

SUPPORTING MATERIALS
The **Gregg College Typing, Series Five** system includes the following additional components for use with either Typing 75 or Gregg Typing for Colleges.

Recordings. The Instructional Recordings for Lessons 1–75 consist of 30 cassettes (60 lessons) that provide the instructions for keyboard presentation, skill building practice, introduction to production typing (letters, reports, forms, and tabulations), and timed writings for the entire first semester. There is also a set of 12 cassettes (24 lessons) entitled Keyboard Presentation Tapes, designed for use only with those lessons in which new keys are introduced. The Instructional Recordings for Lessons 76–150 consist of 15 cassettes that provide the instructions for all skill building practice, production typing, and timed writings for the entire second semester. The Instructional Recordings for Lessons 151–225 provide the skill building practice, production typing, and timed writings for the entire third semester. In addition, they also contain realistic office-style dictation to accompany each of the integrated office projects. The recordings free the instructor to work with the students individually even in a group-instruction situation. The tapes also provide remedial work at any point in the course or makeup work for students who have been absent.

Progress Folder. Three folders provide a lesson-by-lesson guide to the text activities, performance goals, and related instructional recordings for Lessons 1 through 75, Lessons 76 through 150, and Lessons 151–225.

Instructor's Materials. The special materials provided for the instructor can be used with either the Typing 75 kits or with the Gregg Typing for Colleges texts. These instructional materials include a key to the drills and production exercises for each of the three semesters, a book of transparency masters, and a manual of teaching suggestions. A guide to using Gregg Typing, IPM is also available.

ACKNOWLEDGMENTS
We wish to express our appreciation to all the instructors and students who have used the previous editions and who have contributed much to this Fifth Edition.

THE AUTHORS

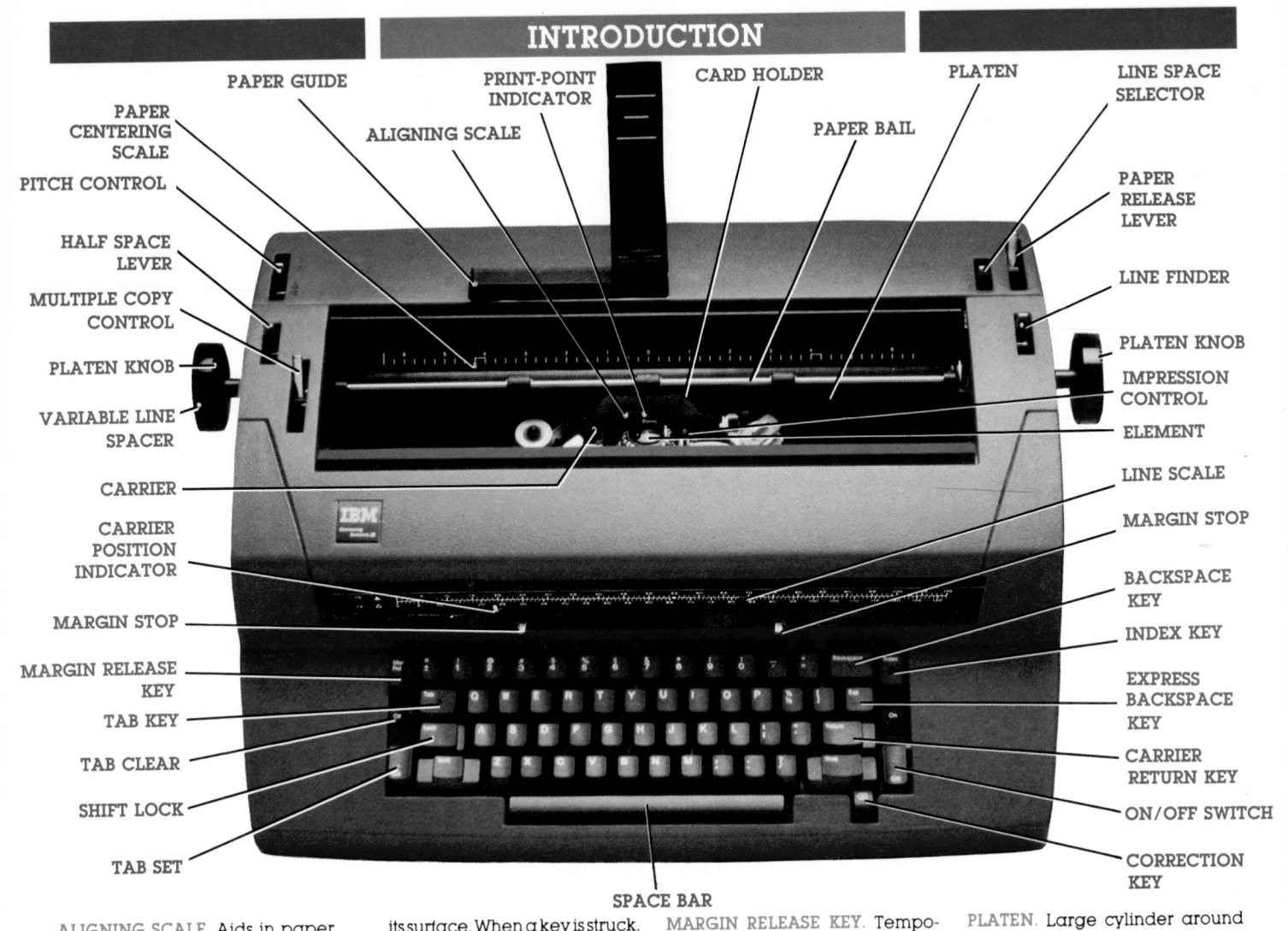

PAPER GUIDE
PRINT-POINT INDICATOR
CARD HOLDER
PLATEN
LINE SPACE SELECTOR
PAPER CENTERING SCALE
ALIGNING SCALE
PAPER BAIL
PAPER RELEASE LEVER
PITCH CONTROL
HALF SPACE LEVER
LINE FINDER
MULTIPLE COPY CONTROL
PLATEN KNOB
PLATEN KNOB
IMPRESSION CONTROL
VARIABLE LINE SPACER
ELEMENT
CARRIER
LINE SCALE
CARRIER POSITION INDICATOR
MARGIN STOP
MARGIN STOP
BACKSPACE KEY
MARGIN RELEASE KEY
INDEX KEY
TAB KEY
EXPRESS BACKSPACE KEY
TAB CLEAR
CARRIER RETURN KEY
SHIFT LOCK
ON/OFF SWITCH
TAB SET
CORRECTION KEY
SPACE BAR

ALIGNING SCALE. Aids in paper realignment.

BACKSPACE KEY. Moves carrier to the left 1 space at a time. Continues backspacing as long as it is depressed.

CARD HOLDER. Holds cards and envelopes against the platen.

CARRIER. Moves from left to right, carrying the typing element across the paper.

CARRIER POSITION INDICATOR. Points to the place on the line scale at which the machine is ready to print.

CARRIER RETURN KEY. Returns carrier to the start of a new line. Continues advancing the paper as long as it is depressed.

CORRECTION KEY (only on selected models). Backspaces to error and raises lift-off tape to working position.

ELEMENT. A ball containing letters, numbers, and symbols on

its surface. When a key is struck, the element turns and prints the corresponding character.

EXPRESS BACKSPACE KEY. Moves carrier rapidly to the left without advancing the paper.

HALF SPACE LEVER. Moves carrier a half space to the left.

IMPRESSION CONTROL (to the right of the element). Controls the force with which the element strikes the paper.

INDEX KEY. Advances the paper without returning carrier to the left margin.

LINE FINDER. Permits leaving the original typing line temporarily to type a superscript, subscript, and so on.

LINE SCALE. Indicates horizontal spaces across length of platen. Guides in setting margins and tab stops.

LINE SPACE SELECTOR. Controls the amount of space between lines of type.

MARGIN RELEASE KEY. Temporarily unlocks the margin.

MARGIN STOPS. Used to set left and right margins.

MULTIPLE COPY CONTROL. Adjusts the position of the platen for varying thickness of typing material (such as carbon packs).

ON/OFF SWITCH. Controls power to the motor.

PAPER BAIL. Holds paper against the platen.

PAPER CENTERING SCALE. Aids in centering any width of paper in the machine.

PAPER GUIDE. Guides and aligns paper as it is inserted into the machine.

PAPER RELEASE LEVER. Used to remove or straighten paper.

PITCH CONTROL (only on selected models). Switches the horizontal spacing between 10 pitch (pica) and 12 pitch (elite).

PLATEN. Large cylinder around which the paper is rolled.

PLATEN KNOBS. Used to turn the platen by hand.

PRINT-POINT INDICATOR. Shows the exact point on the line at which the machine will print.

SHIFT LOCK. Locks the shift key in position so that the machine prints in all capitals.

SPACE BAR. Moves carrier to the right 1 space at a time. Continues spacing as long as it is depressed.

TAB CLEAR. Removes tab stops.

TAB KEY. Releases the carrier so it moves to a point where a tab stop has been set.

TAB SET. Sets tab stops at desired points.

VARIABLE LINE SPACER. Used to make slight vertical adjustments.

The *Series Five* program has been specially designed to help you develop your typewriting skills through a carefully planned, step-by-step process. To be sure that you understand the terms, procedures, and directions used throughout this book, read this introduction and refer to it whenever you have a question or problem.

PROCEDURES AND SIGNALS

STARTING A LESSON

¹Line: 60 spaces ²Tab: 5
³Spacing: single ⁴Drills: 3X
⁵Proofguide: 49
⁶Workguide: 155
⁷Tape: 31A
⁸Goals: To improve speed/accuracy; to make correct word-division and line-ending decisions.

Each lesson heading includes a display to tell what machine adjustments are needed at the start of the lesson and what supplementary materials will be needed somewhere in the lesson. For instance, the example in the margin tells you to (1) use a 60-space line, (2) set a tab stop for a 5-space paragraph indention, (3) use single spacing, and (4) type each drill line three times. In addition, (5) the proof, or key, for this lesson is on Proofguide page 49, and (6) the forms you will need to type the production jobs are on Workguide page 155. (7) The recorded instruction for the lesson is on Tape 31A, and (8) your goal for the lesson will be to improve speed/accuracy and word division skills.

USING COACHNOTES

20 ↓12
→ Mr. Edward Whitman
Smith & Whitman Inc.
1047 Fifth Avenue
New York, NY 10028

LEAVE 1 SPACE BETWEEN STATE AND ZIP CODE.

Marginal notes and arrows are sometimes used to remind you of line length, spacing, and so on. These aids are gradually reduced as you gain experience in typing each kind of job.

MARGINAL NOTES. Some jobs have special explanations with them, positioned as near to the point of use as possible. Always look for and read marginal notes before you begin to type.

ARROWS. *Horizontal arrows* (→) indicate the point at which to begin typing. For example, →*20* means to begin typing 20 spaces from the left edge. *Center arrows* (*CENTER* →) are sometimes used to show you the vertical center of the job. *Down arrows* (↓) indicate how many lines down the next line should be typed. For example, ↓*12* means to begin typing on line 12.

BUILDING SKILL

aw awaken awhile   aw awaken awhile
aw awaken awhile   se severe seized
aw awaken awhile   rd ordeal burden

se severe seized   aw awaken awhile
se severe seized   se severe seized
se severe seized   rd ordeal burden

rd ordeal burden   aw awaken awhile
rd ordeal burden   se severe seized
rd ordeal burden   rd ordeal burden

WARMUPS. Line 1 of each lesson's Warmup builds speed, line 2 builds accuracy, and line 3 builds skill in number typing. The three lines of the Warmup provide practice on all the number and alphabetic keys.

DRILLS. When typing drill lines:

For speed gain, repeat each *individual* line the designated number of times.

For accuracy gain, repeat each *group* of lines (as though it were a paragraph) the designated number of times.

TIMED WRITINGS. All timed writings in this text are the exact length needed to reach the speed goal that is set for each unit, as shown on the first page of each Part. Thus if you finish the timed writing, you know you have reached your speed goal.

The syllabic intensity (the average number of syllables per word) of all timed writings is between 1.30 and 1.40 in Lessons 1–75, between 1.40 and 1.50 in Lessons 76–150, and between 1.50 and 1.60 in Lessons 151–225.

FIGURING SPEED

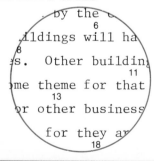
...by the c
⁶
...ildings will ha
⁸
...s. Other building
¹¹
...me theme for that
¹³
...r other business
...for they ar
¹⁸

Your speed on a timed writing is the number of words you typed divided by the number of minutes you typed. Round off a fraction to the nearest whole number.

SPEED MARKERS. All timed writings in this book contain small numbers above the copy. When you take a 5-minute timed writing, your speed is prefigured for you: the highest number that you reach is your *wam* (word-a-minute) speed.

PRODUCTION WORD COUNT (PWC). All word counts given in the production jobs include credit for nonprinting machine operations: (1) triple count for anything centered or underscored, (2) 5 strokes for an extra carrier/carriage return or use of the tabulator, and (3) 10 strokes for any hand operation, such as setting a tab stop.

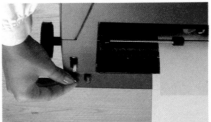

COUNTING THE SPACES

Does	"Jim	asked,
my	meeting	start
at	12:30	today?"

When a key or the space bar is tapped, the carrier or carriage advances 1 space. On most typewriters each space is the same size because most machines space uniformly, as though they were printing on graph paper. These spaces can be counted by using the line scale. This scale shows a number every fifth or tenth space so that you can find any particular space across the width of the paper.

BASIC MACHINE ADJUSTMENTS

Each machine also has a special marker (called the carrier position indicator or the print-point indicator) that points to the space at which the machine is ready to print. For example, if the marker points to 58, the machine is ready to print at 58.

PICA AND ELITE SPACING

aaaaaaaaaaaa Pica
aaaaaaaaaaaa Elite

Typewriters are generally equipped with either pica or elite type size. Pica type is larger and prints 10 characters to an inch. Elite type prints 12 characters to an inch. Thus a full line of typing on standard paper that is 8½ inches wide will contain 85 pica characters (8½ × 10) or 102 elite characters (8½ × 12).

Find out which type size your machine has by typing the letter a 12 times and comparing your typed copy with the illustration at the left.

INSERTING AND REMOVING THE PAPER

Before you insert the paper, confirm the paper guide setting. Then follow these steps:

1. Pull paper bail forward or up.
2. With your left hand, place the paper behind the platen and against the paper guide. Use your right hand to turn the right platen knob clockwise to draw in the paper. Advance the paper until about a third of the sheet is visible.
3. Check that the paper is straight by aligning the left edges of the front and the back against the paper guide.
4. If the paper does not align, pull the paper release lever forward, straighten the paper, and then push the paper release lever back.
5. Place the paper bail back against the paper. Adjust the small rollers to divide the paper evenly. (To prepare to type, turn the paper back until about a quarter inch shows above the paper bail.)
6. To remove the paper, pull the paper bail forward. Then pull the paper release lever with your right hand as you silently draw out the paper with your left hand. Finally return the paper release lever to its normal position.

SETTING THE LINE SPACE SELECTOR

The amount of space between lines of typing is controlled by the line space selector. Set it at 1 for single spacing (*no* blank space between lines) or at 2 for double spacing (*1* blank line between typed lines).

Some machines also have 1½, 2½, or 3 (triple) spacing.

If your machine is set for single spacing and you want to leave a blank line between different parts of your work (for example, when going from one drill to the next), simply return the carrier or carriage twice instead of once.

SETTING MARGIN STOPS

MARGIN STOPS. Margin stops for most typewriters can be set by simply pushing in the left and right margin stops and sliding them to the correct settings on the line scale. If this procedure does not work on the machine you are using, refer to the operating instructions provided by the manufacturer or ask your instructor for assistance.

CENTERING POINT

Three common methods for selecting a centering point are explained below:

1. Set the paper guide at 0 and insert a sheet of paper. If you are using a pica machine, the centering point is 42. On an elite machine, it is 51. (Use 50 to simplify your calculations.)

2. The second method is to use 50 as the centering point for *any* machine, pica or elite. Follow these steps to determine where the paper guide belongs:

a. Mark the center of a sheet of paper by creasing it.

b. Insert the sheet and center the crease at 50.

c. Move the paper guide until its blade edge is against the left edge of the paper.

(Note on the margin scale where you have set the paper guide and be sure it is in the same position whenever you begin typing.)

3. Another method is to use the center of the platen as the centering point. (The center is usually marked by a small dot on the line scale.) If you use the center of the platen as your centering point, move the paper guide to the mark indicated on the paper scale.

PLANNING MARGINS

Placement guides for letters and reports are commonly expressed in inches. The conversions necessary for you to know are as follows:

CONVERTING INCHES TO SPACES

	4"	5"	6"
Number of inches in the line			
Pica spaces (10 per inch)	40	50	60
Elite spaces (12 per inch)	48	60	72
Elite line, "rounded off"	50	60	70

To determine the left margin, subtract half the desired line length from the center point. To set the right margin, add half the desired line length to the center point plus 5 extra spaces to allow for line-ending decisions.

COMMON MARGIN SETTINGS

Line Length	Center at 50		Center at 42	
	Left	Right	Left	Right
40 spaces	30	75	22	67
50 spaces	25	80	17	72
60 spaces	20	85	12	77
70 spaces	15	90	7	82

CENTERING

HORIZONTAL. To center a word or group of words:

1. Move the carrier or carriage to the center.
2. Say each pair of strokes to yourself (including spaces) and depress the backspace key once for each pair of strokes. Do not backspace for an odd letter left over at the end.
3. Starting at the point to which you have backspaced, type the material.

SPREAD. To spread-center a word or line, leave 1 space between letters and 3 spaces between words. An easy way to do this is to backspace once for *each* stroke and space between words, *except* the last one.

VERTICAL. Most typewriters provide 6 lines of space to a vertical inch. A standard sheet of paper, 11 inches long, provides 11 × 6 = 66 possible lines of type. To center the material within the 66 lines:

1. Count the lines (including blank ones) that the material will occupy when typed.
2. Subtract that number from 66 lines (33 on a half sheet).
3. Divide the difference by 2 (drop any fraction) to get the number of the line on which to begin typing.

NOTE: For material to *look* centered, the bottom margin should be a line or two deeper than the top margin.

SETTING TAB STOPS

Setting tab stops using the machine's tabulator mechanism will enable you to indent consistently. To set tab stops:

1. Confirm margin settings.
2. Clear all tab stops already set. Move the carrier or carriage to the right margin and then hold down the tab clear key as you return the carrier or carriage.
3. To set a new tab, depress the space bar the number of spaces you wish to indent (usually 5) and press the tab set key.
4. To test the setting, return the carrier or carriage to the left margin and then firmly depress the tab key. The carrier or carriage should move directly to the point where you set the tab stop.

DAILY ROUTINE

Perform these steps at the start of each class:

1. Arrange your work area: typing paper at the left of the typewriter, front edge of the typewriter even with front edge of the table, book at the right of the typewriter and tilted for ease of reading.

2. Open the textbook to the correct lesson and note the directions in the heading.

3. Detach the designated Workguide and Proofguide pages.

4. Check that the paper guide is in the correct position.

5. Set the line space lever, margin stops, and tab stops as specified in the directions in the lesson heading.

6. Insert a sheet of paper; straighten it if necessary.

7. Assume the correct typing position, place your hands on home keys, and prepare to type.

TYPING POSTURE

Typing speed and accuracy are both affected by your posture.

Body centered opposite the J key, leaning forward.

Head erect, turned to face the book.

Feet apart and firmly braced.

Wrists straight and fingers curved. Position your finger tips on the home keys: left hand on A, S, D, and F; right hand on J, K, L, and ; (semicolon).

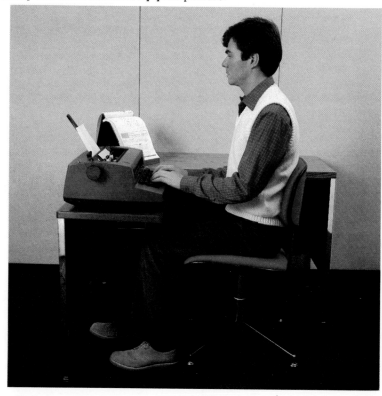

WORD PROCESSING

The symbol at the left is designed to call your attention to information about word processing concepts or applications that you will encounter throughout this text. These special notations are provided to help you understand how word processing equipment functions if used in place of a typewriter to format various production assignments.

Although you may not have access to word processing equipment at this time, you should be familiar with its capabilities: you can be sure that you will have occasion to use it—either in school or on the job—in the very near future.

LETTERS

MODIFIED-BLOCK (Standard Punctuation)

MODIFIED-BLOCK WITH INDENTED
PARAGRAPHS (Standard Punctuation)

BLOCK (Open Punctuation)

SIMPLIFIED

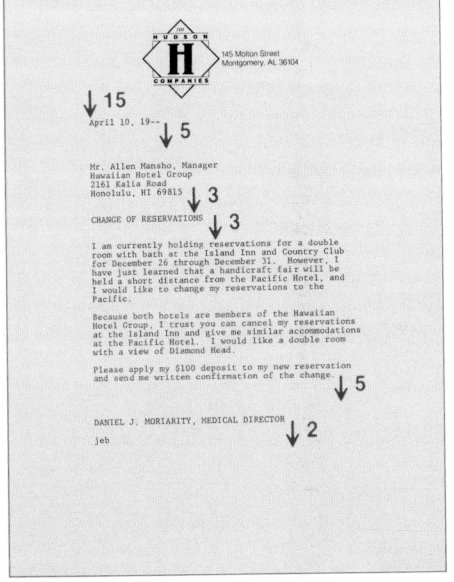

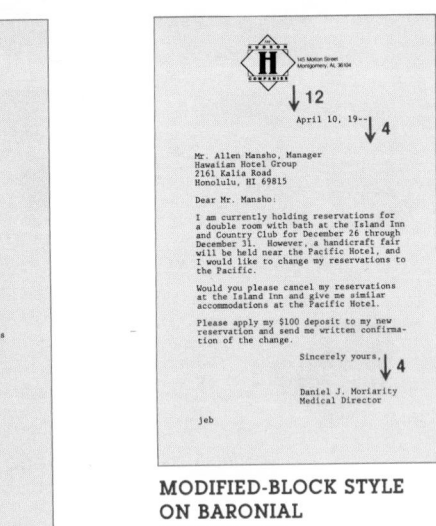

MODIFIED-BLOCK STYLE ON
MONARCH STATIONERY

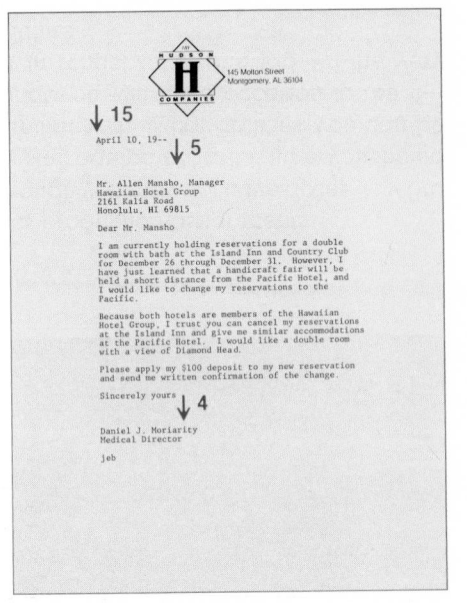

MODIFIED-BLOCK STYLE
ON BARONIAL
STATIONERY

LETTER STYLES

Modified-Block. Date and closing lines begin at center.

Modified-Block With Indented Paragraphs. Date and closing lines begin at center; paragraphs are indented 5 or more spaces.

Block. All lines begin at left margin.

Simplified. All lines begin at left margin. Salutation and complimentary closing are omitted. Subject line and writer's identification are typed in all-capital letters.

PUNCTUATION STYLES

Standard. Contains a colon after the salutation and a comma after the complimentary closing.

Open. Contains no punctuation after these two lines.

STATIONERY SIZES

Standard: 8½ × 11 inches; line length: 50 pica/60 elite

Monarch: 7¼ × 10½ inches; line length: 50 pica/60 elite

Baronial: 5½ × 8½ inches; line length: 40 pica/50 elite

```
                 November 3, 19--  ↓2
                 EXPRESS MAIL  ↓3

Northland Industries
124 South 67 Street
Baton Rouge, LA 70801  ↓2
Attention:  Legal Department  ↓2
Ladies and Gentlemen:  ↓2
Subject:  Aramco Proposal  ↓2
We have carefully reviewed the plan submitted by
Aramco on October 15 and have found that it does not
```

```
will then schedule a meeting with the three of you
so that we can make final plans.

                 Sincerely yours,  ↓2
                 FERRIS ELECTRONICS, INC.  ↓4


                 Eugene Ferris, President
elw
Enclosure
cc Cecelia Esquer  ↓2
PS:  If you would like me to schedule the meeting
during our spring conference, please let me know.
```

LETTER PARTS

Mailing Notation. A mailing notation is typed in solid capitals a double space below the date.

Attention Line. An attention line is sometimes used when a letter is addressed to a company rather than to an individual. It is typed after the inside address, with 1 blank line above and below it. An appropriate salutation for a letter containing an attention line is either *Ladies and Gentlemen:*, or *Gentlemen:*, or *Ladies:*.

Subject Line. A subject line is sometimes used to indicate the topic of the letter. Either the words *Subject, Re,* or *In Re* may be used. The subject line is typed below the salutation, with 1 blank line above and below it.

Company Name in Closing Lines. If the company name is included in the closing lines, it should be typed in all-capital letters below the complimentary closing, with 1 blank line above and 3 blank lines after it.

Enclosure Notation. Whenever an item is to be enclosed with the letter, an enclosure notation should be used. It is typed a single space below the reference initials. For more than one item, type *2 Enclosures, 3 Enclosures,* and so on.

Carbon Copy Notation. If someone other than the addressee is to receive a copy of the letter, a carbon copy (*cc*) notation is typed on the line below the reference initials (or on the line below the enclosure notation if there is one).

If the writer of the letter sends a copy to someone and does not want the addressee to know about it, a "blind" carbon copy (*bcc*) notation is typed only on the carbon copies of the letter. A bcc notation may be typed on line 7 at the left margin or a double space below the last line of the closing lines.

Postscript Notation. If a postscript is added to the letter, it is typed as the last item in the letter, preceded by 1 blank line. If the paragraphs in the letter are indented, the first line of the postscript should be indented as well.

```
↓7
Mr. Alan P. Wunsch
Page 2
September 15, 19--  ↓3

facilities that could be used for promoting the motel.
You will be receiving a copy of the promotional bro-
```

```
↓7
Mr. Alan P. Wunsch    Page 2    September 15, 19--  ↓3

facilities that could be used for promoting the motel.
You will be receiving a copy of the promotional bro-
chures in a few days.  Please make any suggestions
```

Two-Page Letters. One-page letters that contain more than 225 words and all two-page letters should be typed on a 6-inch line (60 pica/70 elite). The bottom margin should be at least 1 inch, and the top margin for the second page (which is typed on plain paper) should also be 1 inch. The heading (consisting of the addressee's name, the page number, and the date) may be blocked at the left margin or displayed in one line across the page.

```
the anniversary sale.  I've enclosed the following
items for your consideration and approval:  ↓2
1.  A news release on the history of your company.  ↓2
2.  The script for three 30-second radio spots to
    be aired over local radio stations in August.  ↓2
Please give me a call after you have had a chance
to study these items so that I can begin to prepare
```

Enumeration. An enumeration in the body of the letter is begun at the left margin, and turnover lines are indented 4 spaces. Leave 2 spaces following the number and period. Lines within an enumeration are single-spaced, with double spacing between the items.

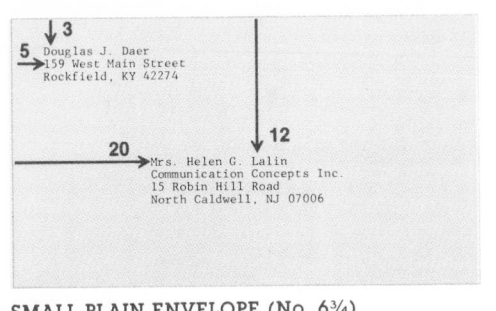

SMALL PLAIN ENVELOPE (No. 6¾)

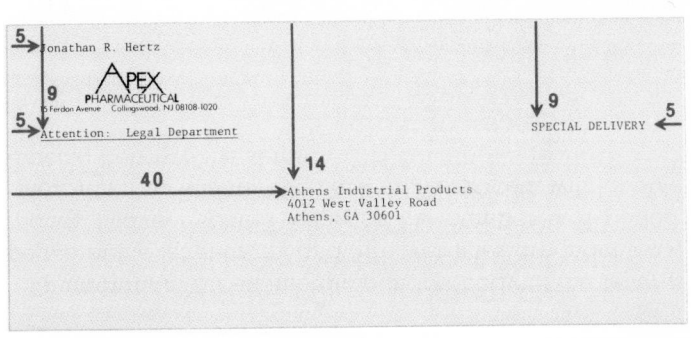

LARGE BUSINESS ENVELOPE (No. 10)

RETURN ADDRESS. If it is printed, center or block the writer's name over it. To type a return address, begin ½ inch (about 5 spaces) from the left edge on line 3; block and single-space the lines. The personal title *Mr.* or *Ms.* should not be used.

ON-ARRIVAL DIRECTIONS. Type attention lines and terms such as *Personal* on line 9 in underscored capital and lowercase letters, aligned on the left with the return address.

SPECIAL MAIL SERVICE. Type on line 9, to end ½ inch (about 5 spaces) from the right edge, any special requests such as *Special Delivery* or *Airmail* (overseas only).

ADDRESS. Begin the name and address on a postal card or small envelope (No. 6¾ is 6½ × 3⅝ inches) on line 12, 2 inches (about 20 spaces) from the left edge; begin the name and address on a large envelope (No. 10 is 9½ × 4⅛ inches) on line 14, 4 inches (about 40 spaces) from the edge. Single-space and block all lines, with city, state, and ZIP Code on the same line. The state name should be typed with its two-letter abbreviation with 1 space before the ZIP Code.

MEMORANDUMS

INTEROFFICE MEMORANDUM (Plain Paper)

INTEROFFICE MEMORANDUM (Printed Form)

When typing an interoffice memorandum on plain paper or on letterhead stationery, use a 5-inch line (50 pica/60 elite). Begin typing the heading information on line 7 (half sheet) or on line 13 (full sheet).

When typing a memorandum on a printed form, set the left margin at the point where the heading information aligns and set the right margin to equal the left (by estimate). Type the insertions 2 or 3 spaces after the guide words, and align the words at the bottom with the guide words.

Separate the body and the heading by 2 blank lines. The writer's initials, if used, are typed either at the center or aligned with the date. Reference initials should be placed at the left margin a double space below the last line of the body or the writer's initials.

TABLES

TITLE. Centered in all-capital letters and single-spaced.

SUBTITLE. Centered a double space below the title.

BODY. Centered horizontally, with 6 blank spaces between columns; single-spaced or double-spaced.

COLUMN. Word columns align at the left; number columns align at the right.

```
              COSTS OF DOING BUSINESS
               IN THE WESTERN REGION      ↓2
             Average Cost per Unit Sold   ↓3

                                          Cost
             Component      Increase     This Year

         Manufacturing      16.9%         $236

         Taxes               8.7%          125

         Personnel          15.8%          110

         Advertising         8.0%           81

         Other              12.5%            9

         TOTALS             61.9%         $561
```

COLUMN HEADINGS. Centered and underscored over the column.
NOTE: The $ sign appears only before the first number and the total.

The % sign is repeated after each number if the column heading does not clearly indicate that the figures under it are percentages.

FORMATTING A TABLE

1. Select the key line, an imaginary line made up of the longest item in each column or column heading plus 6 blank spaces between columns.

2. From the center of the paper, backspace once for every 2 characters or spaces in the key line (ignore any extra stroke), and set the left margin at the point to which you have backspaced.

3. From the left margin, space across the paper once for *each* letter and space in the longest item of the first column plus the 6 blank spaces, and set a tab stop. Repeat the procedure for each column.

4. To determine on which line from the top to begin typing, subtract the number of lines (including blank lines) in the table from either 66 (a full sheet of paper) or 33 (half sheet) and divide by 2. Drop any fraction.

FORMATTING SPECIAL TABLES

Ruled Tables. In order to allow 1 blank line above and below each horizontal rule in a ruled table, single-space *before* each rule and double-space *after* each rule. Begin the horizontal rule at the left margin and extend it exactly even with the last character at the right.

Indent table footnotes 5 spaces. (In open tables, use a 1-inch line to separate a footnote from the table body.)

Boxed Tables. A boxed table contains both horizontal and vertical rules. The vertical rules are drawn with a black pen and ruler after the table has been typed. The boxed format is always used if a table has a braced head—a head that applies to more than one column. The braced head is centered over the column heads it spans.

If a table has a number, it is centered a double space above the title in upper- and lowercase letters.

FORMATTING COLUMN HEADS

For a heading that is narrower than the column, center the heading over the column.

1. Subtract the number of spaces in the column head from the number of spaces in the longest item of the column.

2. Divide the answer by 2 (drop any fraction) and indent the column head that number of spaces. In the example above, $13 - 9 = 4$ and $4 \div 2 = 2$. Indent the column head 2 spaces.

For a heading that is wider than the column, center the column under the heading.

1. Subtract the number of spaces in the longest item in the column from the number of spaces in the heading.

2. Divide the answer by 2 (drop any fraction) and indent the column that number of spaces. In the example above, $8 - 5 = 3$ and $3 \div 2 = 1\frac{1}{2}$ (drop the fraction). Indent the column 1 space.

```
      PROPOSED SALARY INCREASES*
         Effective July 1, 19--   ↓1

    Name          Increase      New Salary  ↓2
                                            ↓1
Chase, Paul G.     $ 1,708      $ 30,168    ↓2
Frazier, Maurice     4,090        44,990
Johnson, Sandra A.   2,800        30,800
McDonald, Janice     4,512        42,112
Moratti, Lori L.     1,749        30,894
Wilson, Michael      1,324        34,424
                                            ↓1
TOTAL              $16,183      $213,388     ↓2
                                            ↓1
    *Subject to Board approval.             ↓2
```
RULED TABLE

```
                    Table 1-7  ↓2
               PRODUCTION SUMMARY  ↓1

                         Shift ↓1        ↓2
Model
Series    First     Second    Third    ↓2
                                        ↓2
  100     2,040      1,780     1,470   ↓2
  200     1,359      1,168       986
  300     1,063        863       529
  400       859        745       485
  500       267        235       169   ↓2
                                        ↓1
TOTAL     5,588      4,791     3,639   ↓2
                                        ↓1
```
BOXED TABLE

↓16

OFFICE COMMUNICATION SERVICES AND DEVICES ↓13

A Report Prepared for

BEAS 201: Administrative Management

Professor Richard Newberry ↓13

Prepared by

Anna Duarte

November 21, 19--

TITLE PAGE

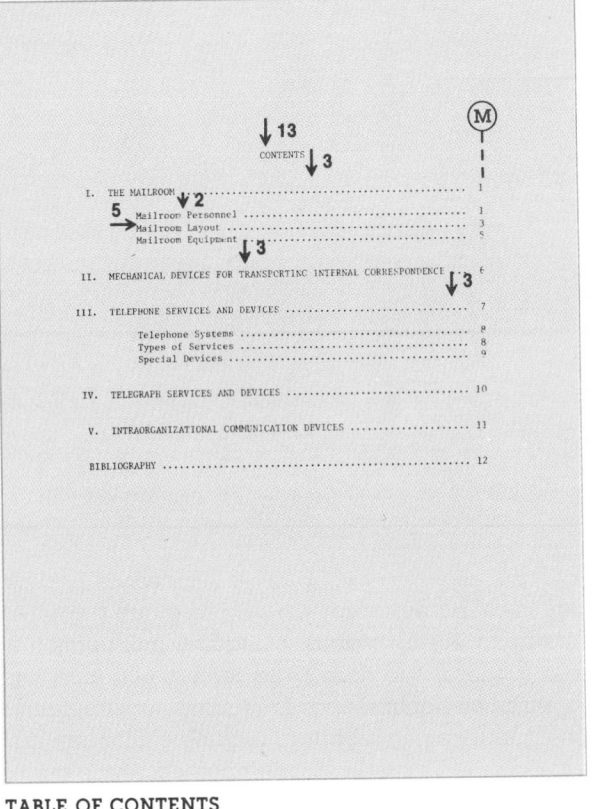

↓13

CONTENTS ↓3

I. THE MAILROOM ↓2 1

     5 → Mailroom Personnel 1
     Mailroom Layout 3
     Mailroom Equipment ↓3 5

II. MECHANICAL DEVICES FOR TRANSPORTING INTERNAL CORRESPONDENCE ↓3 6

III. TELEPHONE SERVICES AND DEVICES 7

     Telephone Systems 8
     Types of Services 8
     Special Devices 9

IV. TELEGRAPH SERVICES AND DEVICES 10

V. INTRAORGANIZATIONAL COMMUNICATION DEVICES 11

BIBLIOGRAPHY 12

TABLE OF CONTENTS

↓13

TYPING FORMAL REPORTS ↓2

By Alan Schwartz ↓3

Typing formal reports is not a difficult task if you just take the time to study the technical aspects involved. This report discusses report headings, page numbers, margins, and footnotes. ↓3

HEADINGS ↓2

The major heading in a report is the title. It should be centered in all-capital letters on line 13. The body of the report begins on the third line below the title or by-line.

Side Headings. A side heading (such as the one shown above) is typed at the left margin in all-capital letters. There should be 2 blank lines above the side heading and 1 blank line below it.

Paragraph Headings. Paragraph headings are indented and typed a double space below the preceding paragraph. The words of the headings are capitalized, underscored, and followed by a period. The text begins on the same line. ↓3

PAGE NUMBERING ↓2

The first page of the body of the report is counted as page 1 but is not numbered. All the other pages are numbered at the top right on line 7, with the first line of text beginning on line 10. The page number of a special section (such as the bibliography) is centered 5 lines from the bottom of the page.

UNBOUND REPORT (Page 1)

↓7

Page 2 ↓3

MARGINS

The following margins should be used for a report: ↓2

1. A 2-inch top margin on the first page and a 1-inch top margin on all other pages of the body of the report. ↓2

2. A 1-inch bottom margin on all pages.

3. A 6-inch line (60 pica spaces and 70 elite spaces). ↓3

FOOTNOTES

Footnotes are used to supply the reader with specific references to sources and to provide any supplementary information.[1] Quotations from these sources should be footnoted. Concerning direct quotations, Turabian advises, "Short . . . quotations should be incorporated into the text of the paper and enclosed in double quotation marks."[2] With regard to longer quotations, Tyne gives this guideline: ↓2 5 →

5 → A quotation that runs four or more typewritten lines should be set off from the text in single spacing and indented five spaces from both margins, with no quotation marks at the beginning or end. Double-space before and after the quotation.[3] ↓2

Footnote citations are typed at the bottom of the same page on which the references occur and are separated from the text by a line of underscores 2 inches long. Single-space before and double-space after the divider line. Each footnote is indented and single-spaced, with double spacing used between footnotes. ↓1

↓2

1. William Coyle, Research Papers, 5th ed., Bobbs-Merrill Educational Publishing, Indianapolis, 1980, p. 123. ↓2

2. Kate L. Turabian, A Manual for Writers of Term Papers, Theses, and Dissertations, 4th ed., The University of Chicago Press, Chicago, 1973, p. 64.

3. Robert L. Tyne, "Let's Agree on the Basics," Journal of Academic Research, Vol. 18, No. 3, p. 46, September 1982.

UNBOUND REPORT WITH FOOTNOTES (Page 2)

Whenever you use the words or ideas of another person in a report, you must provide the reader with the source of the author's work. This is commonly done by using (1) author/year citations, (2) endnotes, and (3) footnotes. ↓3

AUTHOR/YEAR CITATIONS ↓3

Smith (1982) recommends the use of author/year citations. In this method, the last name of the author and the year of publication are inserted within parentheses at an appropriate point in the text. However, if the name of the author occurs in the textual discussion, only the year of publication is cited within parentheses. The reader can then easily refer to the bibliography to find the needed references.

Advantages. One of the reasons given for the growing popularity of this style of citation is that it gives the most important information about the source right in the body of the text so that the reader does not have to search for it; yet this method is not as distracting to the reader as footnotes might be (Reif and Wostophul, 1980).

Another advantage often cited is that this style is easier for the typist to format; thus fewer errors are likely to result (Bruner, 1979).

Quotations. Spavin (1971, p. 34) states, "When using a direct quotation, the writer should also insert the page number of the quotation within parentheses." Other authorities suggest including a page reference whenever any specific item of information is given; that is, omitting the page reference when the source as a whole is being cited but including it whenever only a certain item of information from the source is being cited.

LEFT-BOUND REPORT WITH AUTHOR/YEAR STYLE OF REFERENCES

MARGINS

The following margins should be used for a report: ↓2

1. A 2-inch top margin on the first page and a 1-inch top margin on all other pages of the body of the report. ↓2

2. A 1-inch bottom margin on all pages. ↓2

3. A 6-inch line (60 pica spaces and 70 elite spaces). ↓2

If the report is to be bound at the left, the left margin must be larger to accommodate the binding. The easiest way to provide for the extra space is to move the paper guide and paper 1/4 inch to the left. Type all report pages, including the title page and bibliography, with this wider left margin. ↓3

ENDNOTES

Endnotes are citations placed at the end of a report. They perform the same function as footnotes. Footnotes are used to supply the reader with specific references to sources and to provide any supplementary information.[1] Quotations from these sources should be noted. Concerning direct quotations, Turabian advises, "Short . . . quotations should be incorporated into the text of the paper and enclosed in double quotation marks."[2] With regard to longer quotations, Tyne gives this guideline:

5→ A quotation that runs four or more typewritten lines should be set off from the text in single spacing and indented five spaces from both margins, with no quotation marks at the beginning or end. Double-space before and after the quotation.[3] ←5 ↓2
↓2

Endnotes are typed on a separate page. The notes are single-spaced, with double spacing between them. The identifying number is typed on the line (not as a superior figure), followed by a period and 2 spaces.

LEFT-BOUND REPORT WITH ENDNOTE REFERENCES

↓13
NOTES ↓3

1. William Coyle, Research Papers, 5th ed., Bobbs-Merrill Educational Publishing, Indianapolis, 1980, p. 123. ↓2

2. Kate L. Turabian, A Manual for Writers of Term Papers, Theses, and Dissertations, 4th ed., The University of Chicago Press, Chicago, 1973, p. 64.

3. Robert L. Tyne, "Let's Agree on the Basics," Journal of Academic Research, Vol. 18, No. 3, p. 46, September 1982.

4. A secondary use of footnotes or endnotes is to provide additional information that is worthwhile to include but that would disrupt the flow of thought if introduced into the text. This is an example of such a note.

5. Robert Lipsom, "Who Thought of It First?" The Wall Street Journal, January 18, 1982, p. 1, col. 4.

6. Turabian, p. 69.

8
↑5

ENDNOTES

↓13
BIBLIOGRAPHY ↓3

Black, James, How to Get Results From Interviews, McGraw-Hill Book
10→ Company, New York, 1970. ↓2

Box, W. F., "A Job Seeker's Viewpoint," The Personnel Administrator, September 1977, pp. 51-55.

Distributive Education Clubs of America, Preparing for the Job Interview, Educational Association Clearinghouse, San Francisco, 1981.

Kahn, R. L., and C. F. Cannell, The Dynamics of Interviewing, John Wiley & Sons, Inc., New York, 1968.

Weiss, Judith, et al., "An Inquiry Into the Effects of Listening," Modern Business Communication, Vol. 14, No. 8, pp. 25-32, December 1981.

"Yes—Interviewing Skills Can Be Taught," Current Business, June 19, 1983, pp. 39-42.

9
↑5

BIBLIOGRAPHY

REFERENCE SECTION

WORD DIVISION

It is generally not necessary to divide a word at the end of a line. If it is necessary, however, the three absolute rules of word division must always be observed. If possible, the five preferential rules should also be observed.

ABSOLUTE RULES

1. Do not divide words pronounced as one syllable (*straight, shopped*), contractions (*couldn't, doesn't*), or abbreviations (*UNESCO, c.o.d.*).
2. Divide words only between syllables. If you are uncertain where a syllable ends, consult a dictionary.
3. Leave at least three characters (the last will be a hyphen) on the upper line and carry at least three characters (the last three characters) to the next line. Thus *de- tract* and *bet- ter,* but not *a- round* or *luck- y.*

PREFERENTIAL RULES

4. Divide compound words either at the hyphen (*self- sacrifice*) or where the two words join to make a solid compound. Thus *after- noon,* not *af- ternoon.*
5. If a one-letter syllable occurs in the middle of a word, divide after it; thus *criti- cal* is preferred to *crit- ical.* However, if two separately sounded vowels occur together, divide between them; thus *vari- ation* is preferred to *varia- tion.*
6. Divide after, not within, a prefix. Divide before, not within, a suffix. Thus *inter- fere* is preferred to *in- terfere* and *pay- able* is preferred to *paya- ble.*
7. Avoid dividing elements that are read as units, such as dates (*May 5*), amounts (*$8 million* or *$8,000,000*), titles and names (*Mr. Hess*), reference numbers (*page 5* or *Unit 3*), and so on.
8. Avoid dividing (a) after more than two consecutive lines have ended with a hyphen, (b) at the end of the first line and last line of a page, and (c) a proper noun.

PROOFREADERS' MARKS

Proofreaders' Mark	Draft	Final Copy	Proofreaders' Mark	Draft	Final Copy
Delete	a true fact	a fact	Single-space ss	first line / second line	first line second line
Don't delete	a true story	a true story	Double-space ds	first line / second line	first line second line
Delete and close up	co operation	cooperation	Make new paragraph ¶	If he is	If he is
Capitalize	Fifth avenue	Fifth Avenue	Transpose	to quickly go	to go quickly
Use lowercase letter	our President	our president	Insert word	and it is	and so it is
Spell out	the only 1	the only one	Insert punctuation	today and	today, and
Make it a period	no way	no way.	Insert space #	already to	all ready to
Move as shown	no other way	no other way	Omit space	court room	courtroom
Move to the left	It is not	It is not	Change word	and if she	and so she
Move to the right	It is not	It is not			
Indent 5 spaces	It is not	It is not			

ERROR CORRECTION

TYPING ERASER. A typewriter eraser can be used to correct an error.

1. Turn the platen to move the error into position for easy correction.
2. To keep eraser crumbs from falling into the mechanism, move the carrier or carriage to the extreme left or right.
3. Use a stiff typewriter eraser and a *light* up-and-down motion to erase the error.
4. Return to the typing line and type the correction.

CORRECTION PAPER. Slips of paper that contain a light coating of chalk can also be used to correct an error.

1. Backspace to the error and place the correction paper (coated side toward the typing paper) between the typing paper and the typewriter ribbon.
2. Retype the error. The chalk from the correction paper will conceal the error.
3. Remove the correction paper, backspace, and type the correction.

CORRECTION FLUID. Correction fluid, like correction paper, covers the error.

1. Turn the paper forward or backward.
2. Brush the fluid sparingly over the error.
3. Let the fluid dry.
4. Type the correction.

CORRECTION RIBBON. Typewriters with correction capabilities contain a correction ribbon as well as a special backspace key that engages the correction ribbon.

1. Use the special backspace key to backspace to the error.
2. Retype the error so that the coating on the correction ribbon lifts the error off the typing page.
3. Type the correction.

PUNCTUATION

COMMAS

1. Use a comma after an introductory expression (that is, a word, phrase, or clause that comes before the subject and verb of the independent clause).

Yes, I will be happy to accept the assignment.
When I return to the office, I shall call you.
But: I shall call you when I return to the office.

2. Use commas to separate names used in direct address.

Thank you, Mr. Aranda, for your prompt reply.
I was sorry to learn of your decision, Jane.

3. Use commas to separate three or more items in a series when the last item is preceded by *and, or,* or *nor.*

I will be gone on Monday, Tuesday, and Wednesday.
We immediately unlocked the door, went inside, and started working.

4. Use a comma to separate the two independent clauses in a compound sentence when they are joined by *and, but, or,* or *nor.*

I normally have six workers present, but two of them are ill.
Janice graduated in May, and she began working for us in June.
But: Janice graduated in May and began working for us in June.

5. Use commas to set off a nonessential expression (that is, a word, phrase, or clause that may be omitted without changing the basic meaning or the grammatical completeness of the sentence).

Francis, who has had some experience, should apply for the job.
But: Anyone who has had some experience should apply for the job.
The shipment was sent on Tuesday, before your letter arrived.
But: The shipment was sent before your letter arrived.

6. Use commas to separate the year in a complete date.

The meeting was held on March 1, 1983, in Canada.
But: The meeting was held on March 1 in Canada.

7. When two adjectives modify the same noun, use a comma to separate the adjectives if they are not joined by *and.* (**Note:** If the first adjective modifies the combined idea of the second adjective plus the noun, do not separate the adjectives by a comma.)

She is a quiet, efficient worker.
But: She is a quiet and efficient worker.
He drove a small, uncomfortable car.
But: He drove a dark green car.

8. Use commas to set off an expression in apposition (that is, a word, phrase, or clause that identifies or explains other terms).

Our receptionist, Mr. Dalton, will show you the way.
A meeting was held on Monday, June 14, in Ohio.

9. Use commas to set off a transitional expression (such as *therefore*) or an independent comment (such as *of course*).

I believe, however, that you have met Ms. Carson-Leslie.
We will, by the way, be happy to help with the project.

10. Use commas to separate the name of a state or country following a city name.

I moved to Akron, Ohio, in November.
But: I moved to Akron in November.
Next year's meeting will be in Rome, Italy, in the fall.

SEMICOLONS

11. Use a semicolon to separate two independent clauses that are not joined by *and, but, or,* or *nor.*

Byron was willing to cooperate; Philip was not.
But: Byron was willing to cooperate, but Philip was not.

12. Use a semicolon to separate items in a series if any of the items already contain commas.

We have branch offices in Detroit, Michigan; Des Moines, Iowa; and Newark, New Jersey.

COLONS

13. When a clause contains an expression such as *the following, as follows,* or *these* and is followed by a series of explanatory words, use a colon between the clause and the series.

The major consideration is as follows: the rate of return must be adequate.
The two major considerations are these: the rate of return and liquidity.
But: The two major considerations are the rate of return and liquidity.

HYPHENS

14. Hyphenate a compound adjective (two or more words that function as a unit to describe a noun) that comes *before*

NUMBER EXPRESSION

GENERAL RULES

1. Spell out numbers 1 through 10 and use figures for numbers above 10.

I typed three pages.

Trent interviewed ten people.

Only 16 people attended the conference.

2. If two or more *related* numbers both below and above 10 are used in the same sentence, use figures for all numbers.

The vote was 5 for New York and 16 for Houston.

3. To express even millions or billions, use the following style:

30 million (**Not:** 30,000,000)

10.4 billion (**Not:** 10,400,000,000)

4. When two numbers come together in a sentence and one is a compound adjective, spell out the shorter one and express the longer one in figures.

5. Spell out fractions that stand alone and use figures for mixed numbers.

three-fourths of the members   18⅔ inches

6¾ inches

6. Spell out a number at the beginning of a sentence.

Thirty-one people signed the petition.

Three and one-half inches of rain fell.

7. Use commas to separate thousands, millions, and billions.

6,821   4,915,603   13,530,100,000

ADDRESSES

8. Use figures in house or building numbers.

284 Elm Street   8 Plaza Circle

APOSTROPHES

17. To make a singular noun possessive, place the apostrophe before the s.

a company's reputation   the person's job

Mr. Smith's talk   the doctor's office

18. To make a possessive from a singular noun that ends in an s sound, be guided by the way the word is pronounced. If a new syllable is formed by making the noun possessive, add an apostrophe and an s (*my boss's telephone, an actress's costume*). If the addition of the extra syllable would make a word that is hard to pronounce, add only the apostrophe (*Mr. Hastings' car, Mrs. Simmons' career*).

19. To make a plural noun *not* ending in s possessive, place the apostrophe before the s.

the men's duties   the children's toys

20. To make a possessive from a plural noun ending in s, place the apostrophe after the s.

the two companies' assets   the Smiths' children

both girls' dresses   the doctors' offices

21. Do not use an apostrophe with possessive pronouns.

The victory is yours.

The dog wants its dinner.

But: It's time for dinner.

a noun. **Exception:** If the first word is an adverb ending in *-ly*, do not hyphenate such adjectives.

The well-known author autographed her book.

But: That author is well known.

Our store features only up-to-date styles.

But: Our styles are all up to date.

He bought a poorly constructed house.

UNDERSCORES AND QUOTATION MARKS

15. Underscore titles of complete published works and use quotation marks around titles that represent only part of a complete published work.

Read the chapter entitled "The Effective Business Letter" for tomorrow.

We advertised in The New York Times.

I read an article entitled "Reflections" in today's Arizona Republic.

PERIODS

16. Use a period to end a sentence that is a polite request, suggestion, or command if you expect the reader to respond by acting rather than by giving a yes-or-no answer.

Will you please send us your check today.

May I please have the Jones file for the meeting.

9. Spell out numbered streets 1 through 10 and use figures for numbered streets above 10. Omit *st, d,* or *th* if a word such as *East* precedes the street number.

310 Fourth Avenue   310 14th Street
310 North 14 Street

AMOUNTS OF MONEY

10. Do not use a decimal with even amounts of money.

$360 (**Not:** $360.00)

11. Use the word *cents* for amounts under $1.

68 cents (**Not:** $.68 or 68¢)

12. To express even millions or billions of dollars, use the following style.

$32 million (**Not:** $32,000,000)
$10.7 billion (**Not:** $10,700,000,000)

DATES

13. Use *st, d,* or *th* only if the day precedes the month.

She starts work on the 15th of November.
But: She starts work on November 15.

TIME

14. Use figures to express time, whether with *o'clock* or with *a.m.* and *p.m.* (The abbreviations *a.m.* and *p.m.* should be typed in small letters without spaces.)

11 o'clock (**Not:** eleven o'clock)
Every day he arrives at his office at 9 a.m.
She got home at 7:30 p.m. yesterday.

PERCENTAGES

15. Express percentages in figures and spell out the word *percent.*

8 percent
16.5 percent

Note: The percent sign (%) may be used when typing tables.

AGES AND ANNIVERSARIES

16. When ages are used as significant statistics, express them in figures. Otherwise, spell them out.

You may vote at the age of 18.
He will retire when he reaches 65 years of age.
My daughter is thirteen years old.
Her grandfather is seventy-eight years old.

17. Spell out ordinals (*first, second,* and so on) in birthdays and anniversaries. However, if more than two words would be needed, use figures.

our second anniversary
our sixty-fifth anniversary
our 130th anniversary

CAPITALIZATION

1. Capitalize every proper noun and every adjective derived from a proper noun. A proper noun is the official name of a particular person, place, or thing. In general, do not capitalize prepositions of fewer than four letters (such as *of*). The articles *a* and *an* are not capitalized; the article *the* is capitalized only under special circumstances.

the United States of America   Temple University
East Lansing, Michigan   the Canadian border
New York City   Friday, January 18
New Year's Day   *The New York Times*

2. Capitalize common organizational terms such as *advertising department* and *finance committee* when they are the actual names of units within the writer's own organization and are modified by the word *the.*

The Board of Directors of our firm will meet at noon.
Our board of directors approved the expansion.
The board of directors of his firm refused.

3. Capitalize all official titles when they precede personal names. Do *not* capitalize official titles when the personal name that follows is in apposition and is set off by commas, when the title follows a personal name, or when the title is used in place of a personal name.

President J. Russell Nelson
our president, J. Russell Nelson,
J. Russell Nelson, president,
The president of the company

4. Capitalize *north, south, east,* and *west* only when they designate definite regions or are an integral part of a proper name.

I live in the East.
That young pianist defected to the West.
Martha is from North Carolina.
This house faces east.
We traveled west for three hours.

ABBREVIATIONS

CAPITALIZATION AND HYPHENATION

1. Abbreviations usually follow the capitalization and hyphenation of the full words for which they stand.

Mon. Monday	a.m. ante meridiem	D.C. District of Columbia
ft-lb foot-pound		

PUNCTUATION AND SPACING WITH ABBREVIATIONS

2. In lowercase abbreviations made up of single initials, use a period after each initial but no space after each internal period.

a.m.   i.e.   e.g.

3. In all-capital abbreviations and acronyms made up of single initials, do not use periods or internal spaces.

UNESCO   IQ   IBM   SEC   AWOL

Exception: Retain the periods in abbreviations of geographical names, academic degrees, and a few miscellaneous expressions.

U.K.   B.A.   A.D.   R.S.V.P.   P.O.

4. Leave one space following an abbreviation within a sentence unless another mark of punctuation follows immediately.

I arrived at 6 a.m. and left at 9 p.m. for Chicago.

PERSONAL NAMES AND INITIALS

5. Use a period and one space following each initial of a person's name; however, when personal initials stand alone, type them without periods or spaces.

JFK   R. J. Pulaski   John T. Smith

6a. Always use the following abbreviated titles when they are used with personal names.

Mr.	Messrs. (plural of *Mr.*)
Mrs.	Mmes. (plural of *Mrs.*)
Ms.	Mses. or Mss. (plural of *Ms.*)
Dr.	Drs. (plural of *Dr.*)

b. In general, spell out all other titles used with personal names.

Professor Joan Adams   President Kean

MEASUREMENTS

7a. In nontechnical writing, spell out units of measure.

8½ by 11 inches	a 175-acre estate
a 10-gallon container	8 yards of carpeting

---

5. Capitalize a noun followed by a number or letter.

Table 4   page 4   Room 39
Policy C305   Flight 156   paragraph 6

Exception: Do not capitalize the nouns *page, paragraph,* or *size.*

6. In titles of published works and in headings, capitalize (*a*) the first and last words, (*b*) the first word following a colon or dash, and (*c*) all other words *except* articles (*the, a, an*), short conjunctions (*and, but, or*), and prepositions that contain three or fewer letters (*in, for, to*).

"An Achievement to Be Proud Of"

Fixed-Rate Mortgages: A Reexamination

7. Capitalize the first word of a quoted sentence.

According to Rooney, "Interest rates should begin to drop by the third quarter."

8. Capitalize the first word of each item displayed in an enumerated list.

Please rank each applicant in terms of the following:

1. Education
2. Experience
3. Personality

9. Do not capitalize (*a*) the first word of an indirect quotation, (*b*) the names of school courses that are not proper nouns, or (*c*) the names of seasons.

John said that he would leave in the spring.

She is taking English and business communications this semester.

But: Did you pass Math 140?

ABBREVIATIONS

Mr. Jones works in Washington, D.C., but his home is in Maryland.

But: Baker, on the other hand, believes that high interest rates are "here to stay."

b. Abbreviate units of measure when they occur frequently, as in technical or scientific work, forms, and tables. Do not use periods.

3 yd   6 gal   8 lb   15 ft 2 in

8. The most common metric measurements are derived from three basic units and several prefixes. The abbreviations for these terms are given in parentheses.

Basic Units:	meter (m) liter (L)
	gram (g)

Prefixes Indicating Fractions:	deci (d)	1/10
	centi (c)	1/100
	milli (m)	1/1000
Prefixes Indicating Multiples:	deka (da)	10
	hecto (h)	100
	kilo (k)	1000

Examples:	dm	decimeter	dam	dekameter
	cg	centigram	hg	hectogram
	mm	millimeter	km	kilometer

GRAMMAR

SUBJECTS AND VERBS

1. When two or more subjects are joined by *or, either/or, nor, neither/nor,* or *not only/but also:*
a. If both subjects are singular, use a singular verb.
b. If both subjects are plural, use a plural verb.
c. If one subject is singular and one is plural, it is best to place the plural subject immediately before the verb and use a plural verb.

Neither the manager nor the assistant was at his desk.
Neither the managers nor the assistants were at their desks.
Neither the manager nor the assistants were at their desks.

2. The following pronouns are always singular and take singular verbs: *each, either, neither, much,* and pronouns ending in *-body, -thing,* and *-one.*

Each has a different view of his or her job.
Neither of the women is doing her job well.
Everybody is required to finish his or her work.

3. When establishing agreement between subject and verb, disregard intervening phrases and clauses.

Only one of the secretaries is working on that job.
The secretary, not the typists, is working on that job.
The secretary, as well as the typists, is working on that job.

4. Verbs in the subjunctive mood (those that talk of conditions that are improbable, doubtful, or contrary to fact) usually require the plural form.

I wish the story were true.
If I were he, I would try again.

PRONOUNS

5. Use a singular pronoun with a singular antecedent (the word for which the pronoun stands) and a plural pronoun with a plural antecedent.

Either Marie or Sonia must give up her office.
Neither the bosses nor their aides reached their goals.

(Note also the examples used in the Subjects and Verbs section.)

6. Use nominative pronouns (*I, he, she, we, they,* and so on) as subjects of a sentence and after the verb *to be.*

The manager and he are working on the report.
Mr. Jones wants to know if Larry and I are finished.
It was he who wrote the report.

7. Use objective pronouns (*me, him, her, us, them,* and so on) as objects in a sentence.

Beth telephoned Mr. Smith and me.
The information is for Josh and her.

ADJECTIVES AND ADVERBS

8. Use comparative adjectives and adverbs (*-er, more,* and *less*) in referring to two persons, places, or things; use superlative adjectives and adverbs (*-est, most,* and *least*) in referring to more than two.

She is the faster of the two workers.
She is the fastest of the three workers.
He is the more experienced of the two workers.
He is the most experienced of the three workers.

TEST 9-D
REPORT 90
REPORT WITH ENUMERATION

Paper: Workguide 557

Please prepare the following report with an enumeration. As a heading use my name, Joseph S. Garrett, J.D., with Attorney-at-Law right underneath. As a subtitle use Office Formatting Policies. Leave a 1-inch top margin.

the following lists identify for this firm those legal documents that may be formatted on prepared forms and those that are to be formatted on ruled legal paper . . . in accordance with current practice . . . 8½-inch by 11-inch paper is to be used for ruled legal paper as well as for all prepared forms . . .

(*Let's put in a side heading now that reads PREPARED FORMS*) unless the administrative secretary on duty permits otherwise . . . all the following legal documents are to be formatted on prepared forms . . . (*double-space the enumerations*) 1 . . . deed . . . 2 . . . power of attorney . . . 3 . . . release and indemnity agreement . . . 4 . . . subpoena . . . 5 . . . summons . . . (*Let's put in another side heading now that reads RULED LEGAL PAPER*) all the following legal documents . . . plus others not included in the above list . . . are to be formatted on 8½-inch by 11-inch ruled legal paper . . . 1 . . . affidavit . . . 2 . . . agreement . . . 3 . . . answer . . . 4 . . . complaint . . . 5 . . . contract . . . 6 . . . interrogatories . . . 7 . . . last will and testament.

TEST 9-E
TABLE 70
RULED TABLE

Paper: Workguide 559

Inventory Shortages

March 31, 19---

QUANTITY	DESCRIPTION	PRICE	COST
2	Centrifugal Pump, #4p620	$394.00	$394.00
12	EL-210 Text/LabManual s	8.27	99.24
1	EX-112 Photo-Electric Controller With Maunal	195.00	195.00
2	Magnetic Starters--NEMA 14-- 230 Volts--3 Poles, #5X149	65.66	131.32
12	Heater Elements--Model T32A, #5X2244	3.45	41.40
TOTAL			$903.01

PART 1

THE TYPEWRITER ■ THE ALPHABET AND NUMBER KEYS

OBJECTIVES FOR PART 1

Part 1 is designed to enable you to demonstrate the following abilities when you take the test in Lesson 25:

1. Touch Typing. To operate the letter and number keys with correct fingering and return and indent the carrier or carriage with your eyes on the copy.

2. Machine Adjustments. To correctly set and reset the paper guide, margin stops, tabulator stops, and line space selector, and to position the carrier or carriage.

3. Checking. To proofread your typed work against a key, mark and count errors, and compute typing speed.

4. Technical Knowledge. To answer correctly at least 90 percent of the questions on an objective test.

5. Centering. To center typed material both vertically and horizontally.

6. Enumerations. To format enumerations correctly.

7. Skill Rate. To type at the following speed and accuracy levels by the end of each unit:

Unit	No. of Minutes	Minimum Speed	Maximum Errors
2	1	16	3
3	2	22	5
4	2	25	5

8. Word Processing Information. To understand how word processing equipment would function if used to format various production assignments.

April 21, 19--

Dr. Janice L. Cooper
Membership Chairperson
Paterson Medical Association
2320 Getty Avenue
Paterson, NJ 07503

Dear Dr. Cooper:

As you requested, Dr. Jenny S. Leon and I have contacted the four physicians listed below who are new to the medical community of Paterson. They are now residents of Paterson and want to become active members of the Paterson Medical Association. Application forms and checks are enclosed for each person.

Name	Address	Phone ~~Telephone~~
John A. King	225 Eighth Avenue	555-4210
Amy M. Menge	6670 Braun Avenue	555-3781
Ruth H. Cohen	330 Arch Street	555-9265
Peter Chan	15 Vine Street	555-9347

All are practicing at the Park Medical Clinic, located at 5804 Eastside Park, Paterson, NJ 07504. The telephone number is 555-4728.

Please let us know if there are other physicians for whom you would like us to serve as sponsors.

Sincerely yours,

Manuel J. Garcia, M.D.

cc Dr. Reuben S. Audree, President
Paterson Medical Association

<table>
<tr><td>
Line: 40 spaces   Drills: 2X
Spacing: single
Proofguide: 1
Workguide: 5–6, 41
Tape: 1A or K1A*

* K = Keyboard Presentation Tapes
</td></tr>
</table>

LESSON 1
HOME KEYS

SPACE BAR

Goals: To control the home keys (A S D F J K L ;) and to control the space bar.

With all fingers held motionless in the home position, poise your right thumb about ¼ inch above the space bar. (Left-handers: Use your left thumb if it seems more comfortable.) Tap the space bar in its center and bounce your thumb off.

1-A. PRACTICE THE SPACE BAR

Space once (*tap the space bar once*) ... twice (*tap the space bar twice*) ... once ... once ... twice ... once ... twice ... once ... twice ... twice ... once ... once ... Repeat.

Strike the *center* of the space bar.

Practice using the return key until you can do so with confidence and without raising your eyes from the book.

1-B. PRACTICE THE CARRIER OR CARRIAGE RETURN

In a quick, stabbing motion (1) extend the fourth finger of your right hand to the return key; (2) lightly tap the return key, causing the carrier or carriage to return automatically; and (3) "zip" the finger back to its home-key position.

Space once ... twice ... once ... twice ... Return! Home! (*fingers on home keys*) ... Repeat.

Using your right thumb and both forefingers (with all other fingers kept in home position), type these three lines. Tap the keys lightly. Do not space after the last letter in the line before the return.

1-C. PRACTICE THE FOREFINGER KEYS

Left forefinger on F key
Right thumb on space bar

   fff fff ff ff f f ff ff f f

Right forefinger on J key
Right thumb on space bar

   jjj jjj jj jj j j jj jj j j

Left forefinger on F key
Right forefinger on J key
Right thumb on space bar

   fff jjj ff jj f j ff jj f j

LESSON 225
TEST 9: PROGRESS TEST ON PART 9

TEST 9-A
5-MINUTE TIMED WRITING

Paper: Workguide 549
Line: 60 spaces
Spacing: double
Tab: 5
Start: line 9

One of my old acquaintances still talks about the high   12
level of enthusiasm in physical fitness which was generated   24
more than a decade ago. Millions of people throughout this   36
nation developed their own exercise rituals, which included   48
various competitive sports activities as well as individual   60
forms of stretching. We were all amazed at the high number   72
of people who began to jog or even entered competitive run—   84
ning events. Ages ran from the teens to the seventies.   95

It is good to see that so many have continued with the   107
types of routines that they feel are right for them. Also,   119
hundreds of thousands of young people have joined the ranks   131
each year. Many have joined fitness programs through which   143
teams compete for points on a weekly or monthly basis. One   155
earns points according to a scale that seems to be accepted   167
by fitness enthusiasts throughout the country. As would be   179
expected, a person earns more points by running for an hour   191
than by walking. Also, the points that are awarded reflect   203
the benefit that is achieved by the body, particularly with   215
respect to strengthening the lungs and the heart.   225

In addition to the physical benefits one receives when   237
sticking to a schedule of disciplined physical activity, an   249
additional side benefit accrues. Without exception, all of   261
my physically active friends say that their emotional state   273
is better.   275

| 1 | 2 | 3 | 4 | 5 | 6 | 7 | 8 | 9 | 10 | 11 | 12

LEFT HAND
Forefinger   F
Second finger   D
Third finger   S
Fourth finger   A

RIGHT HAND
J   Forefinger
K   Second finger
L   Third finger
;   Fourth finger
Space bar   Thumb

SPACE BAR

1-D. PRACTICE THE F AND J KEYS

Use forefingers on F and J keys. Tap the space bar with your thumb.

1   fff   fff   jjj   jjj   fff   jjj   ff   jj   ff   jj   f   j
    fff   fff   jjj   jjj   fff   jjj   ff   jj   ff   jj   f   j

Leave 1 blank line (return twice) before you start a new drill.

1-E. PRACTICE THE D AND K KEYS

Use second fingers.

2   ddd   ddd   kkk   kkk   ddd   kkk   dd   kk   dd   kk   d   k
    ddd   ddd   kkk   kkk   ddd   kkk   dd   kk   dd   kk   d   k

1-F. PRACTICE THE S AND L KEYS

Use third fingers.

3   sss   sss   lll   lll   sss   lll   ss   ll   ss   ll   s   l
    sss   sss   lll   lll   sss   lll   ss   ll   ss   ll   s   l

Tap the return key without looking up.

1-G. PRACTICE THE A AND ; KEYS

Use fourth fingers.

4   aaa   aaa   ;;;   ;;;   aaa   ;;;   aa   ;;   aa   ;;   a   ;
    aaa   aaa   ;;;   ;;;   aaa   ;;;   aa   ;;   aa   ;;   a   ;

1-H. WORD BUILDING: SHORT WORDS

Type lines 5–11 twice, leaving a blank line after each pair. Note word patterns.

5   aaa   ddd   add   add   aaa   lll   all   all   add   all

6   aaa   sss   kkk   ask   jjj   aaa   lll   jal   ask   jal

7   ddd   aaa   ddd   dad   lll   aaa   ddd   lad   dad   lad

1-I. WORD BUILDING: LONGER WORDS

8   a   as   ask   asks   asks;   f   fa   fal   fall   falls

Space once after a semicolon.

9   a   al   ala   alas   alas;   f   fl   fla   flas   flask

10   a   ad   add   adds   adds;   s   sa   sal   sala   salad

Compare your Lesson 1 typing with that shown on Workguide pages 5–6, and then complete Workguide page 41 or 42.

1-J. SKILL MEASUREMENT

11   ask dad;   as sad as a lass;   add a salad;

JOB 15
LETTER 94
LETTER WITH BCC

Paper: Workguide 543–544

During your phone conversation with Mr. Clayton, he asked you to confirm in writing the fact that his bill was paid in cash on January 24. Mr. Clayton's current address is 4725 Lupton Lane, Paterson, NJ 07508. You now compose a letter of apology to Mr. Clayton, confirming receipt of his cash payment on the day of his appointment. You decide to send a blind carbon copy to Dr. Leon.

JOB 16
REPORT 88
HUMAN RELATIONS

Paper: plain

Mr. King, obviously very angry, approaches your desk. "I just can't understand how you people can stay in business here. I had an appointment to see Dr. Garcia at 11 o'clock, and it's now after 11:30. If I were that rude to my customers down at the shop, I wouldn't stay in business a month. Don't you know my time's valuable to me? It's costing me good money to sit here in this office." Obviously Mr. King does not understand that good medical treatment cannot be scheduled to the minute. Describe how you would handle this situation.

JOB 17
REPORT 89
HUMAN RELATIONS

Paper: plain

Ms. Rita M. Robinson telephones from somewhere in Pennsylvania. She is returning home from a spring vacation with her family. Ms. Robinson complains of severe pains in her chest and wants Dr. Garcia to examine her as soon as she returns to Paterson this afternoon. How would you handle this telephone call? Prepare a brief report of your conversation with Ms. Robinson.

JOB 18
LETTER 95
LETTER WITH ATTENTION LINE

Paper: Workguide 545–546

Please type the following letter to Modern Pharmaceuticals, Inc., 4520 Wainwright Avenue, Syracuse, NY 10312. Use the attention line "Mr. Ordell E. Grinager." In the closing, type "Sincerely yours" and my name followed by the letters *R.N.*

I wrote this letter in a great hurry, and so please check any spelling, grammatical, and punctuation errors I might have made.

Ladies and Gentlemen:

As you know, we have been purchasing pharmacueticals from your company for over ten years. In your latest two pencillin shipments, your Invoices 58913 and 59061, all twelve boxes carried dates that had expired over six months ago. We have returned both shipments for credit and recieved replacement orders with currant dates.

Base on the good relationship we have had in the passed, I am confident that you will want to check your inventory immediately and discard all other outdated merchandise. Prompt action on your part will safe both your company and our office the time and trouble of returning future shipments. If you have any questions about this matter please feel free to call me.

LESSON 2
NEW KEYS

SPACE BAR

Goal: To control H, E, O, and R keys.

From now on, your fingers are named for the home keys on which they rest. For example, the D finger is the second finger on the left hand.

2-A. WARMUP

1 fff jjj ddd kkk sss lll aaa ;;; fff jjj
2 lll aaa ddd lad sad aaa sss kkk ask fad

2-B. PRACTICE THE H KEY

Use J finger.

3 jjj jhj hhh jjj jhj hhh jjj jhj hhh jhj
4 jhj had had jhj has has jhj ash ash jhj
5 jhj ha; ha; jhj hah hah jhj aha aha jhj
6 hash half sash lash dash hall shad shah

Dotted lines spotlight the reach path you are practicing.

2-C. PRACTICE THE E KEY

Use D finger.

7 ddd ded eee ddd ded eee ddd ded eee ded
8 ded led led ded fee fee ded lee lee ded
9 ded lea lea ded fed fed ded see see ded

E with H

10 heel hake head heal hale heed held shed

2-D. PRACTICE THE O KEY

Use L finger.

11 lll lol ooo lll lol ooo lll lol ooo lol
12 lol sod sod lol old old lol odd odd lol

O with H

13 lol hod hod lol hoe hoe lol oh; oh; lol

O with E

14 does foes hoes dose odes oleo lose shoe

2-E. PRACTICE THE R KEY

Use F finger.

15 fff frf rrr fff frf rrr fff frf rrr frf

R with H

16 frf her her frf rah rah frf red red frf

R with E

17 frf are are frf err err frf era era frf

R with O

18 door soar roar oars rods fore role roll

JOB 11
(Continued)

Here's the rest of the report of consultation for Robert M. Sanchez. Type it on plain paper, using the patient's name, hospital number, and consultation date as a heading.

This is a continuation of the report of consultation for Robert M. Sanchez, Hospital Number 890-32. The last sentence I dictated ended with "interpreted by the radiologist as a questionable right midlung infiltrate."

pertinent features of his examination include the fact that he is in traction of his left leg . . . he has a broken jaw and is dysarthric . . . he does not have jugular venous distention or cervical lymphadenopathy . . . and his lungs are perfectly clear to auscultation and percussion . . . he has been lying on his back for most of his stay . . . he had resting tachycardia of 102 during my examination with a normal belly exam . . .

JOB 12   Paper: plain
REPORT 86
HUMAN RELATIONS

As you are transcribing your report, a woman approaches your desk and says, "I'm Robby Gray's mother, and he's here for his checkup. I've got to run out for a few minutes, and so I'm just going to leave him and his sister here in the waiting room. They are no trouble at all, and I'll be back in time to talk to the doctor when Robby's checkup is finished." On plain paper, describe how you would handle this situation.

After you have dealt with Mrs. Gray, you continue transcribing the Sanchez report.

his right leg . . . which is accessible to examination . . . has no signs of tenderness or clinical evidence for a deep-venous thrombosis . . . (*Operator, that's all for the history of Mr. Sanchez. Now let's type a side heading in all-capital letters, IMPRESSIONS AND DISCUSSIONS, followed by a colon.*) it is likely that his hypoxia can be accounted for as microatelectasis caused by his forced bedrest and pos-

tural stasis . . . the timing is somewhat appropriate for pulmonary emboli . . . i would like to culture his sputum and urine to see if that is a source of his fever . . . i doubt if he is currently suffering from asthmatic symptomatology but would start bronchodilator therapy to treat possible microatelectasis . . . he could be developing an acute pneumonia . . . and i would suggest follow-up X rays . . . (*paragraph*) transport and timing for his lung scan may be difficult because of his traction . . . i would like to discuss this further . . . if the lung scan is unremarkable . . . i think we should watch him for a day or two to make sure that he is not developing pneumonia and then proceed with the operation.

JOB 13   Paper: Workguide 541–542
LETTER 93
COVER LETTER WITH SUBJECT LINE AND POSTSCRIPT

Dr. Garcia conferred with Dr. Trident this morning, and they agreed to consult with another physician, Dr. Edward E. Tai, Marathon County Hospital, Paterson, NJ 07504, on the Sanchez case. Please prepare a brief cover letter to Dr. Tai for forwarding a copy of the Sanchez consultation report. Also, tell him that Dr. Trident and Dr. Garcia are looking forward to discussing the case with him as soon as it can be arranged. Please add a postscript in which Dr. Garcia extends congratulations to Dr. Tai for his excellent article in the March issue of the *New England Journal of Medicine*.

JOB 14   Paper: plain
REPORT 87
HUMAN RELATIONS

It is obvious that Mr. Frederick B. Clayton is extremely upset when he telephones to complain about a letter that he received three days ago. His language is quite abusive. With great patience on your part, you finally find out that the letter was a request for a $55 payment that is two months overdue. Mr. Clayton insists that he paid the bill in cash on the day he saw Dr. Leon and claims that he has a paid receipt to prove it. Type a brief report describing how you would handle this situation. (The office records show that he is indeed correct. The bill was paid on January 24.)

2-F. WORD FAMILIES

Do not pause at the vertical lines that mark off the word families.

19 hear rear fear ear; |sell fell jell dell

20 fade jade lade ade; |real seal deal heal

21 rare hare fare are; |sole dole role hole

2-G. SKILL MEASUREMENT

2-G. Try to complete two copies of line 22 in 1 minute. Try 3 times.

22 he asked for jade; she sold fresh food;

Line: 40 spaces Drills: 2X	LESSON 3	
Spacing: single	**NEW KEYS**	
Proofguide: 1		
Tape: 3A or K3A		SPACE BAR

Goal: To control M, T, I, and C keys.

3-A. WARMUP

1 fff jjj ddd kkk sss lll aaa ;;; fff jjj

2 jhj has ded led lol old frf far her ash

3-B. PRACTICE THE M KEY

Use J finger.

3 jjj jmj mmm jjj jmj mmm jjj jmj mmm jmj

Dotted lines spotlight the reach path you are practicing.

4 jmj jam jam jmj mar mar jmj mom mom jmj

5 same fame dame lame room more mess from

6 ream mess mash mars foam arms elms roam

3-C. PRACTICE THE T KEY

Use F finger.

7 fff ftf ttt fff ftf ttt fff ftf ttt ftf

8 ftf tar tar ftf ate ate ftf sat sat ftf

9 tart dart loot hoot soot seat feat jets

T with M

10 tame mate moot most meet meat mart mats

REPORT OF CONSULTATION

Because there are many errors in the report, please retype it and make any necessary corrections. Make two copies of the report.

The first page of this report of consultation was prepared for Dr. Garcia yesterday by a temporary office assistant.

When Dr. Garcia has finished dictating the rest of the report, I'll bring it to you to transcribe.

WP The dictionary feature of a word processor is particularly important when specialized terminology is used. Between 10,000 and 20,000 technical terms can be stored to check the spelling of a medical document.

REPORT OF CONSULTATION

NAME: Robert M. Sanchez

ROOM NUMBER: 328

HOSPITAL NUMBER: 890-32

ATTENDING PHYSICIAN: Dr. Perry L. Trident

CONSULTING PHYSICIAN: Dr. Manuel J. Garcia

DATE: April 9, 19--

REASON FOR CONSULTATION: Hypoxia

HISTORY: This 43-year-old gentlemen was admitted five days ago after a severe motor vehicle accidnet in which he sustained multiple fractures and lacerations. He is currently being cared for by Dr. Perry L. Trident. Dr. trident had ordered a pre-op blood gas for a planned jaw reconstruction pinning operation tomorrow morning, and a PO2 on room air was 64. For that reason I had been asked to interview the patient and make suggestions.

On interviewing him, I found that he was difficult to talk to becuas he was dysarthric from his jaw fracture. He was treated at the Mayo Clinic several years ago and received allergy hyposensitization shots. He was also told that he had mild asthma. Apparently his allergic symptoms were hay fever-allergic rhinitis type symptomatology. He had had no problems with his asthma and had required no bronchodilator therapy for several years. He is 43 years old and otherwise healthy, with no known allergies or previous diseases. He had nasal polyps oiperated on at the Mayo clinic and had a herniorrhaphy performed by a Dr. Jonson.

The nurses recorded axillary tepmeratures in the gentlemn up to 101.2. he was also noted to have resting tachycardia of 102, and this afternoon he coughed up a small amount of brighrt red blood.

He had no complaints of shortness of breath, chest pain, calf pain or tendernes, difficulty swallowing food, or choking episodes. A chest X ray taken this afternoon, done portably, was probably whithin normal limits, but it was interpreted by the radiologist as a questionable right midlung infiltrate.

NOTE: It is natural to make typing errors at this stage. It is better to risk some errors than to break your rhythm or look away from the line you are copying.

If you forget where a key is located, don't look at your fingers. Look at the keyboard chart instead.

SPACE BAR

3-D. PRACTICE THE I KEY

Use K finger.

11 kkk kik iii kkk kik iii kkk kik iii kik

Dotted lines spotlight the reach path you are practicing.

12 kik air air kik fir fir kik sir sir kik

I with M

13 mist mite mire lime dime aims miss time

I with T

14 tire tide kite site kits mitt hilt kilt

3-E. PRACTICE THE C KEY

Use D finger.

15 ddd dcd ccc ddd dcd ccc ddd dcd ccc dcd

C with M

16 mace came come mice calm mock coma clam

C with T

17 cast acts colt cite cart chat cats tack

C with I

18 dice kick lick tick rich itch sick rice

3-F. WORD FAMILIES

19 dear rear fear ear; |told sold fold mold

20 hall fall tall all; |real meal seal deal

21 fade made jade ade; |head hear heal heat

22 dash hash lash ash; |heed seed feed deed

23 lads cads fads ads; |rake sake fake lake

24 rice dice mice ice; |hock lock dock rock

25 core tore sore ore; |mist fist list cist

26 date fate late ate; |toil foil soil coil

3-G. Try to complete two copies of line 27 in 1 minute. Try 3 times.

3-G. SKILL MEASUREMENT

27 the doctor locked the door to the room;

JOB 10
MEMORANDUM 26

Paper: Workguide 537

Saturdays when the office is open. Both Dr. Leon and Dr. Garcia will have very brief interviews with them next Tuesday afternoon. The interviews will have to be fitted into the doctors' regular appointment schedules. Please be sure both doctors get a copy of this memo I've prepared in rough-draft form.

I've scheduled interviews with the four applicants for the opening for a new part-time nurse to work evenings and

TO: Dr. Leon
           Dr. Garcia

FROM: Paula Bradshaw

DATE:

SUBJECT: Interview Schedule

2 #

As you requested, I have screened the applicants for the Nurse/Medical Assistant to work evenings and Saturdays. I have narrowed the list of candidates to four and have set up interviews for next Tues. afternoon, (April 15). Your interview schedule is shown below:

2 #

NURSE/MEDICAL ASSISTANT CANDIDATES

Interview Schedule ⟶

Name	Interview Time for Dr. Leon	Interview Time for Dr. Garcia
Julia M. Castro [1]	2:00 p.m.	2:45 p.m.
John D. Besseman [2]	2:45 p.m.	2:00 p.m.
Eleanor A. Moore [2]	3:30 p.m.	4:15 p.m.
Yolanda Fernandez [1]	4:15 p.m.	3:30 p.m.

1 L.P.N.
2 R.N.

2 #

If there are any changes you would like to make, please let me know. all four applicants have special qualifications, and I am confident you will select a person who will do a fine job in our office.

| Line: 40 spaces   Drills: 2X |
| Spacing: single |
| Proofguide: 3 |
| Workguide: 43 |
| Tape: 4A or K4A |

LESSON 4
NEW KEYS

SPACE BAR

Goals: To control right shift, V, and period keys; to count errors.

4-A. WARMUP

1 aaa ;;; sss lll ddd kkk fff jjj jhj ded

2 lol frf red jmj mat ftf fed kik lid dcd

4-B. PRACTICE THE RIGHT **SHIFT** KEY

To capitalize any letter that is on the left half of the keyboard:
1. With J finger home, press and hold down the right shift key with Sem finger.
2. Strike the letter key.
3. Release the shift key and return fingers to home position.

3 ;;; A;; A;; ;;; S;; S;; ;;; D;; D;; ;;;

4 ;;; Art Art ;;; Sal Sal ;;; Sam Sam ;;;

5 Alda Alma Rick Aldo Carl Dick Elsa Edie

6 Amos Dale Chet Dora Todd Earl Emma Ford

4-C. PRACTICE THE **V** KEY

Use F finger.

7 fff fvf vvv fff fvf vvv fff fvf vvv fvf

8 fvf vie vie fvf eve eve fvf vet vet fvf

9 move live love have lava ever veer vast

V with right shift

10 Vi Vic Val Vera Vida Velma Victor Viola

4-D. PRACTICE THE **.** KEY

Use L finger.

11 lll l.l ... lll l.l ... lll l.l ... l.l

Space once after a period following an abbreviation and twice after a period at the end of a sentence.

12 l.l sr. sr. l.l dr. dr. l.l fr. fr. l.l

Period with right shift

13 l.l Sr. Sr. l.l Dr. Dr. l.l Fr. Fr. l.l

Period with V

14 Dr. Vale asked Val. Val let Art do it.

4-E. BUILD SKILL ON SHORT SENTENCES

Maintain a smooth and steady pace. Speed up on the second copy of each sentence.

15 Fred looked for the red car at the lot.

16 Eva said that Cass had to come to them.

17 Ted asked if he had moved the old mats.

18 Todd felt that Elmer had left for home.

using 4-0 Nylon running sutures ... when all the intraoral wounds were closed and the skin was also closed ... the wounds were covered with Bacitracin ointment ... bandages were loosely applied to external wounds.

JOBS 5–7   Paper: Workguide 531–536
LETTERS 90–92
SIMPLIFIED COLLECTION LETTER

Three of our patients have accounts that are overdue. Please send reminder letters to them. Use Form Letter 10. The names, addresses, dates of last appointment, and amounts owed are on this sheet.

Mr. Stan Cleveland, 1162 South Washington Avenue, Paterson, NJ 07503, January 28, $55

Ms. Pam Cranston, 425 Lake Shore Drive, Paterson, NJ 07508, January 22, $60

Mrs. Betty E. Meehl, 330 Peters Lane, Paterson, NJ 07508, January 26, $90

JOB 8   Paper: plain
REPORT 83
HUMAN RELATIONS

Just as you finish the letter to Mrs. Meehl, a patient, Mr. George V. Krebs, leaves Dr. Garcia's office, walks right past your desk, and puts on his coat to leave. What will you say to him? You find out that Mr. Krebs has forgotten to bring his checkbook, and he says he will send a check immediately upon arriving home. Type a report on how you would handle this situation.

JOB 9   Paper: plain
REPORT 84
ABSTRACTED REPORT

Sometimes our patients need to be reminded about our office hours and payment policies. In addition, I'm not sure they really know what a family practice is. I'd like you to compose, from the information in the procedures manual, a one-page information sheet explaining these three things. Entitle the information sheet "Family Practice Associates" and use three questions as side headings. Type it double-spaced on one page, and begin with the explanation of family practice. We'll duplicate your information sheet and hand it out to both new patients and people who request this information.

FORM LETTER 10

(Date)

> **WP** In some large offices, a word processor may be linked to a mainframe computer so that desired information can be accessed and merged with a form letter or similar document.

(Name)
(Street)
(City, State, ZIP)
                    ↓ 3
OVERDUE ACCOUNT
        ↓ 3
When you left our office after your appointment on (date), you indicated that your payment of (amount) would be put in the mail promptly. However, we have not yet received your check.

Your bill is now (number) months overdue. Is there some reason why we have not received payment? Please send your check for (amount) or call our office about this problem.
                                                        ↓ 5

(Your name)
Medical Office Assistant

Compare with lines 19–21 below.

4-F. COUNTING ERRORS

Dr. (Field)[1] had a hat; Sal liked the (hat,)[2]
Dr. Field had a hat; Sal liked (thehat.)[3]

Tad took at (lea t)[4] three (leases)[5] to Emma.
Tad took least three leases to (to)[7] Emma.

She ordered (jars red.)[8] Fred liked them.
She ordered red jars. (Fred)[10] (kujws)[11] them.

After studying 4-F, do Workguide page 43.

As indicated in the examples above, *count it an error* when:

1. Any stroke is incorrect.
2. Any punctuation after a word is incorrect or omitted.
3. The spacing after a word or after its punctuation is incorrect.
4. Any stroke is so light that it does not show clearly.
5. One stroke is made over another.
6. A word is omitted.
7. A word is repeated.
8. Words are transposed.
9. A direction about spacing, indenting, and so on, is violated.
10. A word contains a capital that does not print completely.
11. Only one error is charged to any one word, no matter how many errors it may contain.

4-G. BUILD SKILL ON SHORT SENTENCES

4-G. After typing each line 2 times, circle and count your errors.

19 Dr. Field had a hat; Sal liked the hat.

20 Tad took at least three leases to Emma.

21 She ordered red jars. Fred liked them.

4-H. SKILL MEASUREMENT

4-H. Try to complete both lines in 1 minute. Try 3 times. Circle and count your errors.

22 Art sold Dave five jackets at the sale.
    Dave asked for five ties to match them.

| Line: 40 spaces   Drills: 2X
Spacing: single
Proofguide: 3
Workguide: 44
Tape: 5A or K5A | LESSON 5
REVIEW | |

Goals: To strengthen all controls; to learn how to measure speed.

5-A. WARMUP

1 Rod asked Tom if he had a dime for Flo.

2 Vi dreamed of her home at the seashore.

3 Ed liked the movie; Al loved the jokes.

JOB 3
FORM 86
APPOINTMENT BOOK ENTRY

Paper: Workguide 527

The telephone rings. After identifying the office with "Family Practice Associates" and your name, you find that Mrs. Edie J. Kraft would like an appointment with Dr. Garcia on Friday afternoon, April 17. You check your appointment book (Workguide 527) for that date and continue your discussion with Mrs. Kraft. You are able to determine a mutually agreeable time and make the appropriate entries in the appointment book. Her telephone number is 555-9173. She has never seen either Dr. Leon or Dr. Garcia before and has been having frequent severe headaches for the last three weeks.

JOB 4
REPORT 82
OPERATIVE REPORT

Paper: Workguide 529 and
plain paper

Dr. Leon referred one of her patients to Dr. Sherwood for surgery, and Dr. Leon would like to have an operative report typed from the cassette the surgeon has sent to the office. Use the operative report form for the first page, type the subsequent pages on plain paper with name of patient, hospital number, and date of operation as headings. The whole report should be single-spaced with appropriate paragraphing.

This is Dr. Cary Sherwood. I will be dictating an operative report for Crystal A. Perry.

hospital number: 349-89 ... room number: 218 ... preoperative diagnosis: fracture of the jaw and multiple facial lacerations ... postoperative diagnosis: same ... operation/procedure: closure of facial lacerations ... anesthesia: general endotracheal ... procedure date: april 9 ... discharge date: *a week from today* ... procedure: after the patient was under satisfactory general endotracheal anesthesia ... the mouth was copiously irrigated and washed along with the face ... there were several fragments of tooth located in the oral cavity ... these were removed ... but there were no whole teeth or suitably sized pieces for reimplantation ... the right central incisor was loosened but still in place ... the next tooth that was intact was the left canine ... all the rest of the teeth in the left side of the mouth were avulsed totally or partially to the point that there was no crown

showing ... (*paragraph*) the teeth in the lower jaw appeared intact ... there were three significant intraoral lacerations ... one at about the level of the third molar in the buccal mucosa that did communicate with the fracture site ... none of the others did communicate with the fracture site ... this single one was closed with running 4-0 Chromic suture ... the other intraoral lacerations were debrided of crushed edges and closed with 4-0 running Chromic sutures ... (*paragraph*) then the lip was examined ... there was an approximately 2 cm segment that had been partially avulsed but was still attached ... because of the numerous lacerations within its mass and the crush injury to the muscle ... it was felt that this portion of the lip was likely to be nonfunctional ... and it would be better to excise this ... leaving the patient with an incision running transversely across the thickness of the lip rather than any longitudinal incisions in the vermilion ... this was debrided ... the mucosa surface of this was debrided ... and then the skin edge surface of the one that turned and ran obliquely out from the edge of the vermilion toward the lobe of the left ear from approximately 2.5 inches was closed in layers ... the muscle of the lip was reapproximated with 2-0 Chromic ... and 4-0 Nylon was used to close the skin ... the lip itself was closed in the vermilion with 4-0 Silk individual sutures ... (*paragraph*) next ... attention was turned to the longer and deeper laceration parallel to the one just closed ... this one ran obliquely upward and might have been in contact with the fracture site from the external aspect ... but this was not clear ... minimal amount of muscle was debrided because some fibers of nerve could be seen running in the depth of the muscle of the cheek ... however ... since this laceration went over the angle of the jaw ... it was likely that this would cause loss of depressor inferiorus muscle function ... whether or not this would return at a later time was not clear ... nonetheless ... minimal debridement was done in the muscle ... the muscle was closed with 3-0 Chromic ... a fairly large amount of skin was missing on the external portion of the wound overlying the mandible ... however ... it was possible to advance this in without undermining by using 4-0 Chromic buried sutures in the fat and dermis ... then skin could be closed primarily after debridement of nonviable edges

5-B. KEYBOARD REVIEW: HOME KEYS

4 Art ark are ade ads|;;; to; do; so; lo;

5 Sol sad sir sit see|lit led lid lot lad

6 Dot doe dim dad die|kit kid irk ark ilk

7 Fir fit fat fee far|jet jot jar jam jr.

5-C. KEYBOARD REVIEW: OTHER KEYS

8 Eat err era eel ere|hit hot had has her

9 Rae rat red rim rid|oak old ode oar off

10 Tam tar too tot the|ire its ill irk sit

11 Car cam cat cot cad|mat mad mom jam ham

12 Vic vie vat vim via|l.l jr. sr. dr. fr.

After studying 5-D, do Workguide page 44.

5-D. MEASURING SPEED

1. Type for an exact number of minutes while someone times you.

2. Find out how many "average" words you have typed. Every 5 strokes count as 1 average word as marked off by the horizontal scales and, in paragraph copy, as cumulatively totaled after each line. The first example below contains (8 + 8 + 4) 20 words. The second example contains (24 + 4) 28 words.

3. Divide the words typed by the minutes typed. If you type 28 words in 2 minutes, for example, you type (28 ÷ 2) 14 wam (words a minute); or in 1 minute (28 ÷ 1) 28 wam; or in ½ minute, (28 ÷ 0.5) 56 wam.

Any material shown with a word-count scale may be used for timed-writing practice.

Compare with line 15.

```
Vi heard Al ask her for the little car.
Vi heard Al ask her for the little car.
Vi heard Al ask her
|  1  |  2  |  3  |  4  |  5  |  6  |  7  |  8
```

Compare with paragraph 16.

```
Sarah liked the meal he cooked for them
at home.  She asked for fresh fish.  Al
served each a sea sole after the salad.
Sarah liked the meal
|  1  |  2  |  3  |  4  |  5  |  6  |  7  |  8
```

5-E. If you can be timed, take a 1-minute timing on each line instead of typing it twice. Compute your speed; circle and count any errors on each timing.

5-E. BUILD SKILL ON SHORT SENTENCES

13 Ella asked Todd if he liked the stores.

14 The Rams took the title from the Stars.

15 Vi heard Al ask her for the little car.

```
|  1  |  2  |  3  |  4  |  5  |  6  |  7  |  8     = 5-stroke words
```

5-F. If you can be timed, take two 1-minute timings instead of typing the paragraph twice. Compute your speed and count errors.

5-F. BUILD SKILL ON SHORT PARAGRAPHS

CUMULATIVE WORDS

16 Sarah liked the meal he cooked for them   8

at home. She asked for fresh fish. Al   16

served each a sea sole after the salad.   24

```
|  1  |  2  |  3  |  4  |  5  |  6  |  7  |  8
```

5-G. Try to complete both lines in 1 minute. Try 3 times. Compute speed and count errors.

5-G. SKILL MEASUREMENT: 1-MINUTE TIMED WRITING

WORDS

17 Doc asked Alma for jars to save for his   8

mother. She had Chad take them to him.   16

```
|  1  |  2  |  3  |  4  |  5  |  6  |  7  |  8
```

Situation: Today is Friday, April 10, 19—. You are a medical office assistant for Family Practice Associates, 250 McLean Boulevard, Paterson, NJ 07504. You are working for Jenny S. Leon, M.D., and Manuel J. Garcia, M.D. You report directly to the office manager, Paula Bradshaw, R.N.

Your work will include making, changing, and canceling appointments; preparing medical documents; composing or transcribing medical reports, letters, and memorandums; and dealing with patients in person in the reception area or by phone.

Ms. Bradshaw has explained that no matter how carefully the day is planned, interruptions and emergencies will alter your schedule. She has advised you to just rearrange your work and plunge ahead. She has given you the first page of the Family Practice Associates Procedures Manual and asked you to study it carefully before the first patients arrive at 10 a.m.

FAMILY PRACTICE ASSOCIATES PROCEDURES MANUAL

The goal of Family Practice Associates is to maintain good health for the entire family—from the very young to the aged. We realize that an illness can affect not only the patient but family members as well. We want to become acquainted with and treat every member of the family. This will help us to deal more effectively with both the patient and the family when a health problem occurs.

The office is open from 9 a.m. to 5 p.m. Monday through Friday, from 6 to 9 p.m. on Monday and Thursday evenings and from 9 a.m. to noon on Saturdays. An answering service takes all incoming calls when the office is closed and contacts the doctors in emergency situations. Patients are seen by appointment only, and patients requiring immediate care are seen only if the doctors' schedules can be adjusted without causing a prolonged wait for other patients. Patients needing emergency care are referred to Emergency Admissions at Marathon Community Hospital.

When a patient calls for an appointment, the following information must be obtained: (1) name of family member to be seen, (2) age, (3) doctor to be seen, and (4) reason for visit. If a patient does not specify a doctor, an appointment should be made with the doctor who has the most convenient appointment time available.

It is important during the phone call to inform or remind the patient about our policy of collecting payment for services immediately upon completion of the appointment. The patient is given a receipt that also serves as a completed insurance form; the patient is responsible for dealing with the insurance company.

Appointments are to be made by penciling in the patients' names in the appointment book. The hours when no appointments are to be made should be crossed out to ensure that a patient is not scheduled during those hours. The name, phone number, and reason for the appointment should be noted in the book under the name of the appropriate doctor. New patients and physical examinations require one-hour appointments; others are to be scheduled for 30 minutes.

The hours during which each physician is available for appointments are listed in the next column.

	Dr. Leon	Dr. Garcia
Mon.:	10–12, 1–5	10–1, 2–5, 6–9
Tues.:	10–12, 1–5	10–1, 2–5
Wed.:	10–12, 1–5	10–1
Thurs.:	10–12, 1–5, 6–9	off
Fri.:	off	10–1, 2–5
Sat.:	9–12	off

Each day the medical assistant's first task is to prepare an appointment reference sheet for each doctor with a carbon copy. The original is kept on the doctors' desks. The carbon is given to Ms. Bradshaw so that she can pull the necessary patient files. The appointment sheet is formatted on plain paper and includes the appointment time, the patient's name, and the reason for the visit. New patients are identified with an asterisk. As appointments are changed, pen corrections have to be made on the doctors' appointment sheets. Ms. Bradshaw will update her copy of the sheet. The following appointment sheet is provided as a sample:

APPOINTMENTS FOR DR. LEON
Tuesday, February 17

10:00 a.m.	Mark Adams	sore throat
10:30 a.m.	Susan Jacobs*	headaches
11:30 a.m.	Ethel Creith	fever
1:00 p.m.	Jose Badillo	stitches out
1:30 p.m.	Sherry Grond	infected foot
2:00 p.m.	William Jones	flu
2:30 p.m.	Ann Swenson*	well-baby visit
3:30 p.m.	Tommy Garwood	ear infection
4:00 p.m.	Mai Wong	school physical

Unless otherwise specified, letters are to be formatted in modified-block letter style with standard punctuation. The closing lines are as follows:

Sincerely yours,   Sincerely yours,

Jenny S. Leon, M.D.   Manuel J. Garcia, M.D.

JOBS 1–2
TABLES 68–69
OPEN TABLES WITH SUBTITLES
Paper: plain

Using the appointment book for today (Workguide page 525), prepare appointment reference sheets for each doctor. Don't forget to make a carbon copy for me. I'll need it when I pull the files.

Line: 40 spaces	Drills: 2X
Spacing: single	except
Proofguide: 3	as noted
Tape: 6A or K6A	

LESSON 6
CLINIC REVIEW

Goal: To strengthen all controls.

6-A. WARMUP

1 Vera asked Dave if he liked fresh fish.
2 Elmer takes time to edit for Ella Cade.
3 The jacket is at the rear of the store.
    | 1 | 2 | 3 | 4 | 5 | 6 | 7 | 8

6-B. Type each line 2 times. Then make a list of all the letters that you typed incorrectly.

6-B. PRACTICE: KEYBOARD CONTROL

4 Alma told the same jokes Dick had told.
5 Save the three rolls of dimes for Chad.
6 Al took five liters of oil for his car.
7 Sarah came to the office to call David.

6-C. Note the four letters that appear most often on your list of errors. In lines 8–23, find the four corresponding drill lines for those four letters and type each of them 3 times. Then type one copy of the whole group (lines 8–23). Rest after typing lines 12 and 17.

6-C. SELECTIVE PRACTICE

8 aa aches Alma avid atom acid asks alive
9 cc cakes Chad calm cook cite came charm
10 dd drive Dave data desk dads dell deals
11 ee eases Ella ears elms etch edit emits
12 ff faith Fred fool fast fair fame fresh

13 hh havoc hood herd home half halt heard
14 ii ivied ills idol irks ides iris items
15 jj joked jest jots jolt jams jade jilts
16 kk kills kite kilt kiss kale keel kilos
17 ll ladle last lead lode look lied laced

18 mm major male miss mess mare make melds
19 oo order oleo odds oils odes oats oasis
20 rr ratio Rita rake ride reel room reads
21 ss salvo Sara seek sits seal side store
22 tt tamed Todd tail tore tilt trot tasks
23 vv verse Vera vale vast viva vest vials

6-D. Take three 1-minute timings. Compute speed; circle and count errors.

6-D. SKILL MEASUREMENT: 1-MINUTE TIMED WRITING

WORDS

24 Carl asked Dot if she liked jokes. She   8
   said she loved to hear him relate them.   16
    | 1 | 2 | 3 | 4 | 5 | 6 | 7 | 8

17 The DeLoach & Orr Company* quoted a price at 20% off $1.40.
18 Invoice amounts were as follows: #3904, $568; #4192, $739.
19 Ahm & Moe's new store can't compete with mail-order prices.
20 Specialty items* are reduced 25% and will now sell for 75¢.
| 1 | 2 | 3 | 4 | 5 | 6 | 7 | 8 | 9 | 10 | 11 | 12

POSTTEST. Repeat the Pretest and compare performance.

219-D. POSTTEST: ALPHABET, NUMBER, AND SYMBOL REVIEW

219-E. SKILL MEASUREMENT: 5-MINUTE TIMED WRITING

219-E. Spacing—double. Take two 5-minute timings. Between them, practice any words with which you had difficulty. Record your score.

21   A great deal of attention has been given by some media 12
to the rapid growth of the health care profession in recent 24
years. For people not interested in becoming a doctor or a 36
nurse, some other very fine careers can be pursued by those 48
who want to be a part of the respected and rewarding health 60
care profession. Qualified medical secretaries will likely 72
find that there are jobs in many clinics and hospitals. In 84
addition, these types of services are needed in the offices 96
of nursing homes, public health departments, medical supply 108
firms, research agencies, and medical publishing companies. 120
Not only must workers in these offices have the skills that 132
are needed in all types of offices, but they must also have 144
knowledge of the terminology and procedures that are unique 156
to the medical field. 160

   Those hiring secretaries for jobs in the medical field 172
have a right to expect special respect for the high ethical 184
standards of the medical profession. There has to be total 196
regard for the confidential nature of every patient's case. 208
The tasks will often vary from office to office. Some will 220
have direct involvement with patients who are ill and quite 232
depressed; compassion and patience are essential. Special- 244
ized programs for preparing people who desire a career in a 256
medical office can be found at business colleges, community 268
colleges, and four-year colleges. 275
| 1 | 2 | 3 | 4 | 5 | 6 | 7 | 8 | 9 | 10 | 11 | 12

220–224. INTEGRATED OFFICE PROJECT: FAMILY PRACTICE ASSOCIATES

Before you begin your assignment at Family Practice Associates, sharpen your language arts skills by completing Workguide pages 363–364. Then complete each of the medical-office jobs in the order in which they are presented. Do not assign priorities to the jobs.

| Line: 40 spaces   Drills: 2X
Spacing: single
Proofguide: 3
Tape: 7A or K7A | LESSON 7
NEW KEYS |  |

Goal: To control N, W, comma, and G keys.

7-A.   WARMUP

1 David felt the jolt; so did the others.

2 Carlos had a small vest for his sister.

3 Ask Sam Dart if he is to take the oath.

| 1 | 2 | 3 | 4 | 5 | 6 | 7 | 8

7-B.   PRACTICE THE N KEY

Use J finger.

4 jjj jnj nnn jjj jnj nnn jjj jnj nnn jnj

5 jnj not not jnj and and jnj den den jnj

6 none noon then main dine even rain soon

7 done tone cane sane nine fine sink rink

7-C.   PRACTICE THE W KEY

Use S finger.

8 sss sws www sss sws www sss sws www sws

9 sws sow sow sws saw saw sws wow wow sws

10 wove wave wait will warm what wool well

W with N

11 wand want went when wink wins wine wind

7-D.   Type 2 times. Try to finish both lines in 1 minute.

7-D.   PROGRESS CHECK

WORDS

12 Ann waited for Walter in the main room.   8

Fran walked in the snow with no effort.   16

| 1 | 2 | 3 | 4 | 5 | 6 | 7 | 8

7-E.   PRACTICE THE , KEY

Use K finger.

13 kkk k,k ,,, kkk k,k ,,, kkk k,k ,,, k,k

14 k,k do, do, k,k if, if, k,k so, so, k,k

Comma with N

15 man, ton, tan, ran, van, fan, men, can,

Comma with W

16 how, sow, saw, tow, row, low, cow, vow,

Space once after a comma.

<table>
<tr><td>
Line: 60 spaces
Spacing: single
Proofguide: 139–140
Workguide: 331–332,
   525–546
Tape: 56B and 57B
</td>
<td>
Tab: 5
Drills: 3X
</td>
<td>
INTEGRATED OFFICE PROJECT: MEDICAL
LESSONS 219–224
</td></tr>
</table>

GOALS FOR UNIT 36

1. Type at least 55 wam for 5 minutes with no more than 5 errors.
2. Improve alphabet, number, and symbol typing skills.
3. Type tables, reports, and letters, applying rules of capitalization and punctuation.
4. Make decisions based on office policies under simulated conditions.
5. Prepare a one-page abstract from information provided in a procedures manual.
6. Type a memorandum that contains a footnoted ruled table.
7. Proofread and retype draft report copy.
8. Make decisions and formulate responses to situations dealing with interpersonal relations.

219-A.   WARMUP

S 1 Mel may wish to pay for the giant dog when he goes to town.
A 2 Merv quickly adjusted the razorlike blades with extra care.
N 3 The house at 5938 Jasper was 17 blocks from 4260 Princeton.
   | 1 | 2 | 3 | 4 | 5 | 6 | 7 | 8 | 9 | 10 | 11 | 12

219-B.   PRETEST: ALPHABET, NUMBER, AND SYMBOL REVIEW

PRETEST.   **Take a 1-minute timing; compute speed and errors.**

4   The judge* ruled that $735 <u>more</u> be paid to Hill & Ree. 12
The defense attorney (Schultz) collected $248.   Phil and/or 24
Kevin cited ordinances #19 and #60 as "extra burdens" to be 36
considered.   Wes will quit if a 10% add-on tax is assessed. 48
   | 1 | 2 | 3 | 4 | 5 | 6 | 7 | 8 | 9 | 10 | 11 | 12

219-C.   PRACTICE: KEYBOARD REVIEW

PRACTICE.   **If you made no errors on the Pretest, type each line 3 times. If you made 1 error or more, type each group of four lines (as though it were a paragraph) 3 times.**

5 Dr. Van Jensen's horse "Skip" won easily; James was elated!
6 Jeffrey, Kay, and Sara moved to Marquette from Grand Forks.
7 The following Vikings were injured: Pelto, Sell, and Hall.
8 Pete used the "semicolon/colon" key like a first-class pro.
   | 1 | 2 | 3 | 4 | 5 | 6 | 7 | 8 | 9 | 10 | 11 | 12

9 The new team (John and Andrew) could <u>not</u> win on that court.
10 Mr. O'Day said the #3 pump and/or the #4 pump aren't right.
11 The All-Stars scored points as follows: 556, 578, and 590.
12 That band (Air Force) played tunes from the "Big Band" era.
   | 1 | 2 | 3 | 4 | 5 | 6 | 7 | 8 | 9 | 10 | 11 | 12

13 The #2 grade was listed 4 @ $1.50; the #3 sold at only 95¢.
14 Bellur and Zaenglein* reported that 78% sold at only $5.50.
15 Bharath & Rich, Inc., bought 600 @ $125.34 and 1,000 @ $98.
16 The 1985 statistics* will show sales were at 97¢ and $1.05.
   | 1 | 2 | 3 | 4 | 5 | 6 | 7 | 8 | 9 | 10 | 11 | 12

7-F. PRACTICE THE G KEY

Use F finger.

17 fff fgf ggg fff fgf ggg fff fgf ggg fgf

G with N

18 gain nags snag ring king sing tong song

G with W

19 gown wing wage glow swig grow grew gnaw

G with comma

20 leg, log, lag, hag, sag, tag, nag, gag,

7-G. Take two 1-minute timings on each of the two notes or make two copies of each. Compute speed; circle and count errors. (NOTE: Beginning with Lesson 8, you will not be reminded to circle errors.)

7-G. SKILL MEASUREMENT: 1-MINUTE TIMED WRITING

		WORDS
21	An adding machine was delivered at noon	8
	in a green carton in care of Art Wilke.	16
22	Val watched the first team as it jogged	8
	to the front of the other eleven teams.	16

| 1 | 2 | 3 | 4 | 5 | 6 | 7 | 8

Line: 40 spaces   Drills: 2X
Spacing: single
Proofguide: 3
Tape: 8A or K8A

LESSON 8
NEW KEYS

SPACE BAR

Goal: To control left shift, U, B, and colon keys.

8-A. WARMUP

1 Sara, Ed, Fred, or Cora will tell Carl.

2 Al liked his move from the first floor.

3 George had a joke he wanted to tell Al.

| 1 | 2 | 3 | 4 | 5 | 6 | 7 | 8

To capitalize any letter that is on the right half of the keyboard:
1. With F finger home, press and hold down the left shift key with A finger.
2. Strike the letter key.
3. Release the shift key and return fingers to home position.

8-B. PRACTICE THE LEFT SHIFT KEY

4 aaa Jaa Jaa aaa Kaa Kaa aaa Laa Laa aaa

5 aaa Jed Jed aaa Mel Mel aaa Ira Ira aaa

6 Lars Jake Irma Lila Matt Hans Omar Lena

7 Olga Iris Lena Kate John Hank Mike Norm

8-C. PRACTICE THE U KEY

Use J finger.

8 jjj juj uuu jjj juj uuu jjj juj uuu juj

9 juj jug jug juj sue sue juj due due juj

10 uses hulk junk nuns guns hums must rust

U with left shift

11 Utah Utica Ural Union Uganda Ulster Ulm

JOB 9
FORM 84
DOCKET SHEET

Paper: Workguide 521

Every day I keep a handwritten record of the time I devote and the expenses I incur for each client. The data are recorded on a docket sheet. At the end of each month or when a particular legal action for a client has been resolved, I'd like you to prepare a typewritten copy of the docket. When a line is drawn below the last entry on a docket page, it indicates that the legal action on that matter has been completed.

DOCKET

CLIENT *James Allen Bocklin*

TYPE OF MATTER *Preparation of Will*

FEE *$60 an hour plus disbursements*

Date	Explanation	Hours	Disburse-ments
3/10/--	*Meeting with Mr. and Mrs. James A. Bocklin to discuss new will*	*1*	
3/12/--	*Meeting with Ms. Rose Nelson, trust officer at Central State Savings Bank and Trust Company*	*1½*	
3/12/--	*Mileage to Alma, Michigan, for meeting with Ms. Nelson*		*$7.50*
3/16/--	*Research in preparation of will*	*1*	
3/16/--	*Dictation of will*	*1*	
3/17/--	*Attendance at signing of will*	*1*	

JOB 10
FORM 85
STATEMENT

Paper: Workguide 523

To prepare the statement, you'll need Mr. Bocklin's address: 724 East Tenth Street, Alma, Michigan, 48801. In the Services column of the statement, you'll have to summarize briefly the explanations from the docket. The fee for each entry, as well as a total figure at the bottom, must be computed.

STATEMENT

Ms. Karen Komoto
538 East Fourth Street
Alma, MI 48801

Date March 2, 19--

To: JOSEPH S. GARRETT, P.C.
ATTORNEY-AT-LAW
Kaufmann Building
10 Kemp Place
Mount Pleasant, MI 48858

Date	Services	Fee or Retainer	Disburse-ments	Total
2/23/--	Meeting to discuss will	$ 60.00		
2/25/--	Meeting with Mr. Keffas	120.00		
2/25/--	Mileage to Alma, Michigan		$7.50	
2/26/--	Research for will	60.00		
2/26/--	Dictation of will	60.00		
2/27/--	Signing of will	60.00		
				$367.50

By curving your finger under whenever reaching downward (like d-to-c and j-to-m), you can make such reaches without moving your hands at all. The result is accuracy and greater speed.

SPACE BAR

8-D. Type 2 times. Try to finish both lines in 1 minute.

8-D. PROGRESS CHECK

12 The light unit was out on their washer.   WORDS 8

  Jack had the new unit at home for Olga.   16

| 1 | 2 | 3 | 4 | 5 | 6 | 7 | 8

8-E. SPACE BAR PRACTICE

13 a s d f g h j k l ; a s d f g h j k l ;

14 fog all how for ice kid let add rot and

15 Red Mel Tad Lou Rod Hal Dee Nan Art Joe

8-F. PRACTICE THE B KEY

Use F finger.

16 fff fbf bbb fff fbf bbb fff fbf bbb fbf

17 fbf big big fbf job job fbf bag bag fbf

B with left shift

18 Kalb Haber Hibbs Haben Uber Mabel Kable

B with U

19 burn bunt buck burg bush bunk bulb bull

The colon is the shift of the semicolon.

8-G. PRACTICE THE : KEY

Use Sem finger.

20 ;;; ;:; ::: ;;; ;:; ::: ;;; ;:; ::: ;:;

Colon with left shift

21 Dear Jo: Dear Lu: Dear Ike: Dear Mo:

Colon with U

22 Dear Mr. or Mrs. Uthe: Dear Mrs. Urie:

Colon with B

23 Dear Ben: Dear Mr. Briggs: Dear Beth:

Space twice after a colon; once after a period following an abbreviation.

8-H. Take two 1-minute timings on each of the two notes or type two copies of each. Compute speed and count errors.

8-H. SKILL MEASUREMENT: 1-MINUTE TIMED WRITING

24 Dear Jack: I would like to discuss the   WORDS 8

  Briggs case with Tom at lunch tomorrow.   16

25 Dear Verna: It would be so nice to get   8

  all of our good friends together again.   16

| 1 | 2 | 3 | 4 | 5 | 6 | 7 | 8

The studio will teach no more than 15 children from (Mt.) Pleasant, ages 3 through 9, during the school year. The director, Sandra Richardson, is a certified elementary school teacher with a master's degree in child care.

A review of the only existing zoning ordinance (1961) appears to exclude schools from the community. Where private schools are involved, exclusion is unwarranted because it is unrelated to the health, safety, morals, or welfare of the community. It has been held in Michigan that a zoning ordinance that excludes nursery schools from the residential districts of the community is unreasonable and invalid (Madison v. Black, 11 Misc. 2d 674). It was pointed out in that matter that Section 142, subdivision 2, of the education law provides that a Board of Education in a Union Free School District may maintain nursery schools that shall be free to resident children, and the court found that because public schools may not be excluded from any residential zone, a municipality may not discriminate against similar private educational institutions. The court went on to say: "An ordinance will be stricken if it attempts to exclude private schools from any residential area where public schools are permitted."

It has also been found that the instruction of a small number of preschool children in a home that is equipped for such purpose is considered to be a school although it is not registered under the Michigan Education Law (People v. Wilson, 121 Misc. 566). The court noted that Webster's dictionary defines a school as "a place in which persons are instructed in arts. . .or any aspect of learning". That is precisely what Early Experiences School attempts to do.

More than thirty years ago, in People v. Wilson, supra, the county court concluded that the value of preschools to children could hardly be questioned by anyone whose children had attended a well-run school of this character and that a preschool program qualifies as an educational use and constitutes a school.

That being the case, it would seem appropriate for this Board to determine that the use described as a professional studio of a teacher would encompass the uses in this application.

Line: 40 spaces Drills: 2X	LESSON 9	
Spacing: single	**NEW KEYS**	
Proofguide: 3		
Tape: 9A or K9A		

Goal: To control P, Q, diagonal, and X keys.

9-A. WARMUP

1 Janice saved the violet for her mother.

2 Bertha, too, is eager to take her turn.

3 Dear Bob: Send the June bill to Verna.
| 1 | 2 | 3 | 4 | 5 | 6 | 7 | 8

9-B. PRACTICE THE P KEY

Use Sem finger.

4 ;;; ;p; ppp ;;; ;p; ppp ;;; ;p; ppp ;p;

5 ;p; dip dip ;p; rip rip ;p; tip tip ;p;

6 trap stop page pain park flop pipe paid

7 pane part pace peep prep step pale palm

9-C. PRACTICE THE Q KEY

Use A finger.

8 aaa aqa qqq aaa aqa qqq aaa aqa qqq aqa

9 aqa que que aqa quo quo aqa qui qui aqa

10 quid quad quest quote quell quota quoit

11 quip quit equip equal quilt quite quill

9-D. Type 2 times. Try to finish both lines in 1 minute.

9-D. PROGRESS CHECK

12 Dear Paula: Pat and Joann paid quite a   WORDS 8

    price for a quart of quince for Pamela.   16
| 1 | 2 | 3 | 4 | 5 | 6 | 7 | 8

9-E. PRACTICE THE / KEY

Use Sem finger.

13 ;;; ;/; /// ;;; ;/; /// ;;; ;/; /// ;/;

14 ;/; his/her ;/; him/her ;/; us/them ;/;

Diagonal with P

15 peal/peel pail/pale pour/pore pole/poll

Diagonal with Q

16 queue/cue quiet/quite quire/choir quad/

JOB 6   Paper: plain
LETTER 89
MODIFIED-BLOCK STYLE

Here's the cassette for a short letter to Michael J. Graci of Rural Route 3 in Winn, MI 48896. Just use plain paper instead of our letterhead because this letter concerns the Citizens for the Economic Development of Isabella County, of which I'm currently the chairman. In the closing, you don't have to use my title.

dear mr graci ... thank you for your interest in citizens for the economic development of isabella county ... we agree with you that the economy of our county has done well during recent years as compared with many other parts of the state and the country ... (*paragraph*) we are also pleased to find that you agree with us that more can be done to promote economic expansion ... there are no dues for those who want to join our organization ... however ... we do welcome donations for covering our operation costs ... we are simply a group of people who want a forum for discussion ... (*paragraph*) we look forward to seeing you at our next meeting.

JOB 7   Paper: plain
TABLE 67
BOXED TABLE WITH BRACED HEADING

Type this table when you have time, and add the handwritten numbers for the current year.

CITIZENS FOR THE ECONOMIC DEVELOPMENT
OF ISABELLA COUNTY

City or Village	Number of Members		
	1975	1980	
Brinton	4	6	21
Leaton	3	5	18
Mount Pleasant	12	24	44
Rosebush	5	7	20
Shepherd	4	6	17
Weidmann	3	5	22
TOTAL	31	53	?

JOB 8   **Here's the rough draft of a statement of application for the Mount Pleasant zoning board**
REPORT 81   **of appeals. Please type it in regular report format.**
STATEMENT OF
APPLICATION

Paper: plain

STATEMENT OF APPLICATION

This is an application for a determination that Early Experiences School, the day care center ~~presently~~ *currently* conducted at 162 Oak Lane, Mount Pleasant, Michigan, is a permitted accessory use under Section 3.3.1.10(b) in that it is a teaching studio.

The school has been in operation for the past four years. The Department of Social Services *in Michigan* requires a determination that the school is a permitted use prior to issuing a certification.

The basic requirements that (i) the studio is incidental to a residential use and limited to not more than one nonresident assistant, (ii) ~~that~~ it does not occupy more than one floor, and (iii) *it is* not devoted to music or dance are all met.

In Additionally, this school will meet all ~~of~~ the stringent requirements of the ~~Michigan State~~ Department of Social Services for day care centers.

(*Continued on next page.*)

9-F. PRACTICE THE [X] KEY

Use S finger.

17 sss sxs xxx sss sxs xxx sss sxs xxx sxs

X with P

18 pix expel pox expand apex expert expire

19 Quinn had an axle break in Xenia, Ohio.

20 Max bought his quince at the A/X Store.

9-G. Take two 1-minute timings on each note or type two copies of each. Compute speed and count errors.

9-G. SKILL MEASUREMENT: 1-MINUTE TIMED WRITING

WORDS

21 Dear Quinn: Please send the checks for   8
    the June grants to us within the month.   16

22 Dear Viola: Please notice that we have   8
    marked the bill n/c for the six driers.   16

| 1 | 2 | 3 | 4 | 5 | 6 | 7 | 8

Line: 40 spaces   Drills: 2X
Spacing: single
Proofguide: 5
Tape: 10A or K10A

LESSON 10
NEW KEYS

Goal: To control hyphen, Z, Y, and ? keys.

10-A. WARMUP

1 Dear Chuck: The grades were excellent.
2 Jane found three pencils at her school.
3 Robbin Maki bought five quarts of milk.

| 1 | 2 | 3 | 4 | 5 | 6 | 7 | 8

10-B. PRACTICE THE [-] KEY

Use Sem finger.

4 ;;; ;p; ;p-; ;--; ;;; ;p; ;p-; ;--; ;-;

5 ;p- ;-; one-sixth ;p- ;-; part-time ;-;

6 left-hand one-fifth half-time one-sixth

7 one-half, one-third, and one-fourth cup

The reach to the hyphen is very long. Keep the J finger in home position to help guide your hand back after reaching to the hyphen.

10-C. PRACTICE THE [Z] KEY

Use A finger.

8 aaa aza zzz aaa aza zzz aaa aza zzz aza

9 aza zoo zoo aza zed zed aza zee zee aza

10 zest doze zoos zing whiz zinc zone Zola

11 Zola Zerba took her car to an A-Z Shop.

disclaimed is hereby given to the Trustee of the Family Trust of the JAMES

ALLEN BOCKLIN TRUST.

IN WITNESS WHEREOF, I have subscribed my name and set my seal

to this, my Last Will and Testament, consisting of (four (4)) typewritten

pages, this ~~19th~~ *17th* day of ~~July, 1975~~. *March, 19--*   *Please check*

James Allen Bocklin (SEAL)
JAMES ALLEN BOCKLIN

Please check

On the day and / year last above written, the foregoing instru-

ment, consisting of (four (4)) typewritten pages, including the page on

which this attestation clause appears, was signed, sealed, published,

and declared as and for his Last Will and Testament by JAMES ALLEN BOCKLIN,

Testator, in the presence of us, and thereupon we, at his request and in

his presence, and in the presence of each other, and believing him to be

of sound mind, have hereunto subscribed our names as witnesses this ~~19th~~ *17th*

day of ~~July, 1975~~. *March, 19--*

Mary A. Hokenson   of 82 Carlisle Court
Mary A. Hokenson

                                             Mount Pleasant, MI 48858

Dale R. Edmonds   of 3504 River Road
Dale R. Edmonds

                                             Mount Pleasant, MI 48858

Cynthia R. Cook   of ~~1780~~ *1476* University Avenue
~~Cynthia R. Cook~~
Esther C. Bernstein

                                             Mount Pleasant, MI 48858

                                             Please check
                                             (PAGE FOUR OF FOUR)

ELBOW CONTROL. Keep your elbows in close, hanging loosely by your sides. They should not swing out. Keep your shoulders relaxed and your fingers curved.

10-D. Type 2 times. Try to finish both lines in 1 minute.

10-D. PROGRESS CHECK

WORDS

12 Dear Zoe: Jim is a well-known speaker,   8

    and he is a whiz when he is ad-libbing.   16
    | 1 | 2 | 3 | 4 | 5 | 6 | 7 | 8

10-E. PRACTICE THE Y KEY

Use J finger.

13 jjj jyj yyy jjj jyj yyy jjj jyj yyy jyj

14 jyj joy joy jyj jay jay jyj yam yam jyj

Y with hyphen

15 yarn-like texture; yo-yo; year-end sale

Y with Z

16 zany lazy zesty dizzy tizzy crazy fuzzy

The question mark is the shift of the diagonal.

10-F. PRACTICE THE ? KEY

Use Sem finger.

17 ;;; ;/; ;/?; ;??; ;;; ;/; ;/?; ;??; ;?;

18 Was it she? Ed? Did they go? Is she?

19 Are you there? Can you be? Will they?

20 Why not? You cannot? He is? He will?

10-G. Take two 1-minute timings on each note or type two copies of each. Compute speed and count errors.

A hyphen is typed without a space before or after it:
1. To show that a word is divided (line 21).
2. To join words in a compound (line 22).
3. To make a dash, using a second hyphen (line 23).

A dash is two hyphens— without a space.

10-G. SKILL MEASUREMENT: 1-MINUTE TIMED WRITING

WORDS

21 Can you plan to write a few credit let-   8

    ters Monday? I hope you have the time.   16

22 Dear Justin: I hear that you are going   8

    to be one of the six new clerk-typists.   16

23 When do you think that Mr. Quinn can go   8

    on a trip--like Zane--for a year or so?   16
    | 1 | 2 | 3 | 4 | 5 | 6 | 7 | 8

JOB 5 (Continued)

I've dictated the rest of Mr. Bocklin's will on this cassette. He's coming in to sign it at eleven tomorrow morning. Please finish typing it so that I can look it over before he comes in.

This is a continuation of the Bocklin will . . . article iii . . . i give and bequeath my personal and household effects of every kind including . . . but not limited to . . . furniture . . . appliances . . . furnishings . . . silverware . . . china . . . books . . . jewelry . . . wearing apparel . . . boats . . . automobiles . . . and other vehicles . . . life insurance policies . . . and all policies of fire . . . burglary . . . property damage . . . and other insurance on or in connection with the use of this property to my wife . . . CAROL ANN BOCKLIN . . . if she shall survive me . . . if my said wife shall not survive me . . . i give and bequeath all of said property to my children surviving me . . . in approximately equal shares . . . provided . . . however . . . the issue surviving me of a deceased child shall take . . . per stirpes . . . the share their parent would have taken had he or she survived me (*paragraph*) in the event no issue survives me . . . then this bequest shall immediately lapse and fail . . . and the property sought to be conveyed herein shall thereafter be governed by the provisions of Article iv below . . . article iv . . . i give . . . devise . . . and bequeath all the rest . . . residue and remainder of my property and estate . . . of which i may die seized or possessed . . . or to which I may be entitled at the time of my death . . . of whatsoever kind or nature . . . real . . . personal . . . or mixed . . . and wheresoever situated . . . hereinafter referred to as the "Residuary Estate . . ." unto the CENTRAL STATE SAVINGS BANK AND TRUST COMPANY . . . Alma . . . Michigan . . . or any successor . . . as Trustee . . . of the JAMES ALLEN BOCKLIN TRUST . . . an Inter Vivos Trust . . . previously executed by me on august 18 . . . 1983 . . . to be held . . . managed . . . and distributed based upon the terms . . . provisions . . . and conditions as provided in said Inter Vivos Trust as it now exists or as it may subsequently be amended . . . article v . . . i hereby appoint and nominate my daughter . . . MARIE BOCKLIN HARRIS . . . as Executor of this my Last Will and Testament . . . and i direct that no bond be required in any jurisdiction of my Executor . . . or any successors . . . in the event she shall predecease me . . . or if . . . for any reason . . . she is unable or unwilling to accept this trust . . . then i appoint and nominate the CENTRAL STATE SAVINGS BANK AND TRUST COMPANY . . . Alma . . . Michigan . . . to be the Executor instead . . . article vi . . . it is my very strongest intent that my estate not be subject to supervised court administration . . . and I therefore direct that such intent be followed as permitted by section 301 . . . et seq. . . . of the Michigan Revised Probate Code . . . being Public Act 642 of Michigan 1978 . . . unless circumstances occur which I could not have anticipated which would require a supervised court administration to protect the interest of my estate and its beneficiaries . . . article vii . . . in the event that my death and that of my said wife shall occur as a result of a common disaster . . . my said wife shall be considered for the purpose of this Will to have survived me . . . article viii . . . my said wife may disclaim in whole or in part any interest passing to her under this Will or otherwise . . . any interest so disclaimed is hereby given to the Trustee of the Family Trust of the JAMES ALLEN BOCKLIN TRUST.

Now please finish the will with IN WITNESS WHEREOF and so on. I've edited the last page of Bocklin's previous will so that you can copy from it. Be sure that all the signature lines are on the same page as the statement the witnesses are to sign.

NOTE: On legal documents, wording that is valid in one state may not be valid in other states.

WP Errors are not permitted in a legal document. To achieve a perfect copy, correct errors on the screen and then print out the perfect document.

Line: 40 spaces	Drills: 2X
Spacing: single	except
Proofguide: 5	as noted
Tape: 11A or K11A	

LESSON 11
REVIEW

Goals: To strengthen all controls; to type paragraph copy.

11-A.   WARMUP

1   Mack bought eight cans of quality corn.
2   Walt Axton liked a variety of pop jazz.

| 1 | 2 | 3 | 4 | 5 | 6 | 7 | 8

11-B.   INDICATING A NEW PARAGRAPH

When a paragraph is double-spaced, indent the first word 5 spaces. Use the tabulator for this indention. Study the steps for using the tabulator mechanism on page xiv.

When a paragraph is single-spaced, precede it with 1 blank line. The first word may be either indented 5 spaces or blocked at the margin. (See illustrations below.)

```
Dear Mary:

     Thank you for sending the
game to Jim.  He was happy the
game came on his birthday.

     Where did you find such a
zany game?  Everyone has had a
time learning the rules.
```

Double-spaced, indented.

```
Dear Mary

     Thank you for sending the
game to Jim.  He was happy the
game came on his birthday.

     Where did you find such a
zany game?  Everyone has had a
time learning the rules.

     Could you possibly send a
list of other games?  Jim does
like these games.  So do I.
```

Single-spaced, indented.

```
Dear Mary

Thank you for sending the game
to Jim.  He was happy the game
came on his birthday.

Where did you find such a zany
game?  Everyone has had a time
learning the rules.

Could you possibly send a list
of other games?  Jim does like
these games.  So do I.
```

Single-spaced, blocked.

The word counts in this book credit you with 1 word (5 strokes) for each indention and each extra carriage return you must make in a timing.

11-C. Spacing—single; tab— 5. Take a 1-minute timing on each paragraph, or type one complete copy. Compute speed and count errors. Use the tabulator to indent.

11-C.   PRACTICE: KEYBOARD CONTROL

			WORDS
3	5 →	Vicky ordered a dozen jugs and six	8
		rugs from a port in Iraq. They will be	16
		beautiful in a room.	20
4	5 →	The vessel was equipped with extra	8
		boats just in case Liz took many kayaks	16
		for George in Juneau.	20

| 1 | 2 | 3 | 4 | 5 | 6 | 7 | 8

Do not pause at the vertical lines that mark off the phrases.

11-D.   PRACTICE: PHRASES

5   if it|if it is|if it is a|if it is able
6   it is|it is at|it is at a|it is at Alma
7   is to|is to go|is to go a|is to go away

Here's the first page of the Bocklin will. I've almost finished dictating the rest of it. When I'm through, I'll bring the cassette to you right away. This will should be ready by tomorrow morning.

Paper:
 Workguide 511–
 519

LAST WILL AND TESTAMENT

OF

JAMES ALLEN BOCKLIN

I, <u>James Allen Bocklin</u>, in the City of Alma, Michigan, being of

sound mind for the purpose of making disposition upon my death of my

entire estate, real, personal, and mixed, and any estate which I have the

power to dispose of, of whatsoever kind and wheresoever situate, whether

owned and possessed by me at the date of execution hereof, of acquired by

me after such date, do hereby make, publish, and declare this to be my

Last Will and Testament.

Article I

I hereby expressly revoke and cancel any and all Wills, Codicils, or other
testamentary dispositions at any time heretofore made by me.

Article II

I hereby confirm my intention that the beneficial interest in all property, real or personal, tangible or intangible (including joint checking
or savings accts. in any bank or Savings and Loan Association), which is
registered or held, at the time of my death, jointly in the names of myself and any other person (excluding any tenancy in common), shall pass
by right of survivorship or operation of law and outside the terms of

this will to such other person, if he or she survives me. To the extent

that my intention may be defeated by any rule of law, I give, devise, and

bequeath all such jointly held property to such other person or persons

who shall survive me.

PAGE ONE OF FIVE

11-E. PRACTICE: WORD FAMILIES

8 TH their those there they that this the
9 HA hairy halls habit hand halt hams hay
10 Can they sell the hams by halves there?
11 LE lends legal leaps less lean lead let
12 DU ducks ducal dusky dune dumb duke due
13 The duck legs are to be shipped Monday.
14 RE relic reply repay rear read rest red
15 NO noble noted noisy note nose noon not
16 He need not read the reply to the note.

11-F. SKILL MEASUREMENT: 1-MINUTE TIMED WRITING

11-F. Take a 1-minute timing on each paragraph, or type one complete copy. Compute speed and count errors.

WORDS

17 Dear Al: Both the quiz and exam proved   8
to be hard. Joyce felt giving them was   16
a true way to teach.   20

18 Dear Vera: Mary was quick to grasp the   8
pan from Buzz. She had lit the gas jet   16
not expecting anyone.   20

| 1 | 2 | 3 | 4 | 5 | 6 | 7 | 8

Line: 40 spaces   Tab: 5
Spacing: single   Drills: 2X
Proofguide: 5
Tape: 12A or K12A

LESSON 12
CLINIC REVIEW

Goal: To strengthen all controls.

12-A. WARMUP

1 Joel was amazed six had quit the games.
2 The five carts were kept mainly by Lil.

| 1 | 2 | 3 | 4 | 5 | 6 | 7 | 8

12-B. PRACTICE: KEYBOARD CONTROL

12-B. Spacing—double; tab—5. Take a 2-minute timing and note speed and error scores, or type one complete copy.

WORDS

3 5→   The World Series is a sports event   8
baseball fans expect to see. They buzz   16
with the latest acquired facts. As the   24
Series draws near, the fans want to buy   32
tickets to see their team win the game.   40

| 1 | 2 | 3 | 4 | 5 | 6 | 7 | 8

JOB 4

Legal documents have historically been typed on legal-size paper, which measures 8½ inches by 14 inches. These sheets require large file folders and outsize file cabinets. Special attention is required in word processing, microfilming, photocopying, and mechanized filing.

The federal court system has eliminated legal-size files as a cost-cutting measure. As a result, the trend throughout the legal profession is to use 8½-inch by 11-inch paper.

Standard manuscript procedures are used for vertical placement of copy in legal documents. One-page documents are vertically centered on the page. The first page of a multiple-page document has a top margin of 2 inches; subsequent pages have 1-inch top margins. The bottom margins of all pages are from 1 to 1½ inches in depth.

CONTRACT

THIS AGREEMENT, made and concluded this sixteenth day of March, 19--, by and between the firm of Thomas Brothers, Inc., of 2403 Hoffman Court, Mt. Pleasant, Michigan, party of the first part, and Roy D. Gust, 758 Kocar Street, Mt. Pleasant, Michigan, party of the second part.

WITNESSETH

ARTICLE 1. The said party of the 2d part covenants and agrees to and with the party of the 1st part, to furnish his services to the said party of the first part as Sales Representative for the upper peninsula of Michigan for the period of six (6) calendar months, beginning April 1, 19--, and expiring September 30, 19--; and the said party of the second part covenants and agrees to perform all duties incident to such employment.

ARTICLE 2. And the said party of the first part covenants and agrees to pay the said party of the second part, for the same, the sum of twelve thousand dollars ($12,000) in six (6) equal installments of two thousand dollars ($2,000) each, one (1) installment to be paid on the last working day of each month during the stated period of employment. Expenses incurred will also be reimbursed to the party of the second part by the party of the first part on a monthly basis.

IN WITNESS WHEREOF, the parties of this contract have hereunto set their hands and seals, the day and year first above written.

Party of the First Part: Party of the Second Part:

Esther
Elizabeth R. Zimmerman, President   Roy D. Gust
Thomas Brothers, Inc.

Witness to Signature   Witness to Signature

12-C. PRACTICE: PHRASES

Do not pause at the vertical lines that mark off the phrases.

4 if we | if we can | if we can go | if we came
5 so it | so it was | so it was to | so it must
6 as it | as it can | as it can be | as it will

7 the man | the man will | the man will go in
8 was the | was the bill | was the bill to go
9 how can | how can they | how can they be at

10 they went | they went by | they went by her
11 less than | less than it | less than it was
12 they came | they came in | they came in for

12-D. PRACTICE: WORD FAMILIES

13 our hour sour tour your pour four flour
14 ate late fate gate mate date rate crate
15 Our train was an hour late at the gate.

16 ear year tear sear fear hear near clear
17 ill hill fill kill mill pill dill drill
18 Will fear keep Paul from the high hill?

19 ink pink sink link wink mink kink think
20 ail bail tail mail sail jail rail trail
21 Do you think the mail will be too late?

12-E. PRACTICE: TAB INDENTING

12-E. Set a tab stop every 9 spaces from the left margin. Then type lines 22–24, pressing the tab key after typing each word. Type each line twice.

22 at TAB → at TAB → at TAB → at TAB → at
23 hat   hat   hat   hat   hat
24 that   that   that   that   that

12-F. SKILL MEASUREMENT: 2-MINUTE TIMED WRITING

12-F. Spacing—double; tab—5. Take a 2-minute timing and note speed and error scores, or type one complete copy.

	WORDS
25 5 → The Blue Jays won the first game a	8
month ago. The excitement over the win	16
has caused their fans to acquire a blue	24
team pennant. Many of their fans prize	32
these as a way to keep up team spirits.	40

| 1 | 2 | 3 | 4 | 5 | 6 | 7 | 8

214–218. INTEGRATED OFFICE PROJECT: JOSEPH S. GARRETT, ATTORNEY-AT-LAW

Situation: Today is Monday, March 16. You are secretary to Mr. Joseph S. Garrett, attorney-at-law. His office is in the Kaufmann Building at 10 Kemp Place in Mount Pleasant, MI 48858.

While you perform other office tasks for Mr. Garrett, much of your work is directly related to the preparation of legal documents. Mr. Garrett prefers to use the modified-block letter style and standard punctuation. Closing lines are as follows:

                    Sincerely yours,

                    Joseph S. Garrett
                    Attorney-at-Law

FORM 81   Workguide: 501
JOB PRIORITY LIST

Before you begin your work, review the items in this project. Then, on workguide page 501, assign a 1, 2, or 3 priority to each item.

JOBS 1–2   Paper: Workguide 503
FORMS 82–83
VOUCHER CHECKS

I need to have you prepare a couple of voucher checks for me to sign:

The first check is for payment of the March office rent, payable to Monsanto Realty, Inc., 331 Livingston Building, Mount Pleasant, in the amount of $950.

The second check is in the amount of $142.36, payable to Central Office Supply Company for office supplies. The amount is in payment of Invoice 5941. Their office is located at 82 Carson Drive, Mount Pleasant.

JOB 3   Paper: Workguide 505–506
LETTER 88
TWO-PAGE LETTER WITH TABLE

I've dictated a letter to the career counselor at the Mount Pleasant High School. It should go out in the next day or so, but it isn't urgent.

This is a letter to Ruth A. Hartman, Career Counselor, Mount Pleasant High School, 25 Carson Drive, Mount Pleasant.

dear ms. hartman ... i am pleased to have the opportunity to pass on to you and your students some information about career opportunities in the legal profession ... your questions were well thought out and very appropriate ... (*paragraph*) the numbers of people in each of the different job classifications in this region are shown below (*arrange the following information in two columns*) ... attorneys ... 163 ... paralegals ... 14 ... legal assistants ... 5 ... lawyers' assistants ... 2 ... law clerks ... 19 ... legal secretaries ... 106 ... other office support staff ... 77 ... (*paragraph*) the attorneys who are the managers of larger firms are called either senior partners or senior members of the firm ... the attorneys who work for them are usually called associates ... (*paragraph*) paralegals ... legal assistants ... and lawyers' assistants perform pretty much the same function for the firm ... they assist with research as well as other areas of legal work ... some educational institutions have special programs that prepare people for this work ... (*paragraph*) because many law firms in rural areas are quite small ... they often have only one office employee ... that person is usually called a legal secretary and has the responsibility for the operation of the entire office ... (*paragraph*) enclosed is a brochure that tells more about these types of jobs ... if your students have further questions about careers in the legal field ... i would be happy to meet with a group of them at a time we find mutually convenient.

WP Transcribing on a word processor from either shorthand or a transcribing machine is fast and efficient if the wraparound feature is employed because the operator can type at rough-draft speed and does not have to listen for the bell or worry about the right margin.

JOB 4   Paper: Workguide 507–509
REPORT 79
CONTRACT

I've made a few changes on the draft of the employment contract you typed last week. The final contract has to be ready for Zimmerman and Gust to sign at three this afternoon.

| Line: 50 spaces   Tab: 5, center |
| Spacing: single   Drills: 3X |
| Proofguide: 5 |
| Workguide: 3–4, 45 |
| Tape: 13A or K1B |

LESSON 13

SKILL DRIVE

Goals: To improve speed/
accuracy; to center material
horizontally.

S = Speed
A = Accuracy

13-A. WARMUP

S 1 All of the new boys were to be on the job by six.
A 2 Keith was amazed that Pam could quit giving help.
      | 1 | 2 | 3 | 4 | 5 | 6 | 7 | 8 | 9 | 10

13-B. PRETEST: KEYBOARD CONTROL

PRETEST. Take a 1-minute
timing; compute speed and
errors.

3   Only six men paid their dues. Did Fred pull 10
their cards? If not, Fred may wish to do so now. 20
      | 1 | 2 | 3 | 4 | 5 | 6 | 7 | 8 | 9 | 10

13-C. PRACTICE: ALTERNATE HANDS

PRACTICE. If you made 2
or fewer errors on the
Pretest, type each
individual line 3 times;
otherwise, type each group
of lines (as though each
group were a paragraph) 3
times.

4 emblem handle ivory bible clay corn men did or is
5 visual bushel panel handy oaks idle fit fir if so
6 profit dismay right their paid kept she fix of it
7 She made a profit on the bushel of corn she kept.

13-D. PRACTICE: ONE HAND

8 pill card race tear kill fear jump fare upon pull
9 join wade lump east hump weed pony case loop face
10 hill card vest mill date only raft noon dear Fred
11 A pony drew a pink cart uphill in a race at noon.

13-E. PRACTICE: SHIFT KEY

12 Lois Jane Bill Kirk Fred Ruth Dick Lola Jean Hank
13 Kate Anna Tina Carl Norm Olga Zora Bess Reid Cora

POSTTEST. Repeat the Pretest
and compare performance.

13-F. POSTTEST: KEYBOARD CONTROL

13-G. Spacing—double; tab—5.
Take a 2-minute timing or make
one copy. Compute speed and
error scores and record on
Workguide page 3.

13-G. SKILL MEASUREMENT: 2-MINUTE TIMED WRITING

14   Have you ever been on a vacation for a week? 10
Just think of the places you could go if you were 20
given the time.   23
        You would be amazed at how quickly trips can 33
be mapped to some unexpected place.   40
      | 1 | 2 | 3 | 4 | 5 | 6 | 7 | 8 | 9 | 10

213-E. PRACTICE: ' # ; &

15 ' ;'; ;''; ;';'; ;'; ;''; ;';'; ;'; It's I've Bill's firm's
16 # de3 de3# de#ed d#d de3# de#ed d#d #10 #29 #38 #47 and #56
17 ; ;;; ;';l ;'"'; ;;; ;';l ;'"'; ;;; played; flowed; jumped;
18 & ju7 ju7& ju&uj j&j ju7& ju&uj j&j 32 & 54 & 76 & 98 & 100
19 Nielsen & Son won't buy #12; B&J won't buy #13; but I will.
    | 1 | 2 | 3 | 4 | 5 | 6 | 7 | 8 | 9 | 10 | 11 | 12

POSTTEST. Repeat the Pretest
and compare performance.

213-F. POSTTEST: SYMBOL REVIEW

213-G. Spacing—double.
Take two 5-minute timings.
Between them, practice any
words with which you had
difficulty. Record your score.

213-G. SKILL MEASUREMENT: 5-MINUTE TIMED WRITING

20   The job prospects are usually excellent for one who is   12
qualified to work as a legal secretary. For members of the   24
law office team, a professional attitude and appearance are   36
essential. A professional atmosphere must prevail when the   48
secretary interacts with lawyers, the lawyers' clients, the   60
courts, and the public. Lawyers have a right to expect the   72
highest degree of integrity from their secretaries. Every-   84
thing that concerns the clients and the firm's lawyers must   96
be kept in strict confidence.   102

        Only those who have high-level skills will be hired as 114
legal secretaries. No one is surprised to find that typing   126
and shorthand skills are the first ones on the list. It is   138
also no surprise that a legal vocabulary and spelling skill   150
are the types of skills that one will need to work in a law   162
office. There is a need to understand legal procedures and   174
to be familiar with documents and court functions.   184

        Young people must realize that, in addition to working 196
in a law office, one may choose to work in one of the areas   208
of governmental law, in a court system, in insurance, or in   220
the tax field. The unique skills that one needs to work in   232
a legal job can be acquired at business colleges, community   244
colleges, and four-year colleges. Those who do well in the   256
law office will have high ethical standards and be loyal to   268
the firm.   270
    | 1 | 2 | 3 | 4 | 5 | 6 | 7 | 8 | 9 | 10 | 11 | 12

13-H. Do Workguide page 45 before doing 13-H.

13-H. HORIZONTAL CENTERING

To center words across the page:

1. Set the carrier or carriage at the center point of the paper.

2. Find the backspace key in the upper left or right corner of the keyboard. This key is controlled by the nearest little finger.

3. Say the strokes (including spaces) to yourself in pairs, pressing and releasing the backspace key one time for each pair of strokes. For example:

Ma|ry| L|ou|is|e |Ar|no|ld|

CAUTION: If you have a letter left over after calling out the pairs, do *not* backspace for this letter. For example:

Cl|in|t |F.| B|au|me(r)

4. Type the words. They should appear centered on the line.

PRACTICE. Center each of these names.

Mary Louise Arnold
John E. Kraeer
Nancy Omar
Ellis Manack
Jean Alice Alexa
Clint F. Baumer

CHECK: The letter A should align vertically.

Line: 50 spaces Tab: 5, center	LESSON 14
Spacing: single Drills: 3X	
Proofguide: 5	**SKILL DRIVE**
Workguide: 3–4	
Tape: 14A or K2B	

Goals: To improve speed/accuracy; to type in all capitals.

14-A. WARMUP

S 1 June was to be at the store by five to meet Lola.
A 2 Did Paul expect Quinn or George to keep the maze?
   | 1 | 2 | 3 | 4 | 5 | 6 | 7 | 8 | 9 | 10

14-B. PRETEST: KEYBOARD CONTROL

PRETEST. Take a 1-minute timing; compute speed and count errors.

3   The muffler was off the car. Harry placed a 10
call to fix it. All costs are to be on his bill. 20
   | 1 | 2 | 3 | 4 | 5 | 6 | 7 | 8 | 9 | 10

14-C. PRACTICE: PHRASES

PRACTICE. If you made 2 or fewer errors on the Pretest, type each individual line 3 times; otherwise, type each group of lines (as though each group were a paragraph) 3 times.

4 the muffler| the muffler was| the muffler was off a
5 placed a| placed a call| placed a call to| placed it
6 call to| call to fix| call to fix it| call to fix it
7 are to| are to be| are to be on| are to be on it| are

14-D. PRACTICE: DOUBLE LETTERS

8 LL illegal equally falling allows alloys call all
9 FF muffler diffuse effects suffer offers duff off
10 DD toddler caddies muddles saddle toddle adds odd
11 He allowed time for the call to be made to Sally.

Line: 60 spaces   Tab: 5
Spacing: single   Drills: 3X
Proofguide: 137–138
Workguide: 331–332,
501–523
Tape: 54B and 55B

INTEGRATED OFFICE PROJECT: LEGAL
LESSONS 213–218

GOALS FOR UNIT 35

1. Type at least 54 wam for 5 minutes with no more than 5 errors.
2. Improve symbol typing skills.
3. Type letters and legal documents, applying rules of capitalization and punctuation.
4. Type forms and voucher checks.
5. Construct a table from dictated information.
6. Construct a boxed table with braced heading.
7. Develop an understanding of various jobs in a legal office.
8. Set priorities.

213-A. WARMUP

S 1 Len got rid of the rocks in the right field eight days ago.
A 2 Eleven excited citizens enjoyed the quip about melted snow.
N 3 Edward bowled scores of 174, 191, and 203 for a 568 series.
    | 1 | 2 | 3 | 4 | 5 | 6 | 7 | 8 | 9 | 10 | 11 | 12

213-B. PRETEST: SYMBOL REVIEW

PRETEST. **Take a 1-minute timing; compute speed and errors.**

4   The following keys are used quite often: quotation ", 12
colon :, hyphen –, underline _, and apostrophe '. However, 24
the dollar sign $, diagonal /, ampersand &, parentheses (), 36
number #, and percent % keys are used much less frequently. 48
    | 1 | 2 | 3 | 4 | 5 | 6 | 7 | 8 | 9 | 10 | 11 | 12

213-C. PRACTICE: % – " /

PRACTICE. **If you made no errors on the Pretest, type each line 3 times. If you made 1 error or more, type each group of four lines (as though it were a paragraph) 3 times; then type the sentence 3 times.**

5 % ft5 ft5% ft%tf f%f ft5% ft%tf f%f 41% 39% 57% 20% and 86%
6 – ;p– ;p–; ;p–p; ;–; ;p–; ;p–p; ;–; round-faced self-esteem
7 " ;'; ;'"; ;'"'; ;"; ;'"; ;'"'; ;"; "Why?" "Yes." "No, Al,"
8 / ;/; ;//; ;/;/; ;/; ;//; ;/;/; ;/; 1/2 2/3 3/4 2/5 1/6 3/7
9 "One-half or 1/2 equals 50%; one-tenth or 1/10 equals 10%."
    | 1 | 2 | 3 | 4 | 5 | 6 | 7 | 8 | 9 | 10 | 11 | 12

213-D. PRACTICE: : $ _ ( )

10 : ;:; ;::; ;:;:; ;:; ;::; ;:;:; ;:; listed below: follows:
11 $ fr4 fr4$ fr$rf f$f fr4$ fr$rf f$f $64 $770 $2,859 $31,165
12 _ ;p– ;p–_ ;p_p; ;_; ;p–_ ;p_p; ;_; can not be Bert and Pam
13 () 1; lo9(lo(ol l(l ;p0) ;p)p; ;); (east) (38%) (National)
14 The Friday hockey scores: NMU Wildcats 7 and UM Gophers 5.
    | 1 | 2 | 3 | 4 | 5 | 6 | 7 | 8 | 9 | 10 | 11 | 12

14-E. Make two copies. Copy 1: Type each sentence on a separate line. Copy 2: Type each sentence on a separate line, but tab-indent it 5 spaces.

POSTTEST. Repeat the Pretest and compare performance.

14-E. PRACTICE: CARRIER/CARRIAGE RETURN

12 Call me.   Is he going?   Ask him.   See if she can.
13 Why not?   Meet me.   Did you go?   No, sir.   I may.

14-F. POSTTEST: KEYBOARD CONTROL

14-G. Spacing—double; tab—5. Take a 2-minute timing or make one copy. Record score on Workguide page 3.

14-G. SKILL MEASUREMENT: 2-MINUTE TIMED WRITING

14   Have you read the recent books on cooking on 10
trips? They have an amazing quantity of meals to 20
prepare on the next trip. 25
     The books are for sale for just a few cents. 35
Expect the best from her. 40

| 1 | 2 | 3 | 4 | 5 | 6 | 7 | 8 | 9 | 10 |

14-H. TYPING IN ALL CAPITALS

To type in all capitals:
1. Depress the shift lock.
2. Type the word or words.
3. Release the lock by touching the right shift key.

PRACTICE. Center each of these five lines horizontally. The letter E lines up.

An Interview by James Hill on
THE NEW AMERICAN CAR
Designed and Produced by the
EVERHART COMPANY
Tremont, Mississippi

Line: 50 spaces	Tab: 5, center
Spacing: single	Drills: 3X
Proofguide: 5	
Workguide: 3–4, 46	
Tape: 15A or K3B	

LESSON 15
SKILL DRIVE

Goals: To improve speed/accuracy; to center material vertically.

15-A. WARMUP

S 1 If she can go to the zoo, let us know right away.
A 2 Pamela quickly fixed the valve for Bob and Jerry.

| 1 | 2 | 3 | 4 | 5 | 6 | 7 | 8 | 9 | 10 |

15-B. PRETEST: KEYBOARD CONTROL

PRETEST. Take a 1-minute timing; compute speed and errors.

3   The arid country was just the answer for his 10
cold. Jack remained long enough for his lungs to 20
clear. 21

| 1 | 2 | 3 | 4 | 5 | 6 | 7 | 8 | 9 | 10 |

JOB 14   *Start on* ——→ ITINERARY FOR MR. R. KL~~IE~~EN

line 7   February 23-2~~7~~6, 19--

MONDAY, FEBRUARY 23

     7:55 a.m.   Depart Los Angeles, *Los Angeles* International airport
                             ~~on~~ NAL flight 519.

     4:15 p.m.   Arrive *New York* Kennedy International Airport, ~~New~~
                             ~~York.~~ Limousine to Liberty Towers Hotel.

     7:30 p.m.   Dinner with Mr. Frank Tonnelle (Eastern
                             Industries).

TUESDAY, FEBRUARY 24

     8:00 a.m.   Breakfast with Ms. Carol Karwoski (Eastern
                             Industries).

    10:00 a.m.   Presentation to Eastern Industries Board
                             of Directors.

    12:30 p.m.   Lunch with board.

     5:05 p.m.   Depart New York, *La Guardia Airport* on Eastern Commuters
                             Flight ~~240.~~

     6:20 p.m.   *312* Arrive *Boston* Logan Airport, ~~Boston.~~ Reserva-
                             tions at Lo-Port Motel.

     8:00 p.m.   Social Hour--National Electronics Associa-
                             tion Conference, *Mezzanine 10-B.*

WEDNESDAY, FEBRUARY 25

     8:00 a.m.   Opening session of conference--Patriots
                             Ballroom.

    12:00 noon   Luncheon--sit at head table.

     2:00 p.m.   Presentation--Patriots Ballroom.

     6:00 p.m.   Social Hour--Mezzanine 10-B.

     8:00 p.m.   Banquet--Mezzanine 10-A.

THURSDAY, FEBRUARY 26

     8:15   Depart *Boston* Logan Airport, on *NAL* Flight 602.
     ~~8:14~~ a.m.

    10:10 a.m.   Arrive Los Angeles *Los Angeles* International airport.

PRACTICE. If you made 2 or fewer errors on the Pretest, type each individual line 3 times; otherwise, type each group of lines (as though they were a paragraph) 3 times.

15-C. PRACTICE: IN REACHES

4 AR argued arisen armed arena arson army arty arid
5 LU lucent lugged lunge lucky lusty lung lull lugs
6 IN taping remain stain sting train into sing rain
7 The army train was lucky to get into the station.

15-D. PRACTICE: CONSECUTIVE STROKES

8 SW answer swears sweet swift swell swim swam swap
9 OL polled polite poles moles older polo cold tool
10 JU adjust junket judge juicy jumbo jump jury just
11 The judges had decided to pick the sweet flowers.

15-E. PRACTICE: SPACE BAR

12 a b c d e f g h i j k l m n o p q r s t u v w x y

13 an is to go in it is if of so at an by we the and

14 She is to go if he can go to the show in an hour.

POSTTEST. Repeat the Pretest and compare performance.

15-F. POSTTEST: KEYBOARD CONTROL

15-G. Spacing—double; tab—5. Take a 2-minute timing or one copy. Record score on Workguide page 3.

15-G. SKILL MEASUREMENT: 2-MINUTE TIMED WRITING

15   The team added zing to the pep rally. Seven 10
excited students were quick to jest with the four 20
players who were taken to the front of the stage. 30
They were given a plaque by the students, league, 40
and school. 42

| 1 | 2 | 3 | 4 | 5 | 6 | 7 | 8 | 9 | 10

NOTE: Before doing 15-H, do Workguide page 46.

15-H. VERTICAL CENTERING

For material to look centered, the top and bottom margins must appear to be the same. To center a group of lines and to provide for an equal top and bottom margin:

1. Count the lines (including blank ones) that the material will occupy when typed.

2. Subtract that number from the number of lines available on your paper. Most typewriters space 6 lines to an inch. Standard typing paper is 11 inches long. Therefore, 11 × 6 = 66 lines on a full page or 33 lines on a half page.

3. Divide the remainder by 2 (drop any fraction) to find the number of the

line, counting from the top, on which to begin typing.

EXAMPLE: To center 5 double-spaced lines on a half sheet, you need 9 lines (5 typed, 4 blank); 33 − 9 = 24 ÷ 2 = 12. Begin typing on line 12.

PRACTICE. Center the material below on a half sheet. Double-space. Center each line horizontally. The letter A lines up.

LOCAL THEATERS
Alhambra
Lake Shore
CENTER → Spartan Twin
Fox State Lake Quads

CENTER CHECK. To see whether you have correctly centered the work vertically, fold the paper top to bottom and make a crease across the center. The crease should come close to the point indicated by the arrow.

JOBS 9–10   Paper: Workguide 491–494
LETTERS 84–85
COMPOSED LETTERS

Mrs. Schopper has a rush job for you. Please prepare letters to Charles Varnum and Carmen Cabrillo. She has written their addresses on this slip of paper. Enclose a copy of our new price list, and tell them that she plans to accompany Richard Renshaw, our sales representative in the San Francisco area, when he visits them in March. She wants to discuss prospects for a new product line with them.

Mr. Charles T. Varnum, Manager
Varnum Sales & Service
3740 Commercial Street
San Francisco, CA 94108

Miss Carmen M. Cabrillo
Director of Marketing
Mor-Value Hardwares, Inc.
11032 Linares Avenue
San Francisco, CA 94116

JOBS 11–12   Paper: Workguide 495–498
LETTERS 86–87
SIMPLIFIED STYLE

When you've finished the letters to Varnum and Cabrillo, please transcribe the material on this cassette.

This is Mrs. Schopper. I've a few items that can be handled routinely. The first one is a letter to be used in a mass mailing that will be sent to the members of the California Industrial Education Association (CIEA).

dear ciea member ... the purpose of this letter is to introduce you to the industrial training systems that are now being offered by electronic systems, inc ... esi is dedicated to the development and distribution of industrial training systems in the areas of electrical maintenance ... motor control and instrumentation systems ... and programmable controllers ... two basic systems are offered ...

I'm not going to bother to dictate all the information that describes the EL-210 and EL-320. Just copy the two paragraphs that describe them from the letter that I wrote to Ms. Headley in Colorado Springs a few days ago.

Then conclude with the california distributor for esi is crowley & sons ... please contact one of their representatives or our office directly concerning any questions you may have ... our goal is to serve your educational needs in any way that we can.

The second letter is addressed to Mr. Ronald J. Berg, president of the Berg Business Institute, at 2400 Industrial Road, Las Vegas, NV 89102.

dear mr. berg ... i am happy to accept your invitation to speak at your marketing conference in april about the success of our small company in the highly competitive electronics field ...

as you suggest ... my presentation will deal with our tele-sales program that won the national marketing association award in december ... it is my understanding that the presentation is to last one hour and that approximately 300 people will attend ...

thank you for your invitation ... i will contact you at a later date concerning final arrangements.

Please send a carbon copy of the second letter to Stanford T. Owens.

JOB 13   Paper: Workguide 499
MEMORANDUM 25

And finally a memo to Stanford T. Owens, our field representative in Las Vegas. The subject is Speech in Las Vegas.

you will find a copy of a recent letter to mr. ronald j. berg attached ... please contact mr. berg and take care of any details in connection with the trip ... i look forward to seeing you again.

JOB 14   Paper: plain
REPORT 78
ITINERARY

Mr. Klein will be taking a business trip to New York and Boston during the week of February 23. Final arrangements have been completed, and the edited draft of his itinerary is now ready for retyping.

Line: 50 spaces   Tab: 5, center
Spacing: single   Drills: 3X
Proofguide: 7
Workguide: 3—4
Tape: 1B or K4B

LESSON 16
SKILL DRIVE

Goals: To improve speed/accuracy; to center paragraphs.

16-A.   WARMUP

S 1 Ask if Jane is to go to their city by car or bus.
A 2 Mac gave her five or six equal awards for prizes.
      | 1 | 2 | 3 | 4 | 5 | 6 | 7 | 8 | 9 | 10

16-B.   PRETEST: KEYBOARD CONTROL

PRETEST.   Take a 1-minute timing; compute speed and errors.

3   He said the poems were to be edited by Edith 10
   in June. She will need all of her skills to save 20
   them.   21
      | 1 | 2 | 3 | 4 | 5 | 6 | 7 | 8 | 9 | 10

PRACTICE.   If you made 2 or fewer errors on the Pretest, type each individual line 3 times; otherwise, type each group of lines (as though each group were a paragraph) 3 times.

16-C.   PRACTICE: ADJACENT KEYS

4 PO policies poetry poems pools polls port pot pod
5 WE weakness weaver weigh wears weans were wet web
6 SA salaries sailed sales saint sands save sat sap
7 We were to poll the troops as soon as we were in.

16-D.   PRACTICE: UP REACHES

8   ED educated edited Edith edges edict need fed led
9   JU juvenile junior judge juice jumbo June jut jug
10 KI kindness skills kites kinds kitty king kit kin
11 The judge told Dean Kingly to swear to the truth.

16-E.   NOTE: Release the shift lock whenever a stroke that cannot be typed in capitals (a hyphen, for example) appears among the capitalized letters.

16-E.   PRACTICE: SHIFT LOCK

12 They could BUY tickets at LOWE-MANN or ARC-HURON.
13 The ads read SALE--Two GREAT DANES at a low cost.

POSTTEST.   Repeat the Pretest and compare performance.

16-F.   POSTTEST: KEYBOARD CONTROL

16-G.   Spacing—double; tab—5. Record your score.

16-G.   SKILL MEASUREMENT: 2-MINUTE TIMED WRITING

14   The zoo in our city is an exciting place for 10
   kids. They love to watch monkeys jump to catch a 20
   nut.   21
         Many questions are asked. Some want to know 31
   about the kind of food all of the animals will be 41
   fed.   42
      | 1 | 2 | 3 | 4 | 5 | 6 | 7 | 8 | 9 | 10

WP If this table had been stored on electronic media when it was originally typed, it could be easily updated by deleting customers who have paid and moving amounts from column to column.

ELECTRONIC SYSTEMS, INC.

OVERDUE ACCOUNTS

February 28, 19--
~~January 31, 19--~~

Account	60 Days Overdue	~~120~~ 90 Days Overdue	Total Overdue
Ms. Jenna Cray, Manager Redford International 2245 Hanover Palo Alto, CA 94306	$ 420.50 →		$ 420.50
Mr. Robert E. Boyum ET Systems 3340 Brockton Avenue Riverside, CA 92501	1,460.00 →	~~$ 325.00~~	*1,460.00* ~~1,785.00~~
~~Mr. James G. LaFave~~ ~~Technical Center~~ ~~5200 Folsom Boulevard~~ ~~Sacramento, CA 95819~~		~~2,105.00~~	~~2,105.00~~
Miss Frances Janofski, Head Janofski Training School 6050 Del Loma North San Gabriel, CA 91775	740.25 →		740.25
Mr. Alfred I. Haydon Haydon Institute 460 East Military Road Tacoma, WA 98445	1,080.35 →	~~60.45~~	*1,080.35* ~~1,140.80~~
Mr. Allen Bekins, Manager ECTA, Inc. 2130 Canby Street, S.W. Portland, OR 97219	572.80 →		572.80
~~EEE, Inc.~~ ~~8225 Roosevelt Way, NE~~ ~~Seattle, WA 98115~~	~~1,320.60~~	~~962.30~~	~~2,282.90~~
Mr. Jay Ritter, Instructor Institute of Technology 1480 South Lowell Boulevard Denver, CO 80219	*542.25* 835.80 →		*1,378.05* ~~835.80~~
TOTALS	~~$6,430.30~~ ?	~~$3,452.75~~ ?	~~$9,883.05~~ ?

16-H. PARAGRAPH CENTERING

Paragraphs are sometimes centered vertically and horizontally on half or full pages. For instance, this is often done for bulletin-board displays.

1. VERTICAL CENTERING. Use the steps you already know: (*a*) count the lines the display will fill (including any blank lines), (*b*) subtract that number from the lines available on the paper, and (*c*) divide by 2. For example, to center the paragraph in the Pretest (16-B on page 24) single-spaced on a half page: 33 − 3 = 30; and 30 ÷ 2 = 15, the line on which to begin typing.

2. HORIZONTAL CENTERING. To center a paragraph horizontally, determine where to set the left margin: Select an average full line and center it by backspacing from the middle of the paper.

PRACTICE 1. Center the Pretest, 16-B, on a half sheet. Include the title *EDITING*. Use single-spacing, with 1 blank line below the title.

PRACTICE 2. Center the 2-minute timing, 16-G, on a half sheet. Include the title *OUR ZOO*. Use double spacing. Leave 2 blank lines between the title and the first paragraph.

Line: 50 spaces	Tab: 5, center
Spacing: single	Drills: 3X
Proofguide: 7	
Workguide: 3–4	
Tape: 2B or K5B	

LESSON 17
SKILL DRIVE

Goals: To improve speed/accuracy; to block-center material.

17-A. WARMUP

S 1 The banker was to send a short note to all of us.
A 2 Jack Powell was quite vexed by such lazy farming.
| 1 | 2 | 3 | 4 | 5 | 6 | 7 | 8 | 9 | 10

17-B. PRETEST: KEYBOARD CONTROL

PRETEST. Take a 1-minute timing; compute speed and errors.

3   Have him bake the cake at home. The rack is 10
easy to shift. He can use a quick recipe to save 20
more time.   22
| 1 | 2 | 3 | 4 | 5 | 6 | 7 | 8 | 9 | 10

17-C. PRACTICE: DOWN REACHES

PRACTICE. If you made 2 or fewer errors on the Pretest, type each individual line 3 times; otherwise, type each group of lines (as though each group were a paragraph) 3 times.

4 AV avoids avenue stave naval paves save have avid
5 CA carton carpet carts cable cargo care cake card
6 BA bakery ballot bacon badly balmy back bank bang
7 The cars from the bakery avoided that new avenue.

17-D. PRACTICE: OUT REACHES

8 EA earned leaner nears fears feast east bean easy
9 HI higher shifts hiked shirt shine high hide hill
10 RA trains ratify straw rally rails race rain rack
11 It was easy to shift the rack to the higher land.

Here's a purchase requisition from Walt Schlee, our production superintendent. Mr. Klein has approved it, and so you can type a purchase order to get the items that Walt needs. You can get the prices from the attached price list.

ELECTRONIC SYSTEMS, INC.

1459 Shoreham Drive   Los Angeles, CA 90069

PURCHASE REQUISITION

DEPARTMENT: Production
LOCATION: 2d Floor
PERSON: Walt Schlee

NUMBER: 14155
DATE: February 13, 19--
ACCOUNT: 236714

APPROVAL *Roger S. Klein*

QUANTITY	DESCRIPTION	SUGGESTED PURCHASE SOURCE
10	Drum switches, NEMA 1 enclosure, #2T440	E. R. Boyd, Inc.
28	Centrifugal pumps, #4P620	820 Citrus Lane
12	Rainproof disconnect switches, NEMA D enclosure, #5T872	Pomona, CA 91768
20	Magnetic starters, NEMA 1, 230 volts, 3 poles, #5X149	
12	Heater elements, Model T32A, #5X224	

PURCHASING DEPARTMENT INFORMATION

Order from:

Purchase Order Number:
Date Ordered:
Date Received:

E. R. Boyd, Inc.
820 Citrus Lane
Pomona, CA 91768

PRICE SCHEDULE

Item	Catalog No.	Unit Price
Drum switch, NEMA 1 enclosure	2T440	$ 13.73
Centrifugal pump	4P620	394.65
Rainproof disconnect switch, NEMA D enclosure	5T872	24.83
Magnetic starter, NEMA 1, 230 volts, 3 poles	5X149	65.66
Heater element, Model T32A	5X224	3.45

Sheila Kemp, our accountant, has forwarded to us this draft of the February statement of overdue accounts (see page 317). Remember to check all the totals before typing the final copy.

17-E. Set tab stops every 10 spaces. Use the tab key to go from column to column. Type only once.

17-E. PRACTICE: TABULATOR

12	also	TAB →	band	TAB →	coca	TAB →	deed	TAB →	even
13	five		gate		have		idea		jade
14	keep		land		mane		nine		open
15	pale		quad		rest		sale		type
16	user		very		when		exit		zero

POSTTEST. Repeat the Pretest and compare performance.

17-F. POSTTEST: KEYBOARD CONTROL

17-G. Spacing—double; tab—5. Record your score.

17-G. SKILL MEASUREMENT: 2-MINUTE TIMED WRITING

```
17      Nell was hired as the accountant in the firm  10
    last week.  She had no problems passing the exams  20
    and was expected to be on the job within a month.  30
            She was amazed at how quickly everything was  40
    in place for her job.                               44
    |  1  |  2  |  3  |  4  |  5  |  6  |  7  |  8  |  9  |  10
```

To center a block horizontally, center the longest line in the block; *but to center a paragraph, center the average full line instead of the longest line.*

17-H. BLOCK CENTERING

When several lines are to be listed, center them as a group, or a block:

1. Backspace-center and type the title.

2. Select the longest listed item.

3. Backspace to center that item and set the left margin stop at the point to which you have backspaced.

4. Type the list, beginning each item at the margin stop.

PRACTICE. Block-center the adjacent display on a half sheet of paper. Single-space. Leave 2 blank lines below the title.

PARTS OF A TYPEWRITER

Aligning Scale
Backspace Key
Carrier Position Indicator
Correction Key
Line Space Selector
Margin Stop
Paper Bail
Print-Point Indicator
Carrier Return Key
Shift Lock
Tab Key

Line: 50 spaces Tab: 5, center
Spacing: single Drills: 3X
Proofguide: 7
Workguide: 3–4
Tape: 3B or K6B

LESSON 18

SKILL DRIVE

Goals: To improve speed/accuracy; to spread center.

18-A. WARMUP

```
S  1  Sally asked Dan to go to the ball game next week.
A  2  All quick brown dogs do jump over the lazy foxes.
      |  1  |  2  |  3  |  4  |  5  |  6  |  7  |  8  |  9  |  10
```

JOB 4 Paper: Workguide 483–484

LETTER 82
COMPOSED LETTER

Mr. Klein has just received this purchase order from Gray & Gray Associates. The trainer they ordered will be shipped on schedule, but the text/lab manuals are out of stock. The manuals are at the printer and should be ready in about two weeks. Compose a letter for Mr. Klein's signature, informing Gray & Gray of this situation. You can "salve their wounds" by letting them know that the $3,348 price will be honored because the purchase order was dated before the new price increases. Inform them of the new trainer price and enclose a copy of the new price schedule.

Gray & Gray Associates
475 Hauser Boulevard
Los Angeles, CA 90036

Purchase Order No. 3470

To: Electronic Systems, Inc.
1459 Shoreham Drive
Los Angeles, CA 90069

Date: February 17, 19--

PLEASE SHIP AND BILL US FOR THE GOODS LISTED BELOW.
IF FOR ANY REASON YOU CANNOT DELIVER WITHIN 30 DAYS,
LET US KNOW AT ONCE. PLEASE REFER TO OUR PURCHASE
ORDER NUMBER (ABOVE) IN ALL COMMUNICATIONS.

QUANTITY	DESCRIPTION	CAT. NO.	UNIT PRICE	AMOUNT
1	EL-210 trainer	H-42	3,348.00	3,348.00
10	EL-210 text/lab manual	H-43	12.50	125.00
	TOTAL			3,473.00

NOTE: YOUR BILL TO US SHOULD INDICATE ALL YOUR USUAL DISCOUNTS. PAYMENT WILL BE MADE UPON RECEIPT OF BILL WITH GOODS.

Angela Kim _____ Purchasing Agent

JOB 5 Paper: Workguide 485–486

LETTER 83
COMPOSED LETTER

Mr. Klein calls on the phone.

I've just had a phone conversation with Christine Stortz at the Vocational Training Center in Oceanside, California. Various parts of the EL-320 that we shipped last week were damaged in shipment. Of course, I assured her that replacement parts would be shipped by UPS today. Please prepare a letter for me in which I confirm the details of our phone conversation. Please say what you can to make her feel better.

JOB 6 Paper: Workguide 487

MEMORANDUM 24
COMPOSED MEMORANDUM

Mr. Klein continues:

Then prepare a memo to Jack Mitchell in the parts department telling him to get these replacement parts to UPS right away. I called Jack to explain the situation, but I want to be sure that there is a written record.

18-B. PRETEST: KEYBOARD CONTROL

PRETEST. Take a 1-minute timing; compute speed and errors.

3   The phone was the only one in the inn. Bill 10
must go to the museum and ought to call before he 20
gets back. 22

`|  1  |  2  |  3  |  4  |  5  |  6  |  7  |  8  |  9  |  10`

18-C. PRACTICE: JUMP REACHES

PRACTICE. If you made 2 or fewer errors on the Pretest, type each individual line 3 times; otherwise, type each group of lines (as though they were a paragraph) 3 times.

4 ON lesson common prone bonus phone only lone song
5 IN induce regain index fling paint inns into sing
6 MU museum muddle muddy mulls musty must mute much
7 Emma must leave on the noon train or lease a car.

18-D. PRACTICE: ALPHABETIC WORDS

8 area bomb coca deed ease fear gage high iris jars
9 kiki lilt mama nine oboe pace quad rare sash tune
10 unto volt with axes yoyo zero atom baby coco dyed
11 Did Nancy play the rare oboe with a lilting pace?

18-E. PRACTICE: HYPHEN KEY

12 Vi Allen-Brooks heard the off-the-record comment.
13 Call Robert--he is a master--and get his opinion.
14 Sally developed three well-thought-out proposals.

POSTTEST. Repeat the Pretest and compare performance.

18-F. POSTTEST: KEYBOARD CONTROL

18-G. Spacing—double; tab—5. Record your score.

18-G. SKILL MEASUREMENT: 2-MINUTE TIMED WRITING

15   Hazel Walker expects to be promoted to mana- 10
ger of our store in June. She was first employed 20
with us twelve years ago. 25

       I am sure you will like her as she cannot or 35
will not tolerate the status quo a long time. 44

`|  1  |  2  |  3  |  4  |  5  |  6  |  7  |  8  |  9  |  10`

18-H. SPREAD CENTERING

To spread words in display lines to give greater emphasis, leave 1 space between letters and 3 spaces between words. To spread-center a line, use the standard backspace-centering method (13-H) *or use this shortcut:* From the center, backspace once for each space *except the last* that the line would occupy if it were *not* spread out.

PRACTICE 1. Use the standard method to spread-center these lines.

PRACTICE 2. Use the shortcut method to spread-center these lines.

```
F O R   S A L E
C O M M E R C E
B O O K S T O R E S
O F F I C E
P R O G R A M M E R
```

CHECK: The letter O should align vertically.

ESI ELECTRONIC SYSTEMS, INC.

1459 Shoreham Drive   Los Angeles, CA 90069

February 12, 19--

Ms. Linda A. Headley
Electro-Products, Inc.
3870 Princeton Way
Colorado Springs, CO 80909

Dear ~~Mrs.~~ *Ms.* Headley

Thank you for your interest in Electronic Systems, Inc. EST
is engaged in the development and distribution of training
systems in the areas of electrical maintenance, motor control
and instrumentation systems, and ^programmable controllers. Two basic systems are offered:

The EL-210 MOTOR CONTROL ~~AND~~ INSTRUMENTATION TRAINER. This
comprehensive training system (including both hardware and
software) covers the general area of industrial motor controls.
The EL-210 has found wide acceptance in educational institutions and industrial training programs.

The EL-320 PROGRAMMABLE CONTROLLER TRAINING SYSTEM. This
latest product is also a hardware-oriented and software-
supported training system. The industrial-grade controller
incorporates ram memory, I/O ports, time-delay elements, and a
programming console. ¶ I am hopeful that you will want to
represent our firm in Colorado after reviewing the two brochures
and price schedule that are enclosed. I will telephone you in
about a week to discuss what I think can be a mutually profitable association.

ds Sincerely
ELECTRONIC SYSTEMS, INC.

Elvira G. Schopper
Sales Director

mvf
3 ~~2~~ Enclosures

Line: 50 spaces	Tab: 5		LESSON 19	
Spacing: single	Drills: 3X			
Proofguide: 7			**NUMBER**	
Workguide: 3			**KEYS**	
Tape: 4B or K7B				

Goal: To control 4, 7, 3, and 8 keys.

19-A. WARMUP

S 1 Jane can go to the new show with you if you wish.
A 2 Quickly pack the box with five dozen jars of jam.
| 1 | 2 | 3 | 4 | 5 | 6 | 7 | 8 | 9 | 10

19-B. PRACTICE THE 4 KEY

Use F finger.

3 fr4f fr4f f44f f44f f4f4 f4f4 4 44 444 4,444 4:44
4 44 furs 44 fins 44 fish 44 fell 44 flew 444 funds
5 The 44 markers were taken down by 44 men at 4:44.
6 Jill and I drove 444 miles in 4 days and 4 hours.

19-C. PRACTICE THE 7 KEY

Use J finger.

7 ju7j ju7j j77j j77j j7j7 j7j7 7 77 777 7,777 7:77
8 77 jugs 77 jars 77 jets 77 jogs 77 jams 777 jokes
9 On June 7, the 7 ladies left Camp 7 for Camp 777.

7 with 4

10 At 7:47 the 7:44 arrived on Track 47 with 74 men.

19-D. PROGRESS CHECK: 1-MINUTE TIMED WRITING

11 Only the 747 could take the 77 women 4,444 miles.   10
   The 44 meals cost Joan only 74 cents for 77 days.   20
| 1 | 2 | 3 | 4 | 5 | 6 | 7 | 8 | 9 | 10

19-E. PRACTICE THE 3 KEY

Use D finger.

12 de3d de3d d33d d33d d3d3 d3d3 3 33 333 3,333 3:33
13 33 dots 33 dads 33 dues 33 dogs 33 dips 333 deeds

3 with 4
3 with 7

14 Did she catch 33 or 34 fish in the 34 or 44 days?
15 Ask 73 men if they want 37 seats or 73 for March.

19-F. PRACTICE THE 8 KEY

Use K finger.

16 ki8k ki8k k88k k88k k8k8 k8k8 8 88 888 8,888 8:88
17 88 keys 88 kits 88 kids 888 kilts 8,888 kangaroos

8 with 4
8 with 7
8 with 3

18 Train No. 488 departs at 4:48 or 8:48 at Gate 88.
19 On July 8, the 88 girls left Camp 78 for Camp 87.
20 There were between 38 and 83 jobs on List No. 88.

208–212. INTEGRATED OFFICE PROJECT: ELECTRONIC SYSTEMS, INC.

Situation: Today is Tuesday, February 17. You are working as a secretary in Electronic Systems, Inc., a small company located at 1459 Shoreham Drive, Los Angeles, CA 90069.

You will report to Bruce J. Olsen, administrative assistant to Roger S. Klein, manager of Electronic Systems. You will perform a variety of tasks for various people in the company. Many of these tasks consist of typing letters, memorandums, forms, and tables. All letters from Electronic Systems should be typed in block style with open punctuation. Because there is a high liability potential for this firm, the name of the firm is used in the closing lines of all external communications as follows:

```
Sincerely

ELECTRONIC SYSTEMS, INC.


(Name)
(Title)
```

FORM 79   Paper: Workguide 475
JOB PRIORITY LIST

Before you begin your work, review the items in the project. Then, on Workguide page 475, assign 1, 2, or 3 priority to each item.

JOB 1   Paper: Workguide 477
TABLE 65
PRICE SCHEDULE

Mrs. Elvira G. Schopper, our sales director, has dictated some material on this cassette. Please transcribe it.

This is Mrs. Schopper. Please prepare this new price list as a table. Type it on our letterhead. The title is dealer price schedule. *Date it* effective February 23.

Column headings are item ... catalog number ... dealer cost ... *and* suggested resale price ... *the first entry is* EL-210 trainer ... *the catalog number is* H-42 ... *the dealer cost is* $3,684.00 ... *the suggested resale price is* $5,217.00 ... *the second entry is* EL-210 text/lab manual ... H-43 ... $12.50 ... $17.90 ... *the third entry is* EL-320 training system ... H-56 ... $3,890.00 ... $5,295.00 ... *the next entry is* EL-320 text/lab manual ... H-57 ... $12.50 ... $17.90 ... *the next entry is* proximity sensor ... K-82 ... $695.00 ... $920.00 ... *the final entry is* photoelectric controller ... K-94 ... $325.00 ... $485.00.

JOBS 2–3   Paper: Workguide 479–482
LETTERS 80–81
DRAFT LETTER

Mrs. Schopper has also sent us this note with a letter (see page 314) that she has edited for retyping.

> Please type this letter to Ms. Headley. Then make changes as needed and type the same letter to William G. Ross of 4321 Shoreland Drive South in Seattle, Washington. Look up the ZIP Code for Mr. Ross' address.

WP If the letter on page 314 had been stored on electronic media, the operator would call the letter back to the screen to make corrections on the letter to Ms. Headley. In preparing the letter to Mr. Ross, the operator would keyboard the variables (the inside address and salutation) and use the copy function to pick up the remainder of the letter from the letter to Ms. Headley. Finally, the operator would print out both letters.

19-G. Spacing—double; tab—5. Record your score.

19-G. SKILL MEASUREMENT: 2-MINUTE TIMED WRITING

21   There are four seasons in each year. Spring   10
and fall are liked best by a number of people. A   20
hazy spring or fall day can make you dream of all   30
the wonderful things to expect in just a very few   40
months. A quick trip is one.   46

| 1 | 2 | 3 | 4 | 5 | 6 | 7 | 8 | 9 | 10

Line: 50 spaces   Tab: 5
Spacing: single   Drills: 2X
Proofguide: 9
Workguide: 3
Tape: 5B

LESSON 20
NUMBER REVIEW

SPACE BAR

Goals: To strengthen all controls; to measure speed.

S = Speed
A = Accuracy
N = Numbers

20-A. WARMUP

S 1 She thinks that you will have a good time in May.
A 2 John quickly drew six zippers from the level bag.
N 3 Train 438 will not leave from Gate 37 until 7:47.

| 1 | 2 | 3 | 4 | 5 | 6 | 7 | 8 | 9 | 10

20-B. PRETEST: KEYBOARD CONTROL

PRETEST. Take a 1-minute timing; compute speed and errors.

4   On May 3 or 4 and June 7 or 8, the prize for 10
the six crews will be given. Monthly quotas were 20
kept each time.   23

| 1 | 2 | 3 | 4 | 5 | 6 | 7 | 8 | 9 | 10

20-C. PRACTICE: NUMBER KEYS

PRACTICE. If you made 2 or fewer errors on the Pretest, type each individual line 3 times; otherwise, type each group of lines (as though it were a paragraph) 3 times.

5 The clerk had 38 pencils, 7 pens, and 34 tablets.
6 Check Items 38, 47, 74, 83, and 87 on Invoice 48.
7 Only 37 or 38 children are to go on the 4:37 bus.
8 Gail was to read pages 47, 74, 78, and 83 to him.

20-D. PRACTICE: ALPHABET KEYS

9 Just pack his box with ham and cheese sandwiches.
10 The five dozen quilts and rugs were sold Tuesday.
11 Hazel quietly boxed the frozen packages of beans.
12 The afghan rugs were to be sold to Mr. J. Jancek.

20-E. Make two copies. Copy 1: Type each sentence on a separate line. Copy 2: Type each sentence on a separate line, but tab-indent it 5 spaces.

20-E. PRACTICE: CARRIER/CARRIAGE RETURN

13 You may go. He can go. Ask them. They can too.
14 Did she go? She can go. Ask her. Has she gone?
15 Are they there? If not, why? Why did they stop?

POSTTEST. Repeat the Pretest and compare performance.

20-F. POSTTEST: KEYBOARD CONTROL

207-E. PRACTICE: 7 8 9

15 7 ju7 777 7 jaw, 77 jet, 77 unit, 77 undo, 77 mist, '77 mask
16 8 ki8 888 8 kin, 88 key, 88 iced, 88 isle, 88 knot, 88 keep
17 9 lo9 999 9 lid, 99 led, 99 omen, 99 oath, 99 last, 99 lift
18 7 ju7 77 8 ki8 88 9 lo9 99 7 ju7 77 8 ki8 88 9 lo9 99 7 8 9
19 Lots numbered 7, 8, and 9 were sold in either 1978 or 1979.
| 1 | 2 | 3 | 4 | 5 | 6 | 7 | 8 | 9 | 10 | 11 | 12

POSTTEST. Repeat the Pretest and compare performance.

207-F. POSTTEST: NUMBER REVIEW

207-G. Spacing—double. Take two 5-minute timings. Between them, practice any words with which you had difficulty. Record your score.

207-G. SKILL MEASUREMENT: 5-MINUTE TIMED WRITING

20   When the words that are used in communication tasks of   12
an office are complex, it doesn't take long to realize that   24
a specialized secretary is needed. The technical secretary   36
will find unique job openings that are a lot of fun as well   48
as challenging. As technology advances, the need grows for   60
office workers who have an understanding of both the termi-   72
nology and the processes of the modern world.   81
    Jobs for technical secretaries abound at architectural   93
and construction firms and at research centers and the many 105
electronics industries located across the country. Workers 117
with good skills who are eager may well serve as assistants   129
to architects, scientists, and engineers.   137
    Number skills are important for those who want to work   149
in a technical office. Number typing skills are needed for 161
tables, graphs, and statistical reports. Rules for numeric 173
filing are also important because of their frequent use.   184
    The special skills that are needed by one who wants to   196
work in a technical office job can be gained at a technical 208
institute or at a business college, a community college, or 220
a four-year college. Also, young people may first get jobs 232
as general office workers and later move into jobs that are 244
of a technical nature. Some firms may even provide special 256
training programs to help gain these skills.   265
| 1 | 2 | 3 | 4 | 5 | 6 | 7 | 8 | 9 | 10 | 11 | 12

20-G. Spacing—double; tab—5.
Record your score.

20-G.   SKILL MEASUREMENT: 2-MINUTE TIMED WRITING

16   My friend Jill is a very clever person. She 10
    bought an onyx ring at a low price last week. It 20
    is a quaint ring. When you look at the ring, you 30
    can see many colors reflecting from it. The ring 40
    will always be a prized jewel.   46
    | 1 | 2 | 3 | 4 | 5 | 6 | 7 | 8 | 9 | 10

Line: 50 spaces   Tab: 5,
Spacing: single   center
Proofguide: 9   Drills: 2X
Workguide: 3–4
Tape: 6B or K8B

LESSON 21
NUMBER KEYS

Goals: To control 2, 9, 1, and
0 keys; to review centering.

21-A.   WARMUP

S 1 Will you ask when my new green car will be ready?
A 2 We vexed Jack by quietly helping a dozen farmers.
N 3 At 8:37 she left 43 tapes and 87 scripts for Mel.
      | 1 | 2 | 3 | 4 | 5 | 6 | 7 | 8 | 9 | 10

21-B.   PRACTICE THE ❷ KEY

Use S finger.

4 sw2s sw2s s22s s22s s2s2 s2s2 2 22 222 2,222 2:22
5 22 sons 22 sips 22 sirs 22 subs 22 seas 222 seats
6 All 22 boxes were loaded by 22 teams in Room 222.
7 The 22 players needed 22 pairs of shoes by May 2.

21-C.   PRACTICE THE ❾ KEY

Use L finger.

8 lo9l lo9l 1991 1991 1919 1919 9 99 999 9,999 9:99
9 99 less 99 laps 99 labs 99 lads 99 logs 999 loads
10 Flight 999 is to leave soon at Gate 99 or Gate 9.

9 with 2

11 Our 292 queries to 92 persons got us 292 answers.

21-D.   PROGRESS CHECK: 1-MINUTE TIMED WRITING

12 The 929 men and 229 women were to cast 292 votes. 10
13 All 29 boxes, of 92 varieties, are in the 9 vans. 20
      | 1 | 2 | 3 | 4 | 5 | 6 | 7 | 8 | 9 | 10

Line: 60 spaces	Tab: 5
Spacing: single	Drills: 3X
Proofguide: 137–138	
Workguide: 331–332, 475–499	
Tape: 52B and 53B	

INTEGRATED OFFICE PROJECT: ELECTRONICS
LESSONS 207–212

GOALS FOR UNIT 34

1. Type at least 53 wam for 5 minutes with no more than 5 errors.
2. Improve number typing skills.
3. Edit letters and memos while typing, applying rules of capitalization and punctuation.
4. Compose business letters and interoffice memorandums.
5. Prepare a business form and a report.
6. Construct a table from dictated information.
7. Perform calculations.
8. Apply skill in merging paragraph and statistical data.
9. Set priorities.
10. Follow directions.

207-A. WARMUP

S 1 Jane said that the girls did wish to see the field of corn.
A 2 Several exquisite pots were seized by the angry old monkey.
N 3 There were 257 people in Room 46 at 9:30 a.m. on August 18.
| 1 | 2 | 3 | 4 | 5 | 6 | 7 | 8 | 9 | 10 | 11 | 12

207-B. PRETEST: NUMBER REVIEW

PRETEST. **Take a 1-minute timing; compute speed and errors.**

4   The actual count showed 57,903 in attendance. The old 12
record of 56,824 was broken by 1,079. Of those who were in 24
attendance, 54,328 had purchased tickets. It is quite hard 36
to believe that last year's average crowd was about 31,600. 48
| 1 | 2 | 3 | 4 | 5 | 6 | 7 | 8 | 9 | 10 | 11 | 12

207-C. PRACTICE: 0 1 2 3

PRACTICE. **If you made no errors on the Pretest, type each line 3 times. If you made 1 error or more, type each group of four lines (as though it were a paragraph) 3 times; then type the sentence 3 times.**

5 0 ;p0 000 0 pan, 00 pet, 00 part, 00 pull, 00 pick, 00 poem
6 1 aql 111 1 art, 11 age, 11 quit, 11 quip, 11 zany, 11 zoom
7 2 sw2 222 2 set, 22 sir, 22 want, 22 wear, 22 suit, 22 warm
8 3 de3 333 3 dim, 33 dug, 33 east, 33 eyes, 33 cute, 33 coin
9 About 1,100 auditioned for the 32 female and 23 male parts.
| 1 | 2 | 3 | 4 | 5 | 6 | 7 | 8 | 9 | 10 | 11 | 12

207-D. PRACTICE: 4 5 6

10 4 fr4 444 4 far, 44 for, 44 rail, 44 rugs, 44 very, 44 vats
11 5 fr5 555 5 fed, 55 fig, 55 room, 55 tour, 55 vane, 55 beet
12 6 jy6 666 6 jar, 66 joy, 66 year, 66 your, 66 most, 66 next
13 4 fr4 44 5 fr5 55 6 jy6 66 4 fr4 44 5 ft5 55 6 jy6 66 4 5 6
14 The winters of 1945, 1956, and 1964 were particularly cold.
| 1 | 2 | 3 | 4 | 5 | 6 | 7 | 8 | 9 | 10 | 11 | 12

SPACE BAR

Use A finger, if your machine has a 1 key; otherwise, use the small L as the 1.

1 with 2
1 with 9

21-E.   PRACTICE THE 1 KEY

14 aqla aqla alla alla alal alal 1 ll lll 1,111 1:11
15 ll adds ll aims ll alms ll aids ll arks lll autos
16 The 12 men and 21 women won 12 first place votes.
17 By 1991, there will be 9 new teams in 19 leagues.

Use Sem finger.

0 with 2
0 with 9
0 with 1

21-F.   PRACTICE THE 0 KEY

18 ;p0; ;p0; ;00; ;00; ;0;0 ;0;0 0 00 000 0,000 0:00
19 00 pets 00 pads 00 pegs 00 pits 00 pigs 000 plays
20 The 20 buses were to leave at 2:02 for 20 cities.
21 All 90 clerks were to type 9,090 pages for 9 men.
22 At 11:10 the 10 girls and 101 boys will be bused.

21-G. Spacing—double; tab—5. Record your score.

21-G.   SKILL MEASUREMENT: 2-MINUTE TIMED WRITING

23   This entire day has been puzzling for me. A   10
quite excited young man came to the door as I was   20
leaving for town. He had just run out of gas and   30
wanted me to take him to get more. After we left   40
to buy his gas, we ran out of gas, also.   48

| 1 | 2 | 3 | 4 | 5 | 6 | 7 | 8 | 9 | 10

21-H. This job reviews the skills you need for the test in Lesson 25:

Vertical centering
Paragraph horizontal centering
Spread centering
Block (list) centering.

To practice these skills, center a single-spaced copy on a full sheet. Two blank lines separate the title from the body.

21-H.   CENTERING REVIEW

24   M E E T I N G
                    ↓ 3
The Administrative Services Area is pleased to
announce a special meeting on cost-saving ways
to decrease office expenses. The agenda is as
follows:
        ↓ 2
        Labor: Barbara Donnelly
        Fringe Benefits: William Katz
        Supplies: Charles Greco
        Overhead: Edward Portillo

Paper: plain

Here's the rough draft of the minutes you typed for the monthly sales meeting. I've made some revisions, and so it'll have to be retyped. Each member of our sales staff should receive a copy of the minutes, and I also want a copy for myself.

WP To revise rough-draft copy on a word processor, the operator has to keyboard only the revisions using the insert, delete, and move functions.

Minutes of the Monthly Meeting

Climate Control Sales Staff

January 15, 19--

ATTENDANCE

The monthly meeting of the sales staff of Climate Control was held in the office of Mr. Cole's Mr. Thomas Cole presided at the meeting. The following sales persons were present:

Laura Guidi   Paul Moss
Anna Gells   Samuel Berk
Juan Arroyo

put names in alphabetic order

UNFINISHED BUSINESS

which should be mailed to selected residents in the very near future.

Mr. Cole described the advertising campaign that will be implemented for the new Asbury Wood Burning Stove. He distributed copies of the brochures that have been ordered from S & S Printing.

A discussion was held concerning the commission structure for the past year. A table with commissions for each quarter was distributed. It was decided that the comission structure would be modified next year. The proposals from Mr. Arroyo, Mr. Berk, and Ms. Gells were discussed. The proposals from the rest of the sales staff would be discussed at the next meeting.

make this 2d ¶

New Business

The schedule for handling the Climate exhibit at the Energy Fair was discussed. Mr. Arroyo and Ms. Gells will arrive at the Armory by 8:30 a.m. on Saturday to make certain that the exhibit is properly arranged. They will stay in our exhibit area until 1 p.m. Mr. Berk, Ms. Guidi, and Mr. Moss will arrive at the exhibit area at 12 noon and remain on duty until closing. They will be responsible for taking the exhibit down and returning the materials and supplies to our office headquarters. Since Mr. Cole has major responsibilities for the fair, he will be at the Armory all day. He will not, however, plan to spend much time at the Climate Control exhibit.

in depth.   *January 31.*   *Control*

more #   Respectfully submitted,   *energy*

(Your name)
Secretary to the President

Distribution: Salespersons Staff

LESSON 22

NUMBER REVIEW

Goals: To strengthen all controls; to measure speed.

22-A. WARMUP

S 1 Julie and Bob got ham and cheese for their party.
A 2 My folks proved my expert eloquence was a hazard.
N 3 She asked 342 persons 178 questions in 190 hours.
| 1 | 2 | 3 | 4 | 5 | 6 | 7 | 8 | 9 | 10

22-B. PRETEST: KEYBOARD CONTROL

PRETEST. Take a 1-minute timing; compute speed and errors.

4   We hope to receive 47 or 48 boxes from Apex- 10
Brown Co. on July 17 or 20. Can you ship 39 car- 20
tons first-class now?   24
| 1 | 2 | 3 | 4 | 5 | 6 | 7 | 8 | 9 | 10

22-C. PRACTICE: NUMBER KEYS

PRACTICE. If you made 2 or fewer errors on the Pretest, type each individual line 3 times; otherwise, type each group of lines (as though they were a paragraph) 3 times.

5 Adding 10 and 20 and 30 and 40 and 70 totals 170.
6 On July 17, 1981, 230 girls ran in a 4-mile race.
7 He selected Nos. 10, 28, 39, 47, and 74 to study.
8 Call Shirley at 789-0134 or 789-0138 by 2:30 p.m.

22-D. PRACTICE: ALPHABET KEYS

9   Six jet black vans were quickly sold by the firm.
10 A quick tally shows that taxi drivers are polite.
11 A lazy youth picked two boxes of oranges for her.
12 His team was buoyed by the support of their fans.

22-E. PRACTICE: HYPHEN KEY

13 Next week---say, Tuesday---can you go to the movie?
14 Her great-aunt is a well-known American musician.
15 Apex-Brown Co. likes first- or second-class mail.
16 The student--Ella Garcia--was to fly first-class.

POSTTEST. Repeat the Pretest and compare performance.

22-F. POSTTEST: KEYBOARD CONTROL

SOLAR HEATING AND YOU

fill in → By Thomas Cole and Susan Goelz
(? Lines of 40 spaces)

If the high cost of heating is drain-
ing your budget, you should consider put-
ting the sun to work for you. Solar ~~energy~~ *heating*
can be a simple and inexpensive aide to
your current heating system. ⁋ When you
think of solar heating, you may envision
a complex collection of pump, thermostat,
pipe, and roof-top collectors. Although
this type *of* equipment is used with active
solar energy systems, ~~their~~ *there* are cheaper
and simpler alternatives. Passive solar
energy systems require a minimum of
mechanical equipment and operate without
external power.

Two popular passive solar *air* heating
systems are *and* window-box collectors ~~and~~
(thermosiphoning air panels (TAP). Both
of these systems feature the same four
elements ~~which~~ *that* work together: (1) a
collector made of glass through which
sunlight passes, (2) *n* absorber made of
dark material that the sunlight strikes
after ~~passing through~~ *penetrating* the collector,
(3) a method of distributing heat that
relies on natural heat transfer, and
(4) a control to prevent over-heating or
loss of heat.

Thermosiphoning Air Panels

A TAP is a simple way to bring solar
heat into your ~~house~~ *home*. It is usually positioned against the south-facing wall of
your house. It ~~usually~~ *generally* consists of a collector made of glass or plastic glazing,
an aluminum absorber plate painted black,
a wood frame, and two air vents. ~~When~~ *As* the
sunlight strikes the absorber plate, it is
converted into heat. When the absorber
heats up, the air around it is heated.
This hot air travels through an air passage and enters the house through the upper
vent. Simultaneously, cool air leaves the
house through the lower vent. A simple TAP
can be constructed for less th*a*n $500.

Window-Box Collectors

These passive collectors are very
similar to TAPs, but they are hung from
south-facing windows. They are usually
about 20 square feet in size and, like
TAPs, contain no provision for storing
heat. You can construct a basic window-
box collector for ~~approximately~~ *about* $400.

Summary

If the use of solar energy interests
you, take some time to investigate passive
solar heating systems such as the two dis-
cussed here. ⁋ Although ~~they~~ *solar heating systems* will not replace your furnace, they may allow you to
reduce your heating ~~budget~~ *costs*.

*You can contact the Conservation
and Renewable Energy Inquiry and
Referral Service (CAREIRS),
P. O. Box 8900, Silver Spring,
MD 20907. This organization
provides information on all the
different varieties of solar energy.*

(END)

22-G. Spacing—double; tab—5. Record your score.

22-G. SKILL MEASUREMENT: 2-MINUTE TIMED WRITING

17   Have you ever wanted to have your own snazzy 10
jet black typewriter? You could quickly type the 20
many term papers you write. For just a few cents 30
you can rent such a machine. Check the newspaper 40
to rent one for typing your next papers. 48

| 1 | 2 | 3 | 4 | 5 | 6 | 7 | 8 | 9 | 10

Line: 50 spaces   Tab: 5
Spacing: single   center
Proofguide: 9   Drills: 2X
Workguide: 3–4
Tape: 8B or K9B

LESSON 23
NUMBER KEYS

Goals: To control 5, 6, ½, and ¼ keys; to review centering.

23-A. WARMUP

S 1 Val got a new mink hat for the red and blue gown.
A 2 Her job was to pack a dozen equal boxes by night.
N 3 In 1982 there were 2,934 people in the 173 camps.

| 1 | 2 | 3 | 4 | 5 | 6 | 7 | 8 | 9 | 10

23-B. PRACTICE THE 5 KEY

Use F finger.

4 fr5f fr5f f55f f55f f5f5 f5f5 5 55 555 5,555 5:55
5 55 firs 55 furs 55 fish 55 figs 55 fuss 555 fewer
6 The 55 men caught 55 fish in just 5 days in Iowa.
7 It took just 5 hours and 55 minutes to go to Ada.

23-C. PRACTICE THE 6 KEY

Use J finger.

8 ju6j ju6j j66j j66j j6j6 j6j6 6 66 666 6,666 6:66
9 66 jars 66 jams 66 jets 66 jabs 66 jots 666 jolts
10 We shall need 666 pencils and 66 pens for 66 men.

6 with 5

11 She asked for Rooms 65 and 55; he rang 56 and 66.

23-D. PROGRESS CHECK: 1-MINUTE TIMED WRITING

12 Did the 55 men drive 656 miles on Route 56 or 65? 10
They were seated in Rows 56 and 65 at 6:55 today. 20

| 1 | 2 | 3 | 4 | 5 | 6 | 7 | 8 | 9 | 10

23-E. PRACTICE THE ½ KEY

Use Sem finger.

13 $;\frac{1}{2}\frac{1}{2};$ $;\frac{1}{2}\frac{1}{2};$ $;\frac{1}{2};\frac{1}{2}$ $;\frac{1}{2};\frac{1}{2}$ $\frac{1}{2}$ pay; $\frac{1}{2}$ mile; $\frac{1}{2}$ hour; $\frac{1}{2}$ week

½ with 5

14 She used $4\frac{1}{2}$ gallons to paint $2\frac{1}{2}$ rooms last March.
15 Sue has $5\frac{1}{2}$ hours completed toward the $55\frac{1}{2}$ needed.

½ with 6

16 Please order $6\frac{1}{2}$ dozen pairs of size $6\frac{1}{2}$ shoes now.

JOBS 8–10
POSTAL CARDS 5–7

Paper: Workguide 471–472

Mrs. Justo sent postal cards to all the energy fair exhibitors indicating the numbers of the booths they will occupy on January 31. All the registrants have received the information except for the last three. Booths were assigned based on the order of registration, and so we have to send cards to Cline, Air Design, and Indoor Climate. Check the list of exhibitors for the addresses. When you type the postal cards, use this form message:

(CURRENT DATE)

Dear (NAME):

Thank you for submitting your registration fee for exhibiting at the energy fair at the National Guard Armory on Saturday, January 31.

You have been assigned Booth No. (NUMBER) for your exhibit. Each booth will be identified with a large sign with your company name printed on it. The Armory will be open at 7 a.m.; the fair will begin at 9 a.m.

Thomas Cole
Exhibit Chairperson

JOB 11
LETTER 79
**MODIFIED-BLOCK STYLE
ON BARONIAL STATIONERY**

Paper: Workguide 473–474

I've been working on an article on solar heating. I'm writing the article jointly with Susan Goelz of Solar Ray, Inc., in Holland, Michigan. I've prepared a rough draft; Ms. Goelz will polish it and send it to *Saving Money* magazine for publication. Here's my cover letter. Send it with the rough draft to Ms. Susan Goelz, Solar Ray, Inc., 156 East Eighth Street, Holland, MI 49423.

Dear Susan:

Enclosed is my rough draft of our article. It is by no means polished, but I think it does make some important points about solar heating.

As we discussed, you should take no more than a week editing the article. When you feel that it is ready for publication, call me so that we can discuss the final draft. Then you can send it directly to Ed Wong at *Saving Money* magazine.

I will look forward to your call next week, but if you have any questions, feel free to call me earlier.

JOB 12
REPORT 76
MAGAZINE ARTICLE

Paper: plain

Here's the article on solar heating. I'd like you to type it as soon as possible and send it with the cover letter to Ms. Goelz. Type it on a 40-space line. After you've finished typing it, remember to count the number of lines in the article and type the number on the line below the by-line. And be sure to keep a copy of the article for our reference.

WP If the magazine article on page 309 had been stored on electronic media, you could scroll through each page, make the necessary corrections, and then print out a perfect copy.

Except for ½ and ¼, fractions are constructed with the diagonal:

1/5   8/17

SPACE BAR

In mixed numbers, 1 space precedes the fraction:

7 1/8   2 1/2

If any fraction in a sentence must be constructed, then *all* fractions in that sentence should be.

23-F. PRACTICE THE ¼ KEY

Use Sem finger.
¼ with 5
¼ with 6
Other fractions

17 ;$\frac{1}{2}\frac{1}{4}$; ;$\frac{1}{2}\frac{1}{4}$; ;$\frac{1}{4}$;$\frac{1}{4}$;$\frac{1}{4}$;$\frac{1}{4}$ $\frac{1}{4}$ pay; $\frac{1}{4}$ mile; $\frac{1}{4}$ hour; $\frac{1}{4}$ week
18 He worked 5$\frac{1}{4}$ hours in May and 55$\frac{1}{4}$ hours in March.
19 She had 66$\frac{1}{4}$ boxes of fruit and 6$\frac{1}{4}$ boxes of mints.
20 They had 6 1/4 oz of gold and 8 2/3 oz of silver.

23-G. Spacing—double; tab—5. Record your score.

23-G. SKILL MEASUREMENT: 2-MINUTE TIMED WRITING

21 Have you ever used the want ads in the paper   10
to acquire a new piece of furniture?   One ad will   20
often bring an exceptional response.   Sometimes a   30
prized keepsake will be offered to you.   Using an   40
ad will help you get just what you want in a day.   50

| 1 | 2 | 3 | 4 | 5 | 6 | 7 | 8 | 9 | 10

23-H. Block-center (review page 26) this enumeration on a half sheet. Leave 2 blank lines under the title and 2 blank spaces after each period.

23-H. CENTERING REVIEW

22 CORE COURSES IN BUSINESS ADMINISTRATION ↓3
    1. Accounting
    2. Business Communications
    3. Business Law
    4. Computer Science
    5. Economics
    6. Financial Administration
    7. Management
    8. Marketing

Line: 50 spaces Tab: 5,		
Spacing: single center		
Proofguide: 9 Drills: 2X		
Workguide: 3–4,		
47–48		
Tape: 9B		

LESSON 24

NUMBER REVIEW

SPACE BAR

Goals: To strengthen all controls; to measure speed; to review centering.

After 24-A, do Workguide pages 47–48.

24-A. WARMUP

S 1 Is he to go with them to Akron today or tomorrow?
A 2 Joe quietly picked six razors from the woven bag.
N 3 Adding 10 and 29 and 38 and 47 and 56 totals 180.

| 1 | 2 | 3 | 4 | 5 | 6 | 7 | 8 | 9 | 10

EXHIBITORS AT ENERGY FAIR--JANUARY 31, 19--

National Guard Armory--Albany, NY

Company	Address	Contact Person	Telephone	Booth
Energy Control, Inc.	151 Plum Street, Albany 12202	Peter O'Brien	555-3172	1
Enercon Systems, Inc.	17 Bontam Road, Albany 12201	Susan Daley	555-4127	2
ABC Co[u]nsulting	32 River Street, Troy 12180	Murphy Charles	555-3137	3
Kessel Electronics	Box 315C, Albany 12208	James Dale	555-8390	4
Climate Control Systems	134 Park Place, Albany 12208	Thomas Cole	555-1203	5
Solco Energy	Old Post Road, Albany 12207 (4)	Regina Harris	555-9132	6
Ace Heating	78 Shaker Road, Albany 12203	Robert Islip	555-3956	7
Dynamic Air, Inc.	31 Stagg Road, Delmar 12054	Anna Ferrera	555-4137	8
Portelli Environmental	21 Ferry Street, Troy 12180 (7)	Gina Portelli	555-5739	9
Eastern Heating	50 State Street, Albany 12206	Samuel Grady	555-4139	10
Maximum Comfort, Inc.	37 Barry Drive, Troy 12102	Anne Conroy / Fay Eng (Fred)	555-7921 (6556)	11
Airco Heating	71 Wolf Road, Albany 12205		555-5665	12
H & H Company	2 Stagg Road, Delmar 12054	Jack DeVries	555-1280	13
Total Comfort Heating	17 Circle Lane, Albany 12203	Patricia Smith	555-1490	14
Northeastern Energy	14 Lark Street, Albany 12204	Alan Petrelli	555-9974	15
Kirsch Energy, Inc.	15 State Street, Albany 12207	Steve Klein	555-1496	16
RBW Company, Inc.	16 Broadway, Troy 12180	Pamela Gersch	555-7380	17
Cline Solar Heating	158 Budd Way, Albany 12205	Paul Cline	555-7560 (3155)	18
Air Design Systems	14 Alps Way, Albany 12203	Greg Whyte	555-5133	19
Indoor Climate Systems	69 Cole Lane, Troy 12180	Natasha Popov	555-8321	20

24-B. PRETEST: KEYBOARD CONTROL

PRETEST. Take a 1-minute timing; compute speed and errors.

4   He asked for 857 boxes, 10 × 22, for a ship- 10
ment on June 4. He was amazed at how quickly the 20
boxes got through to him. 25

| 1 | 2 | 3 | 4 | 5 | 6 | 7 | 8 | 9 | 10

24-C. PRACTICE: NUMBER KEYS

PRACTICE: If you made 2 or fewer errors on the Pretest, type each individual line 3 times; otherwise, type each group of lines (as though they were a paragraph) 3 times.

5   Bob had 4 brothers and 6 sisters at the 10 games.
6   On July 14, 857 people were to attend 195 events.
7   The test took 22 hours and 8 minutes to complete.
8   All 33 ships took 79 hours to complete the races.

24-D. PRACTICE: ALPHABET KEYS

9   Jack bought five or six prizes to award to Paula.
10   Mary can distribute the trays among the quintets.
11   Helen asked for a quick order of pizza and juice.
12   Please give my extra luggage to the new bellhops.

24-E. PRACTICE: CARRIER/CARRIAGE RETURN

24-E. Make two copies. Copy 1: Type each sentence on a separate line. Copy 2: Type each sentence on a separate line, but tab-indent it 5 spaces.

13   Can he go? Yes, he can go. Will you meet James?
14   What was the cost? Seven dollars. That is high.
15   Has she stopped? Stopped for what? Her license.
16   It is 5:15. Are you sure? He thinks it is 4:15.

24-F. POSTTEST: KEYBOARD CONTROL

POSTTEST. Repeat the Pretest and compare performance.

24-G. SKILL MEASUREMENT: 2-MINUTE TIMED WRITING

24-G. Spacing—double; tab—5. Record your score.

17   The clerk was amazed at how quickly he could 10
type on the new word processor. It took him just 20
a very short time to learn the functions it could 30
perform. He expected that he would forget how to 40
use it his first time alone, but he did remember. 50

| 1 | 2 | 3 | 4 | 5 | 6 | 7 | 8 | 9 | 10

24-H. CENTERING REVIEW

24-H. Center a double-spaced copy on a half sheet. Line 18 should be spread-centered, and lines 18 and 20 should be typed in all caps.

18   A N N U A L   B E E F   B A R B E C U E

19   in

20   PORTER PARK

21   Tickets on Sale at J. Jackson, Inc.

22   East Lansing

I'm having a meeting with our sales staff next Thursday, January 15, at 2:30. All five salespeople are coming to the meeting, and I'd like to have a copy of this agenda for each of them—and a copy for myself, of course.

WP Even though word processors can print 55 to 90 characters per second, it is usually more economical to photocopy the original document when many copies are needed.

SALES STAFF
Meeting Agenda
Thursday, January 15, 19--

COMMISSION COMPENSATION

1. What are the inequities in our current commission structure?
2. What were the commission amounts for the past year?
3. What changes should be considered in our commission structure for next year?

MAJOR ADVERTISING CAMPAIGN

1. What has been the impact of advertising during the past quarter?
2. What types of advertising will be done in the next quarter?
3. What are your suggestions for advertising in the next year?

ENERGY FAIR

1. What are our plans for the energy fair to be held on January 31?
2. Who will be staffing our booth?
3. Who are the scheduled exhibitors?

Mrs. Justo started to type this table for the sales meeting next Thursday. I filled in the missing figures in pen, but now I need the whole table retyped. I'd like you to type the table in the same boxed style. Please double-check the totals for the third and fourth quarters.

CLIMATE CONTROL SYSTEMS
COMMISSIONS FOR PAST YEAR

Salesperson	Commissions for Each Quarter			
	First	Second	Third	Fourth
Juan Arroyo	$ 4,200	$ 3,890	$ 5,230	$ 4,765
Samuel Berk	3,870	3,925	4,210	4,150
Anna Gells	4,315	3,985	4,340	4,765
Laura Guidi	3,515	3,880	4,220	4,125
Paul Moss	4,440	4,375	5,110	4,765
TOTAL	$20,340	$20,055	$ 23,110	$ 22,570

I'm the chairperson for the energy fair that is scheduled to be held at the National Guard Armory in Albany on Saturday, January 31. Mrs. Justo has been keeping a list of the companies that will be participating in the fair. She typed the list as the reservations for exhibitors came in. Please rearrange the information in a table and put the company names in alphabetic order. Single-space, but group the information in sets of four for easier reading. Since this is a particularly wide table, position it sideways on the page and leave only 4 spaces between columns.

WP The sort feature on a word processor makes it possible to rearrange information in a different order—either alphabetic or numeric.

LESSON 25

TEST 1: PROGRESS TEST ON PART 1

TEST 1-A
2-MINUTE TIMED WRITING
ON ALPHABETIC COPY

Line: 50 spaces
Spacing: double
Tab: 5
Paper: Workguide 51, top
Start: 6 lines from top

One of my favorite things to do is to take a   10

trip by car. Planning the trip is always fun. A   20

quick survey of a map will amaze you with all the   30

places you can go in just six days. Six days off   40

can be a good way to leave behind a lot of grief.   50

| 1 | 2 | 3 | 4 | 5 | 6 | 7 | 8 | 9 | 10

TEST 1-B
2-MINUTE TIMED WRITING
ON COPY WITH NUMBERS

Line: 50 spaces
Spacing: double
Tab: 5
Paper: Workguide 51,
    bottom
Start: 6 lines from top

The Green Company, founded in 1925, has been   10

in business over 58 years. It has been producing   20

47 varieties of products since 1937. In the past   30

24 years, over 8,369,600 cases of beans have been   40

sold in all 50 states and in 6 foreign countries.   50

| 1 | 2 | 3 | 4 | 5 | 6 | 7 | 8 | 9 | 10

TEST 1-C
HORIZONTAL AND VERTICAL
CENTERING

Title displayed:
  Typed all caps
  Spread-centered
  2 blank lines
Line: to center longest line
Spacing: as shown
Tab: center only
Paper: Workguide 53, top
Start: to center on half sheet

F O R   S A L E

The Smith–Hughes Company will be holding its   16

annual office supply sale on August 29. The   25

sale will include such items as: 32

Cabinets   34
Chairs   37
Desks   39
Electronic Calculators   43
Four-Drawer Files   47
General Office Supplies   52
Typewriters   54

Dear Homeowner:

Unless you are very wealthy, the cost of heating your home is a major expense each winter. And like many of your neighbors in the Albany area, you probably feel helpless as costs continue to rise year after year.

You no longer have to feel helpless. You can fight back by installing an alternative energy system to supplement your current oil, gas, or electric heating system.

If you call Climate Control today, we will arrange to do a free energy audit especially for your home. There is entirely no obligation on your part. Last year over five hundred families in this area installed alternative energy systems. Like them, you can realize substantial savings by installing a system such as:

[1. A window-box solar room heater to warm your family room or your child's bedroom.

[2. A wood-burning stove to add atmosphere to your recreation room and keep it comfortably warm.

[3. A coal stove to substantially reduce your fuel bills while adding a touch of rustic charm to your living room.

Don't put up with the high cost of heating any longer. Call us today and we'll help you to fight back.

Sincerely yours,
Thomas Cole, President

TEST 1-D
BLOCK CENTERING

Title displayed:
  Typed all caps
  Centered
  2 blank lines
Line: to center longest item
Spacing: single
Tab: center only
Paper: Workguide 53, bottom
Start: to center on half page

SELECTED KEYBOARDING TERMINOLOGY

Additional Character
Automatic Carrier Return
Backspace Correction
Debugging
Execution Instruction
Function Keys
Hardware
Information Processing
Magnetic Keyboard
Random Access Memory

TEST 1-E
LINE CENTERING

Title displayed:
  Typed all caps
  Centered
  2 blank lines
Line: center each line
  separately
Spacing: single
Tab: center only
Paper: Workguide 55, top
Start: to center on half page

JUDGES

Roberta Calens

Gail Felis

Todd Frazier

Ronald Gomez

Douglas Kielbaso

Donald Meaders

Wilma Miller

Vance Whittier

202–206. INTEGRATED OFFICE PROJECT: CLIMATE CONTROL SYSTEMS

Situation: Today is Monday, January 5. You are working as secretary to Thomas Cole, president of Climate Control Systems in Albany, New York. His former secretary, Mrs. Justo, has just moved to California. Mr. Cole founded Climate Control five years ago and has seen the company grow from 3 employees to the current 36 employees. Climate Control is a retail and wholesale distributor of alternative energy systems. The company specializes in helping both residential and industrial customers develop more efficient heating, cooling, and lighting systems by utilizing solar, wood, and coal sources. Mr. Cole is in the midst of organizing a major advertising campaign, as well as helping in the planning for an energy fair for the Greater Albany area.

Some of the work you will be doing has already been typed in rough-draft form by Mrs. Justo; other jobs are handwritten drafts by Mr. Cole. He prefers the modified-block style letter with the following closing:

      Sincerely yours,

      Thomas Cole, President

FORM 76   Paper: Workguide 463
JOB PRIORITY LIST

Before you begin your work, review the items in the project. Then, on Workguide page 463, assign a 1, 2, or 3 priority to each item.

JOB 1   Paper: Workguide 465–466
LETTER 77
MODIFIED-BLOCK STYLE

I've dictated a cover letter for the promotional flier we're sending to the printer. Please transcribe it and send it to Ms. Sharon Sapienza, President, S & S Printing, 517 Fairmont Street, Albany, NY 12207.

it was good to meet with you last week and to finalize the arrangements for the advertising flier that we had planned for climate control . . .

enclosed with this letter is the copy that will be used for the flier . . . notice that i would like the turnover lines of the numbered items to be indented . . .

i will stop by in two days to read the dummy proof that you are going to prepare . . . i would like the 10,000 copies to be ready within the next ten days.

JOBS 2–3   Paper: Workguide 467
FORMS 77–78
INVOICES

Mrs. Justo typed out the information for these two invoices, but she didn't complete the invoices. Please type the invoices and make sure that they go out today.

1.   Invoice 8095 to Mr. and Mrs. George Houser, 17 Diamond Head Road, Albany, NY 12205. Installed Window–Box Air Heater, Model 150––––––––––$295 less deposit of $25.

2.   Invoice 8096 to Ms. Charlene Torrisi, 15 Alpine Way, Albany, NY 12202. Installed Asbury Woodburning Stove, Model 16A, with coal dispenser and cast iron kettle––––––––––$850, plus $45 shipping; less $100 deposit.

WP   A forms package on some word processors enables the operator to store a standard form (invoice, purchase order, and so on) on magnetic media, bring the original to the screen, and keyboard the variables.

JOB 4   Paper: Workguide 469
LETTER 78
MODIFIED-BLOCK STYLE

Please type a copy of the promotional flier that begins "Dear Homeowner" to send to S & S Printing. Follow the instructions I gave in the letter to Ms. Sapienza so that the copy will look like the final printed material as much as possible.

PART 2

SKILL BUILDING ▪ BASIC LETTERS, TABLES, AND REPORTS

OBJECTIVES FOR PART 2

Part 2 is designed to enable you to demonstrate the following
abilities when you take the test in Lesson 50:

1. Touch Typing.   To operate all keys, the tabulator mechanism, and the carrier or carriage return by touch.

2. Technical Knowledge.   To answer correctly at least
90 percent of the questions on an objective test covering
the technical information presented in Part 2, including
word division; uses of symbols; and names of the basic
parts of letters, tables, and reports.

3. Production.   To format correctly various production jobs,
including (*a*) a standard business letter on a letterhead; (*b*) a
three-column table with title, subtitle, and column headings;
and (*c*) a one-page report with side and paragraph headings.

4. Skill Rate.   To type at the following speed and accuracy
levels by the end of each unit:

Unit	No. of Minutes	Minimum Speed	Maximum Errors
5	3	27	5
6	3	28	5
7	3	29	5
8	3	30	5

5. Word Processing Information.   To
understand how word processing
equipment would function if used to
format various production assignments.

201-E.   PRACTICE: IN AND OUT REACHES

15 vacancies obtain baking garage varied offset fast host page
16 imitation debate neater knives fringe wrongs vary earn stay
17 frankness paints decade extras valued damage know gate gear
18 conducted houses gallon saying flying hyphen rear moon gain

19 I conducted a garage sale to earn extra value for my tools.
    | 1 | 2 | 3 | 4 | 5 | 6 | 7 | 8 | 9 | 10 | 11 | 12

POSTTEST. Repeat the Pretest
and compare performance.

201-F. POSTTEST: HORIZONTAL REACHES

201-G. Spacing—double.
Take two 5-minute timings.
Between them, practice any
words with which you had
difficulty. Record your score.

201-G. SKILL MEASUREMENT: 5-MINUTE TIMED WRITING

20   Long lines at gasoline service stations and far higher 12
heating expenses were experienced by many people during the 24
past decade. There were also other indications that it was 36
time for our nation to deal with a number of energy issues. 48
Questions dealing with consumption of energy sources, kinds 60
of energy available, cost of energy needs, and the need for 72
continued research in energy were being asked by government 84
leaders, business people, and homeowners. Let's look at an 96
energy chronology for our country.   103
        Looking back in history, our early settlers made great 115
use of wood as a source of energy. The supply of this form 127
of energy was abundant; however, too much time was expended 139
in obtaining the raw material. Coal came on the scene as a 151
source of energy in the late eighteenth century. Still, it 163
was not until late in the nineteenth century that coal came 175
to be the main source of energy in our nation. Natural gas 187
and oil were discovered in the nineteenth century; however, 199
it was almost eighty years before oil surpassed coal as our 211
major source of energy.   216
        Because of the problems of the past decade, our nation 228
has realized the need for greater research efforts in order 240
to develop new energy sources. Hence attempts to use solar 252
and nuclear energy have been increasing.   260
    | 1 | 2 | 3 | 4 | 5 | 6 | 7 | 8 | 9 | 10 | 11 | 12

Line: 50 spaces   Tab: 5
Spacing: single   Drills: 3X
Proofguide: 11–12
Workguide: 3, 57–58
Tape: 10B, 11B

LESSONS 26/27
SKILL DRIVE

Goals: To improve speed/ accuracy; to make correct word-division and line-ending decisions.

26-A. WARMUP

```
S  1  If I visit the island, I might fish in that lake.
A  2  A new jukebox very quietly plays music by Mozart.
N  3  He arrived May 24, 1976, and left March 25, 1983.
      |  1  |  2  |  3  |  4  |  5  |  6  |  7  |  8  |  9  | 10
```

26-B. PRETEST: VERTICAL REACHES

PRETEST. Take a 1-minute timing; compute speed and errors.

```
   4       After dinner was served aboard the yacht, we 10
       pushed our knives and forks away and yawned.  Kim 20
       then skipped back to the hotel.  The scenic ocean 30
       and valley had been enough excitement for a time. 40
          |  1  |  2  |  3  |  4  |  5  |  6  |  7  |  8  |  9  | 10
```

26-C. PRACTICE: UP REACHES

PRACTICE. If you made 2 or fewer errors on the Pretest, type each line (e.g., lines 5–9) 3 times for speed development. If you made 3 or more errors, type each group of 4 lines (e.g., lines 5–8), as though it were a paragraph, 3 times for accuracy improvement; then type the sentence (e.g., line 9) 3 times.

```
   5  aw awaken lawyer yawned away sawing outlaw straws
   6  se severe seized sequel base served useful choose
   7  rd ordeal burden garden word aboard hazard reward
   8  ki kinder kidney skirts skip baking unkind skinny
   9  After a while the unkind boarder seized my straw.
      |  1  |  2  |  3  |  4  |  5  |  6  |  7  |  8  |  9  | 10
```

26-D. PRACTICE: DOWN REACHES

```
  10  ac accent backed cracks jack vacant unpack actual
  11  kn knocks knight knotty knew knifed kneels kneads
  12  ab abided aboard babies cabs tables enable rabbit
  13  va valley vanish invade vast rivals canvas saliva

  14  She knew about those rabbit tracks in the valley.
      |  1  |  2  |  3  |  4  |  5  |  6  |  7  |  8  |  9  | 10
```

26-E. PRACTICE: JUMP REACHES

```
  15  ve versus verify avenue wave events reveal active
  16  ex excels excite expert exam convex flexed Mexico
  17  no notice normal honors snow annoys cannon domino
  18  ce ceases cereal oceans face scenic decent chance

  19  The next census will prove that no city excelled.
      |  1  |  2  |  3  |  4  |  5  |  6  |  7  |  8  |  9  | 10
```

POSTTEST. Repeat the Pretest and compare performance.

26-F. POSTTEST: VERTICAL REACHES

Line: 60 spaces	Tab: 5
Spacing: single	Drills: 3X
Proofguide: 137–138	
Workguide: 331–332, 463–474	
Tape: 50B and 51B	

INTEGRATED OFFICE PROJECT: ENERGY
LESSONS 201–206

GOALS FOR UNIT 33

1. Type at least 52 wam for 5 minutes with no more than 5 errors.
2. Edit documents while typing, correcting spelling errors and applying rules of grammar, punctuation, and typing style.
3. Type agenda and minutes for a business meeting.
4. Calculate amounts on invoices.
5. Type material for a magazine article.
6. Rearrange material in alphabetic order.
7. Set priorities.
8. Follow directions.

201-A. WARMUP

S 1 She will go downtown to purchase the big map of the island.
A 2 Max realizes by now that Jack Paige worked quite fervently.
N 3 Invoice 21–49 for $56.80 should have been received by 3/27.
| 1 | 2 | 3 | 4 | 5 | 6 | 7 | 8 | 9 | 10 | 11 | 12

201-B. PRETEST: HORIZONTAL REACHES

PRETEST. Take a 1-minute timing; compute speed and errors.

4   A debate was conducted on the dangers of hiking around 12
the edge of the peak. Some boys gave a rave review of this 24
trip. An agent from a local club spurned the raves and was 36
intent on having people hear his pleas for safety and care. 48
| 1 | 2 | 3 | 4 | 5 | 6 | 7 | 8 | 9 | 10 | 11 | 12

201-C. PRACTICE: IN REACHES

PRACTICE. If you made no errors on the Pretest, type each line 3 times. If you made 1 error or more, type each group of four lines (as though it were a paragraph) 3 times; then type the sentence 3 times.

5 ar around cellar market starch beware artery arid card hear
6 oy joyous oyster cloyed envoys tomboy coyote toys yoyo buoy
7 pu pushed spurns impugn wampum punted repute puff spur putt
8 lu lugged plunge dilute stylus lunacy clumsy lush clue lulu
9 When you put your toys around the cellar, do not be clumsy.
| 1 | 2 | 3 | 4 | 5 | 6 | 7 | 8 | 9 | 10 | 11 | 12

201-D. PRACTICE: OUT REACHES

10 ge gently agency legend bugged cringe genial gets ages edge
11 da danger pedals payday pagoda dazzle update data soda dale
12 hi hiking chilly orchid urchin hissed thirty hike chin hint
13 ra razzed tracer piracy rarity scarab tundra rang brag rave
14 He will get data for thirty tracers for the agency to send.
| 1 | 2 | 3 | 4 | 5 | 6 | 7 | 8 | 9 | 10 | 11 | 12

26-G. It is preferable not to divide a word at the end of a line. If it is necessary, however, the three absolute rules of word division must always be observed. If possible, the five preferential rules should also be observed.

26-H. Select the words that can be divided and type them with a hyphen to show where the division should be. Then complete Workguide pages 57–58.

Answers to the practice exercise appear on page 43.

26-I. Since machines vary, check yours now to see how many spaces you have left after the warning bell rings and before your keys lock at the right margin.

26-G. WORD DIVISION

ABSOLUTE RULES

1. Do not divide words pronounced as one syllable (*straight, shopped*), contractions (*couldn't, doesn't*), or abbreviations (*UNESCO, c.o.d.*).

2. Divide words only between syllables. If you are uncertain where a syllable ends, consult a dictionary.

3. Leave at least three characters (the last will be a hyphen) on the upper line and carry at least three characters (the last may be a punctuation mark) to the next line. Thus *de- tract* and *bet- ter*, but not *a- round* or *luck- y*.

PREFERENTIAL RULES

4. Divide compound words either at the hyphen (*self-sacrifice*) or where the two words join to make a solid compound. Thus *after- noon*, not *af- ternoon*.

5. If a one-letter syllable occurs in the middle of a word, divide after it; thus *criti- cal* is preferred to *crit- ical*. However, if two separately sounded vowels occur together, divide between them; thus *vari- ation* is preferred to *varia- tion*.

6. Divide after, not within, a prefix. Divide before, not within, a suffix. Thus *inter- fere* is preferred to *in- terfere* and *pay- able* is preferred to *paya- ble*.

7. Avoid dividing elements that are read as units, such as dates (*May 5*), amounts (*$8 million* or *$8,000,000*), titles and names (*Mr. Hess*), reference numbers (*page 5* or *Unit 3*), and so on.

8. Avoid dividing (*a*) after more than two consecutive lines have ended with a word division, (*b*) at the end of the first and last line of a page, and (*c*) a proper noun.

26-H. WORD-DIVISION PRACTICE

20	stretched	haven't	having
21	slowly	valley	NATO
22	enough	enable	emerged
23	paperweight	self-help	diagram
24	medicine	validate	paragraph
25	ultracritical	readable	Mr. Lester

26-I. LINE-ENDING DECISIONS

When you cannot copy material line for line, you must decide where each line should end. To help you end lines *without looking up*, a bell rings when the carrier or carriage is 8 to 10 spaces from the right margin stop. For example, if you wish lines to end at 75 and have therefore set the margin stop at 80, the bell may ring when the carrier or carriage reaches 70 or 71—signaling that you have 10 spaces left before the keys lock at the margin stop, and only 5 spaces left before you reach the *desired* ending point of 75. When the bell rings, end the line as near to the *desired* line ending as possible (preferably without dividing a word).

For example, if your typewriter gives a 4-space warning, here are some typical line-ending decisions you might encounter:

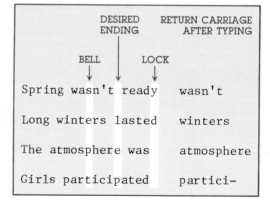

	DESIRED ENDING	RETURN CARRIAGE AFTER TYPING
	BELL LOCK	
Spring wasn't ready		wasn't
Long winters lasted		winters
The atmosphere was		atmosphere
Girls participated		partici-

27-A. Repeat 26-A, page 39. **27-A. WARMUP**

PART 9

INTEGRATED OFFICE PROJECTS · ENERGY, ELECTRONICS, LEGAL, MEDICAL

OBJECTIVES FOR PART 9

Part 9 is a continuation of projects designed to prepare you for working in an office situation. To complete the work satisfactorily, you should demonstrate the following abilities:

1. **Production.** Format correctly various types of business communications from unarranged, rough-draft, and simulated-dictation sources. Edit documents for spelling, grammar, punctuation, and typing style. Use reference sources, set priorities, follow directions, compose correspondence, abstract data, and handle human relations problems.

2. **Technical Knowledge.** Answer correctly at least 95 percent of the questions on an objective test.

3. **Skill Rate.** Type at the following speed and accuracy levels by the end of each unit:

Unit	Minutes	Minimum Speed	Maximum Errors
33	5	52	5
34	5	53	5
35	5	54	5
36	5	55	5

4. **Word Processing Information.** Understand the various functions of word processing.

27-B. PRETEST: DISCRIMINATION PRACTICE

PRETEST. Take a 1-minute timing; compute speed and errors.

26   The skillful drivers managed to build sedans 10
that looked both safer and more secure than their 20
previous models. Neither of the older styles has 30
had as safe a track record as the bold new model. 40
| 1 | 2 | 3 | 4 | 5 | 6 | 7 | 8 | 9 | 10

PRACTICE. If you made 2 or fewer errors on the Pretest, type each line 3 times. If you made 3 or more errors, type each group of 4 lines (as though it were a paragraph) 3 times; then type the sentence 3 times.

NOTE: Discrimination drills help you to type correctly those keys which are most commonly confused. For example: R and T, A and S, M and N.

27-C. PRACTICE: LEFT HAND

27 rtr artery trace barter trade alerts entry assert
28 asa ascent sacks asking safer basics essay biased
29 sds wisdom woods sedans bends beside bands abused
30 rer reacts surer reason error refill purer adhere
31 The safer sedans adhere better to the racetracks.
| 1 | 2 | 3 | 4 | 5 | 6 | 7 | 8 | 9 | 10

27-D. PRACTICE: RIGHT HAND

32 mnm alumni unmet solemn hymns enmesh denim unmade
33 oio oiling diode coined onion biopsy prior avoids
34 olo oldest loans bolder alone colons blown cooled
35 iui genius fruit medium suits radius guide incurs
36 The oldest alumni were suing the fruit merchants.
| 1 | 2 | 3 | 4 | 5 | 6 | 7 | 8 | 9 | 10

27-E. PRACTICE: BOTH HANDS

37 eie eighty diets either liens beings movie unveil
38 ghg ghetto thugs aghast thigh lights shrug hugger
39 yty mighty tying oyster style mystic dirty system
40 sks skates peeks skills tasks unmask banks risked
41 Eighty youths from the school sought movie roles.
| 1 | 2 | 3 | 4 | 5 | 6 | 7 | 3 | 9 | 10

POSTTEST. Repeat the Pretest and compare performance.

27-F. POSTTEST: DISCRIMINATION PRACTICE

27-G. Spacing—double. Compute your speed and count errors. Record your scores.

NOTE: The numbers above each line of copy in 27-G are speed markers for a 3-minute timing. The highest number you reach in 3 minutes is your speed.

27-G. SKILL MEASUREMENT: 3-MINUTE TIMED WRITING

42   You will find that when you begin working in 10
industry, you will not often have to divide words 20
when typing. Often, it is much quicker to simply 30
type the entire word at the end of one line or to 40
carry the entire word to the next line. That way 50
you do not have to puzzle over just how to divide 60
the word between syllables. Still, the rules you 70
have learned should be very useful in your typing 80
later. 81
| 1 | 2 | 3 | 4 | 5 | 6 | 7 | 8 | 9 | 10

↓7
Controlling Telephone Costs

In the past ~~decade~~ *few years*, the whole field of telecommunications has ~~just~~ *expanded* ~~exploded~~ *rapidly*. During this time, many business firms have also ~~seen their~~ *faced rising* telephone costs~~, exploding~~ *business*. A few (suggestions) and (tips) can help a firm trim it's costs.

Review Monthly Statement

Many firms know they get a telephone bill every month, but (it's) necessary to review the basic charges *in order* to determine whether payment is being made for actual pieces and types of equipment that are on hand. Double-check the basic equipment charge ~~for~~ *to* the company.

REVIEW NUMBER OF PHONES

In many businesses, it is common to find a phone on the desk of every employee. Every phone instrument ~~on hand~~ increases ~~your~~ *the* monthly charge. ~~Each phone instrument~~ *and therefore* should be justified. *But four to six employees can often share the same phone without difficulty.*

Review Future Plans

Choose *#* equipment with future growth in mind. Have the foresight to purchase a system that ~~is expandable~~ *can be expanded* through add-on frames or cabinets. Upgrading phone equipment ~~can~~ *will* be less costly if ~~your~~ purchase *such a system is* ~~expandable equipment in the beginning~~.

REVIEW LONG-DISTANCE CALLS

The cost of long-distance calls during business hours is not cheap. Monitor calls made so that all employees will keep costs down. At the same time, a special service might be purchased for frequently called numbers.

LESSONS 28/29
SKILL DRIVE

Goals: To improve speed/ accuracy; to make correct word-division and line-ending decisions.

28-A. WARMUP

S 1 They may work if the auditor signs the amendment.
A 2 Pink jasmines grew very quickly in the Bronx Zoo.
N 3 On April 18–26 we will be open from 7:45 to 9:30.
| 1 | 2 | 3 | 4 | 5 | 6 | 7 | 8 | 9 | 10

28-B. PRETEST: HORIZONTAL REACHES

PRETEST. Take a 1-minute timing; compute speed and errors.

4   The unhappy reader wrote to a favorite youth 10
magazine because he was upset about the amount of 20
unfair advertising. Of course, they wrote him to 30
explain just how their layouts had been designed. 40
| 1 | 2 | 3 | 4 | 5 | 6 | 7 | 8 | 9 | 10

28-C. PRACTICE: IN REACHES

PRACTICE. If you made 2 or fewer errors on the Pretest, type each line 3 times. If you made 3 or more errors, type each group of 4 lines (as though it were a paragraph) 3 times; then type the sentence 3 times.

5 wr wrecks writes wrists wrap wreaks wrench wreath
6 ou ounces output bounce pout course abound enough
7 ad adults adjust blades dead reader inroad thread
8 py pylons sloppy choppy copy grumpy sleepy swampy

9 The dead spy had written out the wrong admission.
| 1 | 2 | 3 | 4 | 5 | 6 | 7 | 8 | 9 | 10

28-D. PRACTICE: OUT REACHES

10 yo yogurt youths myopia yoga beyond canyon tryout
11 fa factor fairly famous sofa infant prefab farmed
12 up upbeat upsets cupful upon superb abrupt holdup
13 ga gained garage gasses saga cigars vagary frugal

14 Your father gave up farming behind my old garage.
| 1 | 2 | 3 | 4 | 5 | 6 | 7 | 8 | 9 | 10

28-E. PRACTICE: IN AND OUT REACHES

15 wracks unwrap wreath coupons couple fouled housed
16 occupy chippy skimpy gadgets adapts badges deaden
17 yonder anyone coyote fabrics fabled facial affair
18 uphold upmost puppet gallops gabled gabbed gasket

19 Did anyone unwrap enough fabrics and blue thread?
| 1 | 2 | 3 | 4 | 5 | 6 | 7 | 8 | 9 | 10

POSTTEST. Repeat the Pretest and compare performance.

28-F. POSTTEST: HORIZONTAL REACHES

the participants at the meeting concerning our presentation dealing with personnel recruitment, selection, and promotion.

As I indicated to you during our brief conversation, I will be pleased to meet with you on Thursday, February 16, at your office. I will plan to arrive at 11 a.m., and I would like you to be my guest at lunch after our meeting.

So that you might have more detailed information about the services that we provide for our clients, I am enclosing a brochure that explains our various services. This should help you to understand how our firm might assist you in meeting your personnel needs. Regarding your particular firm, let me elaborate on the following points:

1. At the present time, we do have a number of potential employees who have the technical background and expertise that you would require in the electrical engineering field.

2. We are able to provide many different services in testing prospective employees. We have personality, aptitude, and specialized skills testing that we can administer.

3. We have files on prospective employees across the board. Professional, technical, administrative support, and clerical workers are available.

4. We have excellent contacts and connections with placement offices in all the colleges, technical institutes, and private business schools in this part of Utah.

We are confident that we can assist you in recruiting and selecting employees who will help your firm grow and prosper. I look forward to describing our services in detail when I meet you.

Sincerely yours, / Harry Foxmoor / President / urs / Enclosure

Table Title: Leisure Time Activities for Administrative Personnel in Northwest Oregon

Table Subtitle: Ranked by "Often" Responses

Leave 4 spaces between columns

Rank	Activity	Often	Sometimes	Never
1	Watching television	64	24	0
2	Reading	59	27	2
3.5	Traveling	58	30	0
3.5	Visiting friends *and relatives*	58	29	1
5	Maintaining living quarters	54	30	4
6	Watching sports *ing events*	52	31	5
7	Listening to music	50	35	3
8	Attending the movies	49	31	8
9	Doing home repairs	45	33	10
10.5	Gardening	44	30	14
10.5	Participating in sports	44	26	18
12	Collecting items for a hobby	36	32	20

28-G. PRACTICE IN MAKING LINE-ENDING DECISIONS

The Pretest in 28-B on page 42 is shown on a 50-space line. Set your margins for a 40-space line and type the passage, deciding for yourself where to end each line. Listen for the bell and *do not look up.* If time permits, repeat this exercise using a 60-space line.

28-H. Select the words that can be divided and type them with a hyphen to show where the division should be (example: *semi-colon*).

Answers to the word division practice appear at the bottom of page 44.

28-H. WORD-DIVISION PRACTICE

20	semicolon	couldn't	mailable
21	hardly	thoughts	$489,000,000
22	return	supersonic	self-control
23	hour	eraser	January 18, 1984
24	overdue	origin	separate
25	along	listen	brother-in-law
26	understand	section	Wallace Goodwin
27	radiation	divide	ideas
28	paperweight	butcher	baby-sitter
29	introduce	belong	aboveground
30	business	U.S.S.R.	knowledge

Answers to practice 26-H, page 40.
20. hav- ing
21. val- ley
22. en- able
23. paper- weight   self- help
    dia- gram
24. medi- cine   vali- date
    para- graph
25. ultra- critical   read- able

28-I. Take a 1-minute timing on the first paragraph to establish your base speed. Then take successive 1-minute timings on the other paragraphs. You must equal or exceed your base speed before moving to the next paragraph.

28-I. SUSTAINED PRACTICE: SYLLABIC INTENSITY

```
31     What is it that makes timed writings hard or   10
   easy?  On one timing you may type quickly, but on   20
   another you may type slowly.  Here is the reason.   30

32     Shorter words that contain just one syllable   10
   are not hard to type; longer words with more syl-   20
   lables are harder.  This explains the difference.   30

33     The number of syllables per word is known as   10
   the syllabic intensity.  The intensity of each of   20
   these lines goes up, increasing their difficulty.   30

34     Although the syllabic intensity of the other   10
   timed writings remains constant, this exercise is   20
   designed to provide practice in difficult typing.   30
```
| 1 | 2 | 3 | 4 | 5 | 6 | 7 | 8 | 9 | 10

29-A. Repeat 28-A, page 42.

29-A. WARMUP

LESSON 200

TEST 8: PROGRESS TEST ON PART 8

TEST 8-A
5-MINUTE TIMED WRITING

Paper: Workguide 453
Line: 60 spaces
Spacing: double
Tab: 5
Start: line 9

The importance of team effort and team play has been a   12
topic of great interest for many different people. Experts   24
who study the behavior of people have undertaken many types   36
of research studies in attempting to evaluate the impact of   48
a unified effort on achievement level. The conclusions are   60
always similar. When a group of people endeavors to meet a   72
common goal, more will be accomplished. This is true in an   84
office, plant, home, school, or church. It is a very valid   96
point in athletics.   100

A number of business firms have recently begun quality   112
circles in their offices. The purpose behind these circles   124
is to encourage small groups of workers to come together to   136
determine whether any procedures and steps that they follow   148
on their jobs can be improved. The small groups give every   160
person in the unit a stake in the operation of the unit. A   172
quality circle recognizes the many benefits of team effort.   184

Of course, the concept of teamwork and team spirit has   196
always played an important role in an athletic event. When   208
they are asked why a championship team has been successful,   220
a lot of observers will point to team spirit and team play.   232
They feel that team effort is far more significant than the   244
talents of individual players.   250

| 1 | 2 | 3 | 4 | 5 | 6 | 7 | 8 | 9 | 10 | 11 | 12 |

TEST 8-B
LETTER 76
MODIFIED-BLOCK STYLE
TWO-PAGE LETTER

Paper: Workguide 455–457

Mrs. Lois Jasper, President / J&R Enterprises / 15 Grover Street / Provo, UT 84601 / Dear Mrs. Jasper:

It was good to meet you last Thursday at the meeting hosted by the Provo Kiwanis and to have an opportunity to describe some of the services that Foxmoor could provide for you. Mr. Jackson and I were extremely pleased with the reception that we received from

(Continued on next page.)

29-B. PRETEST: COMMON LETTER COMBINATIONS

PRETEST. Take a 1-minute timing; compute speed and errors.

The real reason that the free talent contest 10
was canceled was because of a lack of income. It 20
simply became too costly, so we arranged to begin 30
charging a small fee to help defray the expenses. 40

| 1 | 2 | 3 | 4 | 5 | 6 | 7 | 8 | 9 | 10

29-C. PRACTICE: WORD BEGINNINGS

PRACTICE. If you made 2 or fewer errors on the Pretest, type each line 3 times. If you made 3 or more errors, type each group of 4 lines (as though it were a paragraph) 3 times; then type the sentence 3 times.

36 in inches indeed inputs into infers inform indent
37 re recall reacts result real reason record return
38 be became belong begins beat beware belief behalf
39 de devote decent dealer deny decade deduct design
40 Before the debate began, I informed the reviewer.

| 1 | 2 | 3 | 4 | 5 | 6 | 7 | 8 | 9 | 10

29-D. PRACTICE: WORD ENDINGS

41 ly barely fairly calmly only easily deeply weakly
42 ed edited missed agreed deed biased exceed traded
43 nt client moment absent bent quaint extent talent
44 al casual actual formal deal annual mental visual
45 Recently, I nearly missed the quaint formal deal.

| 1 | 2 | 3 | 4 | 5 | 6 | 7 | 8 | 9 | 10

29-E. PRACTICE: OTHER COMBINATIONS

46 fr freeze fringe afraid free defray framed fronts
47 th thanks though ethics both thinks either growth
48 st stable stamps costly best lasted adjust safest
49 ng angels engage danger long change spring wrongs
50 They think our first string was afraid of theirs.

| 1 | 2 | 3 | 4 | 5 | 6 | 7 | 8 | 9 | 10

POSTTEST. Repeat the Pretest and compare performance.

29-F. POSTTEST: COMMON LETTER COMBINATIONS

29-G. Spacing—double. Record your score.

29-G. SKILL MEASUREMENT: 3-MINUTE TIMED WRITING

Answers to practice 28-H, page 43.
20. semi- colon   mail- able
22. re- turn   super- sonic
    self- control
23. January 18,- 1984
24. over- due   ori- gin
    sepa- rate
25. lis- ten   brother- in-law
26. under- stand   sec- tion
    Wallace- Goodwin
27. radi- ation   di- vide
28. paper- weight   baby- sitter
29. intro- duce   be- long
    above- ground
30. busi- ness   knowl- edge

51
$\overset{1}{}$ Word processing personnel$\overset{2}{}$ claim that even as$\overset{3}{}$ 10
complex as$\overset{4}{}$ word processors$\overset{5}{}$ are, it is still not a$\overset{6}{}$ 20
major job$\overset{7}{}$ to train a$\overset{8}{}$ good typist to$\overset{9}{}$ operate these$\overset{10}{}$ 30
machines. Your first$\overset{11}{}$ prerequisite, of$\overset{12}{}$ course, is$\overset{13}{}$ 40
to be an$\overset{14}{}$ expert typist; the second$\overset{15}{}$ requirement is$\overset{16}{}$ 50
good$\overset{17}{}$ English skills; and$\overset{18}{}$ the third$\overset{19}{}$ skill you need$\overset{20}{}$ 60
is knowing how$\overset{21}{}$ to proofread.$\overset{22}{}$ Start today to$\overset{23}{}$ ana- 70
lyze your$\overset{24}{}$ work with care$\overset{25}{}$ to find and correct$\overset{26}{}$ mis- 80
takes.$\overset{27}{}$ 81

| 1 | 2 | 3 | 4 | 5 | 6 | 7 | 8 | 9 | 10

Paper: plain

When I get back to the office, I'll need this report for my meeting with Senator Craig.

Center each line {
Issues Relating to Inter$tate Highway Through 11th District
A Report to Senator Craig
By Carl Paboojian

(and issues)

   I have been collecting information and data concerning the problems
associated with the approval of putting Interstate 2(1)8 through various
town$ in your district. In this report I would like to discus$ the
following two points: economic and environmental concerns.

ECONOMIC CONCERNS
   A number of issues have been raised by ~~local~~ *the* business ~~persons from~~ *communities*
~~both~~ *in* Morris and Sussex Counties. In Morris County, an association of
businesspeople from Flanders has gathered signatures on a petition
expressing concern *that* the interstate highway will take business away from
the m~~s~~any small shops that are now located on the local highway$ that
run$ through town. At the same time, another group of businesspersons
from Franklin *in Sussex County,* has also expressed grave reservations about the affect
of the interstate highway on the shops and local businesses. *on the current highway through town.*

   We have received numerous letters from individuals who own businesses along the proposed highway path ~~from~~ *in* almost every town in your
district, ~~would be effected~~ in addition to the petitions being circu-
lated by these two bodies, Most of these letters detail a specific
concern as to why the Interstate *highway* should not be approved ~~under~~ *until* further
studies *have been* ~~are~~ completed.

ENVIRONMENTAL CONCERNS
   A great deal of correspondence has been recieved ~~about the proposed~~
~~Interstate 281~~ from individuals and groups having an environmental concern. We have 12 petitions from various wild life preservation groups
indicating that they would lend their support to the project only if
certain *provisions for the protection of wildlife* ~~plans~~ are incorporated into the proposal.

Two groups concerned with water supply and management have sent petitions indicating support for the proposed highway on condition that some modifications be included.

Line: 50 spaces   Tab: 5
Spacing: single   Drills: 3X
Proofguide: 13–16
Workguide: 3
Tape: 14B, 15B

LESSONS 30/31
SKILL DRIVE

Goals: To improve speed/accuracy; to locate and correct errors.

30-A. WARMUP

S 1 Did both girls make their formal gowns with bows?
A 2 The disc jockey won six bronze plaques for Alvin.
N 3 Alex made 19,874 points, whereas Joe made 20,365.
  | 1 | 2 | 3 | 4 | 5 | 6 | 7 | 8 | 9 | 10

30-B. PRETEST: CLOSE REACHES

PRETEST. **Take a 1-minute timing; compute speed and errors.**

4   We went hunting with bow and arrow under the 10
huge olive tree near the great swamp. We started 20
to stand in the open but decided we had best hide 30
in the loose grass, where we did a little better. 40
  | 1 | 2 | 3 | 4 | 5 | 6 | 7 | 8 | 9 | 10

30-C. PRACTICE: ADJACENT KEYS

PRACTICE. **If you made 2 or fewer errors on the Pretest, type each line 3 times. If you made 3 or more errors, type each group of 4 lines (as though it were a paragraph) 3 times; then type the sentence 3 times.**

5 rt birth hurts sorts dart party earth alert chart
6 as asked based cases bias tasks basis waste areas
7 op opens copes moped opts drops topic scope stops
8 we wears weave weeks owed weird dwell sweet lower

9 We asked the weaver to stop sorting the clothing.
  | 1 | 2 | 3 | 4 | 5 | 6 | 7 | 8 | 9 | 10

30-D. PRACTICE: CONSECUTIVE STROKES

10 sw swank swamp sweat swap swims sweet swipe swell
11 gr grade graft agree grab great grams grass gross
12 un uncle undid unite noun until funds lunch begun
13 ol older whole bolts oleo colon folds solid extol

14 Uncle Grant thought those sweet rolls were great.
  | 1 | 2 | 3 | 4 | 5 | 6 | 7 | 8 | 9 | 10

30-E. PRACTICE: DOUBLE LETTERS

15 ss bless bossy lasso less amass bliss cross press
16 oo oozed boost goods book loose doors tools stood
17 tt attic otter ditto butt petty mutts putty witty
18 rr array error berry burr hurry sorry ferry merry

19 Jerry used putty and glass to fix the brass door.
  | 1 | 2 | 3 | 4 | 5 | 6 | 7 | 8 | 9 | 10

POSTTEST. Repeat the Pretest and compare performance.

30-F. POSTTEST: CLOSE REACHES

I would like to discuss my itinerary for the third week in December when I meet with Senator Craig the day I get back from my trip. Please type the final draft of this itinerary so that I will have it available when I meet with her.

Start on → ITINERARY FOR CARL PABOOJIAN
line 7

Third Week of December

MONDAY, DECEMBER 15

9 a.m.   *Newton*
                         ~~Trenton~~ Office

8
~~7~~ p.m.   Branchville VFW, Branchville, NJ

TUESDAY, DECEMBER 16

9 a.m.   Hackettstown Office

[11 a.m.   Meet *with* D. Lawrence, Warren County Freeholders
                         About Interstate 281 (Room 4)

2 p.m.   Meet with Victoria Cull*er*, Warren County REA
                         About S-231 (Room 4)

4 P.M.
~~3:30 p.m.~~   Meet with Joseph *K.* Daley, Warren County Elks
                         About S-227 (Room 4)

WEDNESDAY, DECEMBER 17

9 a.m.   Trenton Office

8 p.m.   Warren County Historical Society, *Legion Hall,* Blairstown,
                         NJ

THURSDAY, DECEMBER 18

9 a.m.   Trenton Office

1 p.m.   Meet with John Kelley, Administrative *assistant* ~~Asst.~~
                         ~~For~~ *to* Sen*a*tor Bellini
                         About S-228 (Room C123)

7 p.m.   Hackettstown Schools PTA, *Payne School,* Hackettstown, NJ

FRIDAY, DECEMBER 19

9 a.m.   *Newton*
                         ~~Trenton~~ Office

[11 a.m.   Meet with Jessica Ulinski, Sussex County
                         coordinator for Sen*a*tor Craig Campaign,
                         (Room 111)

30-G. ERROR CORRECTION

An error should be corrected as soon as it is made. Since you may not know when you make an error, however, always proofread your work carefully and correct any errors that you find *before* removing the paper from the typewriter. Correcting errors while the paper is still in the machine is much easier than having to reinsert the paper and align the type.

Use one of the following techniques to correct errors.

TYPING ERASER. (1) Lift the paper bail and turn the platen to move the error into position for easy correction. (2) To keep eraser crumbs from falling into the mechanism, move the carrier or carriage to the extreme left or right—away from the error. (3) Use a stiff ink eraser and a *light*, up-and-down motion to erase the error. (4) Return to the typing line and type the correction.

CORRECTION PAPER. Slips of paper which contain a light coating of chalk can also be used to correct an error. (1) Backspace to the error and place the correction paper between the typing paper and the typewriter ribbon (coated side toward the typing paper). (2) Retype the error. (The chalk from the correction paper will conceal the error.) (3) Remove the correction paper, backspace, and type the correction.

CORRECTION FLUID. Correction fluid works similarly to correction paper in that it covers the error. (1) Turn the paper forward or backward. (2) Brush the fluid sparingly over the error. (3) Let the fluid dry. (4) Type the correction.

CORRECTION RIBBON. Typewriters with correction capabilities contain a correction ribbon as well as a special backspace key which engages the correction ribbon. (1) Use the special backspace key to backspace to the error. (2) Retype the error so that the coating on the correction ribbon lifts the error off the typing page. (3) Type the correction.

30-H. Type lines 20–23 exactly as shown; then make the necessary corrections. Try to make each correction so neatly that it will be impossible to detect.

30-H. ERROR-CORRECTION PRACTICE

20 Sometimes the error appears at the end of a linr.
21 Sometines it occurs at the beginning of the line.
22 And sometimes it appears in tge middle of a line.
23 Wherever an error occrus, find it and correct it.

30-I. Type lines 24–25 three times each. Then take two 1-minute timings on paragraph 26.

30-I. NUMBER PRACTICE

24 aqla alal sw2s s2s2 de3d d3d3 fr4f f4f4 ft5f f5f5
25 jy6j j6j6 ju7j j7j7 ki8k k8k8 lo9l 1919 ;p0; ;0;0

26   John Adams was born on October 30, 1735, and 10
     died on July 4, 1826, at the age of 90; he served 20
     as President from 1797 to 1801. He was succeeded 30
     by Thomas Jefferson who served from 1801 to 1809. 40
     | 1 | 2 | 3 | 4 | 5 | 6 | 7 | 8 | 9 | 10

31-A. Repeat 30-A, page 45.   **31-A. WARMUP**

JOB 9
TABLE 61

Paper: plain

I'm compiling some data for Senator Craig concerning the ten largest cities in New Jersey. Use a road atlas, statistical abstract, or whatever you need to get this information. We'll entitle the table Ten Largest Cities in New Jersey. You'll need three columns. Use the headings Rank, City, and Population. Give the source of your data in a footnote.

JOB 10
MEMO 23

Paper: Workguide 449

I'll be meeting with Senator Craig the day I return from my trip. When I meet with her, I'd like to discuss some of the various projects I've been working on. Please prepare a memo from this draft. Make the subject "Update on Various Activities." Be sure to proofread it carefully and sign my name.

As you know I will be away from the office for a few days. I have scheduled an appointment to meet with you at 10 a.m. on Monday, my first day back in the office. In preparation for that meeting, I would like to share the following information with you:

Campaign Contributions. I have prepare data concerning the contributions you have recieved from individuals throughout your district. I will have a copy of a table giving the names of Contributors who have given $100 through $500 toward your Campaign. In addition, I will be able to give you data about contributors from each of the three counties you represent.

Interstate Highway Report. As you requested, I have prepared a short report on the issues relating to Interstate 281. The report focuses on economic and environmental concerns. I will have a copy of that report when I meet with you.

Largest Cities in New Jersey. I have gathered the data you want on the ten largest cities in New Jersey. When I meet with you, I will give you the population and rank of each city.

31-B. PRETEST: ALTERNATE- AND ONE-HAND REACHES

PRETEST. **Take a 1-minute timing; compute speed and errors.**

27   The chairman turned down the amendment which 10
affected the downtown area. Frankly, the visitor 20
was not impressed. Afterward he reversed his own 30
opinion and agreed to accept the new development. 40
| 1 | 2 | 3 | 4 | 5 | 6 | 7 | 8 | 9 | 10

31-C. PRACTICE: ALTERNATE HANDS

PRACTICE. **If you made 2 or fewer errors on the Pretest, type each line 3 times. If you made 3 or more errors, type each group of 4 lines (as though it were a paragraph) 3 times; then type the sentence 3 times.**

28 bushel signal ancient chairman quantity amendment
29 formal theory element downtown turndown shamrocks
30 handle visual auditor neighbor rigidity authentic
31 profit thrown visitor ornament problems endowment
32 Those fuel problems may signal a big proxy fight.
| 1 | 2 | 3 | 4 | 5 | 6 | 7 | 8 | 9 | 10

31-D. PRACTICE: ONE HAND

33 uphill abstract unhook afterward million regarded
34 poplin affected limply regretted opinion excavate
35 unholy decrease pinion aggravate pumpkin reversed
36 kimono greatest homily cassettes homonym carefree
37 Johnny reserved a minimum of seven seats in July.
| 1 | 2 | 3 | 4 | 5 | 6 | 7 | 8 | 9 | 10

31-E. PRACTICE: BOTH HANDS

38 deeply action develop imported creation affection
39 holder easily frankly kilowatt erection afternoon
40 impact honest illness nominate fraction carefully
41 really number impress reaction hundreds youngster
42 The actions of the honest youngster were tactful.
| 1 | 2 | 3 | 4 | 5 | 6 | 7 | 8 | 9 | 10

POSTTEST. **Repeat the Pretest and compare performance.**

31-F. POSTTEST: ALTERNATE- AND ONE-HAND REACHES

31-G. **Spacing—double. Record your score.**

31-G. SKILL MEASUREMENT: 3-MINUTE TIMED WRITING

43   You should experiment with the various means 10
you have of correcting mistakes. The method that 20
you use may depend upon the color and the quality 30
of the paper, the size of the error, and how many 40
copies you will need to make; one other factor is 50
whether you find your mistakes while the paper is 60
in the machine or after you have removed it. The 70
objective is to make a correction that no one can 80
see. 81
| 1 | 2 | 3 | 4 | 5 | 6 | 7 | 8 | 9 | 10

JOBS 3–5
TABLES 58–60
RULED TABLES

Paper: plain

Using a copy of the large table you just typed, please type three tables showing the contributions from individuals in each county. Use the county name as a subhead. Of course, you'll be eliminating the "County" column altogether. List the contributors based on highest to lowest contribution. For example, in the Morris County table, Marcia Foley will be listed first and William Kruse will be listed last.

JOB 6
LETTER 75
MODIFIED-BLOCK STYLE

Paper: Workguide 445–446

Senator Craig has planned to be a panelist at a meeting in Blairstown. However, she now realizes that she cannot keep this date and asks that I fill in for her. Please send this letter to Mr. Armand Hughes, President, Warren County Historical Society, 117 Mount Hope Road, Blairstown, NJ 07825.

Because of pressing busness in Trenton Senator Craig will not be able to keep her committment to be a panelist at your meeting on Wednesday December 17 at 8 p.m. in the legion hall. Of course, she is most disappointed to cancel her appearance at this late date.

It will be possible for me to rearrange my schedule so that I can substitute for Senator Craig. I would arrange to meet with her prior to attending your meeting in order to be able to reflect her thoughts concerning the questions to be addressed to the panelists.

If you would like me to subsitute for senator Craig please call me at (609) 555-3707 to confirm my participation.

JOBS 7–8
FORMS 74–75
VOUCHER CHECKS

Paper: Workguide 447

We ordered some office supplies and some campaign buttons for Senator Craig's forthcoming campaign. The materials have all been received. Unfortunately, we have misplaced the invoices that accompanied the deliveries. Please issue two checks for our purchases. First, type a check to Circle Paper Supplies at 14 Pompton Road in Butler, NJ 07405 for 10 reams of stationery at $15.95 a ream, 10 boxes of envelopes at $12.50 a box, and 200 poster sheets at $.30 each. After computing the amount of the purchase, add a 6 percent sales tax and $1.50 handling charge. Then type a check to Taylor Novelty Company at 115 Grant Place in Belvidere, NJ 07823 for 500 three-inch campaign buttons at $.75 each and 800 one-inch campaign buttons at $.20 each. Again, add a 6 percent sales tax to the total. Please have these checks ready for me to sign when I return to the office.

| Line: 50 spaces   Tab: center |
| Spacing: single   Drills: 2X |
| Proofguide: 15–18 |
| Workguide: 3–4, 59, 61–69 |
| Tape: 16A or K10B |

LESSONS 32/33
LETTER TYPING

Goals: To control the parentheses and ampersand (&) keys; to format business letters.

32-A.   WARMUP

S 1 Both of my neighbors and I paid a visit to Japan.
A 2 Fay took her quiz and exam with a good black pen.
N 3 On 10/29/83, she typed lines 16–47 in 35 minutes.
| 1 | 2 | 3 | 4 | 5 | 6 | 7 | 8 | 9 | 10

PARENTHESES are the shifts of 9 and 0. Use the L and Sem fingers.

32-B.   PRACTICE THE (AND) KEYS

4 lo9l 19l 19(l l(l l(l ;p0; ;0; ;0););); (l) (12)
5 Please see (1) Bill, (2) Jo, (3) Rob, and (4) Ed.
6 The senator (Mr. Lin) voted for (not against) me.
7 At that time (1982), I argued for Friday (May 9).

AMPERSAND (sign for *and*) is the shift of 7. Use the J finger.

32-C.   PRACTICE THE & KEY

8 ju7j j7j j7&j j&j j7j j&j 5 & 6 & 7 & 8 & 9 & 10.
9 Adams & Sons bought all of the Jones & Ray stock.
10 The case of Webb & Co. vs. Hart & Son will start.
11 Ball & Son opened for business on Friday (May 4).

32-D. Compare this paragraph with the last paragraph of Letter 1 on page 50. Type a list of the words that contain errors, correcting the errors as you type.

32-D.   PROOFREADING SKILLS

12 Western Industrys is growing rapidly, Mr. Cummings and
13 and we will, no doubt, soon be back in teh computer
14 hard ware market in order to stay ahead of the demand
15 for information processing.

32-E. Spacing—double. Record your score.

32-E.   SKILL MEASUREMENT: 3-MINUTE TIMED WRITING

16   In the next section you will learn to format   10
business letters and will use the production word   20
count to compute your speed. The production word   30
count adjusts the standard word count to give you   40
credit for such nonprinting operations as the use   50
of the tab key or the backspace key. This method   60
of computing the word count helps you to equalize   70
your speed on different kinds of copy so that you   80
can compare scores.   84
| 1 | 2 | 3 | 4 | 5 | 6 | 7 | 8 | 9 | 10

WP Instead of using a production word count to measure output, many word processing centers measure output by counting the number of strokes or lines typed.

INDIVIDUAL CONTRIBUTORS FOR SENATOR CRAIG CAMPAIGN

CONTRIBUTIONS OF $100-$500

CONTRIBUTOR	LOCATION	COUNTY	AMOUNT OF CONTRIBUTION	DATE OF CONTRIBUTION
Sall~~e~~y Ayrey	Newton	~~Warren~~ _Sussex_	$ 150	11/2
John Chan	Philipsburg	Warren	200	10/14
Eileen Fitzpatrick	Alpha	Warren	125	11/15
Marcia Foley	Morristown	Morris	500	11/17
(Tom) Griffin	Flanders	Morris	250	10/22
Mary Hillstreet	Washington	Warren	300	11/16
John Holman	Sparta	~~Morris~~ _Sussex_	175	10/31
Patrick Hughes	Chester	Morris	200	10/17
Vincent Jimenez	~~Morris~~ _Mendham_	Morris	275	11/19
Paul Inagaki	Hackettstown	Warren	400	11/28
Ernestine Kowalski	Andover	Sussex	375	11/28
William Kruse	Mendham	Morris	120	11/24
Enzo Marinelli	Hackettstown	Warren	100	10/27
~~Dick~~ _Richard_ Murphy	Lafayette	Sussex	350	11/11
Paula Nardone	Newton	Sussex	400	11/14
Dorthy Nelson	Belvidere	Warren	275	11/7
William Perrine	Dover	Morris	400	10/31
Phyllis Orsini	Hopatcong	Sussex	300	11/21
Charles Plessis	Oxford	Warren	150	11/7
Lois Poller	Franklin	Sussex	100	10/26
Virginia Prugh	Rockaway	Morris	350	11/13
Pedro Ramirez	Whippany	Morris	125	11/17
~~Beverley Robinson~~ _Barbara Robbins_	Branchville	Sussex	275	10/24
Theresa Wilson	Washington	Warren	350	10/26

32-F. BASIC PARTS OF A BUSINESS LETTER

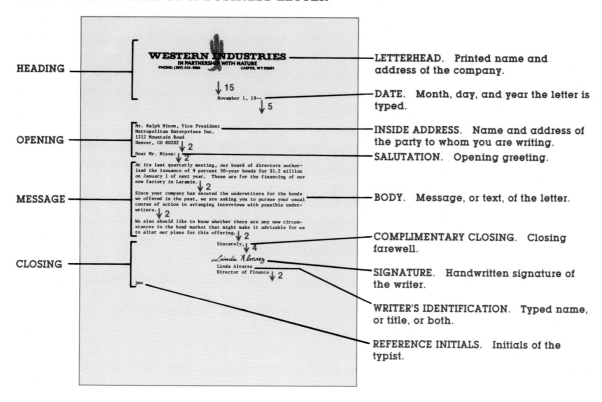

HEADING

LETTERHEAD. Printed name and address of the company.

DATE. Month, day, and year the letter is typed.

OPENING

INSIDE ADDRESS. Name and address of the party to whom you are writing.

SALUTATION. Opening greeting.

MESSAGE

BODY. Message, or text, of the letter.

COMPLIMENTARY CLOSING. Closing farewell.

CLOSING

SIGNATURE. Handwritten signature of the writer.

WRITER'S IDENTIFICATION. Typed name, or title, or both.

REFERENCE INITIALS. Initials of the typist.

32-G. FORMATTING A BUSINESS LETTER

METHOD 1: USING THE VISUAL GUIDE
Detach Workguide page 59, the visual guide for letter placement. Read and follow the directions on it closely. Use the visual guide to develop the judgment you need to estimate placement.

METHOD 2: USING A PLACEMENT FORMULA
1. For letters with fewer than 225 words in the body, set your margins for a 5-inch line (50 pica/60 elite). Set a tab stop at the center point.
2. Type the date on line 15 from the top of the paper, beginning at center.
3. Space down 5 lines and type the inside address at the left margin.
4. Double-space before and after the salutation.

5. Single-space the body of the letter, but double-space between paragraphs.
6. Begin the complimentary closing at center, a double space below the body.
7. Begin the writer's identification at center, 4 lines below the complimentary closing.
NOTE: The space for the writer's signature can be reduced to as few as 2 blank lines or increased to as many as 6 blank lines in order to make the letter appear centered on the page.
8. Type your initials at the left margin a double space below the last line of the writer's identification. Use lowercase letters or solid caps, without periods.
Before typing Letters 1–4, complete Workguide pages 61–62.

32/33-H. BUSINESS LETTERS

Using the visual guide from Workguide page 59 and the letterheads from Workguide pages 63–69, type Letters 1–4 in modified-block style, as illustrated by

Letter 1. All letters in this unit are of average length and require a 5-inch line (50 spaces) for pica machines and a 5-inch line (60 spaces) for elite machines.

Situation: Today is Monday, December 1. You are a typist in the office of State Senator Helena Craig of the 11th district in New Jersey. Her district encompasses parts of Morris, Sussex, and Warren counties. You report directly to Mr. Carl Paboojian, administrative assistant to Senator Craig. Mr. Paboojian likes the modified-block style of letter, with these closing lines:

Sincerely yours,

Carl Paboojian
Administrative Assistant

Mr. Paboojian will be out of the state for the next two days. He has called you into his office to give you some work that must be completed while he is gone. You will have to read through all the work right away so that you can ask him any questions you may have before he leaves the office.

You are expected to make a carbon copy of everything you type. All typewritten copy should be in mailable form. Correct any spelling, grammar, or punctuation errors that you encounter.

FORM 73   Workguide: 441
JOB PRIORITY LIST

Before you begin your work, review the items in the project. Then, on Workguide page 441, assign a 1, 2, or 3 priority to each item.

JOB 1   Paper: Workguide 443–444
LETTER 74
MODIFIED-BLOCK STYLE

Please get this letter in the mail very quickly. The letter will go to Ms. Pauline M. Stephenson, President, Hacketts-town Schools PTA, 171 Schooley Mountain Road, Hacketts-town, NJ 07840. When you finish the letter, sign it for me. Remember to add your initials after my signature.

Dear Ms. Stephenson:

Your invitation to Senator Craig to speak at your meeting on Thursday, December 18, at the Payne School has been recieved.

Senator Craig has had a continuing interest in the progress of the new interstate highway that have been proposed for the outskirts of Hackettstown. She will be please to discuss her recommendations for this interstate highway with the members of your group.

I will be acompanying Senator Craig, and we will plan to arrive at the Payne School by 7 p.m. on December 18. Would you please arrange to have an over head projector available for Senator Craig to use during her presentation.

JOB 2   Paper: plain
TABLE 57
RULED TABLE

I've been working on information about the contributions for Senator Craig's campaign from individuals in her district. Using the rough draft entitled "Individual Contributors for Senator Craig Campaign," (*page 293*) type a final copy of the table. Group the names in sets of three and make an extra copy so that you can use it when you prepare tables of contributions from each of the three counties.

Shown in pica
Line: 5 inches (50 pica/60 elite)
Tab: center
Date: current
Paper: Workguide 63
Proofguide: 15–16

Although there are several ways to format a business letter, the modified-block style shown here is the most commonly used letter style.

WESTERN INDUSTRIES
IN PARTNERSHIP WITH NATURE
PHONE: (307) 555-1086   CASPER, WY 82601

↓15

November 18, 19--   ↓5   4

Mr. Roger A. Cummings   12
Cummings & Wood, Inc.   16
148 Hiland Center Road   21
Cheyenne, WY 82001   25

Leave 1 space between the state and the ZIP Code.

Dear Mr. Cummings: 30

Standard punctuation: Colon after the salutation and comma after the complimentary closing.

Your presentation of the benefits of the Datamate   41
System 6000 (Model A) gave Jack Owens and me much   51
to think about. We were impressed by the competi-   61
tive price of your system, by the relatively low   71
maintenance cost projections, and by your generous   81
trade-in allowance.   85

The production word count (PWC) is given in the right margin. Review 32-E, page 48, for an explanation of PWC.

At this time, however, Western Industries requires   96
a system that has a greater processing capacity than 107
the 6000 offers.   111

Western Industries is growing rapidly, Mr. Cummings, 122
and we will, no doubt, soon be back in the computer 133
hardware market in order to stay ahead of our demand 143
for information processing.   149

Sincerely yours, ↓4   154

Margaret Tam

Mrs. Margaret Tam   163
Data Systems Manager   168
↓2

Type your initials for the reference initials.

dcl   170

Business letter in modified-block style with (1) date and closing lines beginning at center; (2) all other lines beginning at left margin; (3) single spacing.

194-E. PRACTICE: DOUBLE LETTERS

15 ss issued essay tossed messy glossy boss assign toss remiss
16 oo voodoo scoop gloomy igloo lagoon noon bamboo look fooled
17 tt mitten witty spotty attic sitter mitt attach watt pretty
18 rr arrive error mirror worry flurry burr errand purr barrel
19 Our boss arrived at noon and attempted to locate the error.
    | 1 | 2 | 3 | 4 | 5 | 6 | 7 | 8 | 9 | 10 | 11 | 12

POSTTEST. Repeat the Pretest and compare performance.

194-F. POSTTEST: CLOSE REACHES

194-G. Spacing—double. Take two 5-minute timings. Between them, practice any words with which you had difficulty. Record your score.

194-G. SKILL MEASUREMENT: 5-MINUTE TIMING

20
　　　　　　　　　　　　　　　1　　　　　　　　　　　　　　　　2
　　　Since the earliest settlers arrived on our shores, our　12
　　　　　　3　　　　　　　　　　　　　　4
citizens have always had a strong interest in the doings of　24
　　　5　　　　　　　　　　　　6　　　　　　　　　　　　7
government. Whether one mentions national, state, or local　36
　　　　　　　　　　　8　　　　　　　　　　　　9
government, one can be sure that lively discussions will be　48
　　　　　10　　　　　　　　　11　　　　　　　　　　12
generated. One never knows which issue might cause a great　60
　　　　　　　　　13
deal of interest and debate among the voters.　　　　　　　69
　14　　　　　　　　　　　15　　　　　　　　　　　　16
　　　Of course, economic issues or rulings always create an　81
　　　　　　　　　17　　　　　　　　　　18
interest on the part of the taxpayers. Increasing taxes or　93
　　　19　　　　　　　　　　20　　　　　　　　　　21
changing tax laws are two questions which invariably create　105
　　　　　　　22　　　　　　　　　　　　23
a great deal of discussion and debate. Social issues might　117
　　　　　　24　　　　　　　　　　25
also be hotly debated. Our national government spends lots　129
　26　　　　　　　　27　　　　　　　　　　28
of time discussing the issues of unemployment, health care,　141
　　　　　　　　29　　　　　　　30
environment, and poverty. Our state governments attempt to　153
　　　31　　　　　　　　　　　32　　　　　　　　　　33
study the facts on the issues of education, transportation,　165
　　　　　　34　　　　　　　　　　35
and crime. On a local level, much time is spent on zoning,　177
　　　　36　　　　　　　　37
police protection, education, and recreation.　　　　　　186
　　　　　38　　　　　　　　39
　　　Government is a major factor in our society today. It　198
　　40　　　　　　　　41　　　　　　　42
is in the interest of our entire country that we maintain a　210
　　　　　43　　　　　　　　　44
citizenry which will question the many issues being debated　222
　　　45　　　　　　　　46
at the various levels of our government structure. So that　234
　47　　　　　　　48　　　　　　　49
our form of government can always be strong, we must strive　246
　　　　50
for voter awareness.　　　　　　　　　　　　　　　　250
    | 1 | 2 | 3 | 4 | 5 | 6 | 7 | 8 | 9 | 10 | 11 | 12

195–199. INTEGRATED OFFICE PROJECT: OFFICE OF STATE SENATOR HELENA CRAIG

Before you begin your assignment in the office of State Senator Helena Craig, sharpen your language arts skills by completing Workguide pages 361–362.

TITLES IN BUSINESS CORRESPONDENCE

A job title may be typed on the same line as the person's name, on a line by itself, or on the same line as the company name, depending upon which arrangement gives the best visual balance.

Courtesy titles (such as *Mr.* or *Ms.*) are used with both men's and women's names in the inside address. In the closing lines, a courtesy title does not precede a man's name; a woman may include a courtesy title in either her handwritten signature or her typed signature.

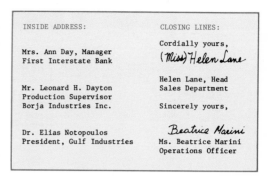

INSIDE ADDRESS:

Mrs. Ann Day, Manager
First Interstate Bank

Mr. Leonard H. Dayton
Production Supervisor
Borja Industries Inc.

Dr. Elias Notopoulos
President, Gulf Industries

CLOSING LINES:

Cordially yours,

(Miss) Helen Lane

Helen Lane, Head
Sales Department

Sincerely yours,

Beatrice Marini

Ms. Beatrice Marini
Operations Officer

LETTER 2
MODIFIED-BLOCK STYLE

Line: 5 inches (50 pica/60 elite)
Tab: center
Date: line 15
Paper: Workguide 65
Proofguide: 15–16

(*Current date*) / Mr. Shelton Graves, Director / Marineland Research Institute / 2608 Shelter Island Drive / San Diego, CA 92106 / Dear Mr. Graves:

Your lease with Western covering 29,775 square feet of tideland area requires periodic rent adjustments. The adjustment in rent for the next period is based upon changes in the Consumer Price Index (CPI) for Los Angeles/Long Beach. The next two-year rental period commences January 1.

The lease requires that the adjustment be directly proportional to the changes in the CPI for the three months immediately preceding the expiration of the lease. When these figures become available in two weeks, your existing land and water rent will be adjusted.

Your next rental invoice will reflect this change. Monthly payments for improvements will remain unchanged.

Sincerely, / Miss Carol Ayers / Property Manager / (*Your initials*)

18
32
34
49
63
77
89
93
108
121
135
147
162
170
186

LETTER 3
MODIFIED-BLOCK STYLE

Paper: Workguide 67
Proofguide: 15–16

WP If you had typed Letter 3 on a word processor, the only part that you would have to retype for Letter 4 would be the inside address and salutation. The body and closing lines could be played out (printed out) automatically from the system's memory, or storage area.

(*Current date*) / Mrs. Allison Lindsey / Administrative Manager / Friedman & Lindsey / 161 South King Street / Honolulu, HI 96813 / Dear Mrs. Lindsey:

As our activities continue to broaden and diversify, it becomes more important for the attorneys here at the national headquarters to be made aware of the many legal matters that are being handled by our various outside legal firms.

We are therefore introducing a program in which quarterly reports are required from the major legal firms with which we do business. The purpose of these reports is to keep our own legal staff abreast of legal matters that affect our company.

I would appreciate it if you would prepare and send to us a report of significant legal matters that your firm has handled on behalf of Western Industries and its subsidiaries during the third quarter of this year.

Yours truly, / Larry Schader / Chief Counsel / (*Your initials*)

17
31
34
49
62
76
82
96
110
124
132
146
160
175
176
193

LETTER 4
MODIFIED-BLOCK STYLE

Paper: Workguide 69
Proofguide: 17–18

(*Current date*) / Mr. Robert Hurston / Attorney-at-Law / Arranda, Fulmer, & Bell / 19 Lumbard Street / San Francisco, CA 94101 / Dear Mr. Hurston:

Use the same body and closing lines as in Letter 3 above.

18
31
33
192

Line: 60 spaces	Tab: 5
Spacing: single	Drills: 3X
Proofguide: 135–136	
Workguide: 441–449	
Tape: 48B and 49B	

INTEGRATED OFFICE PROJECT: GOVERNMENT
LESSONS 194–199

GOALS FOR UNIT 32

1. Type at least 50 wam for 5 minutes with no more than 5 errors.
2. Edit documents while typing, correcting spelling errors and applying rules of grammar, punctuation, and typing style.
3. Calculate invoice extension/sales tax charge.
4. Collect business information, using reference works.
5. Extract information from a table and format new copy.
6. Set priorities.
7. Follow directions.

194-A. WARMUP

S 1 When you visit the island, you may want to do some fishing.
A 2 Vic quickly mixed the frozen strawberries with grape juice.
N 3 On the 23d, we won 60 to 48; on the 27th, we lost 51 to 59.
        | 1 | 2 | 3 | 4 | 5 | 6 | 7 | 8 | 9 | 10 | 11 | 12

194-B. PRETEST: CLOSE REACHES

PRETEST. **Take a 1-minute timing; compute speed and errors.**

4   The bosses were worried about assets.   Therefore, they 12
agreed to switch and adopt a new funding approach.   The old 24
tools for investing were tossed aside and attempts were set 36
in motion to make efforts to attract new sources for funds. 48
        | 1 | 2 | 3 | 4 | 5 | 6 | 7 | 8 | 9 | 10 | 11 | 12

194-C. PRACTICE: ADJACENT KEYS

PRACTICE. **If you made no errors on the Pretest, type each line 3 times. If you made 1 error or more, type each group of four lines (as though it were a paragraph) 3 times; then type the sentence 3 times.**

5 rt artist earth barter short blurts cart yogurt hurt sporty
6 as ascend asset mascot flash erased mash splash bias canvas
7 op option optic copier adopt proper open snoopy loop tiptop
8 we weekly jewel twenty sweet fewest went answer owed weight
9 Twenty copies of the sporty canvas were adopted in a flash.
        | 1 | 2 | 3 | 4 | 5 | 6 | 7 | 8 | 9 | 10 | 11 | 12

194-D. PRACTICE: CONSECUTIVE STROKES

10 sw switch sweet answer swarm sweeps swap swatch swim swings
11 gr graded grant agreed angry degree grew hungry ogre gravel
12 un united undue funded swung brunch unit around noun outrun
13 ol oldest olive colder color woolen sold revolt tool symbol
14 The older unit was sold, and we agreed to switch the funds.
        | 1 | 2 | 3 | 4 | 5 | 6 | 7 | 8 | 9 | 10 | 11 | 12

Line: 50 spaces	Tab: center
Spacing: single	Drills: 2X
Proofguide: 17–18	
Workguide: 3–4	
Tape: 17A or K10B	

LETTER TYPING

Goals: To control the apostrophe and quotation mark keys; to format personal-business letters.

34-A. WARMUP

S 1 The problem is their profit is spent for enamels.
A 2 Evy conquered six black and white jumping zebras.
N 3 Jane flew 6,219 miles from 8:30 a.m. to 7:45 p.m.
    | 1 | 2 | 3 | 4 | 5 | 6 | 7 | 8 | 9 | 10

APOSTROPHE is to the right of the semicolon. Use the Sem finger.

34-B. PRACTICE THE ' KEY

4 ;'; ''' ;'; ''' It's John's job to get Ray's car.
5 I'll use Joe's bat and Rob's ball for Amy's game.
6 The class of '82 can't have its reunion at Bob's.

QUOTATION is the shift of the apostrophe. Use the Sem finger.

34-C. PRACTICE THE " KEY

7 ;'; """ ;"; """ Is "anyone" or "any one" correct?
8 I saw "Face the Nation" and "Meet the Press" too.
9 Use my "Fragile" and "Insured" stamps on the box.

Study rules 1–2 before typing lines 10–13.

34-D. PLACEMENT OF QUOTATION MARKS

1. The closing quotation mark is typed *after* a period or comma, but it is typed *before* a colon or semicolon. *Always*.

2. The closing quotation mark is typed *after* a question mark or exclamation point if the quoted material is a question or an exclamation; otherwise, the quotation mark is typed *before* the question mark or exclamation point.

10 The sign in front read "Hansen's Hideaway Hotel."
11 "Come in," he said. Didn't she look "different"?
12 Mac was acting "strange"; the question was "Why?"
13 Mark these "Rush": invoices, memos, and letters.

34-E. Spacing—double. Record your score.

34-E. SKILL MEASUREMENT: 3-MINUTE TIMED WRITING

14   It is likely that at some point you have had 10
to write to someone in business or the government 20
about some personal matter. Perhaps you wrote to 30
a firm about the jacket you ordered which did not 40
quite fit you or to a government agent about get— 50
ting a tax refund or to a publisher to order some 60
magazines. Now you should not have to write such 70
letters by hand but can type them instead, making 80
the task go faster. 84
    | 1 | 2 | 3 | 4 | 5 | 6 | 7 | 8 | 9 | 10

The last item I want you to type is a short report I'll be giving Mr. Alpart on Monday morning. Here's the rough draft. If there are any questions about this or any of the other jobs I have given you, please see me in my office as soon as possible. I'll be leaving in about 45 minutes.

<u>Potential for New Branch in Arlington</u>

A Report to Jerome Alpart
By Deborah Sisco   *Center each line*

This is a short up date on the feasability of opening a new branch in Arlington.

<u>Available Space</u>

Vagell Realty has checked three different cites. In each case, the location is in an area zoned for business. The sites have an average of 660 square feet of office space. Each of the sites has *ample* parking space around the building.

<u>Population</u>

The current population of Arlington itself is about 150,000. The density of population in the serrounding *towns and* cities is extremely high. In addition, there is an *un*usually high travel frequency because of the large goverment population in this location.

<u>Competition</u>

There are currently 37 travel agencies located in Arlington. In addition, there are another 42 travel agencies with *in* a 15-mile radios of the city. However, six of the travel agencies within Arlington have *just* opened within the past year, and two others have recently changed owner ship.

34/35-F. FORMATTING A PERSONAL-BUSINESS LETTER

Personal-business letters are written to conduct one's own personal business affairs. Since they are typed on plain paper, the writer's return address must be typed as part of the heading. As shown below, the return address is typed on lines 13 and 14, with the date on line 15; all begin at center.

Using plain paper backed by the visual guide, type Letters 5–8 in the personal-business style.

LETTER 5
PERSONAL-BUSINESS LETTER IN MODIFIED-BLOCK STYLE

Shown in elite
Paper: plain
Proofguide: 17–18

↓ 13
845 Washburn Avenue   4
Topeka, KS 66606   9
October 17, 19—   13
↓ 5

Green Tree Gardens   21
500 Woodward Avenue   25
Tallahassee, FL 32304   29

Ladies and Gentlemen: 35

If a letter is addressed to a company rather than to an individual, the appropriate salutation is *Gentlemen* or *Ladies and Gentlemen*.

In several of my gardening magazines, I've recently read about   48
a new variety of floribunda rose that was developed in Japan,   61
which is much less susceptible to aphid infestation than most   74
other varieties. This rose has been referred to as both the   86
"Oriental Petal" and the "Natural Wonder," although I believe   99
they are the same variety.   104

Unfortunately, none of the magazine articles gave a source for   118
this rose. Could you please tell me whether your nursery sup-   131
plies this variety and, if so, the colors that are available   143
and the prices. I would be interested in ordering about a   155
dozen plants of various colors.   162

Would you also send me a copy of your latest mail-order   174
catalog of flower, berry, and fruit-tree selections.   185

                        Sincerely yours,   191
                        ↓ 4

Reference initials are not needed in letters that you type for yourself.

                        Arthur H. Baty   198

LETTER 6
PERSONAL-BUSINESS LETTER IN MODIFIED-BLOCK STYLE

Proofguide: 17–18

Using the same return address, date, body, and closing lines, retype Letter 5, this time addressed to Mrs. Flora Green, President / Green Thumb Nurseries / Clinton, IA 52732 / Dear Mrs. Green:

JOB 9
REPORT 70

Paper: plain

This is a handwritten copy of the bulletin board announcement. Please don't let anyone see it. I want it to be a surprise when I post it. Keep it clipped to the other justified and lettered display material and give it to me Monday morning.

NUMBER (use lettered display)
We are delighted to announce that Patricia Nemetz of our Richmond branch is the *NUMBER ONE SALESPERSON* for Old Dominion for this year. She handled bookings/sales of $401,658. We all relize that Pat had to put in a great deal of time and effort to reach this level of accomplishment. Everyone in our organization salutes her for this very notable achievement.
CONGRADULATIONS, PAT!
ONE (use lettered display)
(Be sure to justify lines!)

JOB 10
LETTER 73
MODIFIED-BLOCK STYLE

Paper: Workguide 439–440

JOB 11
TABLE 56
RULED TABLE

Paper: plain

These are rough drafts of a letter and table that must go out in today's mail. They go to Mr. Paul Bartolini, President, Bartolini, Inc., 171 East Broad Street, Richmond, VA 23219. Just use his first name in the salutation and sign the letter for me. Please remember to add your initials right after the signature.

When you type the table, use the heading Old Dominion Travel Agency, Inc. The subheading is Cost and Mileage from Richmond.

It was good to talk with you again last week about the possability of O. D. handling the travel needs of your professional staff members. As you requested, I have put together some information that should enable you to reach a decision regarding the feasability of engaging us to handle the travel needs of your company.

The enclosed table has information about the cost of travel from Richmond to each of the cities in West Virginia that you serve. In adition, I have shown the number of miles to each of these cities, so that you can estamate the driving time you can save.

When I get back to the office, I will give you a call to set up an apointment for discussing this proposal in greater depth.

Please double-space and put in alphabetic order

Destination	Cost	Mileage
Beckley, WV	$115	263
Parkersburg, WV	147	333
Fairmont, WV	118	269
Clarksburg, WV	118	263
Wheeling, WV	146	326
Bluefield, WV	115	264
Morgantown, WV	118	271
Charleston, WV	130	309
Huntington, WV	151	355

LETTER 7
PERSONAL-BUSINESS LETTER IN MODIFIED-BLOCK STYLE

Paper: plain
Proofguide: 17–18

Using the current date, type this letter from Arthur H. Baty (same return address as Letter 5) to Addison-Hill Furnishings / 1800 Commerce Center / Chicago, IL 60627 / Supply a salutation and the closing lines.

On October 3 I ordered a two-drawer file cabinet (Model A210-6-B) from your company. Yesterday I received my order from UPS and found that you had shipped me Model A210-6-C instead.

In the letter that accompanied the shipment, you stated that the model I had ordered was temporarily out of stock and that rather than delaying my order, you sent me the next larger cabinet at no additional cost to me. While I appreciate your thoughtfulness, the larger model does not fit into the space that I have available.

Would you therefore please arrange to have the file cabinet picked up from my home and ship me Model A210-6-B when it is again in stock.

LETTER 8
PERSONAL-BUSINESS LETTER IN MODIFIED-BLOCK STYLE

Paper: plain
Proofguide: 17–18

Use Arthur H. Baty's return address and the current date.

Type the word *Enclosure* at the left margin a double space below the writer's identification to indicate that an item is enclosed with the letter.

NOTE: In a business letter, the enclosure notation is typed a single space below the reference initials.

Mr. Allen Benson, President	14
Benson & Sons, Inc.	18
P. O. Box 488	21
Waterbury, CT 06710	25
Dear Mr. ~~Allen:~~ *Benson*	30

Ms. Robin Klehr, an interior decora*or*ter in Wilmington, has sug- 44
gested that I write to you concerning the availability of a *some* 56
certain pattern of wallpaper that your firm manufactured ~~many~~ 68
years ago. Because I do not know the name of the pattern, I 80
have enclosed a sample of the ~~style.~~ *design* 88

Our living room is papered on three walls with this patt*er*n. 101
Since the paper is so lovely and is still in excellent con- 113
dition, we would like to paper the third *fourth* wall with the same 125
pattern. 127

Would you please let me know if this ~~pattern~~ *paper* is still avail- 140
able and, if so, what the price is for enough rolls to ~~paper~~ 152
a wall that is 8 feet ~~tall~~ *high* by 16 feet wide. *cover* 161

                    Yours truly, 166

                    Arthur H. Baty 173

Enclosure 175

NOTE: Leave 3 spaces between the two columns.

15.1 JUSTIFYING LINES

When a special announcement or display must be prepared, a typist may want to justify the copy; here's information on how to do it:

```
   Justifying typing (making all        Justifying typing (making all
the lines of typing end evenly)      the lines of typing end evenly)
is done as follows:                  is done as follows:
   1. Type a draft, ending all##        1. Type  a  draft,  ending all
lines as close as possible to##      lines as  close  as  possible  to
the point where you wish them##      the  point where  you wish them
to end.  Except for lines which      to end.  Except for lines which
end paragraphs, fill in short##      end paragraphs,  fill  in  short
lines with # signs to show how#      lines with # signs to  show how
many extra spaces will be used.      many extra spaces will be used.
   2. Type the good copy, making        2. Type the good copy, making
sure to insert extra spaces to#      sure to insert extra  spaces to
spread the lines.  Be sure the#      spread the lines.   Be sure the
extra spaces are scattered so##      extra  spaces  are scattered  so
that they do not come together.      that they do not come together.
```

NOTE: You would not use this method when typing regular correspondence, but it is an excellent technique for special typewriting display.

15.2 LETTERED DISPLAY

The most useful form of artistic lettering in display typing is the style shown below, constructed of small m's, arranged with half spacing. If the machine has half spacing, it will be easy to make the letters. Without half spacing, you will find it easiest to do all the m's you need in regular single spacing; then advance the paper a half line and fill in what is missing—the other m's. The basic display is:

```
mmmm        mmmm        mmmm        mmmm        mmmm        mmmm
                                    m    m      m    m           m
mmmm        mmmm        m           mmmm        m    m           m
                                    m    m      m    m           m
m    m      mmmm        mmmm        m    m      mmmm        mmmm

mmmmmmmmmmmmmmmmmmmmmmmmmmmmmmmmmmmmmmmmmmmmmmmmmmmmmmmmmmmmmmmm

mmm    mmmm   mmm    mmmm   mmm    mmm   mmm    m  m   mmm     m    m  m
m  m   m  m   m      m      m  m   m     m      m  m   m  m    m    m m m
mmm    m  m   m      m      mmm    m     mm     mmmm   m  m    m    mmm
m  m   m  m   m  m   m  m   m      m     m  m   m  m   m  m    m m  m m m
m  m   mmmm   mmm    mmmm   mmm    mmmm  mmm    m  m   mmm     mmmm m    m

m        m      m   m    m   mmmm   mmmm   mmmmm   mmmm   mmmm   m  m   m   m
m        m      mm mm    mm  m   m  m   m  m       m   m  m      m  m   m   m
m        m      m m m    m m m    mm    mmm     m  m   m  mmmm   m  m   m m m
m        m      m   m    m   mm    m  m    mm   m  m   m     m   m  m   mmm
mmmm     m      m   m    m   mmmm   mm    mmmm  mmmm   m     mmmm   mmmm m   m
                                          m

m  m   m    m   m  m   mmmmm   mmmmmmm   mmmmmmm   mmmmmm   mmmmmm
m  m   m  m m   m  m       m    mm   mm   mm  mm    m    m   m mm m
m  m   m  m m    mm       m     mmmmmm    mmmmmmm   m    m       mm
m  m   m  m m    m       m      mmmm      mmmmmmm   m    m       mm
mmmmm  m    m   m  m   mmmmm   ,mm  mm    mm  mm   mmmmmmm  mmmm   mmmm
```

LESSONS 36/37

LETTER REVIEW

Goals: To review symbol keys; to format a letter in various styles.

36-A. WARMUP

1 Make the men sign for the eighty bushels of corn.
2 Did they win Jacqueline's five or six big prizes?
3 At 12:30 only 459 men and 687 women were waiting.
| 1 | 2 | 3 | 4 | 5 | 6 | 7 | 8 | 9 | 10

36-B. Take a 1-minute timing on the first paragraph to establish your base speed. Then take successive 1-minute timings on the other paragraphs. You must equal or exceed your base speed before starting the next paragraph.

36-B. SUSTAINED PRACTICE: NUMBERS AND SYMBOLS

4   Jan was upset. It looked as if the business 10
deal was going to fall through despite all of her 20
hard work. If only there were some way she could 30
convince Mr. Armstrong of the worth of her offer. 40

5   She had talked to as many as 20 people about 10
the project she proposed, and at least 17 of them 20
thought Jan's plan just might work. Why couldn't 30
she get Mr. Armstrong to give her ideas a chance? 40

6   Jan planned her attack. If she could get 25 10
or 30 of Mr. Armstrong's own people to agree with 20
her, he couldn't say "no" to the plans. However, 30
he was not known as "Mr. Strong Arm" for nothing. 40

7   Jan hired Todd & Sons (a research firm), and 10
of the 68 people they interviewed, 49 agreed with 20
her. When he was presented with this "evidence," 30
Mr. Armstrong didn't have any reason to disagree. 40
| 1 | 2 | 3 | 4 | 5 | 6 | 7 | 8 | 9 | 10

36-C. Spacing—double. Record your score.

36-C. SKILL MEASUREMENT: 3-MINUTE TIMED WRITING

8   New developments in the office have made the 10
ability to type as much of a required skill for a 20
manager as it has been in the past for a clerical 30
worker. Word processors are now an accepted fix- 40
ture in the office, and many managers in the mod- 50
ern firm have small computers on their desks just 60
for their own use in solving problems. Each per- 70
son must realize that he or she will need to know 80
how to type by touch. 84
| 1 | 2 | 3 | 4 | 5 | 6 | 7 | 8 | 9 | 10

JOBS 3–5
TABLES 53–55
RULED TABLES

Paper: plain

Mr. Alpart will also need the bookings/sales data for the three branches. You'll need to make an individual table for each branch. Make the location of the branch part of the heading. When you extract the names of the salespeople according to branch, please list them based on the highest to lowest bookings for this year. For example, in the Lynchburg table Joseph Liebman will be first and Lois Fico will be last. You'll need to give totals for this year and last year and the total change for each branch. You can calculate the total percent change by dividing the difference between the two columns by the total bookings for last year.

WP On a word processor, it is possible to extract information for each branch by sorting by branch names; the totals can then be calculated using the math capabilities.

JOB 6
MEMORANDUM 22

Paper: Workguide 437

Here's a draft of the memo that goes with the three tables. I'd like you to give this to Mr. Alpart as early as possible on Friday—4 o'clock at the latest. Make the subject Bookings by Branch.

As I indicated in my memo yesterday, I want you to have the information on total bookings / sales for each of the three branches.

Enclosed you will find three tables that give the information you wanted for each of our three branches. You will be able to use this information when you meet with each of the branch managers. In addetion, I am sure you will want to use this data as you prepare your report for the stockholders' meeting.

When I get back from my trip, I will schedule an apointment to meet with you so that we can discuss the implications of the enclosed data.

JOB 7
REPORT 68
JUSTIFIED DISPLAY

Paper: plain, full sheet
Spacing: double
Line: 65 spaces

JOB 8
REPORT 69
LETTERED DISPLAY

Paper: plain, full sheet
Spacing: optional
Style: as shown

I'm planning a series of announcements for our bulletin board and the monthly newsletter. Please practice the justified and lettered displays as described in this copy of the procedures manual. Just follow the instructions given there. I have a bulletin board announcement to assign to you, but before you type the announcement I'd like to be certain that you understand how to justify margins and type lettered displays.

Read the material in the procedures manual (*page 287*) on justified lines and lettered displays. Then copy the displays exactly as shown in the procedures manual. When you copy the justified display, remember to include the # signs in Column 1.

36/37-D.   SUMMARY OF LETTER BASICS

ASSIGNMENT	STYLE	SPECIAL INSTRUCTIONS	WORDS
Letter 9 Plain paper	Formal Proofguide: 19–20	Arrange as shown below, with inside address typed below the signature.	181
Letter 10 Plain paper	Personal-Business Proofguide: 19–20	Type inside address above the salutation, as shown on page 53.	178
Letter 11 Workguide: 71	Modified-Block Proofguide: 19–20	Omit return address; type inside address above the salutation; add your reference initials.	170
Letter 12 Workguide: 73	Modified-Block Proofguide: 19–20	Same as Letter 11, except add this final sentence to paragraph 3: "We hope the enclosed watercolor of the downtown area of Little Rock will remind you of the beauty of our city." Add your reference initials and an enclosure notation.	194

LETTER 9
FORMAL STYLE

Formal style, with the inside address typed at the bottom, is often used for letters to high-ranking officials.

↓ 13

9600 West 12 Street   4
Little Rock, AR 72201   9
November 27, 19--   14
↓ 5

Dear Mrs. Feldman: 22

On behalf of the planning committee that invited you and all   35
my colleagues who enjoyed your speech, I wish to thank you   47
for a most entertaining and educational presentation at our   59
"Listen-to-the-Leaders" conference.   66

The amount of preparation you put into your presentation was   80
obvious; also obvious was the warm and enthusiastic reception   92
accorded you at the conclusion of your remarks.   102

We appreciate your taking the time from your important work   115
to talk to our group and want you to know that we all bene-   127
fited from your presentation.   133

Yours very truly,   138
↓ 4
Charles Prevost

Charles Prevost, Chairman   148
Conference Planning Committee   155
↓ 5

The Honorable Naomi Feldman   164
United States Representative   170
2310 Rayburn House Office Building   177
Washington, DC 20515   181

Personal-business letter in modified-block style shown in formal arrangement.

JOB 2
TABLE 52
RULED TABLE

Paper: plain

The table had been partially completed, and I just filled in the last two columns. The percentages are correct, but please check my addition of the totals. I'd like the names left in sets of four. Be sure it all fits on one sheet of paper. Make extra copies for use as source documents when you type the tables for the individual branches.

Here's the table, Comparative Bookings/Sales of Current Year and Last Year, that goes with the memo.

OLD DOMINION TRAVEL AGENCY, INC.

COMPARATIVE BOOKINGS/SALES OF CURRENT YEAR AND LAST YEAR

Salesperson	Branch	Bookings Last Year	Bookings This Year	Percent Change
Alarco, Joseph	Richmond	$ 284,542	$ 288,650	1.4
Borrelli, Frank	Richmond	215,640	301,640	39.9
Branca, Carol	Roanoke	188,675	288,370	21.0
Buff, Annmarie	Lynchburg	264,300	258,632	-2.1
Cranley, James	Roanoke	315,487	327,065	3.7
Dodds, Kathryn	Richmond	187,065	179,986	-3.8
Elias, Eric	Roanoke	264,294	278,142	5.2
Fico, Lois	Lynchburg	156,822	201,344	28.4
Hakola, June	Lynchburg	272,430	296,516	8.8
Hawkins, Arthur	Richmond	198,467	196,816	-0.8
Iello, Alex	Lynchburg	236,450	301,820	27.6
Jamieson, John	Roanoke	327,840	332,640	1.5
Klein, Gloria	Richmond	197,432	196,566	-0.4
Kozlowski, Sue	Lynchburg	257,830	249,840	-3.1
Liebman, Joseph	Lynchburg	356,321	371,324	4.2
Maio, Olga	Roanoke	254,622	261,342	2.6
Nemetz, Patricia	Richmond	387,563	401,658	3.6
Nicola, Raymond	Roanoke	192,568	165,820	-13.9
Perez, Tania	Lynchburg	257,347	296,341	15.2
Pucci, Mario	Roanoke	315,689	332,567	5.3
Sherlock, Lucy	Richmond	311,675	334,798	7.4
Swier, Susan	Lynchburg	268,898	293,654	9.2
Taylor, Richard	Richmond	208,351	234,609	12.6
Zabady, Felipe	Roanoke	237,401	276,582	16.5
TOTAL	. . . . .	$6,157,709	$6,606,722	7.3

<table>
<tr><td>Line: 50 spaces   Tab: 5, center
Spacing: single   Drills: 2X
Proofguide: 19–21
Workguide: 3–4, 75
Tape: 19A or K11B</td></tr>
</table>

LESSONS 38/39
TABLES

Goals: To control the #, %, and underscore keys; to format simple tables.

38-A. WARMUP

S 1 That city girl had a problem with the giant fish.
A 2 Jack Delaney's very next question was about zoos.
N 3 Phone for 14 tickets on May 29 or 30 at 555-7168.
| 1 | 2 | 3 | 4 | 5 | 6 | 7 | 8 | 9 | 10

NUMBER (sign for *number* before a figure and *pounds* after it) is the shift of 3. Use the D finger.

38-B. PRACTICE THE # KEY

4 ded de3d d3d d3#d d#d d#d #3 #33 #38 d#d d3d #32.
5 I need 33# of #203, 60# of #745, and 85# of #396.
6 Invoice #409 calls for 5# of #1 ink and 8# of #2.

PERCENT is the shift of 5. Use the F finger.

38-C. PRACTICE THE % KEY

7 f5f f5%5 f5f f5%f f%f f%f 5% 15% 52.5% 83.5% 34%.
8 The discount went from 5% to 14% and then to 19%.
9 The markup on Item #18 was changed from 4% to 8%.

UNDERSCORE is the shift of the hyphen. Use the Sem finger.

NOTE: Style points for underscoring:
  Line 11. For <u>not</u>, type the word, backspace, and underscore it; for <u>The Gregg Reference Manual</u>, type the entire title before underscoring it.
  Line 12. To stress individual words, underscore them separately. Do not underscore the punctuation or the spaces between the words.

38-E. Spacing—double. Record your score.

38-D. PRACTICE THE _ KEY

10 ;-; ;_; ;-; ;_; <u>real</u> or <u>really</u>; <u>amount</u> or <u>number</u>;
11 Randy did <u>not</u> consult <u>The Gregg Reference Manual</u>.
12 Do not confuse the words <u>wholly</u>, <u>holy</u>, and <u>holey</u>.

38-E. SKILL MEASUREMENT: 3-MINUTE TIMED WRITING

13   One of the most challenging types of work in 10
the office is that of typing data in column form. 20
This kind of typing requires more thought than do 30
other jobs. When you stop to analyze how a table 40
is executed on the typewriter, you will find that 50
setting it up is just a matter of centering. You 60
simply choose the longest line in each column and 70
then backspace-center those lines, making sure to 80
add six spaces between every column. 87
| 1 | 2 | 3 | 4 | 5 | 6 | 7 | 8 | 9 | 10

WP Word processors have an automatic underscore feature that underscores words, phrases, or entire lines automatically as you type them.

Situation: Today is Wednesday, November 5, 19—. You are working as secretary to Ms. Deborah Sisco, Vice President of Old Dominion Travel, Inc., with headquarters in Richmond, Virginia, and branches in Lynchburg and Roanoke. Ms. Sisco has been asked by the president, Jerome Alpart, to provide him with different types of information he'll need to study before the forthcoming annual stockholders' meeting. In addition, Ms. Sisco has some projects of her own that must be completed.

Ms. Sisco must be out of town on business for the next few days and will not be back in the office until Monday morning. She plans to leave soon after she has assigned the work that must be completed before her return. You will have to read through all the work right away so that you can ask her any questions before she leaves.

Ms. Sisco prefers the modified-block style letter with standard punctuation and this closing:

Sincerely yours,

Deborah Sisco
Vice President

After you have read through all the material and asked questions, you will have to set priorities for the work that is to be completed. Setting priorities is essential in an office situation, where you will be assigned jobs with varying degrees of importance. The work should be done in the order of its importance. To determine the priorities, review the work to be done and then determine the order in which you will do it. The following method of determining priorities is simple but extremely efficient:

1. Rush items
2. Rough drafts
3. Routine correspondence and reports

FORM 72   Workguide: 433
JOB PRIORITY LIST

Before you begin your work, review the items in the project. Then, on Workguide page 433, assign a 1, 2, or 3 priority to each item.

JOB 1   Paper: Workguide 435
MEMORANDUM 21

Mr. Alpart needs some data on bookings/sales by 4 o'clock Thursday. Be sure this memo and the table that goes with it are on his desk by then. I'll give you the table in a few minutes. The subject of the memo is Total Bookings/Sales for Old Dominion Travel.

By the way, I'm rather careless about spelling, and so you'll have to check my writing for spelling errors.

As you requested, I am sending you the information about the total bookings/sales of Old Dominion Travel. Enclosed you will find a table that shows the sales for each salesperson in the three branchs. The information given shows sales for this year compared with sales for last year. In adition, the percent change has been shown for each person.

The information on total bookings of $6,606,722 for this year compared with total bookings of $6,157,709 for last year should please our stockholders. In view of the fact that the 7.3 percent increase exceeds our targeted projection, our salespeople are to be comended.

I know that you are eager to have the information on sales for each of the individual branches. We will have that information on your desk by 4 p.m. Friday afternoon at the latest.

38-F. BASIC PARTS OF A TABLE

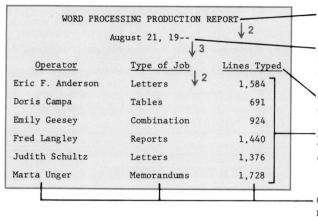

TITLE. Identifies the contents of the table. Center and type in all-capital letters.

SUBTITLE. Sometimes used to give further information about the table. Center a double space below the title, with the first and all principal words capitalized.

COLUMN HEADINGS. Tell what is in each column. Center over the column and underscore; leave 2 blank lines before and 1 blank line after.

BODY. Consists of the columns in the table. Center horizontally, usually with 6 blank spaces between columns; may be either single-spaced or double-spaced.

COLUMN. Is a listing of information. Word columns align at the left, but number columns align at the right.

38-G. FORMATTING A TABLE

Before you begin, *clear all tabs* and move the margins to the extreme left or right.

1. **SELECT THE KEY LINE.** The key line consists of the longest item in each column, plus 6 blank spaces for each open area between columns.

2. **SET LEFT MARGIN STOP.** From the center of the paper, backspace once for every 2 characters or spaces in the key line and set the left margin at the point to which you have backspaced. Example:

se/nt/en/ce/12/34/56/th/ou/gh/12/34/56/ta/bl/es

NOTE: Do not backspace for an extra stroke.

3. **SET TAB STOPS.** Space across the paper once for *each* letter and *each* space in the longest item of the first column plus the 6 blank spaces, and set a tab stop. No matter how many columns there are in the table, use the left margin stop for the first column and a tab stop for each additional column.

4. **COMPUTE THE TOP MARGIN.** To center the table vertically, subtract the number of lines (including blank lines) in the table from either 66 (a full sheet of paper) or 33 (a half sheet) and divide by 2. If a fraction is left, drop it.

EXAMPLE: 33 − 12 = 21; 21 ÷ 2 = 10½; begin on line 10.

5. **TYPE THE TABLE.** Backspace-center the title and type it in all caps. Drop down 3 lines and type the body.

NOTE: Use the tabulator to move from column to column as you type each line.

PRACTICE. Type this short table, centering it double-spaced on a half sheet of paper.

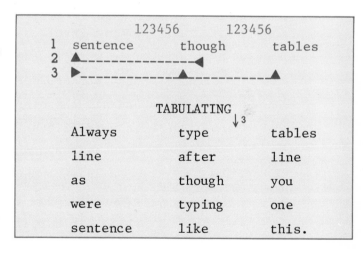

Before typing Tables 1–3, complete Workguide page 75.

38/39-H. TABLES

Type Tables 1–3 on full sheets of paper, double-spacing the body of each table. (Leave the machine on single spacing until you are ready to type the body; *then* adjust for double spacing.)

Remember to clear all tab stops and to move the margins to the extreme left and right before formatting each table.

188-E. PRACTICE: OTHER COMBINATIONS

15 fr freeze fruit afraid fresh defray fret belfry frog frisky
16 th thrown other rather theft apathy this length moth thrust
17 st strive boost estate style dusted stay thrust host strain
18 ng danger angle finger range fringe long stingy ring belong
19 The fruit trees did not seem to belong in this arid estate.
    | 1 | 2 | 3 | 4 | 5 | 6 | 7 | 8 | 9 | 10 | 11 | 12

POSTTEST. Repeat the Pretest and compare performance.

188-F. POSTTEST: COMMON LETTER COMBINATIONS

188-G. Spacing—double. Take two 5-minute timings. Between them, practice any words with which you had difficulty. Record your score.

188-G. SKILL MEASUREMENT: 5-MINUTE TIMED WRITING

20   Many facts and figures are collected in the first year   12
of each new decade in our country. These facts and figures   24
are analyzed by many experts in order that developments and   36
trends may be identified. The data most recently collected   48
has provided us a lot of insight into the new world of work   60
that is forming.   63
        The early history of our nation displayed a great deal 75
of emphasis on farm activities as the major source of work.   87
We were recognized as an agrarian society, with most of our   99
people involved in farm work. Later we began to shift from   111
farm work to the mass production of goods. This meant that   123
many workers were involved in producing coal, steel, autos,   135
and all the other goods that were needed to make us a giant   147
industrial country.   151
        At the present time, we see a major shift taking place 163
once again. The work force has been changing from one that   175
produces goods to one that provides various services. This   187
shift can quickly be observed by noting the number of firms   199
that have been established to take care of the needs of our   211
society. The new high technology that is emerging has been   223
a major force in changing the type of work that we do. The   235
labor market will continue to change in the future.   245
    | 1 | 2 | 3 | 4 | 5 | 6 | 7 | 8 | 9 | 10 | 11 | 12

189–193. INTEGRATED OFFICE PROJECT: OLD DOMINION TRAVEL AGENCY

Before you begin your assignment at Old Dominion Travel Agency, sharpen your language arts skills by completing Workguide pages 359–360.

TABLE 1
3-COLUMN TABLE

Paper: full sheet
Spacing: double
Proofguide: 21

Number columns with decimals align on the decimal point.

REGIONAL SALES AWARDS FOR JUNE ↓2
With Percentage of Increase From May ↓3

Northeastern	Eugene Bonner	16.5
Southern	Cecelia Olivas	21.3
Central	Herbert Sprague	14.8
Mountain Plains	A. R. Edelberg	17.6
Western	Shirley Linn	13.9
Affiliates	Elvira Natalie	19.6

Key Line: Mountain Plains   Herbert Sprague   16.5
          123456   123456

TABLE 2
3-COLUMN TABLE

Paper: full sheet
Spacing: double
Proofguide: 21

Book titles may be typed in all-capital letters or underscored.

SUGGESTED READING LIST

Self-Portrait	Brenda Porter	Roman Press
Twice Blessed	Jane Polinsky	Falcon Books
The Tunnel	Virgil Cheyne	Arroyo, Inc.
No Way But Up	W. B. Townes	Klein Press
Grey Prince	Margaret Kates	Chan-Chung, Inc.
The Animal Book	George Katsaros	Ricci & Son
Spectators	Donald Komoda	Best Books
Personal Investing	C. C. Pearce	Reliable House
Biana's Secret	Viki Tenge	Victory Press
Job Survival Skills	Clara Mayfield	Soulier, Inc.

TABLE 3
2-COLUMN TABLE

Paper: full sheet
Spacing: double
Proofguide: 21

Quality - Circle Steering Committee

Cecil J. Flowers	Die Shop
Donald Levin	Finishing Shop
William G. Nagle	East Annex
Claudia Talbott	Plant C
E. M. Weber	Main Office
Lena Womack	Assembly Shop

<table>
<tr><td>Line: 60 spaces   Tab: 5
Spacing: single   Drills: 3X
Proofguide: 135–136
Workguide: 433–440
Tape: 46B and 47B</td><td>

INTEGRATED OFFICE PROJECT: TRAVEL
LESSONS 188–193

</td></tr>
</table>

GOALS FOR UNIT 31

1. Type at least 49 wam for 5 minutes with no more than 5 errors.
2. Correct commonly misspelled words.
3. Extract information from a table and format new copy.
4. Calculate percentages.
5. Justify lines and use letter display to design an attractive message.
6. Set priorities.
7. Follow directions.

188-A. WARMUP

S 1 Dick paid for half of the ham, but Ken paid for the turkey.
A 2 Liza packed six new bags, quit her job, and moved far away.
N 3 We had 20,875 fans here last night; we have 19,643 tonight.
     | 1 | 2 | 3 | 4 | 5 | 6 | 7 | 8 | 9 | 10 | 11 | 12

188-B. PRETEST: COMMON LETTER COMBINATIONS

PRETEST. Take a 1-minute timing; compute speed and errors.

4   The long delay in striving to get an income index from 12
the leaders would most likely deter a possible repeal plan. 24
They would have to refer this recent revision to that other 36
group before they could argue the need for an equal repeal. 48
     | 1 | 2 | 3 | 4 | 5 | 6 | 7 | 8 | 9 | 10 | 11 | 12

188-C. PRACTICE: WORD BEGINNINGS

PRACTICE. If you made no errors on the Pretest, type each line 3 times. If you made 1 error or more, type each group of four lines (as though it were a paragraph) 3 times; then type the sentence 3 times.

5 in income index insist input invest inch induct into indent
6 re redeem refer reject repay revise rely review ream resign
7 be belong below beyond bench before best became bead behold
8 de decent debug depart deter design dear devote dent delays
9 Before you invest your income, devote some time for review.
   | 1 | 2 | 3 | 4 | 5 | 6 | 7 | 8 | 9 | 10 | 11 | 12

188-D. PRACTICE: WORD ENDINGS

10 ly likely reply lately imply surely only hourly duly boldly
11 ed argued acted obeyed saved heeded sued crated need scored
12 nt invent agent amount spent recent lent cement sent urgent
13 al appeal vital repeal equal social meal denial deal mental
14 Surely, only the need for the urgent appeal saved the plan.
   | 1 | 2 | 3 | 4 | 5 | 6 | 7 | 8 | 9 | 10 | 11 | 12

Line: 50 spaces   Tab: 5, center
Spacing: single   Drills: 2X
Proofguide: 21–22
Workguide: 3–4, 76
Tape: 20A or K11B

LESSONS 40/41
TABLES

Goals: To control the $, ¢, and @ keys; to format tables with column headings.

40-A. WARMUP

S 1 The girl worked with vigor to make the right cut.
A 2 Six lazy bluejays squawked at my four grapevines.
N 3 Read pages 497–568 before your 12:30 drama class.
  | 1 | 2 | 3 | 4 | 5 | 6 | 7 | 8 | 9 | 10

DOLLAR is the shift of 4. Use the F finger.

40-B. PRACTICE THE $ KEY

4 frf fr4f f4f f4$f f$f f$f $4 $43 $44 f$f f4f $45.
5 The $8 books were on sale for $6, a saving of $2.
6 The items cost $44, $58.32, $16, $100, and $7.99.

CENT is the shift of 6. Use the J finger.

40-C. PRACTICE THE ¢ KEY

7 j6j j6¢j j6j j¢j j¢j He charged 6¢, 16¢, and 26¢.
8 The new pencils cost 10¢, 29¢, 38¢, 47¢, and 56¢.
9 The 8¢ items were on sale for 6¢, a saving of 2¢.

AT is the shift of 2. Use the S finger.

40-D. PRACTICE THE @ KEY

10 s2s s2@s s2s s@s s@s I sold 8 @ 16¢ and 10 @ 19¢.
11 Try to get 15 @ 39¢, 48 @ 25¢, and 67 @ 20¢ each.
12 Order 12 items @ $86 and another 165 items @ $26.

40-E. Paragraph 13 contains all the symbols you have learned thus far. Practice it until you can type the three lines with no more than 1 error and without looking at your keys.

40-E. SYMBOL PRACTICE

13 Didn't Cox & Sons send us Invoice #97 for $30.65?
   Do not forget to mark this order "Rush," although
   it costs 42¢ (or 19%) more to mail @ 18¢ a pound.
  | 1 | 2 | 3 | 4 | 5 | 6 | 7 | 8 | 9 | 10

40-F. Spacing—double. Record your score.

40-F. SKILL MEASUREMENT: 3-MINUTE TIMED WRITING

14   An important point to remember when you type 10
numbers or symbols is to type them accurately and 20
to type without looking at the keyboard. You can 30
surely realize how much extra time will be needed 40
if you have to glance down at the keys each time. 50
Do not worry for now about typing numbers or sym— 60
bols with speed; that will come later. Just con- 70
centrate on accuracy and technique. By doing so, 80
your eventual skill will be assured. 87
  | 1 | 2 | 3 | 4 | 5 | 6 | 7 | 8 | 9 | 10

As you requested at the (Sept.) staff meeting, I have surveyed the employees of Glover Industries to determine their banking habits and preferences. The purpose of the memorandum is to report to you the results of this survey.

PROCEDURES

The questionnaire was ~~sent~~ *mailed* to a 10 percent random sample of all Glover employees on October 6. Two weeks later, on October 20, a follow-up postcard was mailed. Out of the 372 employees surveyed, 228 returned usable questionnaires, for a response rate of 61 percent, which is considered a high rate, *of return*.

FINDINGS

As shown in exhibit A, only one-fourth of the employees now have an account with Citizens. Thus, of the 3,720 total employees at Glover, 2,77~~3~~4 do not bank with us, and they represent a lucrative market for us to tap.

Nearly 90 percent of the employees now use a commercial bank, while about a third use the employee credit union. Surprisingly, 18 of the respondents (8 percent) do not use any type of banking institution at all. These data are shown in the bar chart in Exhibit B.

About 45% of the employees choose a bank that was near their office, and another 14 percent chose a bank that was on their way to and from work. Thus, the fact that Citizens is located at One Jefferson Square, where Glover Industries is moving, should be a powerful incentive for these people to switch to our bank.

However, only 27 percent of the employees have ~~switched~~ *changed* banks within the past three years, so there might be some resistance to ~~switching~~ *changing* banks when they move to Jefferson Square. Of those who have ~~switched~~ *changed* banks, the two major reasons were relocation of residence (53 percent) and dissatisfaction with bank service (29 percent). Typical comments from those who have ~~switched~~ *changed* banks are shown in Exhibit C.

Finally, ~~and most importantly,~~ I think, the three most important banking services as perceived by the employees are (in order) free checking, a bank credit card, and a check guarantee card. Over three-fourths of the employees listed these three services as very important. The rankings of the other services are shown in Exhibit D.

SUMMARY AND CONCLUSIONS

Nearly 75 percent of the Glover employees are not now customers at Citizens, although nearly all of them do use a commercial bank. They chose a bank that is ~~convenient to~~ *near* their office and very few of them have ~~switched~~ *changed* banks recently. The three services they value most are free checking, bank credit cards, and check guarantee cards.

In conclusion, many Glover employees are not now our customers; they want a bank that is convenient, and they value most the three services that Citizens ~~presently~~ *now* offers. All three of these major findings would indicate that a well-developed campaign to attract Glover employees to our bank when they move to Jefferson Square would be a profitable undertaking.

If you have any questions about this survey or if you would like further information, I ~~will~~ *would* be happy to discuss this research project with you.

40-G. FORMATTING TABLES WITH COLUMN HEADS

A table with column heads is formatted almost like simpler tables (as described on page 58):

1. Select the key line.
2. Backspace-center to set left margin.
3. Space across to set column tab stops.
4. Compute top margin and insert paper. But you must pause *between steps 3 and 4* to note how many spaces to indent each column head from the start of its column (or, if the column head is wider than its column, to note how many spaces to indent the column from the start of the head).

Pencil in each indention reminder on the copy so that you will not forget to make each indention. As you type the table and reach the point where each reminder applies, space in accordingly. Study this table:

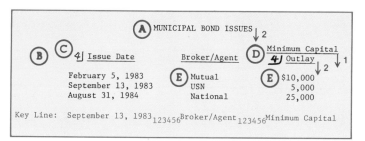

The above table illustrates the following technical points:

A. TITLE.   Centered, typed in all-capital letters.

B. COLUMN HEADS.   Centered, underscored, capitalized, preceded by 2 blank lines, followed by 1 blank line.

C. ANNOTATIONS.   Marked on problem copy to remind typist to indent.

D. TWO-LINE COLUMN HEAD.   Aligned with other headings *at bottom*, underscored completely (both lines), preceded by 1 blank line *if* it "clears" the title (by 2 blank lines if it is under the title). Center the shorter line of the column head on the longer line; center the longer line over the column.

E. TAB CHANGE.   At the start of a narrow column, clear the heading tab stop and set a stop at a point appropriate for centering the column under the heading. NOTE: Count the dollar sign in the column width if it makes centering easier. In this example it is not counted. A dollar sign appears only at the top and in a totals line (if there is one) at the bottom of the column.

NOTE: If the body is to be double-spaced, stay with single spacing through all the headings before shifting to double spacing.

Short Centered Column Heads

1. Subtract the number of spaces in the column head from the number of spaces in the longest item of the column.
2. Divide the answer by 2 (drop any fraction) and indent the column head that number of spaces. In the example, 18 − 10 = 8 and 8 ÷ 2 = 4. Indent the column head 4 spaces.

Long Centered Column Heads

1. Subtract the number of spaces in the longest item in the column from the number of spaces in the column head.
2. Divide the answer by 2 (drop any fraction) and indent the column that number of spaces. In the example, 12 − 8 = 4 and 4 ÷ 2 = 2. Indent the column 2 spaces.

40/41-H. TABLES WITH COLUMN HEADINGS

Complete Workguide page 76. Then type Tables 4–7 on half sheets of paper (33 lines available). For those tables that are double-spaced, leave your machine on single spacing until after typing the column headings; then switch to double spacing to type the body.

TABLE 4
3-COLUMN TABLE WITH
SHORT COLUMN HEADINGS

Paper: half sheet
Spacing: double
Proofguide: 21

DEADLINES FOR ANNUAL REPORT

Part	Draft	Final
Letter From the Chairman	August 11	September 1
Financial Statements	August 15	September 4
Highlights of the Year	August 20	September 9
Major New Products	September 9	October 8

Key Line: Letter From the Chairman₁₂₃₄₅₆September 9₁₂₃₄₅₆September 1

JOB 8
TABLE 51
RULED TABLE

Paper: plain

WP On a word processor, vertical centering of a table is done after it is typed. To center a table vertically, check the format scale for the last vertical line typed and insert at the top of the table half the number of lines remaining.

Would you please type this ruled table showing the results of part four of the questionnaire. You'll need the copy of the survey you filled in by hand or a copy of Exhibit A. I've already rearranged the responses in descending order according to the number of respondents who marked the item "Very Important." Compute the percentages for each item by dividing the numbers on your copy of the questionnaire by 228. Round off the percentages to the nearest whole number and make sure the horizontal columns add up to 100. You may want to use a calculator to do this.

Center the table vertically and horizontally on a sheet of plain paper.

Exhibit D (all caps)

Importance of Banking Services

Service	Very Important	Moderately Important	Unimportant
Free checking	96%	4%	0%
Bank credit card	82%	14%	4%
Check guarantee card	76%	14%	10%
Total teller machines			
Drive-in service			
Convenient installment loans			
Personal banker			
Overdrawing privileges			
Trust department			
Telephone transfer			

Please finish computing the percentages.

JOB 9
MEMORANDUM 20
2-PAGE MEMORANDUM REPORT

Paper: plain

Now then let's finish up this research project by sending the results to the president, Mrs. Marianne Jennings. The results are presented in the memorandum report that I'm giving you in rough-draft form. The subject of this memorandum is Glover Industries Survey. Please date the memorandum November 29 and use single spacing and regular side headings. After you have typed and proofread the memorandum, please attach Exhibits A to D behind the memorandum.

TABLE 5
3-COLUMN TABLE WITH SHORT COLUMN HEADINGS

Paper: half sheet
Spacing: double
Proofguide: 21

Word columns align at the left.

WP Some word processors have a column-layout feature that automatically aligns column headings with word and number columns.

SCHEDULE OF BRANCH-MANAGER MEETINGS
All Meetings to Start at 10 a.m.

Date	Location	Hotel
February 14	Monterey	Doubletree Inn
March 14	Anaheim	Disneyland Hotel
April 11	San Diego	Plaza International
May 16	San Francisco	Jack Tar Hotel
September 12	Long Beach	Queen Mary Hyatt
October 10	Palm Springs	Riviera Hotel
November 14	Lake Tahoe	Harrah's
December 12	Los Angeles	Century Plaza

TABLE 6
4-COLUMN TABLE WITH LONG COLUMN HEADINGS

Paper: half sheet
Spacing: double
Proofguide: 21

Number columns align at the right.

FLIGHT INFORMATION
Phoenix to New York City

Airline	Flight	Departs (a.m.)	Arrives (p.m.)
AA	154	7:45	4:04
REP	630	8:45	4:50
TWA	192	9:00	4:37
AA	34	10:15	6:46
TWA	346	10:50	7:59
UA	232	11:10	8:23
UA	634	11:50	7:35

TABLE 7
3-COLUMN TABLE WITH SHORT AND LONG COLUMN HEADINGS

Paper: half sheet
Spacing: single
Proofguide: 21

The dollar sign is not repeated in a column of figures. The percent sign *is* repeated, unless the title or the column heading is labeled *Percentage*. (See page 59, Table 1 and page 64, Table 9.)

MUNICIPAL BOND ISSUES
(All Amounts in Thousands)

Issue Date	Amount	Interest Rate
February 5, 1981	$1,034	10.7%
September 3, 1981	1,300	8.3%
August 31, 1982	786	12.6%
October 1, 1982	1,045	12.8%
November 5, 1982	900	12.0%
May 30, 1983	1,750	10.2%
September 1, 1983	1,200	10.2%

Key Line: September 3, 1981₁₂₃₄₅₆$1,034₁₂₃₄₅₆Interest Rate

Paper: plain

six handwritten comments we received for Question 5 of the questionnaire. Please type an enumeration of only the handwritten comments. Although we do not want to change the respondents' thoughts, I would like you to correct errors in grammar, punctuation, and typing style as you type the enumeration.

This report should be labeled EXHIBIT C: RESPONDENT REASONS FOR CHANGING BANKS. I've taped together the

---

_____ Relocation of bank
✓ Dissatisfaction with bank service
_____ Other (Please specify _____)

The bank employees at my old bank couldn't add. 3 times last year my bank-statement was incorrect, once by 10 dollars.

---

5. If you have changed banks within the past three years, what was the major reason for the change?
_____ Relocation of residence
_____ Relocation of bank
✓ Dissatisfaction with bank service
_____ Other (Please specify _____)

One of the teller's there was all ways rude to me. He didn't seem to know or care about the affect his actions had on the banks reputation.

_____ Dissatisfaction with bank service
✓ Other (Please specify *my old bank did not offer a*) *credit card so I switched to a first class bank that did.*

_____ Dissatisfaction with bank service
✓ Other (Please specify _____)

Two things caused me to change banks; a new bank opened closer to my home, and my old bank closed their drive-in teller window.

Even though my old bank was alright I changed to Cascade Bank last Spring because my old bank charged 18 cents for each check I wrote. As long as I keep a minimum balance of $300 in my Cascade Bank Account there is no charge for writing checks.

---

5. If you have changed banks within the past three years, what was the major reason for the change?
_____ Relocation of residence
_____ Relocation of bank
✓ Dissatisfaction with bank service
_____ Other (Please specify _____)

Although Alpine National bank was the largest of the two banks I tried neither of the two banks were very helpful, and I finally chose a bank that was farther from my home.

REVIEW

Line: 50 spaces   Tab: 5, center
Spacing: single   Drills: 2X
Proofguide: 23–24
Workguide: 3–4, 77
Tape: 21A

Goals: To improve speed/accuracy on numbers and symbols; to format tables with two-line column headings.

42-A. WARMUP

S 1 Both of the towns are soon due for a visit by me.
A 2 Jack quietly gave the dog owner his prize boxers.
N 3 I won $846 on August 31 and $790 on September 25.

| 1 | 2 | 3 | 4 | 5 | 6 | 7 | 8 | 9 | 10

42-B. Take a 1-minute timing on the first paragraph to establish your base speed. Then take successive 1-minute timings on the other paragraphs. You must equal or exceed your base speed before starting the next paragraph.

42-B. SUSTAINED PRACTICE: NUMBERS AND SYMBOLS

4   No one (not even Johnson & Edwards) knew why 10
the date of the trial had been changed from May 9 20
to May 23. It couldn't have been a worse choice. 30

5   We had been trying since 12:45 to get a copy 10
of Document #108, which we needed. We even tried 20
to pay $18.76 to have it sent "Special Delivery." 30

6   Document #108 showed that the defendants had 10
purchased 65 shares of McGuire & Company stock at 20
$4.75, which was 43¢ (9%) more than it was worth. 30

| 1 | 2 | 3 | 4 | 5 | 6 | 7 | 8 | 9 | 10

42-C. Spacing—double. Record your score.

42-C. SKILL MEASUREMENT: 3-MINUTE TIMED WRITING

7   Stop just a moment sometime and analyze your 10
typing position. Your back should be held erect, 20
and your body should lean forward slightly. Your 30
wrists should be low, with your fingers curved so 40
that you can strike the keys quickly; your elbows 50
must be relaxed. Hold your head straight, turned 60
to face the book, which should be at the right of 70
your typewriter and elevated for ease of reading. 80
Have someone watch you as you type. 87

| 1 | 2 | 3 | 4 | 5 | 6 | 7 | 8 | 9 | 10

42/43-D. LETTER AND TABLE REVIEW

Type the letter and tables on page 64 in the formats indicated. Review page 49 (formatting a business letter), page 58 (formatting a table), and page 61 (formatting tables with column heads) if necessary. And remember, you may also refer to the Proofguide whenever you are uncertain about correct format.

JOB 4
LETTER 72
COMPOSED LETTER

Paper: Workguide 431–432

Now, to get this survey in the mails, would you please send all these materials to Jamie Carr, the research assistant at Survey Sitters, P.O. Box 79, Boise 83707.

Tell Mr. Carr that I'm enclosing the materials (one copy of the questionnaire, the cover letter, and the postal card) for the survey I discussed with him last week.

Please ask him to do the following (and you should enumerate these items):

1. Duplicate 400 copies of each item on 20-pound white paper stock, using offset duplication.

2. Send out copies of the letter and the postal card on the dates shown on the documents. He should use bulk mail, presorted according to ZIP Code.

3. Enclose with the letter one copy of the questionnaire as well as a No. 9 return envelope with our name and address printed on it. He should use our postage-paid permit No. 86.

Remind him that he should already have two sets of mailing labels, which were sent directly to him by Aileen Hollowell at Glover Industries.

Finally, please thank Mr. Carr for agreeing to handle this project on such short notice and ask him to send the bill, along with receipts for any expenditures over $25, directly to me. Date the letter October 3 and I'll sign it.

JOB 5
REPORT 65
QUESTIONNAIRE WITH FILL-INS

Paper: 2 copies of questionnaire from Job 1

I think we've got all the replies to the Glover Industries survey we're going to get. It's been a month since we sent the questionnaire out. Actually, the returns are pretty good: out of the 372 employees surveyed, 228 responded.

If you would get two copies of the questionnaire you filed, I'll read out the results to you. You can write in the results on one copy and type them right on the second copy. Label the typed copy EXHIBIT A: SURVEY RESULTS.

1. 58 yes; 170 no

2. 201 commercial bank; 52 savings and loan association; 75 employee credit union; 6 other; and 18 none

3. 70 near home; 102 near office; 12 near shopping; 31 on way to and from work; and 13 other

4. Overdrawing privileges: 20, 187, and 21
   Telephone transfer: 6, 20, and 202
   Free checking: 219, 9, and 0
   Total teller machines: 151, 45, and 32
   Convenient installment loans: 143, 56, and 29
   Personal banker: 40, 32, and 156

Bank credit card: 188, 32, and 8
Check guarantee card: 174, 32, and 22
Drive-in service: 148, 47, and 33
Trust department: 13, 45, and 170

5. 33 relocation of residence; 4 relocation of bank; 18 dissatisfaction with bank service; and 7 other

JOB 6
REPORT 66
BAR CHART

Paper: plain

I think Question 2 about the types of banking institutions the Glover employees now use is going to be of particular interest to the president. Would you please prepare a bar chart showing this information. Use the instructions and sample from the Citizens State Bank procedures manual below to make the bar chart. First, you'll have to compute the percentages by dividing the number of respondents who checked each alternative by the total number of respondents—228. Round off all percentages to the nearest whole number and show the percentages in increments of 10. Label this chart EXHIBIT B: TYPES OF BANKING INSTITUTIONS.

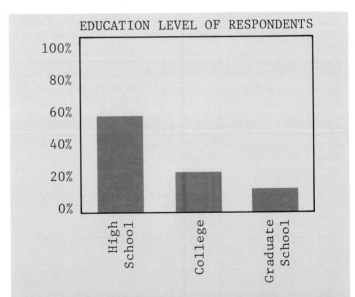

Bar charts are used to show graphically the relationship between different sets of data. The width of the bars should be the same; the height shows the percentage values. Center the chart by eye judgment on the page and draw the lines using either the underscore key or black ink. The bar labels at the bottom may be typed horizontally (if you have room), or you may turn the paper sideways to type them, making sure that all lines end at the same point.

LETTER 13
MODIFIED-BLOCK STYLE

Line: 5 inches (50 pica/60 elite)
Tab: center
Date: line 15
Paper: Workguide 77
Proofguide: 23–24

The enclosure notation is typed at the left margin a single space below the reference initials:

DSO
Enclosure

(*Current date*) / Dr. Raymond Stuart, Chairman / Department of Ad-	17
ministrative Services / The Ohio State University / 1659 North High Street	31
/ Columbus, OH 43210 / Dear Dr. Stuart:	40
During the months of May and June, we surveyed all 619 of our	53
employees, using the job-satisfaction scale that you developed. Be-	67
cause you were so generous in providing us with a copy of this scale,	81
we should like you to have the enclosed copy of the preliminary re-	94
sults of the survey.	98
We are sending the complete results to Elwood & Lee, a consulting	112
firm that has done other research for us in the past. We are asking	126
them to provide us with a detailed interpretation of the findings and	140
to make recommendations for changes that would make our com-	152
pany an even more attractive place in which to work.	163
I shall be happy to supply you with a confidential copy of their re-	177
port when it is completed if you would find it helpful in your further	192
work on this attitude scale.	198
Cordially, / Ruth Tse, Manager / Personnel Department / (*Your ini-*	215
tials) / Enclosure	218

TABLE 8
3-COLUMN TABLE

Paper: full sheet
Spacing: double
Proofguide: 23

Center and single-space each line of a two-line title. The first line should be longer than the second line.

SCHEDULE OF PARTICIPATION IN
JOB-SATISFACTION SURVEY
↓3

Unit or Department	Date	Number Surveyed
Executive	May 3	87
Sales	May 4	143
Word Processing	May 9	24
Maintenance	May 17	19
Development	June 8	48
Manufacturing	June 14	298

Key Line: Word Processing   June 14   Surveyed
                    123456   123456

TABLE 9
4-COLUMN TABLE

Paper: full sheet
Spacing: double
Proofguide: 23

PERCENTAGE OF WORKERS SATISFIED
WITH VARIOUS JOB FACTORS
↓3

Job Factor	All Workers	White-Collar Workers	Blue-Collar Workers
Challenge	73.0	78.5	68.2
Resources	68.4	64.5	71.9
Financial Rewards	64.2	57.4	72.5
Co-Workers	63.4	60.9	67.0
Comfort	54.4	60.3	47.5

Key Line: Financial Rewards   Workers   White-Collar   Blue-Collar
                      123456   123456   123456

WP On a word processor, it is possible to move blocks of copy anywhere within the document.

Glover Industries ~~Questionnaire~~ *Survey*

1. Do you currently have an account at Citizens? *or* *State Bank*?

      _____ No
      _____ Yes

3. 2. Where is your main bank located?

      _____ Near home
      _____ Near office
      _____ Near shopping
      _____ On way ~~from~~ *to* and ~~to~~ *from* work
      _____ Other (Please specify _____)

2. 3. At which of the following ~~banks~~ *financial institutions* do you currently have an account?

      _____ Commercial bank   (*Please check all institutions*
      _____ Savings and loan association   *that apply.*)
      _____ Employee Credit Union
      _____ Other (Please specify _____)
      _____ None

4. How important do you consider ~~each of~~ the following banking services?
   (3 1 = very important; 2 = moderately important; 1 3 = unimportant)

	1	2	3
Over drawing privileges	___	___	___
Telephone transfer	___	___	___
Free checking	___	___	___
Total teller machines	___	___	___
Convenient loans *installment*	___	___	___
Personal banker	___	___	___
Bank credit card *Check guarantee*	___	___	___
Drive-in service *card*	___	___	___
Trust department	___	___	___

5. If you have ~~switched~~ *changed* banks within the past ③ years, what was the major reason for the change?

      _____ Relocation of residence
      _____ Relocation of bank
      _____ Dissatisfaction with bank service
      _____ Other (please specify _____)

   (*Leave 3 blank lines*)

   Thank you so much for your cooperation. Please return this questionnaire in the enclosed envelope.

Line: 60 spaces   Tab: 5
Spacing: single   Drills: 2X
Proofguide: 23–26
Workguide: 3–4, 79, 81–82
Tape: 22A or K12B

LESSONS 44/45

REPORT TYPING

Goals: To control the *, !, =, and + keys; to type rough-draft copy; to format one-page reports.

44-A. WARMUP

S 1 Bob also owns six new shirts and eight pairs of blue socks.
A 2 Franz jumps on the bandwagon for no new taxes very quickly.
N 3 From 1897 to 1946, 2,305 people were born with the disease.
   | 1 | 2 | 3 | 4 | 5 | 6 | 7 | 8 | 9 | 10 | 11 | 12

ASTERISK is the shift of 8. Use the K finger.

EXCLAMATION is the shift of 1. Use the A finger.

44-B. PRACTICE THE ⊛, ❗, ＝, AND ＋ KEYS

4 k8k k*k k8k k*k *** His article* quoted Mason** and Poe.***
5 The * sign, the asterisk, is used for reference purposes.**

6 ala a!a ala a!a !!! Now! No! It can't be so! Impossible!
7 The countdown was steady: Five! Four! Three! Two! One!

8 ;=; ;=; === ;=; === A = 140, B = 90, C = 63, D = 24, E = 5.
9 ;=; ;=+ ;+; ;+; +++ How much is 14 + 1 + 2 + 3 + 4 + 5 + 6?
10 1 + 3 = 4; 83 + 6 = 89; 4 + 5 = 9; 42 + 6 = 48; 3 + 8 = 11.

PLUS is the shift of the EQUALS. Use the Sem finger.

Space once before and after mathematical symbols such as + and =.

44-C. Set a tab 5 spaces to the right of center. Then practice each line until you can type it with no more than 1 error and without looking at your keys.

44-C. SYMBOL PRACTICE

11 Lee & Poe met Day & Fox. TAB → Buy (a) ink or (b) pens.
12 I'll get Roger's papers.   "No," I said, "I'll go."
13 Order 23# of #39 and #6.   David scored 75% to 85%.
14 Is pour or pore correct?   Both rooms cost $40-$45.
15 The pads cost 6¢ and 8¢.   Buy 10 @ $14 and 8 @ $9.
16 I quoted Gill* and Li.**   Hurrah! We won! 23-21!
17 X = 4, Y = 1, and Z = 3.   What is 4 + 13 + 25 + 6?

44-D. Spacing—double. Record your score.

44-D. SKILL MEASUREMENT: 3-MINUTE TIMED WRITING

18 Throughout your college career, you will frequently be 12
asked to write reports. Now that you can touch-type, there 24
is no excuse for you to turn in a report that is written by 36
hand. In addition to being faster, a typed report will em- 48
phasize a professional appearance. In this section and the 60
following lessons, you will learn how to type several kinds 72
of manuscripts. This skill will help you both in class now 84
and later when you get a job. 90
   | 1 | 2 | 3 | 4 | 5 | 6 | 7 | 8 | 9 | 10 | 11 | 12

Situation: Today is Wednesday, October 1. You are secretary to Mr. Andrew Willoughby, assistant director of market research at Citizens State Bank in Boise, Idaho. Mr. Willoughby prefers the modified-block style of letter, with these closing lines:

```
        Sincerely,


        Andrew Willoughby
        Market Research Department
```

JOB 1   Paper: stencil or spirit master
REPORT 64
QUESTIONNAIRE

I've been working for several weeks on a survey for Glover Industries. I think I finally have it the way I want it. (*See page 277 for the rough draft of the survey.*) Although we'll be sending the final version out for printing, I'll need some copies for in-house use. Please type this questionnaire on either a spirit master or a stencil and run off about 25 copies for in-house use. Use standard report margins, but single-space the lines within each item and double-space between each item.

Be sure to file three or four copies for use in analyzing the survey after it has been returned.

JOB 2   Paper: Workguide 427
LETTER 71
COVER LETTER

Now we'll need a cover letter to accompany the questionnaire explaining why we're asking for this information. Let's date the letter October 6, 19—. Since this is a form letter, there won't be any inside address; simply start the salutation at the point where the inside address normally starts. Use the subject line Banking Habits and Preferences.

dear glover employee ... congratulations on glover's forthcoming move to one jefferson square ... jefferson square is the most prestigious commercial park in the entire state of idaho ... and you should enjoy your pleasant and modern surroundings as well as the availability of excellent shopping and restaurants nearby ...

citizens state bank ... located in the heart of one jefferson square ... has been serving the banking needs of employees in this center for over ten years

... and we would like to serve your banking needs as well ...

won't you please take a few minutes to let us know what your banking needs are by answering the enclosed questionnaire ... the information gained from this survey of glover employees will enable us to develop a customized banking service package geared specifically to your needs ... no other bank in the area offers such personalized service ...

Now insert the closing lines and add this postscript:

if you are not currently a customer of citizens state bank and would like to learn more about our regular services ... call us at 555-1076 and ask for a free copy of our newcomer's package.

JOB 3   Paper: Workguide 429
POSTAL CARD 4
FOLLOW-UP REMINDER

While we're at it, why don't we get the follow-up postal card ready for the printer. Type it on the postal card form supplied (*see Workguide page 429*). On the address side, simply type our return address, and Survey Sitters will put on the address labels. Date the card two weeks after October 6. Here's my handwritten draft.

Dear Glover Employee:

Remember us? We wrote you two weeks ago asking you to complete a short questionnaire concerning your banking habits and preferences. If you have not already done so, won't you please take a few minutes to complete this questionnaire and return it to us. The information you provide will enable us to provide better service to Glover employees.

Andrew Willoughby
Market Research Department

44-E. BASIC PARTS OF A REPORT

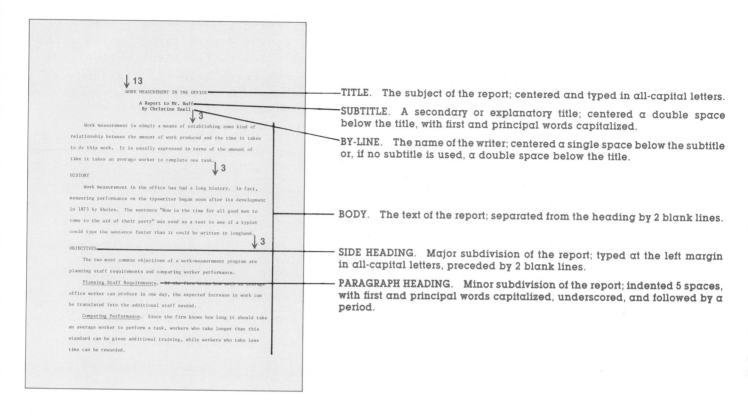

TITLE.   The subject of the report; centered and typed in all-capital letters.

SUBTITLE.   A secondary or explanatory title; centered a double space below the title, with first and principal words capitalized.

BY-LINE.   The name of the writer; centered a single space below the subtitle or, if no subtitle is used, a double space below the title.

BODY.   The text of the report; separated from the heading by 2 blank lines.

SIDE HEADING.   Major subdivision of the report; typed at the left margin in all-capital letters, preceded by 2 blank lines.

PARAGRAPH HEADING.   Minor subdivision of the report; indented 5 spaces, with first and principal words capitalized, underscored, and followed by a period.

44-F.   FORMATTING A ONE-PAGE REPORT

LINE LENGTH.   6 inches (60 pica/70 elite)

TAB STOPS.   Always set two—one for indenting paragraphs and one for centering heading lines.

TOP MARGIN.   2 inches; center the title on line 13.

SPACING.   Always use single spacing until you begin typing the body of the report; then change if the body is to be double-spaced.

BOTTOM GUARD.   Before inserting the paper, pencil in two very light lines (to be erased later): one line about an inch from the bottom to indicate where the last line of typing should go, and a second line about

an inch higher to serve as a warning.

NOTE: The easiest way to format a report is to use a *visual guide*—a sheet on which the margins are marked off in heavy lines. When this sheet is placed behind the paper on which you will type, the ruled lines show through to indicate the correct placement of margins and copy. Workguide page 79 is a visual guide for use in formatting reports.

Before typing Reports 1–3, complete Workguide pages 81–82.

44-G.   PROOFREADERS' MARKS

Study the proofreaders' marks shown below, which are used by writers and typists to indicate changes in typed work when they are revising the copy for final typing. These marks are used in the jobs in this lesson.

Proofreaders' Mark	Draft	Final Copy	Proofreaders' Mark	Draft	Final Copy
⌒ Omit space	court⌒room	courtroom	∧ Insert word	and ᷾so it is	and so it is
∪ Transpose	to ⌐quickly go⌐	to go quickly	✐ Delete	a ~~true~~ fact	a fact
⌐ Paragraph	⌐ If he is	If he is	≡ Capitalize	Fifth a̱venue	Fifth Avenue

182-E. PRACTICE: BOTH HANDS

15 eie veil unveil movie beings liens either piece eighty diet
16 ghg huge bought shrug lights thigh aghast hedge ghetto sigh
17 yty toys system empty mystic style yogurt tying youths myth
18 sks keys risked banks unmask kilos skills keeps skates risk
19 A youthful skater skillfully tried to jump the high hedges.

| 1 | 2 | 3 | 4 | 5 | 6 | 7 | 8 | 9 | 10 | 11 | 12

POSTTEST. Repeat the Pretest and compare performance.

182-F. POSTTEST: DISCRIMINATION PRACTICE

182-G. Spacing—double. Take two 5-minute timings. Between them, practice any words with which you had difficulty. Record your score.

182-G. SKILL MEASUREMENT: 5-MINUTE TIMED WRITING

20 When just a few copies of a typed document are needed, 12
you will often make the copies by using either carbon paper 24
or a photocopy machine. If more copies are needed, you may 36
send the documents to your reprographics department or to a 48
printer. However, you may sometimes be asked to make these 60
copies yourself by using either spirit masters or stencils. 72
Spirit masters are used on a fluid duplication machine 84
to make up to a few hundred copies. You type on the master 96
just as you would on regular paper. To correct errors, you 108
must remove the carbon deposit from the back of the master, 120
using a knife or a special fluid that dissolves the carbon. 132
Next you type the corrections, using a new patch of carbon. 144
Stencils are typed when a sizable number of copies are 156
needed and a better quality copy is desired. Before typing 168
stencils, you should reset your ribbon–control lever to the 180
stencil setting. You correct errors on stencils by coating 192
them with correction fluid and then typing the correct data 204
after the fluid has dried. Proofread the spirit master and 216
stencil carefully before removing them from the typewriter, 228
because it is difficult to reinsert and realign the papers. 240

| 1 | 2 | 3 | 4 | 5 | 6 | 7 | 8 | 9 | 10 | 11 | 12

183–187. INTEGRATED OFFICE PROJECT: CITIZENS STATE BANK

Before you begin your assignment at Citizens State Bank, reread the information in 182-G concerning how to type a spirit master or a stencil. Assemble all your materials, including your work-guide pages, plain paper, and either a blank spirit master or a stencil.

44/45-H. ONE-PAGE REPORTS

Type Reports 1–3, using double spacing and making the corrections indicated by the proofreaders' marks.

The word count at the right credits you for all centering, indenting, and other required machine operations.

REPORT 1
Line: 6 inches (60 pica/70 elite)
Spacing: double
Paper: plain
Visual Guide:
  Workguide 79
Tab: 5, center
Proofguide: 23–24

Triple-space before side headings and double-space after them.

WP Word processors have insert ($\wedge$) and delete ($\mathscr{e}$) keys that allow a unit of text (a character, word, paragraph, and so on) to be automatically inserted into or deleted from the existing text.

↓ 13	
NONVERBAL COMMUNICATION	14
a Report on Body Language	32
By Kent Baty ↓ 3	42

Such non verbal communications as facial expressions, pos- 56

ture, and gestures contribute much to our oral communications. 69

These conscious or unconscious body movements may either re- 81

actually
inforce or contradict what we have to say. ↓ 3 90

PERSONAL SPACE ↓ 2 95

We all seem to carry a deep sense of needing some personal 103

space around us, which we guard against intruders. Likewise, 115

we also try not to intrude on the personal space of others. 125

personal
The higher one's status, the more space one is allowed. 138

FACIAL EXPRESSIONS 144

meanings.
Facial expressions can convey a whole range of messages. 156

Even the absence of a facial expression can convey a message. 169

For example, if I tell you a joke and you do not smile, that 181

tells me that you did not think that my joke was very funny. 194

GESTURES AND POSTURE 200

through
We can also communicate our moods with gestures and 212

posture. Keeping our heads down may tell people to leave us 224

alone. Crossing our arms may indicate that we do not believe 237

what someone is saying. However, all nonverbal communications 249

should only be considered in the light of the whole situation. 262

<table>
<tr><td>

Line: 60 spaces Tab: 5
Spacing: single Drills: 3X
Proofguide: 133–135
Workguide: 427–432
Tape: 57A and 58A
</td></tr>
</table>

INTEGRATED OFFICE PROJECT: BANKING
LESSONS 182–187

GOALS FOR UNIT 30

1. Type at least 48 wam for 5 minutes with no more than 5 errors.
2. Edit documents while typing, applying rules of grammar, punctuation, and typing style.
3. Compose a business letter.
4. Type and run off either a spirit master or a stencil.
5. Prepare visual aids for a business report.
6. Calculate percentages.
7. Follow a research project through from start to finish.

182-A. WARMUP

S 1 The busy auditors paid their usual visit to sign the forms.
A 2 I quizzed Edgar Jenkins about two extremely complex topics.
N 3 Only 14 of the 36 people had read pages 197–208 by June 25.
| 1 | 2 | 3 | 4 | 5 | 6 | 7 | 8 | 9 | 10 | 11 | 12

182-B. PRETEST: DISCRIMINATION PRACTICE

PRETEST. **Take a 1-minute timing; compute speed and errors.**

4   The alert admiral flew solo over the quiet coalfields. 12
He was aghast to discover that either his fuel gauge was in 24
error or he had only eight liters of gas left; by remaining 36
alert, he avoided skidding into the dirty old river bottom. 48
| 1 | 2 | 3 | 4 | 5 | 6 | 7 | 8 | 9 | 10 | 11 | 12

PRACTICE. **If you made no errors on the Pretest, type each line 3 times. If you made 1 error or more, type each group of four lines (as though it were a paragraph) 3 times; then type the sentence 3 times.**

NOTE: **Discrimination drills help you to type correctly those keys which are most commonly confused. For example, R and T, A and S, M and N.**

182-C. PRACTICE: LEFT HAND

5 rtr trap assert entry alerts trade barter trace artery port
6 asa sand biased essay basics safer asking sacks ascent asks
7 sds desk abused ideas beside dense sedans desks wisdom beds
8 rer rear adhere alert refill error reason erase reacts read
9 Alert the rear sedan about the sand trap beside that entry.
| 1 | 2 | 3 | 4 | 5 | 6 | 7 | 8 | 9 | 10 | 11 | 12

182-D. PRACTICE: RIGHT HAND

10 mnm amen mainly denim manner norms solemn named alumni mane
11 oio idol avoids prior points irony coined doing oiling boil
12 olo polo cooled blown colons alone bolder loans oldest solo
13 iui quid incurs guide radius using medium unity genius unit
14 The old guide points out Manet's genius in a bolder manner.
| 1 | 2 | 3 | 4 | 5 | 6 | 7 | 8 | 9 | 10 | 11 | 12

REPORT 2
Spacing: double
Paper: plain
Visual Guide:
    Workguide 79
Proofguide: 25–26

Because of the corrections, you will have to listen for the bell and decide when to end each line.

Using proofreaders' marks to revise and edit a document prior to producing a final copy is called *editing*.

| WP | Information that is sent to a word processing department for processing is called *Input*. Examples of input are longhand, shorthand, and machine dictation. As illustrated in Report 1, changes (called revisions) are often made in a document once it is typed. Since the original document is stored on a tape or disk in the word processor, only the changed material must be retyped.

PARTS OF A REPORT   11

Cecelia Esquer   22

    A long class report often contains several *special* parts in ad-   37

dition to the body of the report. Some of these parts come   49

before the body and some come after *it.* ~~the body~~   58

INTRODUCTORY PARTS   63

The main parts of the report that ~~should~~ come before the body   75

are the title page and the table of contents.   85

    <u>Title page</u>. The title page is the cover page for a long   101

report. It identifies the author, title, and date of the re-   113

port, as well as the course for which the report is prepared.   126

    <u>Table of Contents</u>. The table of contents lists the main   145

sections of the report and tells on which page of the report   157

each of these sections can be found. If a report consists of   170

only a few pages, a table of contents *is* ~~are~~ not needed.   181

<u>Bibliography</u>   185

    The bibliography comes at the end of the report. It lists   198

all the journals, ~~books, and other~~ sources that the writer re-   205

ferred to when preparing the report. The purpose of this sec-   217

tion of the report is to allow the reader to *study any of* ~~refer to~~ these   230

publications if further information is needed. There fore,   241

enough information must be given to allow the reader to locate   253

each source *in the library.*   259

REPORT 3
Paper: plain
Visual Guide:
    Workguide 79
Proofguide: 25–26

Retype Report 2, making these changes: (1) add the subtitle *A Report for Typing 1,* and (2) delete the paragraph headings (but keep the side headings).

any figure that you desire, but 6 lines per inch is the normal setting
and the one that we recommend for most typing.

10.4--Printer Output Mode *Add underscores wherever indicated*

This field allows you to determine how the print will appear on the
page. Three selections are available: normal, flush, and centered.
In normal type (N), the left margin will be flush and the right margin
will be ragged. In flush type (F), the print will be justified at both
margins. In centered type (C), each line will be centered between the
left and right margins.
List these enumerations

10.5--Word Wrap Hot Zone

Word wrap refers to the automatic carrier feature. As you approach the
end of a line, the system will begin looking for a place to end that
line without dividing a word. You are able to select the point at which
the system will do this. We recommend a setting of 5, but you may choose
any number between 0 and 9. Entering 0 into this field will disable
the automatic word wrap; that is, you will have to return the carrier
manually at the end of each line. A setting of 0 is recommended only
if you are keyboarding columns of numbers in a table.

*(If you want to divide a word, see
Section 11.2 for automatic hyphenation
feature.)*

10.6--Default Settings

Your starting menu comes with default settings. These are the selections that automatically appear on the page-layout panel when it first
appears on the screen. You can, of course, change these default settings
to whatever settings are needed most often in your office *for the particular job.*

You may find that you have two or more different types of documents
that you prepare frequently--for example, letters typed on regular-
size stationery and letters typed on monarch stationery. Rather than
changing the settings in the panel before each document is prepared,
you may find it more convenient to keep two disks, one for regular
stationery and one for monarch stationery.

To change the default settings:

1. Enter your choices into the panel.

    (or Function-1)
2. Press Control-1. Your default settings have now been entered
    into the panel and will appear until you again make a change.

LESSONS 46/47

ENUMERATIONS

Goals: To construct special
symbols; to format
enumerations.

46-A.   WARMUP

S 1   The goal of their amendment is to make the city neighborly.
A 2   Vince paid me for fixing Mr. Bank's quartz watch last July.
N 3   On 10/4 Jones paid 257% of the stock's par value of $83.60.
       | 1 | 2 | 3 | 4 | 5 | 6 | 7 | 8 | 9 | 10 | 11 | 12

46-B. Before making good
copies of each example,
practice them all.

46-B.   CONSTRUCTING SPECIAL SYMBOLS

times	4 What is 2 x 2?	Small letter x.
minus	5 $106 - 14 = 92.$	Hyphen.
divided by	6 $144 \div 12 = 12.$	Colon, backspace, hyphen.
fractions	7 $9/10 = 90/100.$	Numerator, diagonal, denominator.
feet and inches	8 John is 6' 2".	Apostrophe (feet), quotation mark (inches).
minutes and seconds	9 15' 30" to go.	Apostrophe (minutes), quotation mark (seconds).
superior figures	10 $4^3 + 5^2 = 89^a.$	Number or letter typed above line (turn platen by hand).
inferior figures	11 H_2O was water.	Number or letter typed below line (turn platen by hand).
military zero	12 Leave at 18Ø0.	Zero, backspace, diagonal.
degrees	13 Freeze at 0^oC.	Small letter o typed above line (turn platen by hand).
exclamation	14 I can't do it!	Period, backspace, apostrophe.
brackets	15 He /W̲i̲l̲l̲i̲a̲m̲s̲/.	Diagonals, with underscores facing inside.
roman numerals	16 Chapter XLVII.	Capitals of I, V, X, L, C, and M.

46-C. Spacing—double.
Record your score.

46-C.   SKILL MEASUREMENT: 3-MINUTE TIMED WRITING

17   The guides you have been given in this text for typing   12
reports represent only one way to organize them. There are   24
other correct ways as well. For example, instead of typing   36
a major heading at your left margin, you may want to center   48
and underline it. Instead of using the line lengths given,   60
you may want to use side margins equal to one inch. Or you   72
may want to leave a blank line between the subtitle and the   84
by-line. Just be consistent.   90
       | 1 | 2 | 3 | 4 | 5 | 6 | 7 | 8 | 9 | 10 | 11 | 12

WP   When you backspace on
a word processor while
typing, you erase the text that
was backspaced over.
Therefore, word processors have
a special overstrike key that
allows you to type one
character over another to
construct special symbols that
are composed of two characters,
such as the "divided by" sign
above.

JOB 6

(DATE)

WP The merge function of a word processor can combine a form letter stored on magnetic media with stored names and addresses.

(NAME)
(STREET)
(CITY, STATE, ZIP)

Dear (NAME):

How many times have you said to yourself, "The last thing I need to do is spend more money on insurance"? And you may be right. In fact, (NAME), you may be paying too much money for the automobile insurance coverage you are ~~now~~ receiving.
                                                        currently

WP The delete function of a word processor enables the operator to remove a letter, word, line, paragraph, page, or an entire document.

Now you can join many of your neighbors from (CITY, STATE) in reducing your automobile insurance premiums. Just send us a copy of your current automobile *insurance* policy, and Ambassador will be happy to provide you with a ~~quote~~ *quotation* for an ~~annual~~ premium for comparable or better coverage.

Of Course,
There is no charge for this service, and you are under no obligation to switch to Ambassador's policy. But we look forward, (NAME), to showing you how ~~Ambassador~~ *we* might help you save some of your hard-earned money.

                    Sincerely,

                    Carmen Ayala
                    Marketing Manager

JOB 7
REPORT 63
OPERATOR'S MANUAL

Paper: plain

Please type these revisions for the operator's manual for word processing equipment (*page 273*). This will be in our standard report format, but will require two pages, and so be sure to consult the Word Processing Center Procedures Manual for instructions on typing page headings.

46/47-D. FORMATTING ENUMERATIONS

Before you type the assignments in this section, read the instructions and the information provided in Reports 4 and 6 carefully. Then type Reports 4–7.

REPORT 4
ENUMERATION

Paper: plain
Line: 6 inches
   (60 pica/70 elite)
Tab: 4
Proofguide: 25–26

↓13

ENUMERATIONS ↓3   8

1. Any series of numbered items can be classified as an enumeration.   24
    However, to most people the word means a displayed listing like   38
    this one, with the numbers standing out at the left. ↓2   50

2. The numbers are typed at the left margin and are followed by a   65
    period and 2 spaces. A tab stop is set 4 spaces in from the   78
    left margin to help align the turnover lines of copy.   91

3. If most items take one line or less, they are single-spaced with   106
    no blank lines left between them. However, if most of the items   120
    require more than one line (as in this enumeration), they are   133
    single-spaced with 1 blank line left between items.   145

4. The periods following the numbers should align vertically. Thus   160
    the left margin must be reset 1 space to the left if the enumera-   174
    tion runs to 10 or more items.   182

REPORT 5
OUTLINE

Paper: plain
Tabs: 4, 8
Proofguide: 25–26
Center horizontally

Use the margin release lever to backspace for roman numerals II and III. The periods align vertically.

↓13

(M) (T) (T)   GETTING A JOB ↓3   9

I.   LEARNING ABOUT EMPLOYMENT ↓2   17

      A.   Analyzing Yourself   23
      B.   Finding Out About Job Opportunities   33
      C.   Matching Job Requirements With Qualifications ↓3   44

II.   WRITING ABOUT EMPLOYMENT ↓2   54

      A.   Data Sheet   59
      B.   Employment Letters   65
           1.   Application letter   71
           2.   Letter of recommendation   79
           3.   Follow-up letter ↓3   86

III. TALKING ABOUT EMPLOYMENT ↓2   96

      A.   Interview Skills   102
           1.   Types of interviews   109
           2.   Preparation for interviews   117
      B.   Listening Skills   122

Key Line: I.   C.   Matching Job Requirements With Qualifications

Operator, this is Karen Scanlon-Brown, Vice President—Marketing. Please prepare a rough draft of a memorandum to Michael Whitehead, President; the subject is Agent Bonus Plan.

as you know ... about two years ago our market research department conducted an industry survey and found that ambassador was competitive in terms of the commissions we pay our agents for writing insurance ...

because of the structure of our compensation plan ... we are finding that we have no trouble attracting beginning agents to our company ... but we tend to lose too many of our experienced agents to other companies ... especially the high volume sellers ... the cost in terms of lost customers ... training expense ... and employee morale is substantial ...

for this reason I feel that it is necessary for us to develop ... in addition to our basic commission ... a bonus plan that will encourage and reward high volume agents ... i will develop and submit a proposed plan for you to review within the next few weeks.

JOB 4   Paper: plain
TABLE 49

Type the table, Agent Bonus Plan, that I sent you with the cassette tape. Type it on a separate sheet of plain paper. Thank you.

JOB 5   Paper: plain
MEMORANDUM 19
TABLE 50

Here's another dictation cassette from Ms. Scanlon-Brown. I believe it is the final version of the memo and table you typed earlier.

Operator, this is Karen Scanlon-Brown, Vice President—Marketing. Please prepare a final copy of my memorandum to President Whitehead about the proposed agent bonus plan. Please delete the last sentence beginning "I will develop and submit ..." and so on, and substitute this sentence instead: "Would you please let me have your reactions to the bonuses proposed below." Then type the table below the last paragraph of the memorandum. Thank you.

JOB 6   Paper: plain
LETTER 70
FORM LETTER WITH VARIABLES

Insurance is a paper-intensive industry, and a lot of paperwork is involved in soliciting business, processing policies, handling claims, and the like. To save time, we use form letters whenever possible.

Ms. Ayala from the Marketing Department has asked us to type the rough draft of a new solicitation letter for automobile insurance (*page 272*). If it is approved by Mr. Whitehead, it will be used as one of a series of form letters that is "personalized" by the word processor and sent to prospective customers.

AGENT BONUS PLAN

Effective January 1, 19--

First-Year Commissions	Bonus for First Year	Bonus for Renewal Years
$1 — $3,000	15%	5%
$3,001 – $6,000	19%	6%
$6,001 – $10,000	22%	7%
$10,001 – $15,000	24%	8%
$15,001 and over	25%	10%

PREPARING a BIBLIOGRAPHY   15

by Violet Ellis   27

The bibliography lists all of the sources that the writer used in   43

preparing the report. The sources are alphabetically arranged accord-   58

ing to the last name of the first author. The following guide lines   71

should be followed in typing a bibliography.   80

Single-space the items within each enumeration but double-space between items.

Indent turnover lines 4 spaces.

1. Use the same line length that is used for the body of the report: 95
    60 pica/70 elite.   101

2. Center the title in all capital letters on line 13; leave 2 lines blank 117
    between the title and the body.   126

3. Arrange the information for books in this order: author, title of   140
    the book (underscored), publisher, place of publication, and date.   155

4. Arrange the information for journal articles in this order: author, title 170
    of the article (enclosed in quotation marks), title of the journal   187
    (underscored), volume number, issue number, page numbers, date.   203

5. Begin the first line of each entry at the left margin. Indent all turn-over lines 5 or 10 spaces. 215
                                                                          225

¶ The bibliography is the last part of the report to   237
be prepared and is placed at the end of the report. Then   247
all pages are proofread one last time, arranged in   259
order, and turned in.   263

↓13
BIBLIOGRAPHY   7
↓3

Black, James, How to Get Results From Interviews, McGraw-Hill Book   36
      Company, New York, 1970. ↓2   42

Box, W. F., "A Job Seeker's Viewpoint," The Personnel Administrator,   64
      September 1977, pp. 51-55.   71

Distributive Education Clubs of America, Preparing for the Job Inter-   96
      view, Educational Association Clearinghouse, San Francisco,   111
      1981.   113

Kahn, R. L., and C. F. Cannell, The Dynamics of Interviewing, John   139
      Wiley & Sons, Inc., New York, 1968.   147

Weiss, Judith, et al., "An Inquiry Into the Effects of Listening,"   162
      Modern Business Communication, Vol. 14, No. 8, pp. 25-32,   186
      December 1981.   190

"Yes--Interviewing Skills Can Be Taught," Current Business, June 19,   211
      1983, pp. 39-42.   216

JOB 2

Mr. Albert Granger/Granger Auto Supply/
1102 Grand Avenue/Kansas City, MO 64106

Dear Mr. Granger

(circled note) Insert necessary punctuation SJR

    I am pleased to learn that you are installing a sprinkler system in your warehouse. Such a system is a great help in preventing the spread of fire and in extinguishing fires.

    Any water damage to your warehouse or its contents resulting from the use of the sprinkler system during a fire is covered by your present fire policy with our company. However we suggest that you add a rider to your policy to cover accidental damage to your sprinkler system. Your sprinkler could be damaged by freezing pipes excessive vibration caused by machinery or other accidents and any water damage thus resulting would not be covered by your present policy.

    If you would like to learn more about the provisions and cost of this type of policy give Bill Reif your local agent a call at 555-1067.

Sincerely

Stanley J. Reinhart
Customer Service

PC Bill Reif

JOB 3
MEMORANDUM 18

Paper: plain

Please transcribe the dictation (*page 271*) I have left on your desk. You can play back the dictation on the transcribing machine. There are controls on the machine that allow you to stop the dictation while you catch up typing or to replay certain parts you may have missed.

Some of the originators whose dictation you'll be transcribing indicate paragraphs, punctuation, and the like, but others do not, and so you'll have to be careful.

If you have any questions about the job, consult the Word Processing Center Procedures Manual.

LESSONS 48/49
REVIEW

Goal: To format a business letter, table, and report for review.

48-A. WARMUP

S 1 They also wish to visit one of the lakes if they go by air.
A 2 Jack required an extra big size of shade for his new lamps.
N 3 We sold 156 fish and 279 beef plates for a total of $3,084.
| 1 | 2 | 3 | 4 | 5 | 6 | 7 | 8 | 9 | 10 | 11 | 12

48-B. Practice this paragraph until you can type it with no more than 1 error and without looking at your keys. Then take several 1-minute timings.

48-B. SYMBOL/NUMBER PRACTICE

4   Lee & Perkins (a supply firm) ordered 458# of our all-   12
purpose cement @ 69¢ a pound. Doesn't this represent a 30% 24
increase from their April 17 order? "It does not," I said. 36
| 1 | 2 | 3 | 4 | 5 | 6 | 7 | 8 | 9 | 10 | 11 | 12

48-C. Spacing—double.
Record your score.

48-C. SKILL MEASUREMENT: 3-MINUTE TIMED WRITING

5   Business people emphasize that the qualities they look 12
for most often in their new workers are the ability to make 24
decisions and a willingness to take responsibility. People 36
who excel in these two skills will have the best chance for 48
the best jobs. Begin now to learn how to judge what has to 60
be done to complete an assignment. And never turn in a job 72
unless you are sure you have done the very best job you can 84
do. Take pride in your work.   90
| 1 | 2 | 3 | 4 | 5 | 6 | 7 | 8 | 9 | 10 | 11 | 12

48/49-D. BUSINESS LETTER WITH TWO ENCLOSURES

Before typing these jobs, review business letter typing (pages 49–50), table typing (pages 58 and 61), and report typing (pages 66–67) if necessary.

LETTER 14
MODIFIED-BLOCK LETTER

Paper: Workguide 83
Proofguide: 27–28

(*Current date*) / Mr. Richard VanAllen / Invest Associates / 250 Church   18
Street / New York, NY 10013 / Dear Mr. VanAllen: 28
   I am happy to provide you with the information that you requested   42
to help you evaluate our firm's stocks as an investment.   53
   Since you already have our latest financial statements and annual   68
report, I am enclosing a table showing our major new products and   81
a short report showing the status of our research activities.   93
   I feel confident that after studying these documents, as well as our   108
annual report, you will wish to recommend American Home stock as   121
a safe and profitable investment for your clients.   132
   Sincerely, / Esther Myers-Abbott / Public Relations Specialist / (*Your* 151
initials) / 2 Enclosures   155

When a letter has more than one enclosure, use the correct numeral and the plural *Enclosures*. Example: *2 Enclosures*.

Situation: Today is Monday, September 15. You are working in the word processing center of Ambassador Insurance Company. Jobs come to the center in different forms. They may be handwritten drafts, dictation, rough drafts, or form letters and memos with variable information.

Your supervisor in the word processing center is Mrs. Mary Baughn, and she is responsible for assigning the jobs that come in. Study carefully the Ambassador Word Processing Center Procedures Manual (page 268) so that you will know how to type and submit the jobs that will be assigned to you.

The person who composes and sends the documents to the center is referred to as the *word originator* (also called *principal* or *author*).

FORM 71   Workguide: 421
OPERATOR'S LOG

Jobs that come into the word processing center are assigned different priorities. "Rush" jobs are completed ahead of routine jobs so that the total time such a job is in the word processing center (*turnaround time*) is short. The turnaround time on your log sheet is the total time the job was in your hands. The instructions for completing this job are given in the log itself and in the Word Processing Center Procedures Manual. You should log in a job as soon as it has been assigned to you by your supervisor, Mrs. Baughn, and begin work immediately.

JOBS 1–2   Paper: Workguide 423–426
LETTERS 68–69
BLOCK STYLE, OPEN PUNCTUATION

Ambassador Insurance operates a 24-hour toll-free hot line so that customers and potential customers can call for a direct answer to their insurance questions. When the office is not open, the questions are handled by a recording device and answered by letter. The company requires that these questions be answered within 48 hours. For this reason, when they come to us in the word processing center, they are given a "rush" priority.

I've just received two such letters from Stan Reinhart, and I'd like you to begin typing the replies as quickly as possible.

JOB 1

Mrs. Adele Heinze
1236 Sandusky Avenue, Apt. 12-G
Kansas City, KS 66102

Dear Mrs. Heinze

We are pleased to inform you that the recent accidental damage to your neighbor's stereo system which was caused by your daughter is covered under your homeowner's policy. Accidental property damage caused by you or members of your immediate family is automatically covered under your particular policy.

We hope you will continue to take advantage of our information hot line to get all your insurance questions answered.

Sincerely

Stanley J. Reinhart
Customer Service

TABLE 10

Paper: full sheet
Spacing: double
Proofguide: 27

NEW PRODUCT INTRODUCTION
American Home Products

Product	Brand Name	Date of Introduction
Air Freshener	Lemon Drop	January
Smoke Detector	House Guard	March
Slow Cooker	Kitchen Helper	March
Moisture Meter	Plant Magic	April
Kitchen Timer	3-2-1 Timer	August
Spice Rack	Sugar & Spice	October
Fireplace Tools	Fireside	October

REPORT 8

Paper: plain
Spacing: double
Line: 6 inches (60 pica/70 elite)
Proofguide: 27–28

RESEARCH ACTIVITIES OF AMERICAN HOME PRODUCTS ... 28
Samuel J. Sutton, Research Director ... 49

The purpose of this report is to provide information on three new ... 65
developments designed to provide both our customers and us with ... 77
information about our products. ... 84

TEST KITCHEN ... 88

Our test kitchen has been completely redesigned and enlarged. Our ... 102
new 500 square-foot facility contains the latest innovations in kitchen ... 117
appliances, lighting, and convenience. This kitchen will be used to test ... 132
new products and recipes. ... 137

HOT LINE ... 140

New toll-free telephone numbers have been established for use by ... 154
all customers who have questions about our products. The numbers ... 167
are: ... 168

Block-center the display lines.
(Review page 26 if necessary.)
Double-space before and triple-space after the display lines.

New York City: 555-1000 ... 184
Elsewhere: (800) 555-1000 ... 189

CONSUMER PANEL ... 193

For the first time American Products is using a consumer panel of 50 ... 208
typical homemakers to field-test all new products before they are of- ... 222
fered to the public. Each participant will keep accurate records of the ... 237
advantages and disadvantages of the product being tested, and ... 249
product modifications will be made when necessary. ... 259

LOGGING DOCUMENTS IN AND OUT

When you are assigned a job to type in the word processing center, your first step is to log in the job on your operator's log by writing in the date and time beside the job number. You should do this before gathering together your supplies, reading the format or input instructions, and inserting the paper into the machine, because all these functions take up part of the time devoted to the job.

FORMATTING DOCUMENTS

The major reason for installing the word processing center at Ambassador was to increase office efficiency. One of the ways in which this is achieved is through the use of standardized formats for frequently typed documents. This way the writers do not have to indicate a format for the work they send to the center, and the operators do not have to decide which style to use. Unless otherwise directed, always use the following formats for processing documents that come to the center.

Standard Letter Format. Use the block-style letter, open punctuation, and a 60-space line. The 60-space line is used for all letters—short, average, and long, and the date always begins on line 15.

Ambassador has found that it is more economical to make any needed copies of documents by photocopying rather than by carbon copies. Thus, unless you are instructed otherwise, do not make carbon copies of any documents. Assume that an administrative secretary will make the needed photocopies. For the copy notation, use the letters "pc" (photocopy) rather than "cc" (carbon copy).

Because the mail-distribution center at Ambassador presorts all outgoing mail by ZIP Code (thus qualifying for a lower postage rate), the standard format for envelopes is to type all lines in solid capitals with no punctuation whatever.

Standard Memorandum Format. All memorandums should be typed on a full sheet of plain paper, using a 60-space line, blocked paragraphs, and a 2-inch top margin. Any items to be included with the memos are attached to the memo itself, and the notation "Attachment" is used.

Standard Report Format. Some of the reports prepared in the Ambassador Word Processing Center are procedures manuals. Type the pages of procedures manuals single-spaced, using blocked paragraphs, a 70-space line, and 1-inch top and bottom margins.

A header line (which identifies the report section number, section title, and page number) is typed at the top of each page. Odd-numbered pages are numbered at the right on the header line, and even-numbered pages are numbered at the left. Triple-space after the header line and before major report headings. Major headings are underlined and are followed by a double space.

Begin enumerations at the left margin, with turnover lines indented 4 spaces. Double-space before and after each enumerated item, but single-space the lines within each enumerated item.

The final typed copy of these reports should be "camera-ready"; that is, the pages should be proofread very carefully and should contain no errors, smudges, or wrinkles, so that they can be sent directly to the reprographics department for duplication.

Standard Rough-Draft Format. Rough-draft copies are temporary copies; after they have been revised, they will be retyped in final form. Thus you should type rough drafts at a fast rate and correct any errors by the *backspace-strikeover method*—when you make an error, simply backspace and type over the incorrect letters with the correct letters. Of course, you would never do this on a final copy; but correcting the error this way saves time and lets the writer know that you have recognized the error and will correct it on the final copy.

Because errors corrected this way are not always legible, you should not use the backspace-strikeover method to correct errors in proper names and numbers—even on a rough draft. Such errors should be corrected by using the X or hyphen key to mark through the error and then typing the correct word or number.

Always double-space rough drafts and indent the paragraphs 5 spaces—even if the final copy is to be single-spaced with blocked paragraphs. Use the same line length as will be used for the final copy.

After typing a rough draft, proofread the document and correct any errors you overlooked by using standard proofreaders' marks.

STORING DOCUMENTS

Unless you are instructed otherwise, type your name, the job number, and the current date at the left margin on the first three lines of each document after you have proofread and corrected all errors. Then store these jobs, in numeric order, in a file folder labeled with your name, followed by "Work Completed."

LESSON 50

TEST 2: PROGRESS TEST ON PART 2

TEST 2-A
3-MINUTE TIMED WRITING

Line: 60 spaces
Spacing: double
Tab: 5
Paper: Workguide 87
Start: 6 lines from top

```
         1              2                3              4
You have now finished the first production sequence in      12
            5         6              7             8
your typing class and have learned how to organize and type  24
              9           10              11            12
the most typical kinds of letters, tables, and manuscripts.  36
         13              14            15              16
In the next part of the course you will refine your ability  48
         17            18              19            20
to produce typed jobs similar to those found in the office.  60
            21            22              23          24
However, first you will need to devote some of your time to  72
         25            26            27            28
increasing your stroking speed.  The next several pages are  84
              29          30
designed to help you do this.                                90
| 1 | 2 | 3 | 4 | 5 | 6 | 7 | 8 | 9 | 10 | 11 | 12
```

TEST 2-B
LETTER 15
MODIFIED-BLOCK STYLE

Paper: Workguide 89

(*Current date*) / Miss Angela Kirk / Assistant to the President / Military   19
Supply Corporation / Highway 83 / Lawton, OK 73501 / Dear Miss Kirk: 33

    Yes, we can supply your firm with recycled paper of the quality   46
needed for stationery to be used by your top corporate officers. Two   60
samples of this kind of paper are enclosed. Costs are comparable to   74
those of nonrecycled paper of the same quality.   84

    Each of these two grades of paper will hold ink from a ball-point   98
pen, fountain pen, or felt-tip marker without blotting. At the bottom of   113
the paper, you may choose to imprint either the recycling symbol or   127
a statement, in small type, about the use of recycled paper.   139

    You may expect a schedule of two months from the date you order   153
the stationery with your company logo and address to the date of the   167
actual delivery.   170

    Sincerely, / Troy Temple / Customer Service / (*Your initials*) / 2   188
Enclosures   190

176-E. PRACTICE: JUMP REACHES

15 ve veiled avert vector every velour even vendor over vested
16 ex expire sexes flexed vexed convex text reflex next expose
17 no noodle annoy normal tenor nosier snow notice anon notify
18 ce celery facet cellar voice census aces center iced cereal

19 Even a normal voice was extremely noisy over in the cellar.
| 1 | 2 | 3 | 4 | 5 | 6 | 7 | 8 | 9 | 10 | 11 | 12

POSTTEST. Repeat the Pretest and compare performance.

176-F. POSTTEST: VERTICAL REACHES

176-G. SKILL MEASUREMENT: 5-MINUTE TIMED WRITING

176-G. Spacing—double. Take two 5-minute timings. Between them, practice any words with which you had difficulty. Record your score.

20   Welcome to Ambassador Insurance Company. You might be 12
already somewhat familiar with the insurance field. If you 24
own a car, it is probably insured against theft and against 36
damage it may cause in an accident. You may have a medical 48
insurance policy that can help pay medical bills in case of 60
illness. Or maybe you own a life insurance policy. So you 72
already know some of the terms or jargon used in insurance. 84
Working at Ambassador should familiarize you with the kinds 96
of typing tasks that are typical in many insurance offices. 108
        The job assignment in this unit is to work in the word 120
processing center. The kind of jobs you will be completing 132
could be typed either on a regular typewriter or on a text— 144
editing typewriter. At Ambassador, one of your assignments 156
will be typing a form letter with variable information; an— 168
other will be typing a rough draft; a third will be merging 180
documents. Two of the most important skills needed in this 192
work, in addition to typing skill, are strong language arts 204
skills and the ability to follow instructions. Pay special 216
attention to these areas as you type the jobs in this unit. 228
Always take pride in the work you do.   235
| 1 | 2 | 3 | 4 | 5 | 6 | 7 | 8 | 9 | 10 | 11 | 12

177–181. INTEGRATED OFFICE PROJECT: AMBASSADOR INSURANCE COMPANY

Before you begin to do your assignments at Ambassador Insurance Company, sharpen your language arts skills in punctuation, capitalization, grammar, number expression, and abbreviations by completing Workguide pages 355–358. Then study carefully the page from the procedures manual for the Ambassador Word Processing Center on page 268 so that you will know how to type and submit the jobs that will be assigned to you. After you have done that, turn to Job 1 on page 269 and begin your first assignment.

MARKET-SHARE ANALYSIS
Lawn Mower Sales

Brand	Number	Percent
Yard King	118,500	19.3
Ellis	115,000	18.7
Handyman	114,500	18.6
Tashiro 100	111,000	18.0
Grass Eater	89,000	14.5
Taylor Electric	54,000	8.8
Pro Master	13,000	2.1

SPECIAL RESPONSIBILITIES OF THE SUPERVISOR   26

By Suzanne DuPont   38

In addition to routine responsibilities, supervisors have *two* special   54

duties regarding attendance and health problems.   64

ATTENDANCE PROBLEMS   69

Over a period of time, ~~these types of problems~~ *tardiness and absenteeism* can be *quite* costly to   84

the organization. Although some tardiness and absences are unavoidable,   99

studies have shown that the most common reason for them is a lack of   112

job satisfaction. ~~on the job~~   116

HEALTH PROBLEMS   120

Because supervisors are in close contact with *their* subordinates, many organi-   137

zations are now asking them to observe their workers for any signs of   151

alcoholism, *or drug abuse.*   157

Alcoholism. In the past, many firms discharged employees when it   175

was discovered that they had an alcohol problem. But today, many firms   189

have developed quite effective programs to treat alcohol-related illness.   204

Drug abuse. Because the symptoms of drug abuse may be less obvious   223

initially than those of alcohol abuse, it is a more difficult task for   237

the supervisor to detect drug abuse. Once the supervisor has evidence   251

that there is drug abuse, he *or she* generally refers the person to some one   266

who can provide the professional assistance needed.   276

Line: 60 spaces   Tab: 5
Spacing: single   Drills: 3X
Proofguide: 133–134
Workguide: 421–426
Tape: 55A and 56A

INTEGRATED OFFICE PROJECT: INSURANCE
LESSONS 176–181

GOALS FOR UNIT 29

1. Type at least 47 wam for 5 minutes with no more than 5 errors.
2. Apply the rules of punctuation, capitalization, number expression, and abbreviations in typing documents.
3. Use standardized formats for typing documents.
4. Type rough drafts, using the backspace-strikeover method of correcting errors.
5. Type a form letter for insertion of variable information.
6. Mark overlooked errors on rough drafts by using proofreaders' marks.
7. Follow directions.

176-A. WARMUP

S   1   Do they own those downtown firms that make maps of islands?
A   2   Victor Koufax squeezed the exquisite blue and gold jonquil.
N   3   We won the March 29 game by 106–98 in front of 34,725 fans.
   | 1 | 2 | 3 | 4 | 5 | 6 | 7 | 8 | 9 | 10 | 11 | 12

176-B. PRETEST: VERTICAL REACHES

PRETEST. **Take a 1-minute timing; compute speed and errors.**

4   A noisy blackbird flew back over my snow–filled valley 12
with enough straw to build a very large nest in that vacant 24
lot next to the garden. He next flew over the border of my 36
lawn and grabbed several hard seeds attached to the leaves. 48
   | 1 | 2 | 3 | 4 | 5 | 6 | 7 | 8 | 9 | 10 | 11 | 12

176-C. PRACTICE: UP REACHES

PRACTICE. **If you made no errors on the Pretest, type each line 3 times. If you made 1 error or more, type each group of 4 lines (as though it were a paragraph) 3 times; then type the sentence 3 times.**

5   aw awhile crawl awning straw lawful lawn brawny flaw seaway
6   se ceased based secure vases absent used wisely hose select
7   rd border hardy ardent horde ordain bird ordeal ward accord
8   ki kidnap skies kindly khaki kiting skin akimbo kilo napkin
9   The brawny kid ordered khaki trousers and a hard straw hat.
   | 1 | 2 | 3 | 4 | 5 | 6 | 7 | 8 | 9 | 10 | 11 | 12

176-D. PRACTICE: DOWN REACHES

10   ac accent black accept enact access ache acquit pace acumen
11   kn knight knelt knacks known knifed knew kneads knot knells
12   ab abused cable abduct labor ablaze tabs abound abut absurd
13   va vacant naval vacuum rival vagary oval valise vary valley
14   Her rival knew about a canvas valise in back of the tracks.
   | 1 | 2 | 3 | 4 | 5 | 6 | 7 | 8 | 9 | 10 | 11 | 12

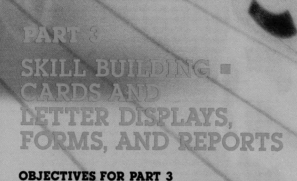

OBJECTIVES FOR PART 3

Part 3 is designed to enable you to demonstrate the following abilities when you take the test in Lesson 75:

1. Touch typing. To operate all keys, return and indent the carrier or carriage, position the carrier or carriage for the date line and closing lines of a letter, and tabulate the columns of an invoice by touch.

2. Technical Knowledge. To answer correctly at least 90 percent of the questions on an objective test covering the technical information presented in Part 3, including proofreaders' marks, footnote styles, and carbon copy notations.

3. Production. To format correctly from unarranged or rough-draft copy: (a) interoffice memorandums on plain paper and on printed forms, (b) postal cards and envelopes, (c) invoices with multiple columns and numbers, (d) a job application form and personal data sheet, and (e) one- and two-page reports with and without footnotes.

4. Skill Rate. To type at the following speed and accuracy levels by the end of each unit:

Unit	No. of Minutes	Minimum Speed	Maximum Errors
9	5	32	5
10	5	33	5
11	5	34	5
12	5	35	5

5. Word Processing Information. To understand how word processing equipment would function if used to format various production assignments.

PART 8

INTEGRATED OFFICE PROJECTS • INSURANCE, BANKING, TRAVEL, GOVERNMENT

OBJECTIVES FOR PART 8

Part 8 is designed to introduce you to the type of work you would encounter in an office situation. To complete the work satisfactorily, you should demonstrate the following abilities:

1. Production. Format business communications from unarranged, rough-draft, and simulated-dictation sources. Edit documents for spelling, grammar, punctuation, and typing style. Use reference sources, set priorities, follow directions, and compose letters.

2. Technical Knowledge. Answer correctly 95 percent of the questions on an objective test.

3. Skill Rate. Type at the following speed and accuracy levels:

Unit	No. of Minutes	Minimum Speed	Maximum Errors
29	5	47	5
30	5	48	5
31	5	49	5
32	5	50	5

4. Word Processing Information. Understand the various functions of word processing.

Line: 60 spaces   Tab: 5
Spacing: single   Drills: 3X
Proofguide: 29–30
Workguide: 3
Tape: 24A, 25A

LESSONS 51/52
SKILL DRIVE

Goals: To improve speed/accuracy; to center on a printed line.

51-A. WARMUP

S 1 When typing lines with easy words, try to boost your speed.
A 2 Jack gave the frozen box of quality shrimp to the servants.
N 3 Sue paid $346.50 for the 17 skirts, 29 tops, and 8 jackets.
| 1 | 2 | 3 | 4 | 5 | 6 | 7 | 8 | 9 | 10 | 11 | 12

51-B. PRETEST: VERTICAL REACHES

PRETEST. Take a 1-minute timing; compute speed and errors.

4   A judge and banker were united in making plans to help 12
an estate on matters of money. After scanning the records, 24
they drew up and developed plans for a unified credit base. 36
| 1 | 2 | 3 | 4 | 5 | 6 | 7 | 8 | 9 | 10 | 11 | 12

51-C. PRACTICE: UP REACHES

PRACTICE. If you made 2 or fewer errors on the Pretest, type each line (e.g., lines 5–9) 3 times for speed development. If you made 3 or more errors, type each group of 4 lines (e.g., lines 5–8), as though it were a paragraph, 3 times for accuracy improvement; then type the sentence (e.g., line 9) 3 times.

5 at attend batter attach battle matter elated that flat brat
6 dr dressy driven adroit drivel redraw dragon drag drop drip
7 es estate jester vessel lowest stress escape best test less
8 ju juices jungle injury junior unjust judged jump jute junk
9 The batter escaped injury when that bat was dropped on him.
| 1 | 2 | 3 | 4 | 5 | 6 | 7 | 8 | 9 | 10 | 11 | 12

51-D. PRACTICE: DOWN REACHES

10 ca catnip cavity scared decade locate carpet cake scan cafe
11 nk shrink anklet sinker unkind banker drinks pink honk inky
12 ba batter rebate bazaar embark barter urbane bane tuba baby
13 sc scales scarab escape screen school scrape scab scar scan
14 A pink carpet at a school bazaar was scanned by the banker.
| 1 | 2 | 3 | 4 | 5 | 6 | 7 | 8 | 9 | 10 | 11 | 12

51-E. PRACTICE: JUMP REACHES

15 cr secret cradle decree crater outcry crayon crab acre crew
16 on onward cotton yonder sonnet reason nylons only upon tone
17 ev evolve severe uneven evicts revive eleven even levy evil
18 ni nickel knight monies enigma ninety united nice unit knit
19 A united crew went secretly onward even through the outcry.
| 1 | 2 | 3 | 4 | 5 | 6 | 7 | 8 | 9 | 10 | 11 | 12

POSTTEST. Repeat the Pretest and compare performance.

51-F. POSTTEST: VERTICAL REACHES

TO: William Collins   5
                     Field Manager   9

FROM: Robert A. Hunter   15
                     Vice-President for Sales   21

DATE: February 20, 19--   28

SUBJECT: New Suncrest desk line   35

Copies of a letter that we recently received from the Suncrest   50
furniture company and my reply are enclosed. Please note that   62
Mr. Capello has been informed that you will contact him within   75
two weeks. Although Suncrest is a small company at the present,   86
there is a real possibility that sales from Suncrest could   97
sky rocket with the success of this new line of desks. Please   110
help us in determining an apropriate credit level for Suncrest   123
by sending us information in two areas.   131

Plant Capacity   136

Not only must we be concerned about the the physical facility   148
and machinery for assembly, It is equally important that an   162
assessment be made of the supply of both unskilled and skilled   173
labor available for such expansion.   180

Market Potential   186

Although I have a great deal of respect for Mr. Capello's   196
management skills, we must be assured that the percieved   208
market is in fact real. We shouldn't assume that an apro-   219
priate Feasibility Study has been conducted. It is essential   232
that we have access to all research data if we are to validate   244
the findings of their marketing consultants.   254

Please provide weekly reports on this important project.   266

kak   268
2 Enclosures   270

NOTE: If you are not sure of the position that a line of underscores will occupy or how far above it letters will print, type the alphabet and underscore it; then note the *exact* relation of the letters to the underscore and of the underscore to the aligning scale on your machine.

Remove the paper, reinsert it, and add five underscores to the line you originally typed.

51-G. CENTERING ON A PRINTED LINE

There are two steps to typing and centering something on a printed line:

STEP 1. Adjust the paper so that the line is in the position that a line of underscores would occupy. (See the note in the left margin.)

To adjust the paper slightly up or down, turn the platen with your right hand while your left hand presses the variable spacer in the left platen knob. To loosen the paper for adjustments, use the paper release.

The line is too high.

The line is too low.

The line is just right.

STEP 2. Determine how many spaces to indent the typing from the start of the

line: set the carrier or carriage at the start of the printed line, tap the space bar once for each space that the typed line will fill, and then (counting the strokes now) continue spacing to the end of the line to find out how many spaces remain to be divided around the name.

? Pepe Alonso ?

Pepe Alonso1234567

123Pepe Alonso1234

PRACTICE. Using a pen and ruler, draw ten straight lines varying from 3 to 4 inches long on a sheet of paper. Then insert the paper and center your full name on each line.

51-H. Type lines 20–27, correcting the one misspelled word in each line.

51-H. SPELLING SKILLS

20 The accommodations for an anniversary party were excellant.
21 The recent ocassion can be remembered with justified pride.
22 The individual received a blue receipt for the merchandize.
23 Managment has always been a very attractive career choice.

24 The similar procedure was quite familar to the individual.
25 Her acceptence speech was applauded by those in attendance.
26 A proprietor must secure a lisence to operate a restaurant.
27 Each performer had a seperate dressing room near the stage.

51-I. Clear your machine of all tabs. Then set five new tab stops every 10 spaces. Type lines 28–31, tabulating across from column to column.

51-I. TABULATOR PRACTICE

28 awake   check   elite   soggy   civic   vague
29 swish   color   extra   refer   sense   error
30 knock   month   puppy   youth   peach   usual
31 noble   ninth   local   joint   might   level

52-A. Repeat 51-A, page 77.

52-A. WARMUP

52-B. PRETEST: DISCRIMINATION PRACTICE

PRETEST. Take a 1-minute timing; compute speed and errors.

32   News of the brave deed traveled fast. I invite you to 12
join our flag and ribbon ceremony. Your family might enjoy 24
pondering this noble feat at a sunrise service at the lake. 36
    | 1 | 2 | 3 | 4 | 5 | 6 | 7 | 8 | 9 | 10 | 11 | 12

TEXAS HARDWOODS, INC.

24780 Pecan Creek Drive   Houston, TX 77043
Telephone: (713) 555-4625

February 20, 19--   4

Mr. Alfred S. Capello   12
Suncrest Furniture (Co.)   17
7160 Oakhurst Lane   21
Beaumont, *TX 77707*   25

Dear Mr. Capello   29

Subject: *New* Suncrest Desk Line   37

Your recent letter created a ~~lot~~ *great deal* of interest in the offices   51
here at Texas hardwoods. We agree that a new line of desks   63
for home use will be well recieved by consumers throughout *both maple and*   75
the region. We further agree that your plans to produce oak   90
models are indeed sound.   96

Our plant here in Houston has been designed to process wood   109
for distribution in ~~sheet~~ dimensions specified by you or in   121
part*ial*ly finished pieces ready for final finishing and assembly.   134
We shall be happy to help you make the choice most suitable   146
for you at a later date. A pamphlet that describes the two   158
options is enclosed for your review. ¶ As a preliminary step   171
toward achieving an early start-up date, Mr. William Collins,   183
our Field Manager in your district, will be contacting you   195
within two weeks. He has been with us for over fifteen years   208
and is particularly qualified to help you ~~finalize~~ your pro-   219
duction plans. We shall look forward to a long and mutually   232
profitable association with you. *complete*   238

Sincerely yours,   244

Robert A. Hunter   251
Vice-President for Sales   257

      259
kak   261
Enclosure   264
cc William Collins

PRACTICE. If you made 2 or fewer errors on the Pretest, type each line 3 times. If you made 2 or more errors, type each group of 4 lines (as though it were a paragraph) 3 times; then type the sentence 3 times.

NOTE: Discrimination drills help you to type correctly those keys which are most commonly confused. For example: V and B, W and E, K and L.

52-C. PRACTICE: LEFT HAND

33 vbv verb bevy brat very barn vibe brave bevel beaver behave
34 wew drew weak news wear sews weep sewer weave strewn weight
35 ded dead weed deed fade beds deep grade delve stated debate
36 fgf figs golf flag goof frog gulf feign gaffe finger gifted

37 A brave golfer debated whether to swerve from a deep grade.
    | 1 | 2 | 3 | 4 | 5 | 6 | 7 | 8 | 9 | 10 | 11 | 12

52-D. PRACTICE: RIGHT HAND

38 klk lack kill lake keel bilk kilt stalk skill locker pickle
39 uyu buoy your ugly yule buys busy young study eulogy unduly
40 pop open poem cope pole copy pool roped pound snoopy ponder
41 jhj high just hush jobs with ajar thing enjoy health unjust

42 The busy young man will enjoy his skills at a lake or pool.
    | 1 | 2 | 3 | 4 | 5 | 6 | 7 | 8 | 9 | 10 | 11 | 12

52-E. PRACTICE: BOTH HANDS

43 rur runt four rust your guru user round usurp cruise nature
44 bnb been numb barn snub burn band noble banks ribbon nibble
45 eie diet veil tier rein lieu wine feign grief chiefs reigns
46 ghg hang high hung sigh nigh gush thing might ghetto though

47 Most cruises might invite you to nibble and snub your diet.
    | 1 | 2 | 3 | 4 | 5 | 6 | 7 | 8 | 9 | 10 | 11 | 12

POSTTEST. Repeat the Pretest on page 78 and compare performance.

52-F. POSTTEST: DISCRIMINATION PRACTICE

52-G. Spacing—double. Compute your speed and count errors. Record your score.

52-G. SKILL MEASUREMENT: 5-MINUTE TIMED WRITING

48   Expert typists are like trained athletes. Both have a   12
skill obtained through plenty of practice and using correct   24
technique. They have refined their movements and thus have   36
no wasted motions. They can concentrate on their work with   48
ease because they are not tense. They also realize that it   60
is important to practice often, each day if possible. They   72
really do enjoy perfecting their skill.   80

        To be an expert typist, one must always use the proper   92
technique. It is important to sit with good posture. Feet   104
should be flat on floor, slightly apart for balance. While   116
typing, hold the fingers up and curved; keep the wrists low   128
but off the frame of the typewriter. Most valuable of all,   140
keep eyes on copy. If you do all of these things each time   152
you type, you can become an expert too.   160
    | 1 | 2 | 3 | 4 | 5 | 6 | 7 | 8 | 9 | 10 | 11 | 12

The General Information Test for Part 7 is on Workguide pages 411–412.

LESSON 175

TEST 7: PROGRESS TEST ON PART 7

TEST 7-A
5-MINUTE TIMED WRITING

Paper: Workguide 413
Line: 60 spaces
Spacing: double
Tab: 5
Start: line 9

```
          1                                    2
    More and more people are retiring at an earlier age as        12
         3                              4
a result of supplementary retirement programs that business       24
    5                          6                          7
firms and government agencies provide.  This is true at the       36
              8                          9
same time that their life expectancy continues to grow.  It       48
        10                          11                  12
is obvious then that the number of years in retirement will       60
                            13                        14
increase because of these two factors.  Many healthy people       72
              15                      16
find themselves at this juncture in their lives with plenty       84
     17                        18                          19
of free time and nothing to do.  As one approaches the time       96
                        20                          21
of retirement, it may be too late to acquire new interests,      108
            22                          23                  24
hobbies, and recreational skills.  All of us should analyze      120
                                25                    26
our activities and build new interests throughout our lives      132
                    27                      28
so that we are ready for retirement when the time comes.         143
          29                          30                      31
    My neighbor Ernie, a recent retiree, has acquired many       155
                        32                      33
diverse interests.  Although he enjoys reading and watching      167
              34                          35
sports spectaculars on television, he also plays tennis and      179
     36                          37                          38
sails his beautiful boat.  He doesn't stay indoors when the      191
                            39                      40
wintry weather comes.  He will often be found skiing either      203
              41                          42                      43
on the exciting slopes or the nearby trails.  All of us can      215
                            44                          45
take lessons from Ernie in planning for retirement.             225
| 1 | 2 | 3 | 4 | 5 | 6 | 7 | 8 | 9 | 10 | 11 | 12
```

TEST 7-B
TABLE 48

Open Table
Paper: Workguide 415
Spacing: double

PRODUCTION
SHIFT ∧ COMPARISONS
Quarter
(Last Half of 19--)

Month	Day Shift	Late Shift	Totals
Oct.	225	202	427
Nov.	218	199	417
Dec.	212	180	392
	~~218~~	~~199~~	~~417~~

Line: 60 spaces   Tab: 5
Spacing: single   Drills: 3X
Proofguide: 29–32
Workguide: 3
Tape: 26A, 27A

LESSONS 53/54

SKILL DRIVE

Goals: To improve speed/accuracy; to make typed insertions.

53-A. WARMUP

S 1 You may do your best work when you are happy with yourself.
A 2 The juniors who excelled did not find the quiz very taxing.
N 3 Order 10, 29, 38, 47, and 56 yards of the colored material.
| 1 | 2 | 3 | 4 | 5 | 6 | 7 | 8 | 9 | 10 | 11 | 12

53-B. PRETEST: HORIZONTAL REACHES

PRETEST. **Take a 1-minute timing; compute speed and errors.**

4   The artists and writers who enjoy the months of winter$_{12}$
employ their genius to dabble in things that will then help$_{24}$
their output and bring luster to achievements for the year.$_{36}$
| 1 | 2 | 3 | 4 | 5 | 6 | 7 | 8 | 9 | 10 | 11 | 12

53-C. PRACTICE: IN REACHES

PRACTICE. **If you made 2 or fewer errors on the Pretest, type each line 3 times. If you made 3 or more errors, type each group of 4 lines (as though it were a paragraph) 3 times; then type the sentence 3 times.**

5 ar artist bursar arctic tartar harder barter bear dark army
6 oy oyster employ voyage deploy coyote convoy buoy boys ahoy
7 pu punish spunky pupils output puddle spurge push spun purr
8 lu lumber allure luster glumly allude salute plus lung glue

9 Employers salute pupils and like to push for harder output.
| 1 | 2 | 3 | 4 | 5 | 6 | 7 | 8 | 9 | 10 | 11 | 12

53-D. PRACTICE: OUT REACHES

10 ge genius bigger grange nugget gender gauges huge gear aged
11 da dabble update dagger medals dainty sedate damp soda dash
12 hi hidden awhile hinder things hither behind high ship thin
13 ra rather hurrah strain camera rascal strand rate cram drag

14 The rascal hid the dainty nuggets behind the biggest crate.
| 1 | 2 | 3 | 4 | 5 | 6 | 7 | 8 | 9 | 10 | 11 | 12

53-E. PRACTICE: IN AND OUT REACHES

15 searching thread cannon forget update months legs whom bags
16 pamphlets patent zoning backed labels skates area nine year
17 employees larger adapts eating writer modest ours acts upon
18 lucrative images pulled babies learns winter dark twin baby

19 The employees were searching the area for larger pamphlets.
| 1 | 2 | 3 | 4 | 5 | 6 | 7 | 8 | 9 | 10 | 11 | 12

POSTTEST. **Repeat the Pretest and compare performance.**

53-F. POSTTEST: HORIZONTAL REACHES

Finish typing the pages for the correspondence manual.

REPORT 59
BOUND REPORT:
APPENDIX (10)
TABLE 47

Paper: plain, full sheet
Proofguide: 131–132

Start on line 13

APPENDIX A
↓3

PARTS OF THE BUSINESS LETTER
↓1

↓2

Standard Parts	Supplemental Parts ↓1 ↓2
1. Letter head	1. P(r)esonal or Notation *Confidential*
2. Date Line	2. Reference Line
3. Inside Address	3. Attention Line
4. Salutation	4. Subject Line
5. Body	5. Company Signature
6. Complimentary Closing	6. Enclosure Notation
7. Writer's Identification	7. Mailing Notation
8. Reference Initials	8. Carbon Copy notation
	9. Post script

↓1

REPORT 60
BOUND REPORT:
TABLE OF
CONTENTS

Paper: plain, full sheet
Line: 6 inches (60 pica/70 elite)
Proofguide: 131–132

Prepare a table of contents, similar to the one shown below, for the correspondence manual you typed in Unit 28.

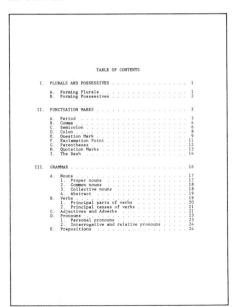

REPORT 61
BOUND REPORT:
TITLE PAGE

Paper: plain, full sheet
Proofguide: 133–134

Prepare a title page for your correspondence manual that is similar to the one shown below.

REPORT 62
BOUND REPORT:
BIBLIOGRAPHY
(11)

Paper: plain, full sheet
Line: 6 inches (60 pica/70 elite)
Proofguide: 133–134

Prepare a bibliography for your correspondence manual that is similar to the one shown below.

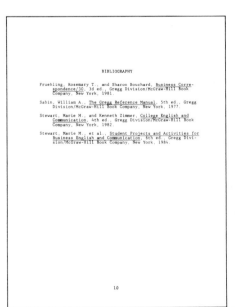

53-G. TYPED INSERTIONS

The aligning scale on your typewriter is used regularly when you type corrections and when you type on printed business forms and cards. Type the alphabet on your machine, and compare your typing and the aligning scale for two things:

① → abcdefghijklmnopqr
②

1. To align insertions vertically, you must know exactly how much space (if any) there is between the typing and the aligning scale.

2. To align insertions horizontally, you must know exactly how nearly the markers on the scale come to the center of the letters (easiest to check are i, l, m, I, T, period, and colon).

PRACTICE 1. Type this name (with space left for the omitted letters) in five places on a sheet of paper:

Ms. V rg n a H. W ll amson

Remove the paper, reinsert it, and fill in the missing letters:

☒ Ms. V^{i}rg$_i$n$_i$a H. W$_i$lliamson
☑ Ms. Virginia H. Williamson

Use the variable spacer (in the left cylinder knob) for vertical adjustments of the paper. Use the paper release for horizontal adjustments.

PRACTICE 2. Type *TO:* and *FROM:* in four different places on the paper. Remove the paper, reinsert and align it, and then type your name 2 or 3 spaces after each of the colons.

53-H. SPELLING SKILLS

20 Accurecy in typewriting can bring you additional dividends.
21 Their school calender has numerous activities for the week.
22 It was apparant that a number of students failed that test.
23 A great many individuals would catagorize you as a liberal.

24 There income tax return had major allowances for liability.
25 Personnel in their sales department were greatful for help.
26 The definate decision was endorsed by the entire committee.
27 A practical solution to the personel problems was reached.

53-I. SHIFT LOCK PRACTICE

28 NY, NJ, PA, and DE are known as the MIDDLE ATLANTIC STATES.
29 The new company, BENTLEY STEEL, is located in ANDERSON, IN.
30 MS. ANGELA GOMEZ, 1516 KENNEDY BOULEVARD, won the election.
31 MANAGEMENT INFORMATION SYSTEMS--MIS--is our new department.

54-A. WARMUP

54-B. PRETEST: COMMON LETTER COMBINATIONS

32   It is hard to find a single person who will forget the 12
elation of trying to compete carefully in some event. Most 24
likely, a constant search for a brand new event is evident. 36
 | 1 | 2 | 3 | 4 | 5 | 6 | 7 | 8 | 9 | 10 | 11 | 12

| Line: 60 spaces   Tab: 5 |
| Spacing: single   Drills: 3X |
| Proofguide: 131–134 |
| Workguide: 331–332 |
| Tape: 54A |

LESSONS 173/174
FORMAL REPORT (Continued)

Goal: To complete the correspondence manual.

173-A. WARMUP

S   1   The six of them may cut half of the corn in that big field.
A   2   Frederick creatively equipped a jalopy with dazzling speed.
N   3   The 45 teachers and 761 students arrived at 8:30 on May 29.

| 1 | 2 | 3 | 4 | 5 | 6 | 7 | 8 | 9 | 10 | 11 | 12

173-B. SKILL DRILL: INFREQUENT LETTER PRACTICE

Y   4   Twenty youths eagerly awaited many sunny days of this type.
   5   Rory may try to fly to Yonkers if they buy the shiny plane.
Z   6   A dozen puzzled zebras were seized by a dozen dizzy guards.
   7   Zeke was amazed at the huge size of the dozen crazy prizes.

| 1 | 2 | 3 | 4 | 5 | 6 | 7 | 8 | 9 | 10 | 11 | 12

173-C. SKILL MEASUREMENT: 5-MINUTE TIMED WRITING

173-C. **Spacing—double. Take two 5-minute timings. Between them, practice any words with which you had difficulty. Record your score.**

8   Although I like the feel of money in my purse, it will   12
be a happy day for me when our society no longer uses money   24
for financial transactions. I was totally embarrassed last   36
week at a fast-food restaurant when my personal check and a   48
credit card were both refused. With only fifty cents in my   60
wallet, my face turned red as I mumbled an apology and left   72
empty-handed. After this experience, I will adjust quickly   84
to a society in which all money equivalents are transferred   96
electronically. I do realize, however, that hard cold cash   108
will quite likely be used for many years to come.   118
     Most people are amazed at how extensive the electronic   130
transfer of funds has become. The dollar amount of my pay—   142
check has been automatically deposited to my account at the   154
bank for about twenty years. The amounts of my car payment   166
and house payment have been paper transfers at the bank for   178
the last ten years. All of my utility bills are handled in   190
the same way. More and more retail payments are handled in   202
this way. There can be little doubt that almost all of our   214
payments will be made in this manner in the years ahead.   225

| 1 | 2 | 3 | 4 | 5 | 6 | 7 | 8 | 9 | 10 | 11 | 12

PRACTICE. If you made 2 or fewer errors on the Pretest, type each line 3 times. If you made 3 or more errors, type each group of 4 lines (as though it were a paragraph) 3 times; then type the sentence 3 times.

54-C. PRACTICE: WORD BEGINNINGS

33 for fort forth forget formal format forgive forlorn forgery
34 con cone conch confer convey convoy convert convene connote
35 per pert perch person peruse permit perfect perfume persist
36 com come comma commit common compel compact compile compete

37 Persons who forget to forgive often convey common concerns.
| 1 | 2 | 3 | 4 | 5 | 6 | 7 | 8 | 9 | 10 | 11 | 12

54-D. PRACTICE: WORD ENDINGS

38 ing seeing saying trying flying earning ringing combing ing
39 ion nation ration action motion elation fashion portion ion
40 ble double enable stable foible payable taxable visible ble
41 ful useful sinful artful lawful careful helpful fearful ful

42 Careful nations are saying their actions should be visible.
| 1 | 2 | 3 | 4 | 5 | 6 | 7 | 8 | 9 | 10 | 11 | 12

54-E. PRACTICE: OTHER COMBINATIONS

43 gl gladly tangle glance single bangle glider glib ogle glue
44 er errand ponder butter errant bakery series ergo mere pier
45 ea search easily bearer appear earthy cereal each seat east
46 br abroad bridge debris brazen abrupt branch brew brat bran

47 A search for the girls included a brief glance in a bakery.
| 1 | 2 | 3 | 4 | 5 | 6 | 7 | 8 | 9 | 10 | 11 | 12

POSTTEST. Repeat the Pretest on page 81 and compare performance.

54-F. POSTTEST: COMMON LETTER COMBINATIONS

54-G. Spacing—double. Record your score.

54-G. SKILL MEASUREMENT: 5-MINUTE TIMED WRITING

48   Everyone should learn how to type. It is a skill that 12
will be useful throughout life. Even if you do not type to 24
earn money, your skill will make life easier. For your own 36
use, being able to type will save time and effort. It will 48
also produce cleaner copy. Thus you should always think of 60
typing rather than writing. You will find it to be faster. 72
    There are many uses for personal typing. For example, 84
you may type letters to friends and people in business. It 96
will make all your words legible. You may type term papers 108
for school. Studies say that higher grades are acquired by 120
students who type papers. You might type your resume along 132
with a letter of application. It might get you a good job. 144
Your personal skill might even be a good stepping-stone for 156
zeroing in on a job. 160
| 1 | 2 | 3 | 4 | 5 | 6 | 7 | 8 | 9 | 10 | 11 | 12

Typing "Enclosure" or "Enclosures (4)" is adequate in most situations, but (it's) important to identify enclosures if any are small, if any are valuable (as a check would be), or if someone other than the typist will (mail and seal) the letter. The enclosure notation is omitted only from letters in formal arrangement (inside address below the letter body).

7. The Mailing notation specifies special handling that the letter should receive, if any. This notation should be typed a double space below the date or one line below the reference initials and any enclosure notation.
↓4

Table 4

Mailing Notations

RPG/kl	kl	S. Kline/ms
Enclosure	Certified	By Messenger
Registered	cc Mrs. Brown	cc: W. Jones
Special Delivery	Dr. Alan	M. Loren

↓4

8. The Carbon Copy Notation lets the addressee know that copies were sent to the persons listed. This notation is typed below the enclosure or mialing notation. The two most commonly used arrangements are shown in Table 4.

REMINDER: The bcc notation may also be typed on line 7 at the left margin.

A "blind carbon copy" notation indicates to whom copies are sent without the receiver's knowledge. The "bcc" notation is typed on the blind carbon copy and on the file copy a line below the reference lines at the bottom of the page.

9. The Postscript is used to highlight a particular thought or as an after thought of the writer's. It is typed as a separate paragraph at the bottom of the letter. The letters PS: or PS. (followed by 2 spaces) usually begin the paragraph. It follows the same style as other paragraphs in the letter--either blocked or indented.

Line: 60 spaces   Tab: 5
Spacing: single   Drills: 3X
Proofguide: 31–32
Workguide: 3
Tape: 28A, 29A

LESSONS 55/56
SKILL DRIVE

Goals: To improve speed/ accuracy; to spread and squeeze letters.

55-A. WARMUP

S 1   Just think about what you are doing, and you get more done.
A 2   Chocolate flavored pie is amazingly unique and costs extra.
N 3   Flight 947 left Rome at 10:58 a.m. and was due at 3:26 p.m.
   | 1 | 2 | 3 | 4 | 5 | 6 | 7 | 8 | 9 | 10 | 11 | 12

55-B. PRETEST: CLOSE REACHES

PRETEST. Take a 1-minute timing; compute speed and errors.

4   Many voices joined in agreeing to a travel policy. It 12
was a stormy noon-hour session which made no provisions for 24
possible problems, such as visas, air safety, or insurance. 36
   | 1 | 2 | 3 | 4 | 5 | 6 | 7 | 8 | 9 | 10 | 11 | 12

55-C. PRACTICE: ADJACENT KEYS

PRACTICE. If you made 2 or fewer errors on the Pretest, type each line 3 times. If you made 3 or more errors, type each group of 4 lines (as though it were a paragraph) 3 times; then type the sentence 3 times.

5   tr trader stride trance poetry travel stripe tray trap trot
6   sa satire bursar saddle unsafe safety salads salt visa saga
7   po police sports policy oppose potion tripod pole spot hypo
8   oi boiler joined choice spoils voices foiled boil oily soil

9   The police joined a safety travel campaign by their choice.
   | 1 | 2 | 3 | 4 | 5 | 6 | 7 | 8 | 9 | 10 | 11 | 12

55-D. PRACTICE: CONSECUTIVE STROKES

10 ft caftan gifted soften lofted bereft rafter left lift sift
11 my myriad stormy mystic myself myopic myrtle myth army limy
12 ny nylons anyone brainy anyhow brawny anyway bony many onyx
13 lo locate allows sloven lotion slouch lounge look solo slow

14 We looked as many rafters were lifted at a stormy location.
   | 1 | 2 | 3 | 4 | 5 | 6 | 7 | 8 | 9 | 10 | 11 | 12

55-E. PRACTICE: DOUBLE LETTERS

15 ee keeper agreed sleepy greedy deeply speedy coffee decrees
16 ll teller refill billet allied taller pulley billed dollars
17 nn annoys dinner cannot runner tunnel tennis annual connect
18 pp happen puppet uppers apples pepper zipper supper support

19 A taller teen agreed to a speedy dinner or supper at night.
   | 1 | 2 | 3 | 4 | 5 | 6 | 7 | 8 | 9 | 10 | 11 | 12

POSTTEST. Repeat the Pretest and compare performance.

55-F. POSTTEST: CLOSE REACHES

Footnote 6. Compose a footnote using the same source given in footnote 5, but cite page 97.

Quotations that take more than three typed lines are displayed using single spacing and are indented 5 spaces from each margin.

Footnote 7. Make and insert a footnote citing page 252 of the book by Sabin, previously mentioned (see page 253).

REPORT 56
BOUND REPORT (7)
TABLE 45

Proofguide: 131–132

Footnote 8. Make and insert a footnote citing page 97 of the book by Lloyd, previously mentioned (see page 254).

Ellipses. Three periods separated by spaces, called an *ellipsis* (plural: *ellipses*), indicate an omission. If the omission is at the end of a sentence, four periods are used instead of three.

3. The Attention Line is included when a letter is addressed to a company rather than an individual to indicate which dept. or person might best handle it. The attention line is located between the inside address and salutation[6] and is generally blocked at the left. However:

> When an attention line is used . . . , the letter is considered to be addressed to the organization rather than to the person named in the attention line. . . . Whenever possible, omit the attention line and address the letter directly to an individual. . . .[7]

"Gentlemen" is commonly used as a salutation. However, "Ladies" and "Ladies and Gentlemen" are becoming popular.

4. The Subject Line is located between the salutation and the body. It is generally blocked at the left margin and is typed in capital and lowercase letters. It is usually preceded by "Subject" or by "Re" or "In Re."

5. The Company Signature is normally used to indicate that the obligation set forth in the letter is that of the company rather than the writer. It may, however, be used to stretch a letter. The name of the company "is typed in all caps a double space below . . . the complimentary closing"[8] and is started at the same point.

6. THE Enclosure Notation is a reminder to both the sender and the receiver of a letter that something is enclosed in the envelope. Notations like those in Table 3 are typed one line below the reference initials.

Table 3

SOME CORRECT FORMS OF ENCLOSURE NOTATIONS

One Enclosure	MORE than one	Enumerated
Enclosure	3 Enclosures	Enclosures:
Enc.	3 Enc.	Bill
1 Enc.	Enc. 3	Check
1 Enclosure	Enclosures (3)	Enclosures:
Invoice Enclosed	Enclosures: 3	1. Invoice
Check Enclosed	Enclosures--3	2. Check

(Continued on next page.)

55-G. SPREADING AND SQUEEZING LETTERS

Spreading and squeezing letters are techniques that are used to make corrections in typewritten work. These techniques are used when a correction requires more space or less space.

SPREADING. To make a correction fill an extra space, move the word a half space to the right, leaving a space and a half before and after it. The best way to do this is determined by the machine you are using: (1) If you have an electric machine with a half-space key or lever, engage the half-space mechanism and type the word. (2) If the machine does not have a half-space mechanism, move the carrier or carriage by hand about a half space.

PRACTICE. Type line 20 as it is. Then remove the word *that* and replace it with the word *the*. Type line 21 as it is. Then remove the word *might* and replace it with the word *will*.

20 By learning how to spread, you will save that page of type.

21 He might go to the restaurant with his friends from school.

SQUEEZING. If an extra letter must be inserted, move the word a half space to the left, leaving a half space before and after it. The same steps discussed above should be followed.

PRACTICE. Type line 22 as it is. Then remove the word *can* and replace it with the word *will*. Type line 23 as it is. Then remove the word *will* and replace it with the word *might*.

22 Squeezing letters takes practice, but it can pay dividends.

23 You will enjoy the opportunity to visit the financial area.

55-H. SPELLING SKILLS

55-H. Change your margins to a 50-space line. Then type the paragraph, selecting the correctly spelled words. All lines end evenly.

24 The members of the (maintenance/maintainance) department of our company will prepare a new (proceedure/procedure) which is to (receive/recieve) consideration by top management before it is (reccomended/recommended) for adoption. The intent is to (acommodate/accommodate) those customers who have not received the (opportunity/oppertunity) to register their complaints.

55-I. CARRIER/CARRIAGE RETURN DRILL

55-I. The opening lines of a letter require the quick operation of the carrier/carriage return. Type the opening lines of the letter in 55-I using the proper carrier/carriage return technique.

(*Current date*) ↓ 5

Mr. Charles Hamilton
2132 North Maple Avenue
San Antonio, TX 78208 ↓ 2

Dear Mr. Hamilton:

56-A. Repeat 55-A, page 83.

56-A. WARMUP

56-B. PRETEST: ALTERNATE- AND ONE-HAND REACHES

PRETEST. Take a 1-minute timing; compute speed and errors.

25 The world must initiate action to have debates on many 12
social issues for the benefit of humanity. Maximum efforts 24
must be made to help all people attain their minimum goals. 36

| 1 | 2 | 3 | 4 | 5 | 6 | 7 | 8 | 9 | 10 | 11 | 12

Continue typing the pages for the correspondence manual.

REPORT 54 (Cont.)
TABLE 44

TECHNICAL NOTES
1. Lines of underscores are often used to divide long tables and displays.
2. For equal space above and below a line, single-space before typing the line and double-space after it.
3. To save space, leave only 2 blank lines in each signature space.

Table 3

APPOPRIATE ARRANGEMENTS FOR CLOSING LINES

Sincerely yours,	Yours very truly,
Manager	Vice President, Sales
Sincerely,	Cordially yours,
Kay River, Director	Secretary to Dr. Grey
Cordially,	Very Truly yours,
THE CASE CORPORATION	WILLIAM SUN CORP.
Mrs. Patricia Case President	William D. Ollila Controller
Yours Truly,	Very cordially yours,
INTERNATIONAL PRINTING, INC.	A C E , I N C .
Donald Snowdon Chairperson	Ms. Rita Pearce Conelly Director, Research Center

REPORT 55
BOUND REPORT (6)

Proofguide: 129–130

B. THE SUPPLEMENTAL LETTER PARTS

Through the years business writers have added many extra parts to the letter as an aid to the reader and/or the writer. These are "supplements" and are not essential in relaying the message to the recepient. A list of these nine additional parts appears in Appendix A.

1. The Personal or Confidential Notation is typed on the second line below the date at the left margin if the letter is of this nature. It is usually typed in all-capital letters.

2. The Reference Line is included in the letterhead of those businesses that keep their records in numeric files. "When Replying, Refer To" is printed; the typist inserts the correct file number. The reply to this letter should include the file number in its subject line.

(Continued on next page.)

PRACTICE. If you made 2 or fewer errors on the Pretest, type each line 3 times. If you made 3 or more errors, type each group of 4 lines (as though it were a paragraph) 3 times; then type the sentence 3 times.

56-C. PRACTICE: ALTERNATE HANDS

26 chap lapel town mantle burnt girl penalty spend bushel also
27 firm world paid emblem fuels buck visible cubic formal corn
28 with amend fuel eighty angle lake problem laugh social down
29 male blend tidy enrich flaps goal auditor rigid profit such

30 The chap had such problems with the eighty bushels of corn!
| 1 | 2 | 3 | 4 | 5 | 6 | 7 | 8 | 9 | 10 | 11 | 12

56-D. PRACTICE: ONE HAND

31 effected homonym acreage nippy eraser hook draws joy debate
32 asserted dessert drafted pupil regret milk great ink facade
33 reserves minimum greeted junky safest pull fewer ump rebate
34 beverage pumpkin catered knoll adverb mink craft oil better

35 Look at the effects of debates on minimum acreage reserves.
| 1 | 2 | 3 | 4 | 5 | 6 | 7 | 8 | 9 | 10 | 11 | 12

56-E. PRACTICE: BOTH HANDS

36 deeply numbers section hundred federally imported affection
37 region mileage cartoon limited certainly immodest carefully
38 evenly pioneer develop kindest afternoon populate detection
39 ounces readily illness destiny kilowatts reaction minimized

40 There were fifteen military houses with attached sun decks.
| 1 | 2 | 3 | 4 | 5 | 6 | 7 | 8 | 9 | 10 | 11 | 12

POSTTEST. Repeat the Pretest on page 84 and compare performance.

56-F. POSTTEST: ALTERNATE- AND ONE-HAND REACHES

56-G. Spacing—double. Record your score.

56-G. SKILL MEASUREMENT: 5-MINUTE TIMED WRITING

41   Americans have been known for their mobility. Figures 12
can be found that would show millions of people changing an 24
address each year. Many of these changes are prompted by a 36
search for a better life and income. Historically, one can 48
observe the moves from the farms to the cities and from the 60
cities to the suburbs. Analyzing the current happenings, a 72
large trend of moving to the South and West would be noted. 84
      Whether such mobility will continue to occur as we use 96
up our space and resources is open to question. Certainly, 108
it can be expected that people will always search for jobs. 120
When seeking a job, it is important to have specific skills 132
and talents. The ability to type is such a skill. Typists 144
are quite mobile. Every paper in the country has many jobs 156
listed for typists. 160
| 1 | 2 | 3 | 4 | 5 | 6 | 7 | 8 | 9 | 10 | 11 | 12

LESSONS 171/172
FORMAL REPORT (Continued)

Goal: To format additional
pages of a formal report.

171-A. WARMUP

S 1 The big chap paid a visit to the city when he got the auto.
A 2 Jacqueline might keep the expensive zippers for future use.
N 3 She planned to return 12 items on invoice #5790 for $4,836.
      | 1 | 2 | 3 | 4 | 5 | 6 | 7 | 8 | 9 | 10 | 11 | 12

171-B. SKILL DRILL: INFREQUENT LETTER PRACTICE

Q 4 I quickly acquired an eloquent quartet for the quiet queen.
   5 She quickly qualified for equal quarterly quotas of quills.
X 6 Dexter expects extra excise taxes in excess of six percent.
   7 Lex expects those extra deluxe taxis in exactly six months.
      | 1 | 2 | 3 | 4 | 5 | 6 | 7 | 8 | 9 | 10 | 11 | 12

171-C. SKILL MEASUREMENT: 5-MINUTE TIMED WRITING

171-C. **Spacing—double.
Take two 5-minute timings.
Between them, practice any
words with which you had
difficulty. Record your score.**

8   A friend who teaches at a university recently informed   12
me that he was amazed at the differences in age between his   24
students today and his students twenty-four years ago, when   36
he began teaching college typing. With few exceptions, the   48
students in those days were between eighteen and twenty-two   60
years old. Since it was customary in those days to carry a   72
full load of credits, almost all the students who completed   84
college did so in four years. I asked my friend if he knew   96
how many acquire degrees in four years today. He said that   108
although the number varied from one institution to another,   120
only a slight majority did at his university.   129
         These changes have not resulted from the enrollment of 141
students at a younger age. Rather, it is not unusual today   153
for a young person to attend college as a full-time student   165
for a year or two, secure employment, and then come back to   177
the campus as a part-time student. Also, we see more older   189
adults returning as both day and evening students. Profes-   201
sors all over the country believe that this blend of people   213
has resulted in classroom discussions that are more lively.   225
      | 1 | 2 | 3 | 4 | 5 | 6 | 7 | 8 | 9 | 10 | 11 | 12

<table>
<tr><td>Line: 60 spaces</td><td>Tab: 5, 10</td></tr>
<tr><td>Spacing: single</td><td>Drills: 2X</td></tr>
<tr><td>Proofguide: 33–34</td><td></td></tr>
<tr><td>Workguide: 3–4, 95–97</td><td></td></tr>
<tr><td>Tape: 30A</td><td></td></tr>
</table>

LESSONS 57/58
MEMORANDUMS

Goal: To format memorandums on plain paper and letterhead stationery.

57-A.   WARMUP

S 1 The key to the problem with both their maps is their shape.
A 2 Six of the women quietly gave the prizes back to the judge.
N 3 Bill got tickets 10, 29, 38, 47, and 56 for tonight's show.
   | 1 | 2 | 3 | 4 | 5 | 6 | 7 | 8 | 9 | 10 | 11 | 12

57-B.   NUMBER PRACTICE

In these *We-23* drills, each number uses the same reaches as the preceding word.

4 we 23 it 85 ore 943 the 563 top 590 yet 635 out 975 two 529
5 et 35 or 94 tie 483 you 697 yet 635 pup 070 rip 480 tip 580
6 up 70 to 59 rot 495 pie 083 owe 923 wit 285 pet 035 wet 235
7 re 43 ie 83 toy 596 pot 095 owl 929 pit 085 yet 635 put 075

57-C. Spacing—double. Record your score.

57-C.   SKILL MEASUREMENT: 5-MINUTE TIMED WRITING

8   A memo is a message sent from one person to another in 12
the same firm; it is an internal letter that does not go to 24
someone outside the firm. Its purpose is to give or to ask 36
for information, just as in a business letter. Because the 48
memos stay within the firm, they do not have to be quite as 60
formal as a letter. They are typed on plain paper, on let— 72
terhead stationery, or on special forms which are set up so 84
that the typist will just zoom along while typing the memo. 96
    Research shows that there is increased use of memos in 108
offices today. With more people working in business now, a 120
need for more data is to be expected. Some memos are writ— 132
ten so as to have a written record of what has happened for 144
future use. For memos to achieve their purpose, the writer 156
must word the message clearly and concisely. 165
   | 1 | 2 | 3 | 4 | 5 | 6 | 7 | 8 | 9 | 10 | 11 | 12

57/58-D.   FORMATTING AN INTEROFFICE MEMORANDUM

An interoffice memorandum is a message from one person to another in the same organization. It may be typed on a special memorandum form, on plain paper, or on letterhead stationery, using either a half sheet or a full sheet of paper. Follow these steps in typing a memorandum on either plain paper or letterhead stationery:

1. Begin typing the heading on line 7 on half sheets of paper and on line 13 on full sheets of paper.

2. Use a 5-inch line (50 pica/60 elite).

3. Set a 10-space tab to align the heading information.

4. Leave 2 blank lines between the heading and the body of the memorandum.

5. Include your reference initials. The writer's initials are optional.

In a display such as the one at the right, center the longest line and align the others with it.

FOOTNOTE ABBREVIATIONS (Cont.)
3. *Ibid.* means "same as the immediately preceding footnote"; if followed by a page number, it means "same book as in the immediately preceding footnote but on a different page, which is . . ."
NOTE: Some books use *loc. cit.* instead of (or interchangeably with) *ibid.* Some books also distinguish between *ibid.* and *loc. cit.,* using *ibid.* only for "same book but different page."

All the Latin footnote abbreviations mentioned on pages 254 and 255 have become so common that, like *etc.,* they are not underscored.

TECHNICAL NOTE
Short footnotes may be typed beside or below one another, whichever is better for the bottom margin on that page.

CAUTION: You must determine where to end page 4 and all succeeding pages.

REPORT 54
BOUND REPORT (5)

Proofguide: 129–130

Ms. Stacey Walker, Manager
Vacationland Resort

Mr. R. Jonathon Richardson
Secretary, Bay Yacht Club

Dr. Lee Wong
Executive Director

4. The Salutation is typed a double space below the inside address. It begins at the left margin and is usually followed by a colon. Only the first word, any title, and any noun are capitalized (*Dear Ms. Creighton* or *My dear Ms. Creighton*).

5. The Body begins a double space below the salutation. It contains the message, which is usually single-spaced with 1 blank line between paragraphs. However, if the letter is very short (50 or fewer words), it may be double-spaced.

6. The Complimentary Closing is the closing phrase of the letter. It begins at the center or the left margin depending on the letter style. Only the first word is capitalized, and the phrase usually is followed by a comma.

7. The Writer's Identification is typed under the blank lines that are provided for the handwritten signature. Illustrations of several arrangements appear in Table 2 on the next page.

Three blank lines are normally left for the signature, but some variation is allowed: the space may be "as few as 2 blank lines"[4] or "up to 6 blank lines,"[5] depending on the length of the letter.

8. The Reference Initials are those of the typist and may be preceded by (1) the dictator's initials if his or her name is not typed under the signature or (2) the dictator's full name if the dictator prefers this style. The most popular forms are *TYP* and *typ* or, if both sets are used, *DIC:TYP* and *DIC/typ.*

---

4. Lloyd, op. cit., p. 57.   5. Ibid.

(Continued on page 257.)

MEMO 1

Paper: plain, half sheet
Line: 50 pica/60 elite
Tab: 10
Proofguide: 33–34

↓7

TO: Maria Rodriguez, Word Processing Center ↓2

FROM: Robert Schleicher, Manager ↓2

DATE: January 4, 19-- ↓2

SUBJECT: Meeting on Affirmative Action ↓3

This will confirm our telephone conversation earlier this morning, in which I indicated that I would like to meet with all managers in our Administrative Support Division concerning progress we have made on our Affirmative Action Program. ↓2

The meeting will begin at 10 a.m. on January 14 and will be held in the conference room on the seventh floor. Please bring with you data on your new hires since July 1 of last year. ↓2

mbe

MEMO 2

Paper: Workguide 95
Line: 50 pica/60 elite
Tab: 10
Proofguide: 33–34

WP Word processors can be programmed to provide whatever top margin you may frequently or consistently require.

RECREATION ASSOCIATES
919 MARKET STREET
PHILADELPHIA, PA 19107
(215) 555-3445

↓13

TO: Robert F. Earle, Vice President ↓2

FROM: Robert Schleicher, Manager ↓2

DATE: January 16, 19-- ↓2

SUBJECT: Affirmative Action ↓3

Our goals and accomplishments regarding Affirmative Action for the past year were reviewed at a meeting on January 14, and the results are impressive. ↓2

We began the year with 136 employees. During the year, 16 workers left the company. We replaced those 16 people and hired 6 more. Of the 22 new employees, 14 were female and 8 were male; 13 were from various ethnic and minority groups. ↓2

The remainder of the meeting dealt with our new procedures and the objectives for this year. ↓2

mbe

1. The Letterhead consists of the company's name, address, and perhaps a telephone number. A letterhead can range anywhere from 6 lines to 18 lines deep, but most are about 9 or 10 lines. When a letterhead is more than 12 lines deep, the date should be typed 3 lines below the bottom of the letterhead.[2]

2. The Date Line includes the month, day, and year that the letter is typed. Never abbreviate the month in a business letter. A comma separates the day and year:

May 24, 1985

The armed forces and some government bureaus use the "military style," with the day before the month:

24 May 1985

Many persons who have served in the military or who have much European correspondence prefer this arrangement.

3. The Inside Address contains the name and address of the addressee. It is usually above the body of the letter, but in social-business letters and in formal letters to high officials and dignitaries it may be typed at the bottom of the letter, below the typewritten signature.[3]

Often the business title of an individual is included in addition to the name. This title may be placed after the name, at the beginning of the next line, or on a line by itself. The line length of the inside address determines the position of the title. Keep these lines as nearly equal as possible.

---

2. Alan C. Lloyd et al., *Gregg College Typing, Series Four,* Gregg Division, McGraw-Hill Book Company, New York, 1979, p. 262.

3. Sabin, op. cit., p. 268.

(Continued on next page.)

MEMO 3

Paper: plain
Half sheet
Proofguide: 33–34

TO: Ray Ling, International Operations / FROM: Charlotte McMullen,   16
Manager / Development for European Market / DATE: March 14, 19— /   31
SUBJECT: Potential for European Plant   40

    I have compiled the data you requested concerning a possible plant   56
site for our European market. The sites under consideration are in   70
London, Madrid, Munich, Paris, and Rome. I compiled most of this   83
information on a trip to these five cities during the month of February.   98

    As we agreed in our telephone conversation earlier this morning, I   112
will send you a comprehensive report on my findings in the next few   126
days, and we will then meet to discuss the report on April 2. / (*Your*   138
initials)   140

MEMO 4

Paper: Workguide 97
Proofguide: 33–34

WP Word processors have a rapid form-fill-in feature that automatically prints each line of the heading for a memo, pausing to allow you to type in the variable information on each line.

TO: Ray Ling, International Operations   9

FROM: Charlotte McMullen, Man~~g~~*a*er   17
         Development for European Market   25

DATE: *March 19, 19--*   31

SUBJECT: European Plant Recommendation   40

In my ~~recent~~ memo of March 14, I indicated that I would be   53

forwarding *to* you my recommendations regarding a site for our   66

European market. During the month of Feb*ru*ary I visited   77

towns and cities near London, Madrid, Munich, Paris, and Rome.   90

The nonskilled labor needed in the production of *many of* our items   103

seemed to be plentiful in all five areas. The technical labor   116

needed in the production of our special lines ~~were~~ *was* available   128

in greater numbers in London and Munich.   136

Possible
~~Plant~~ sites were ~~found and~~ inspected in each of the five areas   148

visited. Costs of leasing and purchasing these sites, costs   161

of renovation to meet our needs, and square footage were all   173

considered. Based on these ~~considerations,~~ *factors,* I would rank the   184

sites ~~this way:~~ *in this order:* Munich, Paris, Madrid, London, and Rome.   196

Our products would have the greatest sales potential in   209

Munich and Paris because of the ~~weather~~ *Climate,* the interest in   220

recreation, and the money available for leisure time.   231

At our April 2 meeting, I will have *a* ~~the~~ detailed analysis of   244

my findings, along with my recommendations, to present to you.   257

jcp   258

Shown in elite
Paper: plain
Line: 6 inches
  (60 pica/
  70 elite)
Tabs: 5, 10, center
Proofguide: 129–130

If an enumeration is introduced by a short line, it may be double-indented— that is, indented 10 spaces.

↓7
CORRESPONDENCE MANUAL   Page 2
                                                                       ↓3

Experienced typists, in actuality, do not waste valuable time counting words or studying a letter-placement table. They devise a pattern for average letters (about 70 percent have fewer than 225 words in the body) and then spread shorter ones and compress longer ones into the space of the average one.

To expand a short letter:

  1. Allow extra space after the date.
  2. Divide the letter into more paragraphs.
  3. Insert a company signature line.
  4. Allow extra space for the signature.
  5. Lower the reference lines.
  6. Use a smaller size of stationery.

To telescope a long letter into less space:

  1. Allow less space after the date.
  2. Divide the letter into fewer paragraphs.
  3. Omit the company signature if possible.
  4. Allow less space for the signature.
  5. Raise the reference lines.

By following these hints, the typist will fit most letters into the space of an average letter. Margins will need to be adjusted only in letters that are very short or very long.
                                                                    ↓3

Part II. Parts of a Letter

Letters used for business correspondence may contain up to 17 different parts.[1] See Appendix A, page 10.
                                                                    ↓3

A. THE STANDARD LETTER PARTS

Eight parts are so standard in every business letter that a letter would be incomplete if any of them were excluded.
                                                                    ↓1
_____
                                                                    ↓2
1. William A. Sabin, The Gregg Reference Manual, 5th ed., Gregg Division, McGraw-Hill Book Company, New York, 1977, pp. 232-260.

NOTE: Footnotes may also be typed with superior numbers—e.g., ¹William . . . .

Line: 60 spaces   Tab: 5
Spacing: single   Drills: 2X
Proofguide: 33–36
Workguide: 3–4, 99–104
Tape: 16B

LESSONS 59/60
POSTAL CARDS AND ENVELOPES

Goals: To improve proofreading skill; to format postal cards and envelopes.

59-A. WARMUP

S 1 The two girls took the day off to see the new show in town.
A 2 We could jeopardize six of the gunboats by two quick moves.
N 3 Invoices #10, #29, #38, #47, and #56 were misplaced by Joe.
   | 1 | 2 | 3 | 4 | 5 | 6 | 7 | 8 | 9 | 10 | 11 | 12

59-B. PROOFREADING SKILLS

Compare the message from this postal card with the message on the postal card on the next page. Type a list of the words that contain errors, correcting the errors as you type.

4 Our Wausa civic Association is curently holding a contes to select the store front window with the must attractive winter sene. The contest will fun from Januery 14 to Febrary 15 and winers will be named ar the Wausau winter ball on Febrary 21. Call me at 555-1939 if you would lik to particpate.

59-C. Spacing—double. Record your score.

59-C. SKILL MEASUREMENT: 5-MINUTE TIMED WRITING

5 In recent years, there has been a huge increase in the 12
volume of mail. Incoming and outgoing mail have both shown 24
the increase in growth. It is a result of the expansion of 36
business communications in general. This has required many 48
businesses to evaluate the procedures and equipment used in 60
handling the mail in an efficient manner. Many changes can 72
be expected in the future regarding the processing of mail. 84
The procedures for handling mail must be analyzed in a 96
careful manner. Of course, the procedures for handling the 108
outgoing and the incoming mail will be different. However, 120
in either case, it is vital that all steps are properly and 132
carefully followed. Recent advances in technology can help 144
make the job of processing the mail much easier. There are 156
many firms waiting to cut their mail costs. 165
   | 1 | 2 | 3 | 4 | 5 | 6 | 7 | 8 | 9 | 10 | 11 | 12

169/170-D. FORMATTING A CORRESPONDENCE MANUAL

Use plain paper to format the correspondence manual. Before you begin, do the Learning Guide on Workguide pages 407–408. Use the visual guide on Workguide page 410.

REPORT 50
BOUND REPORT (1)
TABLE 43

Shown in elite
Paper: plain
Line: 6 inches
  (60 pica/
  70 elite)
Spacing:
  double
Tab: 5, center
Proofguide:
  127–128

↓ 13

CORRESPONDENCE MANUAL
↓ 3

Part I. Letter Placement

Communications experts agree that a letter should be so arranged on the paper that it is pleasing to the eye. The text of the letter should be centered between equal side margins. The bottom margin should be slightly bigger than the side margins. The letter should be "framed" by the margins.

Several formulas for achieving the "framed picture" have been devised; however, no one formula provides the perfect solution for every letter. The lengths of letters, the sizes of stationery, and the depths of letterheads vary too much for an all-inclusive formula.

Table 1 describes one recommended formula that is widely used, but even this one requires adjustments at times.
↓ 4

Table 1

STANDARD LETTER-PLACEMENT GUIDE

Letter Factor	Short and Average	Long
Words in the body	Up to 225	Over 225
Position of date*	Line 15	Line 15
Drop to address	5 lines	5 lines
Length of line	5 inches	6 inches
Length in spaces	50P, 60E	60P, 70E

NOTE: See page 248 for format of ruled tables with footnotes.

*On letterheads more than 2 inches deep, position the date 3 lines below the bottom of the letterhead.

59/60-D. FORMATTING A POSTAL CARD

Study the illustrations and annotations below and in the left panel; then, using the postal card forms on Workguide pages 99–100, type Postal Cards 1–3.

POSTAL CARD 1
Shown in elite
Paper: Workguide 99–100
Line: 45 pica/55 elite
Spacing: single
Tabs: 2
Proofguide: 35–36

RETURN ADDRESS. Blocked on line 3, ½ inch (about 5 spaces) from left edge. The personal title *Mr.* should not be used, but other titles such as *Dr.* or *Mrs.* may be used.

ADDRESS. Blocked on line 12, 2 inches (about 20 spaces) from left edge.

NOTE: Single-space all addresses. Type the city, state, and ZIP Code on one line; leave 1 space between the state abbreviation and the ZIP Code.

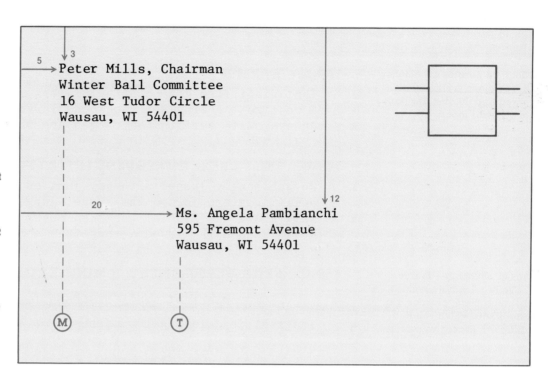

MARGINS. ½ inch (about 5 spaces) on each side. Start the date on line 3 at center.

CLOSING. At center. Leave room for signature if required; otherwise, leave 1 blank line.

REFERENCE INITIALS. Your own.

CARD SIZE. Postal cards are 5½ by 3½ inches (about 140 by 89 millimeters).

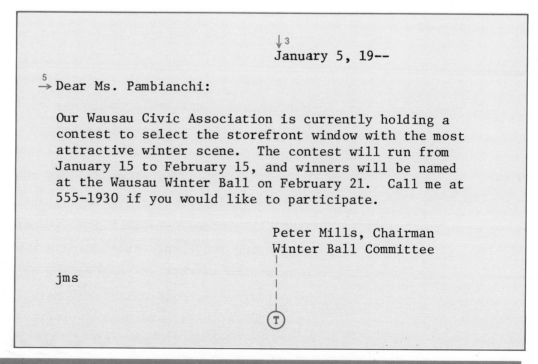

<table>
<tr><td>

Line: 60 spaces   Tab: 5
Spacing: single   Drills: 3X
Proofguide: 127–130
Workguide: 331–332,
   407–408, 410
Tape: 54A

</td><td>

LESSONS 169/170
FORMAL REPORT

</td></tr>
</table>

Goal: To develop proficiency in sustained typing by formatting the first five pages of a formal report.

169-A. WARMUP

S 1 That giant firm got both the big box and the pair of bowls.
A 2 I realize the eloquent backwoods lawyer convinced the jury.
N 3 We are quite certain their ages are 56, 47, 38, 29, and 10.
    | 1 | 2 | 3 | 4 | 5 | 6 | 7 | 8 | 9 | 10 | 11 | 12

169-B. SKILL DRILL: INFREQUENT LETTER PRACTICE

J 4 Jo jubilantly jumped with joy just as Jim joined the major.
   5 Jolly jugglers joined the judge, jury, and jealous jailers.
K 6 Kaye knows the kind of work Ken seeks may keep him looking.
   7 Kevin knew Kirk kicked a rock that struck a flock of ducks.
    | 1 | 2 | 3 | 4 | 5 | 6 | 7 | 8 | 9 | 10 | 11 | 12

169-C. **Spacing—double. Take two 5-minute timings. Between them, practice any words with which you had difficulty. Record your score.**

169-C. SKILL MEASUREMENT: 5-MINUTE TIMED WRITING

8   Some owners of small business firms have not used good 12
judgment in delaying the purchase of a microcomputer. Many 24
others have made the mistake of buying their microcomputers 36
for the wrong reasons. An amazing number of persons do not 48
question the limitations of a computer in helping solve any 60
and all problems. First of all, one should not expect that 72
a computer can resolve the types of problems that require a 84
subjective solution. Also, history tells us that computers 96
won't save money through the elimination of workers. Maybe 108
the biggest surprise for many new microcomputer users is to 120
find out these microcomputers are of no help in solving the 132
complex problems that are tough to define in precise terms. 144
      If a firm's manual procedures are computerized, errors 156
in those old procedures will continue to exist unless steps 168
have been taken to correct them. Apart from the office and 180
accounting functions, some users are very disappointed when 192
they become aware that forecasting and trend analyses can't 204
be performed without historical data. And some buy a piece 216
of hardware that lacks good software programs. 225
    | 1 | 2 | 3 | 4 | 5 | 6 | 7 | 8 | 9 | 10 | 11 | 12

POSTAL CARD 2
Paper: Workguide 99–100
Proofguide: 35–36

POSTAL CARD 3
Paper: Workguide 99–100
Proofguide: 35–36

Mr. Mills would like to send the same message found in Card 1 on the previous page to Mr. Robert Bergh / 324 First Avenue / Wausau WI 54401.

Send a postal card with the following message from Mr. Mills to Ms. Pamela Benton 196 Sullivan Lane / Wausau, WI 54401.

As you undoubtedly know, the Wausau Civic Association is planning its Winter Ball for February 21 at the Phillips Hotel. During that evening, we will announce the winners of our storefront window scenes. Will you encourage the members of your organization to attend this special function? Please call me at 555-1930 for more information.

59/60-E. FORMATTING ENVELOPES

Note: The format used for addressing the large envelope is recommended by the U.S. Postal Service—particularly for bulk mail that will be sorted by an electronic scanning device. The address is typed in all-capital letters with no punctuation, and it also incorporates the proposed nine-digit ZIP Code.

Dr. Margaret C. Johnson ①

APEX PHARMACEUTICAL
15 Ferdon Avenue □ Collingswood, NJ 08108-1020

9 Personal ②

40

↓14
DR WILLIAM C LAUER ③
BENTLEY TECHNOLOGY INC
189 HENDERSON STREET
NORRISTOWN PA 19402-1520

↓9
SPECIAL DELIVERY ④

↑
Standard large envelope, No. 10, is 9½ by 4⅛ inches (about 238 by 103 millimeters).

↓3
5 Samuel B. Jax ①
→157 Lexington Avenue
Ashland, WI 54806

↓9
Confidential ②

20

↓12
→Mr. Paul Festerson, Manager ③
Baldwin & Wallace
17 North Cove Road
Wausau, WI 54401

④ ↓9 REGISTERED

← Standard small envelope, No. 6¾, is 6½ by 3⅝ inches (about 163 by 91 millimeters).

1. **RETURN ADDRESS.** Business envelopes have a return address printed on the envelope. The writer's name may be typed above the address. On a personal letter, the return address begins ½ inch (about 5 spaces) from the left edge on line 3. Lines are single-spaced and blocked at left. The personal title *Mr.* should not be used, but other titles can be.

2. **ON-ARRIVAL DIRECTIONS.** Any on-arrival directions, such as *Personal, Confidential, Please Forward,* or *Hold for Arrival,* should be typed on line 9 and aligned on the left with the return address. These words are typed in capital and lowercase letters and underscored.

3. **ADDRESS.** Begin the name and address on a small envelope on line 12, 2 inches (20 pica/24 elite

spaces) from the left edge; and on a large envelope on line 14, 4 inches (40 pica/48 elite spaces) from the left edge. Single-space and block all lines with city, state, and ZIP Code on the same line. The state name should be typed with its two-letter abbreviation with 1 space before the ZIP Code.

In foreign addresses, indicate the postal zone after the city; type the name of the country on a separate final line, in all capitals.

4. **SPECIAL MAIL SERVICE.** Directions for such mail services as *special delivery, airmail* (overseas only), or *registered* are typed in all-capital letters on line 9. The notation should end ½ inch (about 5 spaces) from the right edge.

167/168-D. TABLES AND FORMS

See Workguide pages 383–384 for a review of table and forms typing.

TABLE 42
OPEN TABLE

Paper: plain, full sheet
Proofguide: 125

FORM 60
RULED REPORT FORM

Workguide: 399
Proofguide: 127

Complete a report form using the information in Table 42.

Leave 6 spaces between columns

Requests for Word Processing Tours
January 19--

Date	Time	Name	Company/*Address*
1/17	9:30 a.m.	Penny Carello	Franklin Hospital 5601 State St Duluth, MN 55808
1/17	1:30 p.m.	Charles P. Bainchi	First Savings 9480 Briar Road Rochester, MN 55901
1/24	9:30 a.m.	K L Taylor	Des Moines Clothing 3615 E Fulton Drive Des Moines, IA 50315
1/24	10:00 a.m.	Susan L. Niven	Lisk/Kallio attorneys 1650 East Franklin Ave Minneapolis, MN 55404
1/24	1:30 p.m.	Thomas P. Fulsher	Fulsher Insurance, Inc 310 E Lawson Avenue St. Paul, MN 55101

FORMS 61–65
ACKNOWLEDGMENT CARDS

Workguide: 401–404
Proofguide: 127–128

Prepare an acknowledgment card for each person listed in Table 42.

 On a word processor, if the constant information of a form is stored on magnetic media, only the variables have to be inserted.

FORMS 66–70
NAME TAGS

Workguide: 405
Proofguide: 127–128

Prepare a name tag for each of the persons whose name appears in Table 42.

LONDGREN'S | Department Store
1450 West Kellogg Boulevard
St. Paul, MN 55102

Dear Ms. Carello:

We would like to confirm the tour of our word processing center that you requested:

        Date: January 17
        Time: 9:30 a.m.

We look forward to seeing you.

          (Your name)

LONDGREN'S
WELCOMES

Penny Carello

ENVELOPE 1 (No. 6¾)
Workguide: 101

ENVELOPE 2 (No. 10)
Workguide: 102

ENVELOPE 3 (No. 10)
Use for letter that follows.
Workguide: 104

From Ann M. Jankiewicz / 385 Belmont Avenue / Asheboro, NC 27203.
Registered to Dr. Earl Gillis / 17 May Street / Asheboro, NC 27203.

From Jacob Kaufman.
To Ms. Marie Buford / 15 St. Joseph Street / Easton, PA 18042.

From Mary B. Alexander, Personnel Manager.
Special Delivery to Liberty Travel Agency / 78 Bond Street / Bloomingdale, TN 37660.

LETTER 16
MODIFIED-BLOCK STYLE

Line: 5 inches (50 pica/60 elite)
Tab: center
Date: current; line 15
Inside address from Envelope 3 above
Paper: Workguide 103
Proofguide: 35–36

Ladies and Gentlemen: We are delighted that it will be 33
possible for you to handle the travel arrangements 43
for our employees who will be visiting Bermuda 53
during the week of February 15. We certainly 62
appreciate your quick and efficient response to our 72
request for information. 78

As it stands now, we will need accommodations 88
for 22 of our employees. Ten double rooms and 12 98
single rooms will be adequate. The group will be 108
flying from the Johnson City Airport. 116

Thank you for handling our request so 124
promptly. We look forward to working with you on 134
this special trip for United Forms Systems 143
employees. Sincerely yours, 156

59/60-F. FOLDING LETTERS FOR LARGE AND SMALL ENVELOPES

To fold a letter for a large (No. 10) envelope:
1. Fold up the bottom third of the letter.
2. Fold the top third down to ½ inch from the bottom edge.
3. Insert the last crease into the envelope first, with the flap facing up.

To fold a letter for a small (No. 6¾) envelope:
1. Fold up the bottom half to ½ inch from the top.
2. Fold the right third over to the left.
3. Fold the left third over to ½ inch from the right edge.
4. Insert the last crease into the envelope first, with the flap facing up.

LESSONS 167/168
TABLES AND FORMS

Goals: To increase basic skills; to improve skill in formatting tables and forms.

167-A. WARMUP

S 1 Both of them wish to row down to the dock by the giant oak.
A 2 That exhibit has priceless jewels and a dozen unique vases.
N 3 I typed 10 and 2 and 9 and 3 and 8 and 4 and 7 and 5 and 6.
  | 1 | 2 | 3 | 4 | 5 | 6 | 7 | 8 | 9 | 10 | 11 | 12

167-B. Take three 1-minute timings. Keep your eyes on the copy.

167-B. SKILL DRILL: NUMBER AND SYMBOL PRACTICE

4 About 3/4 of the #2 oil @ $1.84 was sold! The 20¢ discount 12
(a last-minute decision) was awarded to 65% of the dealers* 24
who have been eligible for "seasonal discounts" since 1979. 36
Don't you think that Hayes & Selby should also be eligible? 48
  | 1 | 2 | 3 | 4 | 5 | 6 | 7 | 8 | 9 | 10 | 11 | 12

167-C. Spacing—double. Take two 5-minute timings. Between them, practice any words with which you had difficulty. Record your score.

167-C. SKILL MEASUREMENT: 5-MINUTE TIMED WRITING

5   It has often been said of some strange-looking animals 12
that they look as though they were designed by a committee. 24
The implication, of course, is that members of a group can- 36
not join together and make good decisions. However, permit 48
one who has been a committee member for many, many years to 60
take exception to the generalization. Experience has shown 72
me that decisions arrived at by committees are usually of a 84
higher quality than those that would have been made or that 96
have been made by the individual members of the group. 107
      But there is a price to be paid when operating through 119
a committee system. If those hours spent in committee work 131
are costed out in a business firm or a governmental agency, 143
it does not take long for the cost to run into the hundreds 155
or even thousands of dollars. Though there may not be dol- 167
lar costs for people involved with nonprofit organizations, 179
there is a price that is paid in terms of human energy that 191
is expended as well as the time that one is away from other 203
interests and the family. Even so, it may well be that the 215
price is justified to achieve superior decisions. 225
  | 1 | 2 | 3 | 4 | 5 | 6 | 7 | 8 | 9 | 10 | 11 | 12

Line: 60 spaces   Tab: 5
Spacing: single   Drills: 2X
Proofguide: 35–38
Workguide: 3–4, 105–110
Tape: 16B

LESSONS 61/62

LETTERS WITH CARBONS

Goals: To improve number typing; to format letters with carbon copies.

61-A. WARMUP

S   1   If the work is handled right, the groups may make a profit.
A   2   Sixty equals only five dozen, but we promised Jackie eight.
N   3   Cabins 10, 29, 38, 47, and 56 were filled while we cruised.
   | 1 | 2 | 3 | 4 | 5 | 6 | 7 | 8 | 9 | 10 | 11 | 12

61-B. Type lines 4–7 two times each. Then take two 1-minute timings. Note that the last two digits of each number are a cumulative word count.

61-B. NUMBER PRACTICE

4   1201 4102 5603 3104 1505 4806 2907 3408 1609 3710 4111 9812
5   5613 6714 7215 8316 3917 2318 1019 4320 6421 8922 3423 5624
6   6425 1426 2727 9028 5429 3930 8231 6832 7233 9134 5535 1836
7   3237 8338 9639 5640 7341 9342 6543 4244 8745 3046 2447 9648

61-C. Spacing—double. Record your score.

61-C. SKILL MEASUREMENT: 5-MINUTE TIMED WRITING

8   Just as memos are internal messages in a firm, letters 12
are external. They are mailed outside the company, and the 24
image they create is very important. The image may be good 36
or poor depending on how the letter looks. The letter must 48
make a good first impression or it may never be read. Neat 60
typing is required to make an attractive letter. Also, the 72
typist must proofread with great care to remove all errors. 84
     A good business letter is a sales letter. It tries to 96
sell a product, a service, or an idea to the reader. To do 108
this, the content must be well organized. This involves an 120
opening, the message, and closing. Writing good letters is 132
not easy, but the skill can be learned. The typist and the 144
writer must work as a team to make an effective letter that 156
will impress the reader right from the start. 165
   | 1 | 2 | 3 | 4 | 5 | 6 | 7 | 8 | 9 | 10 | 11 | 12

61-D. CARBON COPIES

It is good business practice to keep a copy of all typed materials. In addition, a copy may be sent to one or more individuals other than the addressed party. Copies can be made by typing with carbon paper or by a photocopy machine after the document is completed. Whatever method is used, it is necessary to indicate on the original document that copies have been sent to others.

The illustration at the top of the next page shows how carbon paper is used to make extra copies.

Most word processing centers instruct their operators to log the work that comes in and goes out of the center. This procedure allows the manager to find a document at any point in its cycle, measure operators' production, and compile summary reports.

Using the information from Forms 50–57, prepare a log sheet for Pam Crothers and for Harold Mathias, two of the operators in the word processing center.

LONDGREN'S | Department Store
Word Processing Center
Operator's Daily Log

OPERATOR ___Harold Mathias___   DATE ___January 6, 19--___

Time In	Originator	Department	Type of Document	Input Form	Total Lines	Time Out	Total Minutes
7:30	Pat McCray	Shipping	S	L	17	8:08	38

FORMATTING TABLES WITH FOOTNOTES

To format footnotes in unruled and ruled tables, take the following steps:

UNRULED TABLES

1. Separate the footnote from the body of the table with a 1-inch underscore.
2. Single-space before typing the underscore and double-space after typing it.
3. Indent the footnote 5 spaces and type it to the width of the table with single spacing; double-space between footnotes.
4. Type an asterisk or another symbol at the beginning of a footnote to introduce it.

RULED TABLES

1. Type the footnote a double space below the final rule.
2. Follow steps 3 and 4 for unruled tables.

TABLE 41
OPEN TABLE

Paper: plain, full sheet
Spacing: double
Proofguide: 125

WP The automatic functions used to format a table on a word processor include: (1) centering of heading lines, (2) vertical centering of the entire table, (3) horizontal centering of columns, and (4) decimal alignment.

Weekly Productivity Report
Week Ending January 7, 19--

Operator	Hours Worked	Average Lines an Hour	Performance Index*
Pam Crothers	37.00	135	68%
Jose Fuentes	40.00	196	98%
Harold Mathias	35.50	182	91%
Susan O'Connel	33.25	216	108%
Patsy Sandstrom	15.75	139	10%

Standard performance was 200 lines an hour in December 19--.

MAKING CARBON COPIES

When you use carbon paper to make a copy of a letter, memorandum, form, or report, follow the steps that are illustrated below.

WP On a word processor you would make additional copies by (1) inserting a carbon pack into the printer (the piece of equipment that actually types out what you have entered on the word processor) or (2) having the system print out as many copies of the document as you need.

1. Assemble the carbon pack: (a) the sheet of paper on which you will type, (b) the carbon paper (shiny side down), and (c) the onionskin or other thin sheet of paper on which you wish to make the copy.
2. Insert the carbon pack into the typewriter: (a) Straighten the sides and top. (b) Insert the pack into the machine with the carbon side (and the copy paper) facing you. (c) Hold the pack in your left hand and turn the platen smoothly with your right. (d) Before you start to type, check to be sure that the letterhead or top sheet as well as the dull side of the carbon paper is facing you.

LETTER 17
MODIFIED-BLOCK STYLE

Carbons: 1
Paper: Workguide 105–106
Proofguide: 35–36

ERASING ON CARBON COPY. Use a soft (pencil) eraser to erase errors. Place a stiff card under the sheet on which you erase to keep smudges from appearing on the copies beneath. If you find an error after removing your paper, erase and correct each sheet separately.

A carbon copy (cc) notation is added if someone is to get a copy of the letter. Type the notation on the line below the reference initials (or below the enclosure notation if there is one). The initials *cc* should be typed in small letters, with or without a colon following. If a colon is used, leave 2 spaces after the colon.

(Current date)	4
Mr. William Walmach	12
Casual Clothing	15
15 Maple Avenue	18
Cleveland, MS 38732	22
Dear Mr. Walmach:	27

Thank you for your telephone call requesting information 40
about the clothing we carry at Leisure Wear. Under separate 52
cover we have sent you a catalog, which includes all of our 64
clothing lines. 68

Our sales representative in your area, Mr. George Esposito, 81
has received your name and address and will be calling on you 93
within the next few days. He will answer any questions you 105
may have concerning purchases, credit, and deliveries. In 117
addition, he will have sample products to show you. 128

We hope that you will be impressed with our clothing lines 141
and that you will consider purchasing some of our lines for 153
sale in your store. We believe that you would be pleased 164
with the increased sales that you would notice in a short 176
period of time. 179

Sincerely yours, 185

Joan Tomain 191
Sales Manager 195

djm 197
cc George Esposito 201

165/166-D. TABLES AND FORMS

Before typing the tables and forms in this lesson, complete Workguide pages 383–384.

TABLE 39
OPEN TABLE

Paper: plain, full sheet
Spacing: double
Proofguide: 123

TABLE 40
OPEN TABLE

Paper: plain, full sheet
Spacing: double
Proofguide: 123

Type Table 40 with the departments alphabetized. Add a total line at the bottom and compute the amounts.

WORD PROCESSING CENTER
Summary Report by Department
December 19--

Department	No. of Jobs	No. of Authors	Lines	Time Hours/Minutes
Special Services	81	5	3,948	83/12
Accounting	62	5	3,486	79/10
Executive	42	8	1,673	29/20
Purchasing	7	3	182	4/15
Shipping	87	6	4,821	108/30

FORMS 50–57
JOB REQUEST FORMS

Workguide: 391–393
Proofguide: 125–126

Fill in the appropriate information on a job request form for each person who sent work to the word processing center on the morning of January 6. The two operators assigned to the jobs were Pam Crothers and Harold Mathias.

JOB REQUEST FORM

ORIGINATOR Pat McCray   DATE 1/6/--

DEPT. Shipping   NO. OF COPIES 3

DOCUMENT TYPE S   INPUT FORM L

STORAGE REQ.: Permanent _____ One Time X

DIRECTIONS Please store for 2 days.

_____

Document Type   Input Form
L   Letter   D   Dictated
FL Form Letter   L   Longhand
M   Memo   P   Prerecorded
R   Report   RD Rough Draft
S   Statistical

WP CENTER USE

OPERATOR ASSIGNED Harold Mathias

TIME IN 7:30   TIME OUT 8:08

TOTAL LINES 17

Pat McCray from the Shipping Department sent a statistical table written in longhand and asked for 3 copies with storage for 2 days. Harold began the 17-line table at 7:30 and finished it at 8:08.

Steve Carlisle, an executive, sent a letter in longhand and asked for 1 copy with permanent storage. It took Harold from 8:15 to 8:30 to type the 21-line letter.

Kris Swanson from the Purchasing Department sent a rough draft of a 5-page report. He asked for 2 copies and storage for a week. Harold typed the 109-line report between 8:40 and 9:32.

Al Kramer from the Shipping Department brought 4 letters that were dictated on tape. He asked for 1 copy of each with storage for 3 days. The job was assigned to Pam, who began the letters at 8:03 and finished them at 9:10. There were a total of 92 lines.

Sue Ricker from the Accounting Department sent a statistical table in longhand and asked for 5 copies with storage for 2 days. Pam began the table at 9:40 and finished it at 10:33. There were a total of 23 lines.

Alice Gomez, an executive, sent a dictated memo and asked for 15 copies and 1-day storage. Harold began the memo at 9:45 and finished it at 10:10. He typed a total of 15 lines.

John Stone from the Purchasing Department dictated 3 letters. He asked for 1 copy of each with permanent storage, since these were new form letters. Harold typed the 56 lines between 10:15 and 11:02.

Rick Aster from the Shipping Department sent back a 10-page report to be revised. He asked for 1 copy and another week of storage. Pam began revising the report at 11:05 and finished it at 11:20. There were a total of 26 lines.

LETTER 18
MODIFIED-BLOCK STYLE

Date: current
Carbons: 1
Paper: Workguide 107–108
Proofguide: 35–36

Enumerations within a letter are arranged with the numbers at the left margin and turn-over lines indented 4 spaces.

Mr. Robert Holbrook, President	14
Holbrook Brothers, Inc.	19
561 Union ~~Street~~ *Avenue*	23
Shreveport, LA 71103	27

Dear Mr. Holbrook: 32

It was ~~good~~ *nice* to meet you at the recent *trade* show in ~~Memphis~~ *Knoxville* and to 47
have you stop by our ex*h*ibit area. We would be pleased to help 58
meet some needs for l*ei*sure clothing and *to* help increase your 72
sales. As we agreed at that init*i*al meeting, I have *the following*: *(of your)* *(done the)* 87

1. Sent you our credit application form. We must have this 100
   form on file prior to any ship ment of clothing on credit. 112

2. Give*n* your name and address to *m*r. *p*aul *m*iller, one of our 126
   representatives in your area. 133

3. Sent you the sample products you requested. Mr. Miller 146
   will pick them up from you when he makes his *initial* call. 159

Thank you for you*r* interest in our ~~different~~ *various* clothing lines. 172
We hope you will find them to be exactly what you need. 184

                          Sincerely yours, 189

                          Joan Tomain 196
                          Sales Manager 199

djm 201
cc Mr. Paul Miller 205

LETTER 19
MODIFIED-BLOCK STYLE

Carbons: 1
Paper: Workguide 109–110
Proofguide: 37–38

ENUMERATION. Treat each item as a separate paragraph with numbers at left margin and turnover lines indented 4 spaces.

ENVELOPES. Type a No. 10 envelope for Letters 17 and 18. Type a No. 6¾ envelope for Letter 19.

(*Current date*) / Ms. Christine Olsen, President / Romar Textile Mills, Inc. / 20
Hellersville Road / Orangeburg, SC 29115 / Dear Ms. Olsen: 32

   Our production manager has just talked to me regarding the last 46
shipment of cloth we purchased from your mill. He feels that the fab- 59
ric does not meet the specifications we had established. The material 74
was received with Invoice 11-34. The following points should be 87
noted: 1. The width of these rolls is 52" and the specs called for 54". 103
2. The content of the cloth is 30% cotton and 70% polyester; the specs 118
called for 50% cotton and 50% polyester. 3. The color of the rolls re- 135
ceived was Harvard Blue; the specs called for Heaven Blue. 148

   Please have someone from your plant stop by within the next week 162
to clear up this matter. Of course, I am holding up payment on this 175
invoice. 177

   Sincerely yours, / Charles V. Donaldson / Chief Executive Officer / 198
(*Your initials*) / cc Mr. John Krieger, Production Manager 208

Line: 60 spaces   Tab: 5
Spacing: single   Drills: 3X
Proofguide: 123–126
Workguide: 331–332,
   383–384, 391–397
Tape: 53A

LESSONS 165/166
TABLES AND FORMS

Goals: To increase basic skills; to improve skill in formatting tables and forms.

165-A.   WARMUP

S   1   Did their pals burn the coal when they got to the icy city?
A   2   Vivian will be making unique prizes for the major exhibits.
N   3   She will be on Route 67 for 1,308 of the 2,495 total miles.
    | 1 | 2 | 3 | 4 | 5 | 6 | 7 | 8 | 9 | 10 | 11 | 12

165-B.   Take three 1-minute timings. Keep your eyes on the copy.

165-B.   SKILL DRILL: NUMBER AND SYMBOL PRACTICE

4   What high prices!   The tag shows 50# @ $2.49 and 10# @ 78¢.   12
But the new ad* for Frost & Coyne shows prices that are 36%   24
lower.   Let's build an inventory (an up-to-date one) now by   36
buying at these "summer discount prices."   Don't you agree?   48
    | 1 | 2 | 3 | 4 | 5 | 6 | 7 | 8 | 9 | 10 | 11 | 12

165-C.   Spacing—double. Take two 5-minute timings. Between them, practice any words with which you had difficulty. Record your score.

165-C.   SKILL MEASUREMENT: 5-MINUTE TIMED WRITING

5   Ah, the joy of the weekend.   It is truly a rare person   12
who does not look forward with anticipation to a fun-filled   24
and relaxing weekend.   For all too many, this is a reprieve   36
from a sentence of forty hours a week at a job that is both   48
dull and without challenge.   It is so depressing for people   60
who have acquired such an acute dislike for their jobs that   72
the jobs are simply endured in exchange for a paycheck.   It   84
is extremely important that young people give thought at an   96
early age to the zesty pursuit of a career that brings real   108
rewards.   Those working hours should be enjoyable.   118
     I became aware quite recently that there is a parallel   130
situation tolerated by large numbers of people with respect   142
to the geographic location at which they are employed.   The   154
person with a city orientation may find employment opportu-   166
nities in a rural setting.   The reverse is also true; there   178
are many people who are forced to work and live in an urban   190
setting but prefer the relatively uncomplicated life of the   202
small town.   Young people should give attention to the type   214
of community they want as well as to the type of career.   225
    | 1 | 2 | 3 | 4 | 5 | 6 | 7 | 8 | 9 | 10 | 11 | 12

| Line: 60 spaces Tab: 5 |
| Spacing: single Drills: 2X |
| Proofguide: 37–38 |
| Workguide: 3–4, 111–115 |
| Tape: 17B |

LESSONS 63/64
MEMORANDUMS

Goals: To practice symbol keys; to format memorandums on printed forms.

63-A. WARMUP

S 1 The eight of us found a lake that was right by the village.
A 2 Vic quickly mixed frozen strawberries into the grape juice.
N 3 Seats 10, 29, 38, 47, and 56 were unsold for the bus rides.
| 1 | 2 | 3 | 4 | 5 | 6 | 7 | 8 | 9 | 10 | 11 | 12

63-B. **Type lines 4–7 two times each. Then take two 1-minute timings on paragraph 8.**

63-B. SYMBOL PRACTICE

4 sws sw2s s2s s@s s2s@s s2@s frf fr4f f4f f$f f4f$f f4$f $44
5 lol lo9l l9l l(l l9l(l l9(l ded de3d d3d d#d d3d#d d3#d #33
6 juj ju7j j7j j&j j7j&j j7&j frf fr5f f5f f%f f5f%f f5%f 55%
7 ;p; ;p0; ;0; ;); ;0;); ;0); jyj jy6j j6j j¢j j6j¢j j6¢j 66¢

8 Order #2130 was sent to Van & Blake for the following: (1)   12
15 shirts @ $6.75 each; (2) 8 hats @ $9.25 each; (3) 8 ties   24
@ $4.50 each; and (4) 25 shorts @ 95¢ each. The amount for   36
the total invoice was $246.75, which included 5% sales tax.   48
| 1 | 2 | 3 | 4 | 5 | 6 | 7 | 8 | 9 | 10 | 11 | 12

63-C. **Spacing—double. Record your score.**

63-C. SKILL MEASUREMENT: 5-MINUTE TIMED WRITING

9   Success in the world of work is not due to chance. It   12
has to be earned. To start a career will require technical   24
skills. This means a good basic education and perhaps even   36
specialized training. It may mean updating these skills in   48
a world that never stands still. Good workers do more than   60
is expected. They are prompt, neat, and accurate. Working   72
steadily, they will follow through each task to completion.   84
          Technical skills are not enough. To be a success, one   96
must have good human relations skills. A great many people   108
who lose their jobs do so because of their inability to get   120
along well with others. Those who succeed in life know how   132
to make friends. They have a real, warm interest in others   144
and know how to listen. They project the positive, both in   156
thought and action. Success at work depends on ability and   168
attitude.   170
| 1 | 2 | 3 | 4 | 5 | 6 | 7 | 8 | 9 | 10 | 11 | 12

Type the following variables in the order shown below with an asterisk (*) to separate each variable and 1 blank line to separate each set of variables. Do not space before or after the asterisk.

VARIABLES TO INSERT IN LETTER 65

Left margin: 5
Paper: plain
Proofguide: 123

WP Word processing equipment can merge variables with a form letter like the one you typed on the previous page. These variables must be keyboarded in a certain order, depending on the equipment. After you have keyed in the variables, a few commands are all that are needed to have the letter typed automatically.

LETTER 66
MODIFIED-BLOCK STYLE WITH INDENTED PARAGRAPHS

Line: 5 inches (50 pica/ 60 elite)
Tab: 5, center
Paper: Workguide 387–388
Proofguide: 123–124

Type Letter 66 to Gary Pintar, inserting the proper information.

FORMS 43–49
FILL-IN CHARGE ACCOUNT CARD

Workguide: 389
Proofguide: 123–124

Type a fill-in card for each person on the list above by selecting the appropriate information.

Mr. Gary S. Pintar
1024 Suburban Avenue
St. Paul, MN 55106
*Mr. Pintar *Mr. Pintar *$514.38 * 09-873-89 * Mr. Pintar

Mr. Juan Garcia
210 Milford Street
St. Paul, MN 55117
*Mr. Garcia * Mr. Garcia * $752.96 * 87-972-72 * Mr. Garcia

Ms. Jean Sarasin
1408 Ross Avenue
St. Paul, MN 55106
* Ms. Sarasin * Ms. Sarasin * $1,245.04 * 93-721-90 * Ms. Sarasin

Mrs. Betty Lahti
608 Goodhue Street
St. Paul, MN 55102
*Mrs. Lahti * Mrs. Lahti * $346.78 * 74-710-13 * Mrs. Lahti

Miss Susan L. Dawe
280 Cayuga Street
St. Paul, MN 55101
*Miss Dawe * Miss Dawe * $457.26 * 23-801-77 * Miss Dawe

Mr. Clay Abbott
1640 East Sycamore Street
St. Paul, MN 55117
* Mr. Abbott * Mr. Abbott * $183.90 * 46-361-72 * Mr. Abbott

Mr. Willard Epper
1006 Sherburne Avenue
St. Paul, MN 55104
*Mr. Epper * Mr. Epper * $2,008.72 * 75-900-87 * Mr. Epper

Account No. ___09-873-89___

LONDGREN'S | Department Store

Name ___Mr. Gary S. Pintar___

Address ___1024 Suburban Avenue___

___St. Paul, MN 55106___

Signature _____

63/64-D. FORMATTING A MEMORANDUM ON A PRINTED FORM

Although an interoffice memorandum can be typed on plain or letterhead paper, it is generally typed on a form with printed "guides," such as *To, From, Date,* and *Subject.* See the example in Memo 5 below. Remember the following points:

1. The forms are either full-size or half-size sheets of paper. Guide words may appear in any of many different arrangements. Compare the memorandum below with the memorandum forms on Workguide pages 113–115.

2. Set the left margin at the heading aligning point and set the right margin to equal the left (by estimate).

3. Begin the insertions 2 or 3 spaces after the printed guides and align the insertions with the printed words at the *bottom.*

4. Separate the body and heading by 2 blank lines.

5. The writer's initials are typed at center or aligned with the date.

6. Use reference initials and enclosure notations.

MEMO 5
ON PRINTED FORM

Paper: Workguide 111,
     top
Proofguide: 37–38

To: Richard Nickerson
       Personnel Department

From: Sarah Coleman
         Purchasing Department

Subject: Dental Insurance Plan **Date:** April 5, 19-- ↓3

A number of employees in our department have raised questions about the new dental insurance policy that was described in a recent issue of our company news-letter. Apparently, they never received the bro-chure concerning this new fringe benefit. ↓2

Please send me about 25 copies of the brochure that describes the plan, along with the application forms. If I have any questions about the plan after reading the brochure, I will be in touch with you. ↓2

                    SC ↓2

mdp

MEMO 6
ON PRINTED FORM

Paper: Workguide 111,
     bottom
Proofguide: 37–38

The abbreviation *RE* is sometimes used in place of the word *SUBJECT* in a memo or letter.

(*TO:*) Employees in Accounting Department / (*FROM:*) Mildred Quigley /   13
Department Receptionist / (*RE:*) Thomas Catalano Retirement / (*DATE:*)   24
April 10, 19—   27

As you are ~~all~~ aware, thomas catalano will be retiring from our   39
department on June 30, 19--. Tom has been an employee in the   52
Accounting Department for 26 years. He began as a clerk in the   65
accounts receivable division and moved (the ranks through) to   77
his current position as manager of the auditing division.   88

We are planning to hold a ~~nice~~ luncheon on Thursday, May 10,   102
(for Tom) at the Glen view Inn from 12: 30 to 2. If you are   112
interested in attending this luncheon, please see me for   123
the reservation from and details.   132

mdp   (other)   136

163/164-D.   FORM LETTERS AND PRINTED FORMS

Use the visual guide for letter placement (Workguide page 367) when typing correspondence.

LETTER 65
FORM LETTER: MODIFIED-BLOCK STYLE WITH INDENTED PARAGRAPHS

Line: 5 inches (50 pica/ 60 elite)
Tab: 5, center
Paper: Workguide 385
Proofguide: 121–122

Information that is variable should be typed as shown (in parentheses).

WP Word processing equipment can produce form letters that are personalized, with specific information for each individual. "Stop codes" or special commands are keyboarded where the variables are to be inserted.

LONDGREN'S | Department Store

1450 West Kellogg Boulevard
St. Paul, MN 55102

January 5, 19--

(NAME)
(ADDRESS)
(CITY, STATE, ZIP)

Dear (NAME):

Londgren's (Dept.) Store thanks you, (NAME), for your business during the past year. We are pleased that you have selected our store to serve your needs.

Since your purchases amounted to (AMOUNT) during the past year, you are entitled to a free gift. Please select one of the many gifts listed below and stop in at your convenience to receive it.

Purchases	GIFT
$ 101-$250	pen set, Picture Frame
$ 251-$500	Ceramic Vase, Coaster Set
$ 501-$ 750	Wicker Baskets, Teflon Pans
$ 751-$1000	Blanket, Card Table
$1001 and up	Fishing Pole, Blender

Center table

Your temporary card showing (ACCOUNT NUMBER) as your new charge account number is enclosed. You should carry it with you when shopping. Please let us know how we can better satisfy your shopping needs. We are here to serve you, (NAME).

Sincerely,

Phyllis A. Goettleman
President

clo
Enclosure

MEMO 7
ON PRINTED FORM
Paper: Workguide 113
Proofguide: 37–38

ENUMERATION. Treat each item as a separate paragraph with numbers at left margin and turnover lines indented 4 spaces.

(*TO:*) Joseph Youngman / Engineering Department / (*FROM:*) Jody Zamora / Business Services / (*SUBJECT:*) Travel Expenses / (*DATE: Current*)   12 / 22 / 27

In response to your telephone request of yesterday afternoon, I am pleased to share the following information with you concerning our policies on handling travel expenses.   42 / 56 / 64

1. Employees are required to submit travel expenses on a monthly basis. The report should be turned in during the first 10 days of the following month. 2. The current mileage rate for the use of your automobile is 20.5 cents per mile. Receipts must be submitted for all tolls. 3. Receipts for travel by bus, rail, or plane must be submitted with the expense form. 4. Hotel/motel lodgings must not exceed $65 per night. This is the charge prior to tax, etc. Of course, all receipts for such expenses must be submitted. 5. Our maximum allowance for food is $30 per day—$5 for breakfast, $8 for lunch, and $17 for dinner. 6. Miscellaneous expenses must be itemized—telephone, taxi, laundry, etc. 7. The expense form must be approved by your immediate supervisor, John Diaz, prior to submission to our office.   78 / 93 / 108 / 124 / 141 / 159 / 174 / 189 / 203 / 220 / 232 / 245

Enclosed you will find a copy of our expense report form. After you have gone through the process for your first month here, please see me if you have any questions about our policies or procedures in handling travel expenses. / (*Reference initials*) / Enclosure   259 / 274 / 287 / 299

MEMO 8
ON PRINTED FORM
Paper: Workguide 115
Proofguide: 37–38

(*TO:*) Dr. Shirley Livingston / Chemical Research (*FROM:*) Sarah Coleman / Purchasing Department / (*SUBJECT:*) Purchase of Dictating and Duplicating Equipment / (*DATE:*) April 12, 19—   16 / 31 / 43

I have reviewed your purchase requisition forms for a dictating unit and a desk-top copy machine and am returning the order forms to you to get more information before I can place the orders.   53 / 63 / 70 / 79

1. Please submit a cover letter with the order forms giving justification for the orders. Include projected use and number of users. In addition, please justify why equipment now assigned to your division no longer meets your needs.   91 / 103 / 114 / 125 / 132

2. Please include names and addresses of potential vendors for the two pieces of equipment. You might want to include two or three possible sources. You should also include the approximate prices charged by each vendor.   143 / 155 / 167 / 178 / 184

Don't forget your reference initials and enclosure notation.

Line: 60 spaces   Tab: 5
Spacing: single   Drills: 3X
Proofguide: 121–124
Workguide: 331–332,
    367, 385–389
Tape: 53A

LESSONS 163/164
FORM LETTERS AND PRINTED FORMS

Goals: To increase basic skills; to improve skill in typing form letters and forms.

163-A. WARMUP

S 1 Both of the handy men dug where they cut down the big bush.
A 2 The jovial lads were quite excited and seized the parakeet.
N 3 My 32 books weigh 195 pounds; my 48 rocks weigh 670 pounds.
| 1 | 2 | 3 | 4 | 5 | 6 | 7 | 8 | 9 | 10 | 11 | 12

163-B. SKILL DRILL: NUMBER AND SYMBOL PRACTICE

4 aql l sw2 2 de3 3 fr4 4 ft5 5 jy6 6 ju7 7 ki8 8 lo9 9 ;p0 0
5 ala l s2s 2 d3d 3 f4f 4 f5f 5 j6j 6 j7j 7 k8k 8 l9l 9 ;0; 0
6 al! ! s2@ @ d3# # f4$ $ f5% % j6¢ ¢ j7& & k8* * l9((;0))
7 a!a ! s@s @ d#d # f$f $ f%f % j¢j ¢ j&j & k*k * l(l (;);)

163-C. Spacing—double. Take two 5-minute timings. Between them, practice any words with which you had difficulty. Record your score.

163-C. SKILL MEASUREMENT: 5-MINUTE TIMED WRITING

8   Many people who operate small business firms are still 12
undecided about the purchase of a microcomputer. They have 24
yet to be convinced that the expense is justified for their 36
small operations. It may well be that for some quite small 48
firms the use of a service company or the continuation of a 60
manual system is the much better choice. Before finalizing 72
a decision, it is extremely important that consideration be 84
given to the kinds of business problems that a computer can 96
help to solve as well as the types of problems for which it 108
is not appropriate. One can easily see that the accounting 120
area lends itself to computer processing. Financial state- 132
ments, billings, receivables, and payrolls are the types of 144
operations that are appropriately handled by computers.   155
        In addition to the area of accounting, there are other 167
business functions that are appropriate for processing on a 179
computer. These include filing, personnel records, reports 191
of sales and inventory, and countless other clerical opera- 203
tions. Routine work can now be done more efficiently. The 215
office of the future is here for those who want it.   225
| 1 | 2 | 3 | 4 | 5 | 6 | 7 | 8 | 9 | 10 | 11 | 12

LESSONS 65/66
FORMS

Goals: To improve proofreading skill; to format invoices and credit applications.

65-A. WARMUP

S 1 The man may take the land by the lake and sell it for less.
A 2 Jeff amazed the audience by quickly giving six new reports.
N 3 Sue read pages 28–35; Al read pages 64–70; Jo read page 91.
| 1 | 2 | 3 | 4 | 5 | 6 | 7 | 8 | 9 | 10 | 11 | 12

65-B. PROOFREADING SKILLS

Compare this paragraph with the second paragraph of the timed writing in 65-C. Type a list of the words that contain errors, correcting the errors as you type. (NOTE: There are 21 errors in this paragraph.)

4   Al forms have names. For esample. they may be
memos, invoises, purchase orders ect. They are also much
differant kinds of forms. They may consist of one sheet of
paper only or come in sets that make multipel copies at one
time. But forms have one things in comon and that is there
amasing growth. Now some computors read and process forms.
Most likeley they will play an importent role in the futere
of form.

65-C. SKILL MEASUREMENT: 5-MINUTE TIMED WRITING

65-C. Spacing—double. Record your score.

5   American business runs on printed forms. Filling in a 12
form is a way of life in most offices. In fact, almost all 24
business functions require a form at some point. Forms are 36
major time-savers for they help to standardize office work. 48
Forms contain all the information which is constant printed 60
right on them. Then the typist fills in the variable data. 72
Repetitive typing is eliminated when you use printed forms. 84
      All forms have names. For example, they may be called 96
memos, invoices, purchase orders, etc. There are also many 108
different kinds of forms. They may consist of one sheet of 120
paper only or come in sets that make multiple copies at one 132
time. But forms have one thing in common and that is their 144
amazing growth. Now some computers read and process forms. 156
Most likely, they will play an important role in the future 168
of forms.   170
| 1 | 2 | 3 | 4 | 5 | 6 | 7 | 8 | 9 | 10 | 11 | 12

161/162-D.   ORDER-FORM LETTERS

Use plain paper to prepare three variations of an order-form letter.

WP On a word processor, descriptive paragraphs that are used frequently can be stored on magnetic media for easy retrieval and fill-in.

LETTER 62
ORDER-FORM LETTER

Paper: plain
Proofguide: 121–122

Center the order-form letter shown below both vertically and horizontally. If you do not have 1½ spacing on your typewriter, double-space the mailing information lines at the bottom.

LETTER 63
ORDER-FORM LETTER

Paper: plain
Proofguide: 121–122

Retype Letter 62 but change the prices to reflect a 10 percent increase.

LETTER 64
ORDER-FORM LETTER

Paper: plain
Proofguide: 121–122

Retype Letter 63 but omit the Item No. SA-3A entry. (Use the new prices which reflect the 10 percent increase.)

Winter
~~Fall,~~ 19--

Sound Center
1142 Contratto Street
Ironwood, MI 49938
Attention: Ms. Mary Lee Bruno
Ladies and Gentlemen:

Please send the following items: *in the quantities indicated*

Quantity   Item No.   (Description) → *center*

_____   SA-1A   Saturn Stereo Digital Clock Radio. 100% solid-state AM/FM Stereo radio. 2 side-mounted 3-inch speakers. # Walnut finish. ~~$69.50~~ $73.50.

_____   SA-2A   Saturn Stereo Digital clock radio. 100% solid-state AM/FM radio. 3½-inch speakers. Built-in AM/FM radio. Walnut-grained *plastic* finish. $59.50.

_____   SA-3A   Saturn AM/FM Radio. 3 Solid-state Am/Fm. Vernier slide-rule dial. # Three-inch speaker. Black plastic cabinet. $33.50.

_____   JU-3C   Jupiter CB radio. ~~Forty~~ *40* channels with rotary channel indicator, DC powered. ~~One~~-year guarantee. $108.50.

Please ship the above to me under your standard credit terms.

Send to:

Person

Company Name

Street address _____

City, state, Zip _____

65/66-D. FORMATTING AN INVOICE

An invoice is a list of the charges for one delivery of goods or services that is usually typed on a form with printed guide words for positioning heading details and ruled areas for positioning the columns. (See example below.)

1. Invoices come in various sizes and designs.

2. Number columns (Quantity, Unit Price, and Amount) align at the right and are centered visually within each ruled area.

3. Word columns (Description) are aligned at the left, 2 or 3 spaces after the vertical rule.

4. The left margin is set at the first column. Tab stops are set for additional columns.

5. The words *Amount Due* are aligned (tab stop) at the start of the printed word *Description*.

6. The @, ¢, and $ symbols usually are not typed on printed invoice forms, but they are included on typed forms.

7. The typist is responsible for all details.

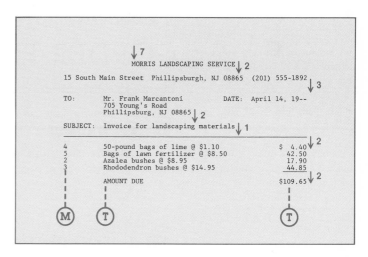

Invoices may also be typed on plain paper. Center the return address and type the date to end at the right margin. Use single spacing and a 60-space line.

FORM 1
INVOICE
Tab: 4
Form: Workguide 117, top
Proofguide: 39

WP For forms that are used frequently in the office, you would adjust the word processor so that it would automatically stop at the first blank space, pause while you typed in the variable information, and then automatically move to the next blank, pause, and so on.

FORMS 2–3
INVOICES (Below)
Forms: Workguide 117, bottom; 119
Proofguide: 39–40

Slimline Communications, Inc.
156 Grand Street   New Britain, CT 06052   (203) 555-8634

TO: Mr. Frank Verrone
Hillside Radio & TV
56 Kennedy Boulevard
Hillside, NJ 07205

DATE: October 16, 19--

INVOICE 86-1893

QUANTITY	DESCRIPTION	UNIT PRICE	AMOUNT
3	Slimline cassette tape recorders, SL-5963	35.50	106.50
10	Slimline AM/FM radios, SL-2136	17.50	175.00
5	Slimline AC/DC cassette recorders with AM/FM radio, SL-8540	42.50	212.50
8	Slimline stereophones, SL-1451	12.95	103.60
	AMOUNT DUE		597.60
	5% SALES TAX		29.88
	TOTAL AMOUNT DUE		627.48

Slimline Invoice 86-1894, current date, to Mr. Charles Kensington, Hillcrest Radio/TV Sales, 51 Westmont Avenue, Mineola, NY 11501 *for:* 2 Slimline 9-inch black/white TV, SL-341 @ 59.75 = 119.50 / 1 Slimline 13-inch color TV, SL-411, @ 210.75 = 210.75 / 1 Slimline video cassette recorder, SL-683 @ 551.50 = 551.50 / 3 Slimline AM/FM Radios, SL-2136 @ 17.50 = 52.50 / AMOUNT DUE 934.25 / 7% SALES TAX 65.40 / TOTAL AMOUNT DUE 999.65.

Slimline Invoice 86-1895, current date, to Gem Electronics, 57 Plymouth Street, Portsmouth, NH 03801 *for:* 6 Slimline Cassette Tape Recorders, SL-5963 @ 35.50 = 213.00 / 10 Slimline Stereophones, SL-1451 @ 12.95 = 129.50 / 5 Slimline AM/FM Clock Radios, SL-2240 @ 24.50 = 122.50 / AMOUNT DUE 465.00 / LESS 10% TRADE DISCOUNT 46.50 / PLUS 5% SALES TAX 20.93 / TOTAL AMOUNT DUE 439.43.

LESSONS 161/162
ORDER-FORM LETTERS

Goal: To format order-form letters.

161-A. WARMUP

S 1 Did the man see the girl when her cow got out of the field?
A 2 Pat was very cozy with extra quilts in back of Joe's truck.
N 3 We saw 10 horses, 29 cows, 38 pigs, 47 goats, and 56 sheep.
| 1 | 2 | 3 | 4 | 5 | 6 | 7 | 8 | 9 | 10 | 11 | 12

161-B. Clear all tabs. Then set three new tab stops 26, 43, and 53 spaces from left margin. Type each line, tabulating across from column to column.

161-B. SKILL DRILL: TABULATOR PRACTICE—ALPHABET AND NUMBERS

4	Gallegho, Alicia	Bayfield	27	$ 683
5	Jackson, Palmer A.	Quincy	25	903
6	Lutz, Raymond E.	Lexington	37	4,116
7	Wong, Frances	Renville	28	8,049

161-C. Spacing—double. Tab—5. Take two 5-minute timings. Between them, practice any words with which you had difficulty. Record your score.

161-C. SKILL MEASUREMENT: 5-MINUTE TIMED WRITING

8   A friend recently queried me about the procedures used 12
by our firm in the selection of new employees. It was soon 24
apparent that the primary question dealt with criteria that 36
are used to select certain individuals for interviews. The 48
application form, a data sheet, and maybe a letter from the 60
applicant are first screened very carefully by at least two 72
of our six personnel assistants. Candidates who seek posi- 84
tions not only have their data analyzed thoroughly but also 96
are judged on the neatness and format of the documents. 107
     Traditional job seekers have filled out an application 119
form, provided a data sheet, and waited for that phone call 131
that too often does not occur. Although there is not total 143
acceptance in the personnel field, an assertive alternative 155
on the part of the job hunter may prove successful. Either 167
a phone call to the company or even a stop at the personnel 179
office may lead to that perfect job. While there are those 191
who react negatively to this approach, the timing of a call 203
or a visit may be crucial. It is not necessarily true that 215
the desirable jobs go to those who patiently wait. 225
| 1 | 2 | 3 | 4 | 5 | 6 | 7 | 8 | 9 | 10 | 11 | 12

65/66-E. CREDIT APPLICATIONS

FORM 4
CREDIT APPLICATION
Form: Workguide 121
Proofguide: 39

An application for credit or for a credit card may differ in form and design, but the information requested is standard. When typing a credit application form, be sure to adjust the paper (use the paper release) so that your typing will appear above the printed line.

APPLICATION FOR CREDIT

NAME Marjorie K. Jenkins

ADDRESS 183 South Lincoln Avenue

Bellevue   NE   68005
Town or City   State   ZIP

HOW LONG AT ABOVE ADDRESS? 10 years

OWN OR RENT? Own

PREVIOUS ADDRESS 15 Jefferson Drive

Plattsmouth   NE   68048
Town or City   State   ZIP

CURRENT EMPLOYER Bellevue Travel Agency

EMPLOYER'S ADDRESS 15 Main Street

Bellevue   NE   68005
Town or City   State   ZIP

POSITION HELD Travel agent

HOW LONG EMPLOYED? 6 years

CURRENT SALARY $1,800 a month

SOCIAL SECURITY NUMBER 151-38-0744

TELEPHONE (402) 555-8624

CHECKING ACCOUNT First National Trust
                         Name of Bank

SAVINGS ACCOUNT Nebraska Savings
                        Name of Bank

OTHER CREDIT OBLIGATIONS

Kress Department Store $250
   Creditor   Amount

Auto Loan--First National Trust $3,550
   Creditor   Amount

NAMES AND ADDRESSES OF TWO REFERENCES

Mr. Jose Paz, P.O. Box 102, Bellevue, NE 68005

Mrs. Amy Lee, P.O. Box 215, Bellevue, NE 68005

APPLICANT'S SIGNATURE *Marjorie K. Jenkins*

Line: 60 spaces   Tab: 5
Spacing: single   Drills: 2X
Proofguide: 39–40
Workguide: 3–4, 123
Tape: 18B

LESSONS 67/68
JOB APPLICATION PAPERS

Goals: To practice symbol keys; to format a personal data sheet and a job application form.

67-A. WARMUP

S 1 The man and boy did not get paid for the day off from work.
A 2 Five big jet planes zoomed quickly by the six steel towers.
N 3 Order 10 orange, 29 tan, 38 gray, 47 red, and 56 blue pens.
      | 1 | 2 | 3 | 4 | 5 | 6 | 7 | 8 | 9 | 10 | 11 | 12

67-B. Type lines 4–7 two times each.

67-B. SYMBOL PRACTICE

4 juj ju7j j7j j&j j7j&j j7&j frf fr5f f5f f%f f5f%f f5%f 15%
5 sws sw2s s2s s@s s2s@s s2@s frf fr4f f4f f$f f4f$f f4$f $41
6 ;p; ;p0; ;0; ;); ;0;); ;0); jyj jy6j j6j j¢j j6j¢j j6¢j 16¢
7 lol lo9l l9l l(l l9l(l l9(l ded de3d d3d d#d d3d#d d3#d #31

MEMORANDUM 15

Paper: Workguide 381
Proofguide: 119–120

This is a memorandum report, a commonly used form for short business reports.

MEMORANDUM 16

Paper: plain, full sheet
Proofguide: 119–120

WP Some word processors have a *bold printing* feature. This feature makes it possible to print certain information, such as headings, darker than the rest of the text.

MID-STATE BAKERIES, INC.
3628 Mount Vernon Drive   Bloomington, IL 61701

↓13

To: Walker F. Folsom, Delivery   7
                                                                          8
From: Warren A. Dahlman, Manager   15
                                                                         16
Date: (Current Date)   22
                                                                         23
Subject: O'Dell's Corner Grocery Account   32

a copy of my follow-up letter to Mr. O'Dell is attached.   34

You reported last Wednesday that you ~~had~~ visited O'Dell's   45
Corner Grocery in Peoria. Please ~~except~~ accept my thanks for your   69
efforts in brining our products to thier attention. You   81
will be pleased *to know* that we have now obtained the following   93
information, which was useful in making credit decisions: 105
                                                            ↓3
                                                                        107

CREDIT INFORMATION   111
                   ↓2   112

All information provided by ~~credit~~ references suggests that   124
O'Dell's has a *sound* reputation for timely payment of its open   137
accounts. We have set a credit limit of $3,500, based on   148
projected purchases. Requests for extension of that amount   160
must be aproved by the credit department.   169
   +#   171
DRIVER RESPONSIBILITIES   176
                                                                        177

You will be responsible for monitoring this new account   188
during the next six months, which is a *unofficial* trial period. If at 202
any time the requested purchases exceed $3,500, Mr. O'Dell   214
must be informed by you that your instructions require cash   226
payment above that amount. However, in the interest of good-   238
will, you will telephone the Credit Department with a request   251
for a temporary credit extension. #Again, thanks *to you* for securing 265
the O'Dell account. Your Incentive Reward will be included   277
in your next pay check.   281
                                                                        282

frs   283
Attachment   285

An attachment is much the same as an enclosure. However, it is usually attached with a paper clip or a staple and not necessarily placed in an envelope for routing.

67-C. Spacing—double. Record
your score.

67-C. SKILL MEASUREMENT: 5-MINUTE TIMED WRITING

8   Temporary help firms developed during the postwar era.   12
Since then, they have grown in size and scope to provide to   24
business millions of workers. Today, temporary help is big   36
business. Companies quite often need extra staff when they   48
have peak work loads or have workers absent. This shortage   60
of workers can be eased by having a temporary service place   72
one of its workers on the job for a day, a week, or longer.   84
The worker, known as a temp, is paid by the hour. The   96
pay scale rises with the level of skill, and those who type   108
earn more than those who do not, and those who can use word   120
processors can earn most of all. Doing temp work is a good   132
way to begin a career, gain experience, improve skills, and   144
make job contacts. A further benefit is that the temporary   156
worker may earn a salary higher than the pay of the regular   168
employee.   170

| 1 | 2 | 3 | 4 | 5 | 6 | 7 | 8 | 9 | 10 | 11 | 12

67/68-D. JOB APPLICATION PAPERS

At some point in one's life, it is necessary to give consideration to applying for a job. Regardless of the employment level desired, it is critical that one prepare employment papers with care and accuracy. Your employment application papers may create the first impression you make during an interview—so prepare them properly! Generally, you will need a letter of application; a personal data sheet, or résumé; and a job application form.

LETTER 20
LETTER OF APPLICATION

**PERSONAL-BUSINESS LETTER
  IN MODIFIED-BLOCK STYLE**
Paper: plain
Proofguide: 39–40

Review page 53 for vertical and horizontal placement of a personal-business letter.

157 Main Street / Clearfield, KY 40313 / April 2, 19— / Mr. Thomas Catalano / Personnel Department / General Insurance Company / 15 South Maple Avenue / Morehead, KY 40351 / Dear Mr. Catalano: 19 30 43

Mrs. Roberta Carr, my instructor in secretarial procedures at Harris Business College, has informed me that you are currently looking for an individual to join your firm as an administrative assistant in the Claims Department.   58 68 82 86

I will be earning a diploma in secretarial science from Harris on May 15. Since I am eager to use my skills and abilities in a well-known company, I would like to be considered for the available position. Enclosed is my personal data sheet.   101 115 129 136

I will call you next week to set up an appointment for an interview.   151

Sincerely yours, / Susan M. Sarafino / Enclosure   166

159/160-D. LETTERS AND MEMORANDUMS

Use Workguide letterheads and plain paper to type the letters and memorandums.

LETTER 60
BLOCK STYLE WITH OPEN PUNCTUATION ON BARONIAL STATIONERY

Carbons: one cc, one bcc, one file
Paper: Workguide 377–378
Proofguide: 119–120

LETTER 61
BLOCK STYLE WITH OPEN PUNCTUATION

Carbons: one cc, one bcc, one file
Paper: Workguide 379–380
Proofguide: 119–120

Retype the letter, this time on standard-size paper.

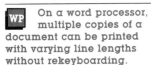 On a word processor, multiple copies of a document can be printed with varying line lengths without rekeyboarding.

The bcc notation is typed after removing the original and any carbon copies that are not to show this information.

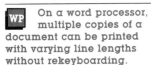 On a word processor, the bcc notation can be added to selected copies without removing the other copies.

REMINDER: The bcc notation may also be typed on line 7 at the left margin.

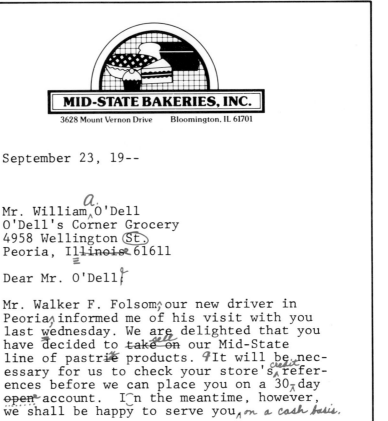

MID-STATE BAKERIES, INC.	
3628 Mount Vernon Drive Bloomington, IL 61701	

September 23, 19--   4

Mr. William a. O'Dell   11
O'Dell's Corner Grocery   16
4958 Wellington St.   21
Peoria, Illinois 61611   24

Dear Mr. O'Dell   28

Mr. Walker F. Folsom, our new driver in   37
Peoria, informed me of his visit with you   46
last wednesday. We are delighted that you   54
have decided to take on sell our Mid-State   61
line of pastrie products. ¶It will be nec-   69
essary for us to check your store's credit refer-   79
ences before we can place you on a 30-day   87
open account. In the meantime, however,   94
we shall be happy to serve you, on a cash basis.   104

Deliveries will be made seven days each   113
week, beginning on a date that you select.   122

Sincerely yours   126

Warren A. Dahlman   133
Manager   134

efk   136
cc Credit Department   140

Sincerel

Warren A
Manager

efk
cc Credi
bcc Mr. Walker F. Folsom

Business letter in block style on baronial stationery, with cc and bcc notations.

**PERSONAL DATA
SHEET**

Shown in elite
Paper: plain
Placement: center
Line: 6-inch (60 pica/70
 elite)
Tab: 15
Proofguide: 39–40

Type the data sheet at
the right or prepare
one for your own use in
applying for a job.

List all items in reverse
chronological order—
most recent first.

Susan M. Sarafino

157 Main Street
Clearfield, KY 40313
606–555–4269 ↓ 3

Education   Harris Business College, Morehead, KY 40351
Degree: A.A. in Secretarial Science, May 1984 ↓ 2

Business Subjects:
 Accounting
 Typing (75 wam)
 Shorthand (120 wam)
 Office Procedures
 Filing
 Transcription
 Communications
 Word Processing ↓ 2

Morehead High School, Morehead, KY
Graduated: June 1982 ↓ 3

Honors,
Awards, and
Activities   Scholarship to Harris Business College; vice president,
Administrative Management Society; member of Ski Club
and Bowling Club ↓ 3

If work experience is
your strongest asset,
list it first.

Work
Experience
(Part-time)   Bates & Wilson, Morehead, KY
Position: Clerk/Stenographer
June 1983–Present
↓ 2

Johnson Fuels, Clearfield, KY
Position: File Clerk/Typist
September 1982–June 1983
↓ 3

Include at least three
references. (Be sure to
receive permission
before using someone's
name as a reference.)

References   Mrs. Roberta Carr, Secretarial Procedures Instructor,
Harris Business College, Morehead, KY 40351 ↓ 2

Ms. Martha Chan, Academic Dean, Harris Business
College, Morehead, KY 40351 ↓ 2

Mr. William Bates, Bates & Wilson, 33 Garrison Street,
Morehead, KY 40351

FORM 6
JOB APPLICATION

Form: Workguide 123
Proofguide: 39

Page 123 of your Workguide contains an employment application form. Fill it in completely with your personal data, as though you were applying for an office job.

Line: 60 spaces   Drills: 3X
Spacing: single
Proofguide: 119–120
Workguide: 331–332,
   377–381
Tape: 52A

LESSONS 159/160
LETTERS AND MEMOS

Goals: To build skill in tabulating; to improve skill in formatting letters and memorandums.

159-A. WARMUP

S   1   She told us that half of the men will turn at the old fork.
A   2   Five citizens of Quebec joined her at an extravagant party.
N   3   The 1849 wagon train had 57 men, 26 women, and 30 children.
| 1 | 2 | 3 | 4 | 5 | 6 | 7 | 8 | 9 | 10 | 11 | 12

159-B. Clear all tabs. Then set four new tab stops every 13 spaces. Type each row, tabulating across from column to column.

159-B. SKILL DRILL: TABULATOR PRACTICE—NUMBERS

4 1,234	2,345	7,890	6,789	4,567
5 3,459	9,201	3,739	4,011	6,681
6 2,480	1,857	5,002	5,482	4,702
7 7,693	8,936	6,793	3,550	2,018

159-C. Spacing—double. Tab—5. Take two 5-minute timings. Between them, practice any words with which you had difficulty. Record your score.

159-C. SKILL MEASUREMENT: 5-MINUTE TIMED WRITING

8   There is no question that a traditional boss–secretary 12
office is not as efficient as we would like to think. Most 24
such offices must deal with a volume of paper that seems to 36
increase each day. The increased costs of processing reams 48
of paper have led many business executives to search for an 60
alternative that might be justified. Word processing is an 72
option that is often seized upon as the way to go. The use 84
of longhand in the office has been a real problem for years 96
as a popular method for capturing ideas. Dictation and the 108
use of text–editing equipment have become alternatives that 120
eliminate repetitive keyboarding and proofreading. 130
     Those who have worked in an office know that there are 142
days filled with uneven work loads. We all agree that such 154
days lead to frustrations and a low production rate for the 166
company. But the work loads are assigned and supervised by 178
a professional supervisor whenever a word processing center 190
is established. Work loads become more even, and there are 202
fewer interruptions. The net result is secretaries who are 214
satisfied, challenged, and highly productive employees. 225
| 1 | 2 | 3 | 4 | 5 | 6 | 7 | 8 | 9 | 10 | 11 | 12

Line: 60 spaces	Tab: 5, center
Spacing: single	Drills: 2X
Proofguide: 41–42	
Workguide: 3–4, 125–126	
Tape: 19B	

LESSONS 69/70
BOUND REPORTS

Goals· To use additional proofreaders' marks; to format a two-page bound report.

69-A. WARMUP

S 1 The eight girls will laugh when the ducks flap their wings.
A 2 The dozen extra blue jugs were quickly moved from the pool.
N 3 Order No. 2947 requested 56 pies to be shipped to 1380 Elm.
| 1 | 2 | 3 | 4 | 5 | 6 | 7 | 8 | 9 | 10 | 11 | 12

69-B. Type lines 4–7 two times each. Then take two 1-minute timings. (Note that the last two digits of each number are a cumulative word count.) After the number practice, take a series of 1-minute timings on paragraph 8.

69-B. NUMBER PRACTICE

4 3701 5602 6703 1204 4405 7806 1907 2108 3709 5110 6911 2312
5 1513 8314 7315 9216 8817 2118 3219 4720 9721 1622 2423 8724
6 7225 5426 3927 1828 7129 2730 4931 8232 8033 9434 1935 3236
7 6837 7238 9439 6440 3841 7142 3343 9944 5145 3146 2247 5048

8 　　Memberships were as follows: 156 members in the Drama 12
Club, 104 members in Zeta Tau, 73 members in Theta Phi, 129 24
members in Ski Club, 83 members in Beta Rho, and 72 members 36
in the Dance Club. This gave a grand total of 617 members. 48
| 1 | 2 | 3 | 4 | 5 | 6 | 7 | 8 | 9 | 10 | 11 | 12

69-C. Spacing—double. Record your score.

69-C. SKILL MEASUREMENT: 5-MINUTE TIMED WRITING

9 　　Reports are important, both in school and in business. 12
Many teachers assign reports in their classes so that their 24
students will delve deeper into subjects. Many schools now 36
require a report in each course in order to improve writing 48
skills. Reports play a major role in business too and form 60
the basis for future actions. This is true today more than 72
ever before. Decisions are often based on written reports. 84
　　Reports give facts and help one to analyze data. They 96
vary in length from one page to many. Form counts, as well 108
as the content, and the neater a report is, the better. In 120
fact, students get higher grades when they type their work, 132
and many teachers accept only typed reports. Some students 144
must hire others to type for them. Since report writing is 156
such a common task, the wise student shall certainly profit 168
by learning how to type accurately. 175
| 1 | 2 | 3 | 4 | 5 | 6 | 7 | 8 | 9 | 10 | 11 | 12

These three letters are also being sent by Melissa K. Jocelyn, marketing director at Administrative Support Services, Inc. She prefers to use *Sincerely yours,* for most letters. But she uses *Cordially,* as the complimentary closing for letters to those with whom she is on a first-name basis. Provide the correct paragraphing for each letter.

LETTER 57
MODIFIED-BLOCK STYLE
WITH INDENTED
PARAGRAPHS

Line: 5 inches
   (50 pica/60 elite)
Paragraphs: 3
Tab: 5, center
Paper: Workguide 371–372
Proofguide: 117–118

This letter is to be sent to Mr. Steven T. Pierce, a 12
personal friend of Ms. Jocelyn. Mr. Pierce is the 20
administrator at Johnson Memorial Hospital lo- 20
cated at 8960 Pompano Lane, Houston, TX 77072. 28
(*Opening lines*) 31

Thanks for the kind words you passed on to 41
Dan Beckman about the statistical report we 50
produced for you last month. The success of 59
our service depends on the opinions of you 67
and our other customers. I thought you might 78
be interested to know that we recently ac- 86
quired a high-speed line printer which ac- 94
cepts magnetic cards as input. I know you 103
were inquiring about the possibility of using 112
your magnetic card typewriters to simply 120
keyboard your large mailings and send them 129
to us for printing. This certainly would save 138
your operators' time. Let me know if you 146
would like to pursue this possibility. Please 157
say hello to Kris. Tom and I are looking for- 166
ward to seeing both of you this winter at the 175
lodge. (*Closing lines*) 195

LETTER 58
MODIFIED-BLOCK STYLE
WITH INDENTED
PARAGRAPHS

Line: 5 inches
   (50 pica/60 elite)
Paragraphs: 3
Tab: 5, center
Paper: Workguide 373–374
Proofguide: 117–118

This letter is to Ms. Juanita Lopez, Stockbroker, 14

Equity Resources, Inc., 7602 Cedar Bayou Road, 23
Baytown, TX 77520. (*Opening lines*) 31

In response to your letter in which you in- 41
quire about producing a monthly letter to be 50
sent to your five hundred regular clients, let 59
me say that we would be most pleased to 67
take on this project. The inside addresses 77
and salutations would be keyboarded and 85
stored in our computer. Each month the form 94
letter would be keyboarded on the text edi- 102
tor only once. We would recall the cus- 110
tomer information from the computer and 118
merge it with the form letter. Our high-speed 127
line printer would then produce an original, 136
personalized letter for each of your cus- 144
tomers. I have given your request to Mr. 154
Daniel Beckman, our office coordinator. He 163
will be contacting you to discuss these plans. 172
(*Closing lines*) 192

LETTER 59
MODIFIED-BLOCK STYLE
WITH INDENTED
PARAGRAPHS

Line: 5 inches
   (50 pica/60 elite)
Paragraphs: 2
Tab: 5, center
Paper: Workguide 375–376
Proofguide: 119–120

This letter is to Ms. Susan P. Connors, Office Man- 14
ager, Kline and Frank Law Offices, 8402 South 23
Shore Drive, Galveston, TX 77550. (*Opening lines*) 34

Yes, we are now in the process of adding 44
the type of consulting service about which 52
you inquired in your recent letter. We will 62
provide word processing consulting services 70
to companies in the Houston area. Our 79
services will range from assisting small firms 89
in the selection of text editing equipment to 98
conducting feasibility studies for implemen- 107
tation of a word processing center in larger 116
firms. This service will be ready to begin 125
operation next month. We will then be in 134
touch with you. (*Closing lines*) 157

69-D. PROOFREADERS' MARKS

Six proofreaders' marks were introduced in Lessons 44/45. Additional proofreaders' marks are presented below. Before you type Report 10, study all the proofreaders' marks and read through the entire report that follows. As you type the report, listen for the margin bell and end each line accordingly. Your typed page will not necessarily end at the same point as the page in the text.

For further practice in using proofreaders' marks, complete Workguide pages 125–126.

Proofreaders' Mark		Draft	Final Copy
SS	Single-space	SS ⌈first line / ⌊second line	first line / second line
ds	Double-space	ds ⌈first line / ⌊second line	first line / second line
¶	Make new paragraph	¶ If he is	If he is
∽	Transpose	to (quickly / go)	to go quickly
∧	Insert word	and ∧it is	and so it is
∧	Insert punctuation	today∧and	today, and
#	Insert space	all#ready to	all ready to
◡	Omit space	court◡room	courtroom
word	Change word	and if she	and so she

Proofreaders' Mark		Draft	Final Copy
♂	Delete	a true fact	a fact
•••	Don't delete	a true story	a true story
ℒ	Delete and close up	co⌿operation	cooperation
≡	Capitalize	Fifth avenue	Fifth Avenue
/	Use lowercase letter	our President	our president
◯	Spell out	the only ①	the only one
⊙	Make it a period	one way⊙	one other way.
♂	Move as shown	no (other) way	no way
[	Move to the left	[It is not	It is not
]	Move to the right	It is not]	It is not
⑤	Indent 5 spaces	⑤It is not	It is not

69/70-E. FORMATTING A TWO-PAGE REPORT (BOUND)

A bound report requires a wider left margin for binding. To format a bound report, (1) use the visual guide on Workguide page 80 or (2) set stops for a 6-inch (60 pica/70 elite) line and shift the paper guide ¼ inch (about 3 spaces) to the left.

The first page of a two-page report is formatted in the same manner as a one-page report. To format the second page: (1) Type the page number (the word *page* is unnecessary) on line 7 at the right margin. (Do not type a page number on the first page.) (2) Begin

```
                                          ↓7
                                           2
                                          ↓3
BOTTOM MARGINS

    The bottom margin on each page should be a minimum of 6
or a maximum of 9 lines deep.  On standard paper with 66 lines,
```

the text of the report on line 10, a triple space below the page number.

REPORT 10
**TWO-PAGE BOUND
  REPORT**

Shown in pica
Paper: plain
Visual guide: Workguide 80
Proofguide: 41–42

```
TYPING A REPORT              Title               9

A Report for Typing I        Subtitle            24
     By (Your name)          By-Line             38
              ↓3

    The standard rules for typing a report, such as a term   52

paper, are illustrated on this and the next page.            62
                                         ↓3

THE SPACING TO USE                                           68

    Single-space all special displays, such as headings that  80

take (2) lines, quotations that are sure to will fill more than two  91

typed lines, footnotes, listings, and so forth.             101
```

157/158-D. MODIFIED-BLOCK LETTERS

Before typing the letters in this lesson, complete Workguide pages 365–366. Use the visual guide for letter placement (Workguide page 367) when typing correspondence.

LETTER 56
MODIFIED-BLOCK STYLE

Shown in elite
Line: 5 inches (50 pica/60 elite)
Tab: center
Paper: Workguide 369–370
Proofguide: 117–118

ADMINISTRATIVE SUPPORT SERVICES, INC.

12301 Turtle Creek Road   Houston, TX 77017   Telephone: (713) 555-9267

September 20, 19—   4

Southwest Insurance Agency   13
7160 Oakhurst Lane   17
Beaumont, TX 77707   21

Attention: Mr. Craig Lindberg   28

Ladies and Gentlemen: 34

Subject: Office Services   40

Administrative Support Services, Inc., would like to welcome   53
you to Beaumont. You will enjoy conducting business in this   65
beautiful and rapidly expanding area in the Lone Star State.   78

Our office performs a variety of office tasks that companies   91
might not have the resources to accomplish on their own. There   104
will surely be periods when your office work load becomes so   116
great that your secretaries become frustrated by the heavy   128
load of overtime work. This could result in low productivity.   140

You will be able to minimize these problems by allowing us   153
to transcribe those stacks of dictated tapes, produce those   165
multiple-page reports, or prepare those hundreds of letters.   178
A pamphlet detailing our services is enclosed for your review.   190
If you would like a free estimate, please contact Mr. Daniel   203
Beckman, our office coordinator.   209

Sincerely yours,   215

Melissa K. Jocelyn   223
Marketing Director   227

kak   229
Enclosure   231
cc Daniel Beckman   235

WP Word processors have an automatic page-break feature that will end one page at the appropriate point to provide the correct bottom margin and then automatically space down to begin typing on the next page, leaving the correct top margin.

Start page 2 here →

Double-space the body of the report unless there is a   113
special reason for single-spacing it (such as the need for   125
saving space in filing or materials in duplicating).   135

Triple-space (that is, leave 2 blank lines) after the   146
heading of any page and before any major sub-heading.   157

Quadruple-space (leaving three blank lines) to seperate   169
a table from the adjacent body of the report.   178

THE MARGINS TO USE   184

Top Margin. The top margin should be 2 inches deep on   200
the first page and 1 inch deep on all the other pages. So typ-   213
ing will begin on Line 13 of the first page and on Line 7 of all   226
additional other pages.   229

Bottom Margin. The bottom margin should be at least   245
one inch deep and maybe up to 1½ inches deep. If the last   257
page of a report is short, then the bottom margin will, of course, be deeper.   272

Side Margins. The side margins should permit a 6-inch   296
line of writing (60 spaces pica, 70 spaces elite), centered   308
in if the report is not to be bound in a note book or binder,   319
but moved a quarter ¼ inch to the right (giving a left margin   330
of 1½ inches and a right margin of 1 inch) if the report is   342
to be so bound.   345

THE PLACEMENT OF Headings   352

The page-1 heading lines should be centered, the title   364
in all caps and other lines in capitall and small letters.   376
Major subheadings may be blocked at the margin (in which case   389
they are called "side headings") or centered. They may be   401
typed in all caps, as in this report, or underscored.   412
paragraph headings are indented and underscored.   423

The page number is omitted on page 1. On other pages, it   435
is typed on line 7 at the right margin, with or without the   447
word "page," and is followed by 2 blank linespaces.   457

| Line: 60 spaces   Drills: 3X |
| Spacing: single |
| Proofguide: 117–120 |
| Workguide: 331–332, |
| 369–376 |
| Tape: 52A |

LESSONS 157/158
LETTERS

Goals: To build skill in tabulating; to improve skill in formatting letters.

157-A. WARMUP

S 1 Four signs showed the way to a town that is now on the map.
A 2 A quaint chap woke up and saw a fox jump the blazing river.
N 3 Our city's population grew from 39,612 to 40,587 in a year.
   | 1 | 2 | 3 | 4 | 5 | 6 | 7 | 8 | 9 | 10 | 11 | 12

157-B. Clear all tabs. Then set four new tab stops every 13 spaces. Type each row, tabulating across from column to column.

157-B. SKILL DRILL: TABULATOR PRACTICE—ALPHABET

4 carts	frame	trait	irony	quart
5 learn	jolly	label	zebra	block
6 named	pilot	labor	poems	waive
7 cough	dream	train	drill	extra

157-C. Spacing—double. Tab—5. Take a 5-minute timing with a 5-second rest after each minute, then a 5-minute timing without stopping. Try to reach the same point on the second timing with 5 or fewer errors. Record your score.

157-C. SKILL MEASUREMENT: 5-MINUTE TIMED WRITING

8   Typists in most offices are required to make a copy of 12
each item of correspondence for the files. The preparation 24
of additional copies for those who need to know the content 36
of the item may be judged necessary. Copies may be carbons 48
or photocopies. It is customary to inform the recipient of 60
the letter, memo, or report that the sender is also mailing 72
extra copies to certain individuals. The carbon copy nota- 84
tion is typed under the typist's reference initials. After 96
the letters "cc," names of copy recipients are then entered 108
either according to rank or else alphabetically.   118
        A blind carbon copy notation might be needed at times. 130
For example, if a customer sends a sizzling letter, you may 142
want to respond with a gentle letter but rush copies of the 154
letter and your response to your local agent with a request 166
that the matter be investigated. To show that the copy was 178
sent without the knowledge of the addressee, you type "bcc" 190
and the field agent's name only on the file copy and on the 202
copy for him or her. The "bcc" notation is then entered at 214
the left margin under the closing lines of the letter.   225
   | 1 | 2 | 3 | 4 | 5 | 6 | 7 | 8 | 9 | 10 | 11 | 12

NOTE: The bcc notation may also be typed on line 7 at the left margin.

Line: 60 spaces   Tab: 5, center
Spacing: single   Drills: 2X
Proofguide: 41—44
Workguide: 3—4, 80
Tape: 20B

LESSONS 71/72

FOOTNOTES

Goals: To format a bound manuscript with footnotes at the bottom of the page; to format a one-page report with endnotes.

71-A. WARMUP

S 1 The neighbor paid the town for the effort to move the tree.
A 2 Dave froze the mixtures in the deep brown jugs too quickly.
N 3 Stubs 19, 20, 37, 56, and 84 were misplaced by the teacher.
| 1 | 2 | 3 | 4 | 5 | 6 | 7 | 8 | 9 | 10 | 11 | 12

71-B. Spacing—double. Record your score.

NOTE: Be sure you read and understand the information in 71-B before going on to 71-C.

71-B. SKILL MEASUREMENT: 5-MINUTE TIMED WRITING

4   Footnotes are often used in reports. Their purpose is 12
to cite the exact source from which data was taken and make 24
it easy for the reader to look up special points. They may 36
also explain ideas. Sometimes the writer must be the judge 48
of whether to footnote or not, but it's always good to give 60
credit where credit is due. Failure to cite direct sources 72
is more severe and may lead to legal problems. Hence it is 84
essential research practice to know when you must footnote. 96
      Footnotes are generally typed at the bottom of a page. 108
The typist should plan ahead so as to have room for all the 120
footnotes. Allow three lines for each footnote. After the 132
last line of text, single-space before typing an underscore 144
line of two inches and then double-space once again. Typed 156
footnotes are single-spaced, with each first line indented. 168
Double-space between the footnotes. 175
| 1 | 2 | 3 | 4 | 5 | 6 | 7 | 8 | 9 | 10 | 11 | 12

71-C. FOOTNOTES AND ENDNOTES

Type the following first page of a bound report (page 108) with footnotes at the bottom of the page. A 2-inch (20 pica/24 elite) underscore line is typed to separate the text from footnotes. Single spacing precedes the underscore line and double spacing follows it. Each footnote is a separate, single-spaced item, with the first line indented 5 spaces. Leave 1 blank line above each footnote.

After you have typed the report with bottom-of-page footnotes, retype the page using endnotes. When using endnotes, place the references on one page at the end of the report. (See the illustration to the right.)

↓ 13
NOTES
↓ 3

    1. William Coyle, Research Papers, 5th ed., Bobbs-Merrill Educational Publishing, Indianapolis, 1980, p. 123.

    2. Kate L. Turabian, A Manual for Writers of Term Papers, Theses, and Dissertations, 4th ed., The University of Chicago Press, Chicago, 1973, p. 64.

    3. Robert L. Tyne, "Let's Agree on the Basics," Journal of Academic Research, Vol. 18, No. 3, p. 46, September 1982.

    4. A secondary use of footnotes or endnotes is to provide additional information that is worthwhile to include but that would disrupt the flow of thought if introduced into the text. This is an example of such a note.

    5. Robert Lipsom, "Who Thought of It First?," The Wall Street Journal, January 18, 1982, p. 1, col. 4.

    6. Turabian, p. 69.

156-D. PRACTICE: ACCURACY

30 Complimentary passes won't be distributed indiscriminately.
31 Several oversized boxers made necessary weight adjustments.
32 The lavender robe seemed excessively exquisite for a boxer.
33 Thirty-nine relatives with ringside tickets jumped for joy.

| 1 | 2 | 3 | 4 | 5 | 6 | 7 | 8 | 9 | 10 | 11 | 12

156-E. PRACTICE: MACHINE MANIPULATION

Backspace key

34 Ms. Lelander's most recent book was entitled <u>Tax Revisions</u>.
35 Edward said that they <u>may</u> join us for a <u>late</u> round of golf.
36 Michael had to prepare <u>four</u> depositions and <u>five</u> contracts.
37 One witness said the car was <u>yellow</u>; one said it was <u>white</u>.

Margin release

38 A decision has been made to shut down one building in March or April.
39 Energy conservation and the slight decrease in sales are the reasons.
40 The savings in utility costs alone for one year could exceed $60,000.
41 Your division must be prepared to relocate no later than February 28.

| 1 | 2 | 3 | 4 | 5 | 6 | 7 | 8 | 9 | 10 | 11 | 12 | 13 | 14

POSTTEST. Repeat the Pretest and compare performance.

156-F. POSTTEST: SELECTIVE PRACTICE

156-G. Spacing—double. Take a 5-minute timing with a 5-second rest after each minute, then a 5-minute timing without stopping. Try to reach the same point on the second timing with 5 or fewer errors. Record your score.

156-G. SKILL MEASUREMENT: 5-MINUTE TIMED WRITING

42   A word processing machine can be used with some of the 12
other types of equipment in the modern office. Information 24
processing is a term used by those firms that integrate two 36
or more pieces of the following: data and word processing, 48
micrographics, and telecommunications. We now see that the 60
linking of text-editing terminals to big computers is quite 72
common. The data processing functions that permit a person 84
to select, sort, and merge are fused with text editing. 95

    A word processor can be used in conjunction with other 107
amazing new techniques that are used to make copies at fast 119
speeds and at costs that are very low. The cost of storing 131
file copies can be adjusted downward when microfilm is used 143
rather than those big files that take up so much space. As 155
filming can bypass the printing stage, both paper and space 167
are saved. Telecommunications is a broad term that is used 179
to include the various alternatives to the traditional mail 191
system for distributing messages. Information is sent over 203
telephone and telegraph lines at high rates of speed, and a 215
message may use tables and graphs as well as words. 225

| 1 | 2 | 3 | 4 | 5 | 6 | 7 | 8 | 9 | 10 | 11 | 12

WP On a word processor, it is not necessary to backspace before underscoring. Instead, the operator enters a command before and after typing the underscored word(s), and the machine underscores automatically.

Report 11:
Type the report shown on this page with footnotes.
Report 12:
Type the report shown on this page replacing the footnotes with endnotes.

Paper: plain
Visual guide:
  Workguide 80
Proofguide: 41–44

WP **Word processors have a special feature that enables you to position footnote numbers quickly and correctly and to automatically leave enough space at the bottom of the page for typing the footnotes.**

NOTE: **Footnotes may also be typed with superior numbers—e.g., [1]Estelle . . . .**

BUSINESS NEEDS EFFECTIVE COMMUNICATORS   23

By (*Your name*)   37

Communication plays a vital role in the daily operations   52

of the business world. The need for better communications   63

skills has long *been* noted by business leaders.[1] effective communi-   79

cation means effective listening, speaking, and writing.[2]   92

Listening   96

All people in business must listen carefully *so* that they will   110

have the information needed to make decisions. One must   121

listen with the mind and decide what to do with the information   134

heard. Listening is the first key to becoming an *effective* communicator.   149

SPEAKING AND WRITING   155

Business *needs* requires workers who can speak and write clearly   167

Whether a person is an entry-level worker, a top executive of   176

the company, or a middle management, individual *or* there will be   184

instances where oral and written communication *is a requirement of the job* will be used   196

To be an effective communicator, in speaking and writing, one   204

must know grammar, punctuation, spelling, vocabulary, and *and*   215

expression. To be successful an individual in business, should *must*   225

posses good speaking and writig skills.   234
        240

1. Estelle L. Popham et al., A Teaching-Learning System   264
for Business Education, McGraw-Hill Book Company, New York,   286
1975, p. 243.   288

2. Kalia Lulow, "Conversations *With* Rosemary T. Fruehling,"   301
Business Education World, May/June, 1980, p. 11.   321

PRACTICE. If you made no errors on the Pretest, type the speed drill lines in 155-C 3 times each; otherwise, type the accuracy drill lines in 155-D 3 times each. Then type each machine manipulation drill line in 155-E 3 times.

155-C. PRACTICE: SPEED

```
5  as if it|got the old|went with them|shall not be|if she can
6  it is as|the man has|they were with|going for it|it may not
7  or it is|had cut the|will wish that|think she is|or had the
8  to do it|may not see|told them that|might not go|as the man
9  is to be|but for the|have seen some|there may be|is for the
   |  1  |  2  |  3  |  4  |  5  |  6  |  7  |  8  |  9  |  10  |  11  |  12
```

155-D. PRACTICE: ACCURACY

```
10  Inquiring students have acquired a dozen mystery thrillers.
11  Indisputable evidence directly linked six major characters.
12  The yelping dogs and whining jaguars arouse my imagination.
13  These haunted houses have creaking doors and eerie squeals.
14  Eleven amazingly extravagant philanthropists were culprits.
   |  1  |  2  |  3  |  4  |  5  |  6  |  7  |  8  |  9  |  10  |  11  |  12
```

155-E. PRACTICE: MACHINE MANIPULATIONS

Shift lock
```
15  His favorite wildlife photography book is ANIMALS AT NIGHT.
16  HOME TEAM and VISITORS signs were both spelled incorrectly.
17  BASIC and PL/1 are two of the older languages still in use.
18  Gwen Stanton and R. B. O'Connell coauthored POWER SOFTWARE.
19  The NO SMOKING and EXIT signs were printed by art students.
   |  1  |  2  |  3  |  4  |  5  |  6  |  7  |  8  |  9  |  10  |  11  |  12
```

Tabulator key

Clear all tabs. Then set two new tab stops 30 and 51 spaces from left margin. Type each row, tabulating across from column to column.

```
20  Chau, Chiu E.              Chairman          3 years
21  Holcomb, Rex A.            Secretary         5 years
22  Kroeger, Teri A.           Treasurer         7 years
23  Pohl, Irene E.             Director         12 years
24  Pulaski, Robert L.         Director          6 years
```

POSTTEST. Repeat the Pretest and compare performance.

155-F. POSTTEST: SELECTIVE PRACTICE

156-A. Repeat 155-A, page 232.

156-A. WARMUP

156-B. PRETEST: SELECTIVE PRACTICE

PRETEST. Take a 1-minute timing; compute speed and errors.

```
25      The control of inventory in our retail stores, as well 12
    as in the warehouses, has become increasingly important.  A 24
    modified Inventory Control Manual will acquaint experienced 36
    workers and job seekers with routinized control procedures. 48
    |  1  |  2  |  3  |  4  |  5  |  6  |  7  |  8  |  9  |  10  |  11  |  12
```

156-C. PRACTICE: SPEED

PRACTICE. If you made no errors on the Pretest, type the speed drill lines in 156-C 3 times each; otherwise, type the accuracy drill lines in 156-D 3 times each. Then type each machine manipulation drill line in 156-E 3 times.

```
26  He may get lost if half of their maps are so worn and torn.
27  She may lend me the blue auto that is for sale if it works.
28  They may make a cane chair for their camp when they return.
29  Eight of the men got to the city for the game at the field.
   |  1  |  2  |  3  |  4  |  5  |  6  |  7  |  8  |  9  |  10  |  11  |  12
```

LESSONS 73/74
REPORT PARTS

Goal: To format (1) a title page for a report and (2) a table of contents.

73-A. WARMUP

```
S  1  The boys will fix the soap dish, and Ruth will pay the fee.
A  2  Six or seven flashing new jet planes quickly zoomed by him.
N  3  When adding $17, $30, $65, $74, and $98, you will get $284.
      |  1  |  2  |  3  |  4  |  5  |  6  |  7  |  8  |  9  |  10  |  11  |  12
```

73-B. Spacing—double. Record your score.

73-B. SKILL MEASUREMENT: 5-MINUTE TIMED WRITING

```
4          By using credit, we can buy now and pay later.  Almost   12
     everyone will use some form of credit in a lifetime whether   24
     it be a loan from a bank, a charge account at a store, or a   36
     credit card.  The rise in the use of credit in modern times   48
     has been truly amazing and is a reversal of the past.  Less   60
     than sixty years ago, the use of credit was a stigma and it   72
     marked people as poor money managers.  At that time, no one   84
     delayed payment, except for major purchases such as a home.   96
           But times change.  Today, you can charge anything from  108
     a new car or boat to a trip around the world.  Business and  120
     government, likewise, have come to depend on credit.  It is  132
     a unique feature of our system—-a tool that has allowed our  144
     economy to expand and has raised our standard of living.  A  156
     look at signs for the future, though, indicates less use of  168
     credit as finance charges increase.                          175
     |  1  |  2  |  3  |  4  |  5  |  6  |  7  |  8  |  9  |  10  |  11  |  12
```

73/74-C. FORMATTING A TITLE PAGE AND A TABLE OF CONTENTS

Reports prepared for college or business often include a title page and a table of contents. The title page should appear centered horizontally and vertically—the information included is variable, depending on whether it is a business or academic report.

The table of contents for a report should be on a separate page. The heading is typed in all-capital letters on line 13. If the report is to be bound on the left, always move the paper ¼ inch (about 3 spaces) to the left to provide a larger left margin.

PRACTICE 1. Format the title page shown on page 110.

PRACTICE 2. Format a title page for Report 10, typed in Lessons 69/70.

154-G. SKILL MEASUREMENT: 5-MINUTE TIMED WRITING

154-G. Spacing—double. Take two 5-minute timings. Between them, practice any words with which you had difficulty. The marker you reach in 5 minutes is your speed. Record your score.

If you cannot be timed, type two copies of the selection.

39   Most persons agree that word processing can be defined 12
as a process whereby one transforms thoughts into words and 24
types them out on the paper with a printer. The process is 36
going on all the time in many offices throughout the world, 48
while the cost for communicating this information continues 60
to skyrocket. The findings of questionnaire studies reveal 72
that an average cost figure for the preparation and mailing 84
of a business letter is over seven dollars. With its extra 96
heavy volume of communications combined with the escalating 108
costs, the modern office must adjust and reorganize most of 120
the old ways in which it captures, processes, and transmits 132
information. There is no doubt that the challenge is real. 144
     The systems approach uses efficient control procedures 156
to aid in the smooth flow of paper in the office. Thoughts 168
are put on a magnetic medium by an author, and then one who 180
is highly skilled will use a text editor to type a document 192
that can be revised later without retyping. File space can 204
be saved with a microfilm or microfiche copy, and the cycle 216
is complete when the original copy is mailed. 225

| 1 | 2 | 3 | 4 | 5 | 6 | 7 | 8 | 9 | 10 | 11 | 12 |

| Line: 60 spaces Tab: 5 |
| Spacing: single Drills: 3X |
| Proofguide: 115–118 |
| Workguide: 331 |
| Tape: 50A and 51A |

LESSONS 155/156
SKILL DRIVE

Goals: To improve speed/accuracy; to improve machine manipulation skills.

155-A. WARMUP

S 1 He may give me the idle bus if he is busy down by the lake.
A 2 Coach Jim requested that we relax (not doze) while playing.
N 3 Lot #20 at 346 Cedar Lane is 89 feet wide by 157 feet long.

| 1 | 2 | 3 | 4 | 5 | 6 | 7 | 8 | 9 | 10 | 11 | 12 |

155-B. PRETEST: SELECTIVE PRACTICE

PRETEST. Take a 1-minute timing; compute speed and errors.

4   Jennifer can produce exact revisions overnight because 12
of her ability to operate the word processing machine. The 24
MANAGEMENT FUNDAMENTALS draft and the new outline for GAMES 36
AND THE WORK ETHIC will zoom out of the machine quite soon. 48

| 1 | 2 | 3 | 4 | 5 | 6 | 7 | 8 | 9 | 10 | 11 | 12 |

REPORT 13
TITLE PAGE

Paper: plain
Tab: center
Style as shown
Proofguide: 43–44

Prepare a title page with the following information: SURVEY OF AFFIRMATIVE ACTION PROGRAMS. A Survey to Determine the Scope, Extent, and Operation of Affirmative Action Programs in Business in Warren County, New Jersey, in 1982–83. Prepared by Charles H. Small, Research Assistant, Personnel Services Department, Data Systems, Inc. April 12, 19—.

REPORT 14
TABLE OF CONTENTS

Paper: plain
Line: 6 inches
   (60 pica/70 elite)
Tab: center
Style as shown
Proofguide: 43–44

LEADERS. **Use leaders (rows of periods that lead the eye across the page) to prepare a table of contents.**

NOTE: **Always leave 1 space** *before* **and** *after* **the row of periods. (Spaces may also be inserted between the periods, but all leaders must align vertically.)**

NOTE: **For roman numerals that take more than 1 space, use the margin release and backspace from the left margin stop.**

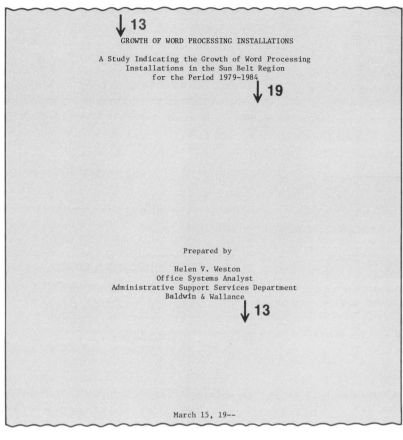

↓13

GROWTH OF WORD PROCESSING INSTALLATIONS

A Study Indicating the Growth of Word Processing
Installations in the Sun Belt Region
for the Period 1979-1984

↓19

Prepared by

Helen V. Weston
Office Systems Analyst
Administrative Support Services Department
Baldwin & Wallance

↓13

March 15, 19--

↓13
CONTENTS ↓3

153-G. Take a 1-minute timing on the first paragraph to establish your base speed. Then take successive 1-minute timings on the other paragraphs. You must equal or exceed your base speed before moving to the next paragraph.

153-G. SUSTAINED PRACTICE: NUMBERS

20   Our goal for the coming year will be to produce 340 of 12
the standard models as compared to 291 last year. We shall 24
need 85 people in that section as compared to 76 last year. 36

21   Goals have been set at 1,895 for the economy model and 12
350 for the deluxe model as compared to the goals 1,770 and 24
264 set for last year. Models produced were 1,684 and 293. 36

22   Production goals for those previous four years totaled 12
2,278, 2,196, 1,930, and 1,875. The number of shop workers 24
totaled 549, 530, 483, and 467, plus the 60 office workers. 36

  | 1 | 2 | 3 | 4 | 5 | 6 | 7 | 8 | 9 | 10 | 11 | 12

154-A. Repeat 153-A, page 230.

154-A. WARMUP

154-B. PRETEST: KEYBOARD REVIEW

PRETEST. Take a 1-minute timing; compute speed and errors.

23   The instructor said that all beginning students should 12
type these keys by touch: diagonal /, percent %, number #, 24
colon :, quotation ", hyphen –, underline _, dollar sign $, 36
semicolon ;, parentheses (), apostrophe ', and ampersand &. 48

  | 1 | 2 | 3 | 4 | 5 | 6 | 7 | 8 | 9 | 10 | 11 | 12

154-C. PRACTICE: % – " /

PRACTICE. If you made no errors on the Pretest, type each line 3 times. If you made 1 error or more, type each group of 4 lines (as though it were a paragraph) 3 times; then type the sentence 3 times.

24 % ft5 ft5% ft%tf f%f ft5% ft%tf f%f 13% 26% 48% 50% and 79%
25 – ;p– ;p–; ;p–p; ;–; ;p–; ;p–p; ;–; self–defense four–wheel
26 " ;'; ;'"; ;'"'; ;"; ;'"; ;'"'; ;"; "Chip" "Tiny" "Scooter"
27 / ;/; ;//; ;/;/; ;/; ;//; ;/;/; ;/; him/her I/we 7/16 19/64
28 "One–half or 1/2 equals 50%; one–tenth or 1/10 equals 10%."

  | 1 | 2 | 3 | 4 | 5 | 6 | 7 | 8 | 9 | 10 | 11 | 12

154-D. PRACTICE: : $ _ ( )

29 : ;:; ;:;:; ;:;:; ;:; ;:;:; ;:;:; ;:; listed below: follows:
30 $ fr4 fr4$ fr$rf f$f fr4$ fr$rf f$f $38 $274 $1,569 $64,032
31 _ ;p– ;p–_ ;p_p; ;_; ;p–_ ;p_p; ;_; may be _if_ we choose _one_
32 ( ) 1; lo9(lo(ol 1(1 ;p0) ;p)p; ;); (large) (physics) (98%)
33 The May 9, 10:30 a.m. futures: $1.89 (rye); $3.76 (wheat).

  | 1 | 2 | 3 | 4 | 5 | 6 | 7 | 8 | 9 | 10 | 11 | 12

154-E. PRACTICE: ' # ; &

34 ' ;'; ;'"; ;';'; ;'; ;'"; ;';'; ;'; I'll it's Kim's Carol's
35 # de3 de3# de#ed d#d de3# de#ed d#d #39 #85 #40 #21 and #76
36 ; ;;; ;';l ;'"'; ;;; ;';l ;'"'; ;;; studied; worked; slept;
37 & ju7 ju7& ju&uj j&j ju7& ju&uj j&j Al & Vi & Jo & Lu & Pat
38 B&J can't buy #17; Cartier & Moss can't buy #18; but I can.

  | 1 | 2 | 3 | 4 | 5 | 6 | 7 | 8 | 9 | 10 | 11 | 12

POSTTEST. Repeat the Pretest and compare performance.

154-F. POSTTEST: KEYBOARD REVIEW

LESSON 75

TEST 3: PROGRESS TEST ON PART 3

TEST 3-A
5-MINUTE TIMED WRITING

Line: 60 spaces
Tab: 5
Paper: Workguide 129
Start: 6 lines from top

```
            1                            2
    The nature of the labor force is quite different today    12
         3                       4
from what it was years ago.  First, there are more women at    24
     5                    6                   7
work.  In fact, about half of the work force is female, and    36
                      8                        9
most of these women work out of necessity.  Second, we have    48
        10                      11                      12
a labor force that is better educated than ever before.  We    60
                     13                      14
also have more and more minority people in different levels    72
                 15                      16
of employment.  Finally, there are more older workers since    84
    17                      18                    19
inflation and higher retirement age keep people on the job.    96
                    20                     21
    Also, the type of work has now changed as business has    108
       22                        23              24
become more complex and mechanized.  Machines are replacing    120
              25                        26
labor.  This means that more goods will be made in far less    132
            27              28
time with fewer workers.  There is a shift now to providing    144
      29                    30                       31
services instead of making goods.  Two out of three workers    156
                  32                      33
are now in the service industry, and the number most likely    168
         34                     35
will grow in the immediate future.    175
|  1  |  2  |  3  |  4  |  5  |  6  |  7  |  8  |  9  |  10  |  11  |  12
```

TEST 3-B
LETTER 21

MODIFIED-BLOCK STYLE

Standard punctuation
Tab: 5, center
Paper: Workguide 131
Visual guide: use if desired

ENUMERATION. The three
enumerations should be treated
as separate paragraphs.

Please send the following letter to Mr. Gerald Underwood / U & B Tool 15
& Dye / 134 Miles Avenue / Warwick, RI 02886 / Dear Mr. Underwood: 28

Thank you for your recent letter inquiring about our data process- 42
ing service for handling your payroll. In response to your questions, I 57
would like to give you the following information: / 1. We would have 71
no problem processing the data for your 23 employees on a weekly 80
basis. / 2. You would be required to submit your payroll data by 4 p.m. 96
on the Tuesday after the week for which checks will be issued. / 3. We 112
are currently serving about 57 firms in the Warwick area, and we 126
would be pleased to give you the names of businesses you might wish 141
to contact. ¶Thank you again for considering Sloan Services. By copy 156
of this letter, I am instructing our sales representative, Gladys Sher- 170
dell, to call you during the next week for an appointment to answer 183
your questions and to give you any other details that you might need 197
prior to making a decision to become one of our clients. Sincerely 213
yours, / Alfred W. Sloan / President / (*Initials*) / cc Gladys Sherdell 229

| Line: 60 spaces   Tab: 5 |
| Spacing: single   Drills: 3X |
| Proofguide: 115–116 |
| Workguide: 331 |
| Tape: 48A and 49A |

LESSONS 153/154
SKILL DRIVE

Goal: To improve speed/
accuracy.

153-A. WARMUP

S 1 They may fix the worn cycle if he pays them with good food.
A 2 That mild earthquake eventually caused a dozen broken jaws.
N 3 I shipped 20 crates each of items #485 and #697 on July 31.
   | 1 | 2 | 3 | 4 | 5 | 6 | 7 | 8 | 9 | 10 | 11 | 12

153-B. PRETEST: KEYBOARD REVIEW

PRETEST. **Take a 1-minute
timing; compute speed and
errors.**

4   We gazed at the sizable figures on the 1984 income tax 12
form. The $32,587 adjusted gross income figure was up $960 24
from the $31,627 figure for 1983. They itemized deductions 36
of $6,540 and yelled for joy when they saved an extra $240. 48
   | 1 | 2 | 3 | 4 | 5 | 6 | 7 | 8 | 9 | 10 | 11 | 12

153-C. PRACTICE: Y Z 0 1

PRACTICE. **If you made no
errors on the Pretest, type
each line 3 times. If you
made 1 error or more, type
each group of 4 lines (as
though it were a paragraph)
3 times; then type the
sentence 3 times.**

5 Y yes yard gray pays spry yearn yeast merely Yakima Yucatan
6 Z zip zero lazy maze size zebra zesty freeze Zurich Zeeland
7 0 ;p0 ;0; 0 pod, 00 pen, 00 pins, 00 pots, 00 putt, 00 past
8 1 aql ala 1 ask, 11 all, 11 quiz, 11 quit, 11 zany, 11 zinc

9 Those 10 lazy zebras laid in the sizable 100' by 100' yard.
   | 1 | 2 | 3 | 4 | 5 | 6 | 7 | 8 | 9 | 10 | 11 | 12

153-D. PRACTICE: 2 3 4 5

10 2 sw2 s2s 2 sit, 22 set, 22 wind, 22 wall, 22 same, 22 worn
11 3 de3 d3d 3 dug, 33 den, 33 ease, 33 ever, 33 cuff, 33 came
12 4 fr4 f4f 4 fog, 44 fir, 44 rose, 44 reed, 44 vein, 44 vote
13 5 fr5 f5f 5 fur, 55 fed, 55 rude, 55 torn, 55 vent, 55 base

14 I displayed 45 texts from 1923, 1924, 1925, 1933, and 1945.
   | 1 | 2 | 3 | 4 | 5 | 6 | 7 | 8 | 9 | 10 | 11 | 12

153-E. PRACTICE: 6 7 8 9

15 6 jy6 j6j 6 jog, 66 jug, 66 yarn, 66 yell, 66 mine, 66 nine
16 7 ju7 j7j 7 jar, 77 jaw, 77 unit, 77 used, 77 mass, 77 much
17 8 ki8 k8k 8 kin, 88 keg, 88 idea, 88 into, 88 knot, 88 keen
18 9 lo9 l9l 9 let, 99 lit, 99 owed, 99 ours, 99 life, 99 last

19 The 1980 sales were $89,766 as compared to $68,797 in 1970.
   | 1 | 2 | 3 | 4 | 5 | 6 | 7 | 8 | 9 | 10 | 11 | 12

POSTTEST. **Repeat the Pretest
and compare performance.**

153-F. POSTTEST: KEYBOARD REVIEW

Spacing: single, with the
 groupings shown
Tab: 4
Form: Workguide 133

Invoice 86-1892, *current date, to* Country Style Furniture, 15 Washington Street, Northampton, MA 01060; *invoice from* Oxford Furniture, Inc., 181 Pine Hill Road, Oxford, NC 27565.

QUANTITY	CAT. NO.	DESCRIPTION	UNIT PRICE	AMOUNT
4	11-009	Bulletin Blackboard	21.50	86.00
2	11-107	Coat Rack & Mirror	31.25	62.50
3	11-121	Spice Rack	27.75	83.25
3	12-081	Canterbury Magazine Rack	47.50	142.50
2	12-121	Coat Rack/Umbrella Stand	51.50	103.00
3	12-311	Storage Ottoman	44.75	134.25
		AMOUNT DUE		611.50
		5% SALES TAX		30.58
		DELIVERY CHARGE		61.15
		TOTAL AMOUNT DUE		703.23

TEST 3-D
REPORT 15

REPORT WITH FOOTNOTES

PAGE 1 OF REPORT

Line: suitable for
 bound report
Spacing: suitable
 for bound
 report
Footnotes: typed
 at bottom
Tab: 5, center
Paper: Workguide
 135

SEVERE SECRETARIAL SHORTAGE   17

By (*Your Name*)   26

American business is faced with a severe short age of secretarial   41
and clerical workers. At a time when the office is becoming more and   55
more critical in the operation of a successful business enterprise,   69
there has arisen
an acute shortage ~~is developing for~~ the workers needed to staff "the 83
nerve/brain center" of any business. This paper will investigate cur-   97
of the
rent data concerning secretarial shortages, historical developments ~~for~~ 112
the   of technology
secretarial profession, ~~technological~~ impact on the future of the sec- 127
retarial profession, and career paths for secretarial workers.   139

CURRENT DATA CONCERNING SECRETARIAL SHORTAGES   150

There are currently 3.5 million people employed as secretaries and   163
stenographers.[1] annual openings are projected through 1990 to be about 180
302,000 per year, which makes this one of the fastest growing areas in   194
the labor force.[2] Many reasons have been given to explain this tremen- 210
dous imbalance of supply and demand. The reasons, however, do not assist 225
a
anyone looking for capable secretary these days.   236
                                                                          240

1. Andrea Feld, "The Vanishing Secretary: Critically Needed, but 257
in Short Supply," Today's Secretary, March 1979, p. 7.   276

2. Maureen Early, "Help Wanted Secretarial," Newsday, January 31, 295
1980, Part II/5.   298

152-D. PRACTICE: Q R S T

40 Q qua quit aqua quip quiz queen quart equity Quincy Quinlan
41 R row rust farm fair acre round roost fourth Ruston Rumania
42 S sun suit lass vase nest slide spare sister Salina Siberia
43 T tip trim late soft tuft trade table stream Topeka Tunisia

44 First, thank Mr. Quinn for those square vases you acquired.
   | 1 | 2 | 3 | 4 | 5 | 6 | 7 | 8 | 9 | 10 | 11 | 12

152-E. PRACTICE: U V W X

45 U use unit true suit fuel usury unite lumber Urbana Ukraine
46 V vat volt pave over five voice viola louver Vernon Vizcaya
47 W won will drew owed sewn worst white thrown Winona Wexford
48 X tax axle text axes exit extra index exceed Dexter Xanthus

49 We have five new usury laws and five or six extra tax laws.
   | 1 | 2 | 3 | 4 | 5 | 6 | 7 | 8 | 9 | 10 | 11 | 12

POSTTEST. **Repeat the Pretest and compare performance.**

152-F. POSTTEST: KEYBOARD REVIEW

152-G. Spacing—double. Take two 5-minute timings. Between them, practice any words with which you had difficulty.

   The small numbers above the copy are speed markers for a 5-minute timed writing. The marker you reach in 5 minutes is your speed. Record your score.

   If you cannot be timed, type two copies of the selection.

152-G. SKILL MEASUREMENT: 5-MINUTE TIMED WRITING

50   There is ample proof that ideas have been captured and 12
put in written form for thousands of years. A usable type- 24
writer was first developed more than one hundred years ago, 36
but the concept of word processing that is so obvious today 48
had its beginning around twenty years ago. Word processing 60
took a huge leap forward at the time International Business 72
Machines introduced a text editor on which typed characters 84
could be stored on a magnetic tape. Error corrections were 96
now handled by simply backspacing and striking over. After 108
the document was entirely recorded, revisions could be made 120
without retyping the document. Then the final correct copy 132
was played back at over twice the rate of an expert typist. 144
      We were all quite amazed at just how quickly an office 156
could change when magnetic typewriters were put in use. As 168
times have changed, so has the modern office. Text editors 180
with visual screens are more and more common. Words can be 192
added or deleted, margins changed, paragraphs moved, or the 204
spelling can be checked--and you see it all in front of you 216
on a screen before it is printed out on paper. 225
   | 1 | 2 | 3 | 4 | 5 | 6 | 7 | 8 | 9 | 10 | 11 | 12

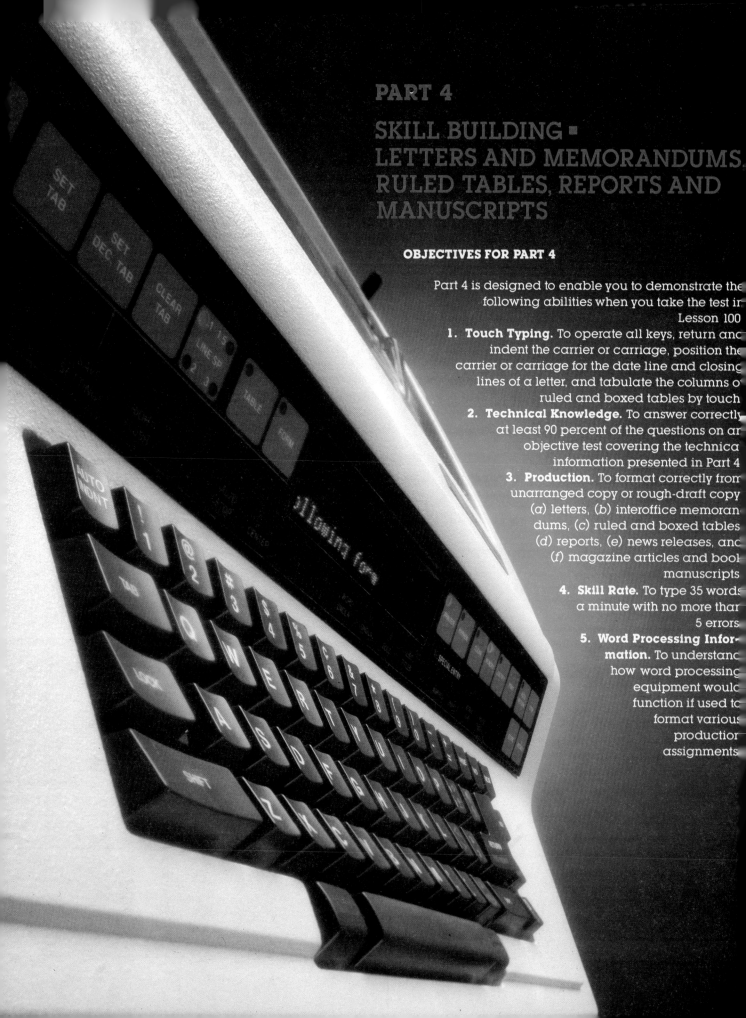

PART 4

SKILL BUILDING ■ LETTERS AND MEMORANDUMS, RULED TABLES, REPORTS AND MANUSCRIPTS

OBJECTIVES FOR PART 4

Part 4 is designed to enable you to demonstrate the following abilities when you take the test in Lesson 100

1. **Touch Typing.** To operate all keys, return and indent the carrier or carriage, position the carrier or carriage for the date line and closing lines of a letter, and tabulate the columns of ruled and boxed tables by touch

2. **Technical Knowledge.** To answer correctly at least 90 percent of the questions on an objective test covering the technical information presented in Part 4

3. **Production.** To format correctly from unarranged copy or rough-draft copy (a) letters, (b) interoffice memorandums, (c) ruled and boxed tables, (d) reports, (e) news releases, and (f) magazine articles and book manuscripts

4. **Skill Rate.** To type 35 words a minute with no more than 5 errors

5. **Word Processing Information.** To understand how word processing equipment would function if used to format various production assignments

151-G. PROOFREADING SKILLS

The need for proofreading skills on the part of office workers has become increasingly apparent. The following paired sentences contain examples of errors that might occur in typed copy. In each case type the first sentence, making the corrections indicated by the proof-readers' marks. (It is suggested that you review the proofreaders' marks on page xv before you begin.) Then type the second sentence, correcting the same types of errors that were demonstrated in the preceding sentence. Compare your sentences with the correct ones shown on Proofguide page 113.

20 Domestc help is in short supply in manyy cities these days.
21 A goood cleaning lady should eb treated like a prized jewl.

22 Some people can not recieve quality medical treatment today.
ss
23 Some life guards beleive the new techniques are appropriate.

24 If they drive the 4 will not get to memphis until noon.
25 When the snow began the 1st car stopped near louisville.

26 That little girls Mother shows complete confidence in her
27 The three boy's Father exposed them to the arts and sports;

28 Most of of those vocal music courses have filed very quickly.
29 Sevral of those students' solos might have to be be canceled.

30 Mrs. Mayo & Ms. Oliver maynot want to perform on friday.
31 The number of $ raised in october wasnot very large.

32 The sun rise over mount yampa was a truly spectacular site.
33 He still plans to fire proof there new house at norway lake.
| 1 | 2 | 3 | 4 | 5 | 6 | 7 | 8 | 9 | 10 | 11 | 12

152-A. Repeat 151-A, page 227.

152-A. WARMUP

PRETEST. **Take a 1-minute timing; compute speed and errors.**

152-B. PRETEST: KEYBOARD REVIEW

34   Business reports have been prepared and distributed in 12
company offices for decades. When answering tax questions, 24
we use annual and quarterly information extensively. We do 36
see more extensive quarterly reports from the computer now. 48
| 1 | 2 | 3 | 4 | 5 | 6 | 7 | 8 | 9 | 10 | 11 | 12

PRACTICE. **If you made no errors on the Pretest, type each line 3 times. If you made 1 error or more, type each group of 4 lines (as though it were a paragraph) 3 times; then type the sentence 3 times.**

152-C. PRACTICE: M N O P

35 M map moon farm tame swim money muddy hammer Mobile Majorca
36 N nut nail lane tune tent train under number Newark Navarre
37 O old over took show root spoon color troops Oxford Okinawa
38 P put poll hope soup cape crepe spoil spider Peoria Prussia

39 Many more people want to play both pinochle and backgammon.
| 1 | 2 | 3 | 4 | 5 | 6 | 7 | 8 | 9 | 10 | 11 | 12

Line: 60 spaces	Tab: 5
Spacing: single	Drills: 3X
Proofguide: 49–51	
Workguide: 155	
Tape: 31A and 32A	

LESSONS 76/77
SKILL DRIVE

Goals: To improve speed/accuracy; to make correct word-division decisions.

S = Speed

A = Accuracy

N = Number

76-A. WARMUP

S   1   The size of the main group will be such that he may not go.
A   2   You find that jobs are executed very quickly if this is so.
N   3   Lannie purchased 10 boxes each of items 29, 38, 47, and 56.
    | 1 | 2 | 3 | 4 | 5 | 6 | 7 | 8 | 9 | 10 | 11 | 12

76-B. PRETEST: KEYBOARD REVIEW

PRETEST. **Take a 1-minute timing; compute speed and errors.**

4   Jorg camped in the Canadian wilderness last fall. The 12
locale from the east bank of Hudson Bay to the Atlantic has 24
been called one of the most beautiful areas of the country. 36
    | 1 | 2 | 3 | 4 | 5 | 6 | 7 | 8 | 9 | 10 | 11 | 12

76-C. PRACTICE: A B C D

PRACTICE. **If you made no more than 1 error on the Pretest, type each individual line 3 times for speed development. If you made 2 or more errors, type each group of lines (as though it were a paragraph) 3 times for accuracy improvement.**

5   A Ada Alan also raft last arena canoe attain meander Amazon
6   B Bob Beth buck able band bacon brown absorb cabinet Boston
7   C Coe Chip cold scan cowl cared actor occult machine Canada
8   D Dad Dave drop adds dent diner adopt nudged address Dublin

9   Barb and Dan canoed in the backwoods of Canada in late May.
    | 1 | 2 | 3 | 4 | 5 | 6 | 7 | 8 | 9 | 10 | 11 | 12

76-D. PRACTICE: E F G H

10   E Eve Ella we eye else teeth engine elevate execute Ecuador
11   F Fay Fred of fly cuff stuff afford factory effects Fairfax
12   G Gil Glen go gig gold lager regard haggard geology Germany
13   H Hal Hope he hit hash harsh health heather highway Hungary

14   Fred and Harry laughed gaily as they flew over the highway.
    | 1 | 2 | 3 | 4 | 5 | 6 | 7 | 8 | 9 | 10 | 11 | 12

76-E. PRACTICE: I J K L

15   I Ida Irma ice did inch inner bikini indices picnics Israel
16   J Jon Judy jog jar jack jetty junior jujitsu conjure Jordan
17   K Kay Kent key kin kink skill kayaks jackals kickoff Kokomo
18   L Lou Lane lot all lull allow locale alfalfa lullaby Lowell

19   Leslie jogged by the lake while Kay and Jo played jai alai.
    | 1 | 2 | 3 | 4 | 5 | 6 | 7 | 8 | 9 | 10 | 11 | 12

POSTTEST. **Repeat the Pretest and compare performance.**

76-F. POSTTEST: KEYBOARD REVIEW

Line: 60 spaces   Tab: 5
Spacing: single   Drills: 3X
Proofguide: 113–115
Workguide: 331
Tape: 46A and 47A

LESSONS 151/152
SKILL DRIVE

Goals: To improve speed/accuracy; to improve proofreading skills.

S = Speed
A = Accuracy
N = Number

151-A.   WARMUP

S   1   She may visit the little coop that is down by the big lake.
A   2   After eating a huge jar of cookies, Roxy quietly dozed off.
N   3   They were 65 or 70 miles south of Freeway #429 at 8:31 a.m.
    | 1 | 2 | 3 | 4 | 5 | 6 | 7 | 8 | 9 | 10 | 11 | 12

151-B.   PRETEST: KEYBOARD REVIEW

PRETEST.   Take a 1-minute timing; compute speed and errors.

4   We just knew there would be multitudes of birds at the 12
feeders on such a fine day. First came the bossy bluejays, 24
followed by the chatty chickadees and frisky nuthatches. A 36
flock of huge grosbeaks then gathered to eat what was left. 48
| 1 | 2 | 3 | 4 | 5 | 6 | 7 | 8 | 9 | 10 | 11 | 12

151-C.   PRACTICE: A B C D

PRACTICE. If you made no errors on the Pretest, type each line (e.g., lines 5–9) 3 times for speed development. If you made 1 error or more, type each group of 4 lines (e.g., lines 5–8), as though it were a paragraph, 3 times for accuracy improvement; then type the sentence (e.g., line 9) 3 times.

5   A ate aunt fast trap jade alert above laughs Athens America
6   B bet boat bell able bird about below cables Bangor Bolivia
7   C cup chip coat acre such crate climb castle Camden Corsica
8   D dot draw drop raid fade draft drain dollar Dayton Denmark
9   Cary Baird cannot buy Dave's beach ball for Al with a dime.
| 1 | 2 | 3 | 4 | 5 | 6 | 7 | 8 | 9 | 10 | 11 | 12

151-D.   PRACTICE: E F G H

10   E elm even lead heat seed earns equal saddle Eugene England
11   F fix fast loaf cuff leaf foamy feast profit Fresno Finland
12   G get game brag wage rage guilt great wagons Goshen Grenada
13   H hop halt both ship wash happy haste ashore Hudson Hungary

14   Eve and Fern Gates bragged when they saw Hal fix that roof.
| 1 | 2 | 3 | 4 | 5 | 6 | 7 | 8 | 9 | 10 | 11 | 12

151-E.   PRACTICE: I J K L

15   I its item side pine wide igloo index joined Irving Iceland
16   J jam jump join just jury jewel jelly adjust Juneau Jamaica
17   K kit keep know sink dark knock knife taking Kearny Kashmir
18   L lap left lion pail help light lever cattle Linden Lapland

19   Kevin knew Inez would join Jim just as he left Lake Forest.
| 1 | 2 | 3 | 4 | 5 | 6 | 7 | 8 | 9 | 10 | 11 | 12

POSTTEST. Repeat the Pretest and compare performance.

151-F.   POSTTEST: KEYBOARD REVIEW

76-G. REVIEW OF WORD-DIVISION RULES

If you need to divide a word at the end of a line, follow these rules:

ABSOLUTE RULES

1. Do not divide words pronounced as one syllable (*brought, mailed*), contractions (*won't, wouldn't*), or abbreviations (*NASA, f.o.b.*).

2. Divide words only between syllables. If you are uncertain where a syllable ends, consult a dictionary.

3. Leave at least three characters (the last will be a hyphen) on the upper line and carry at least three characters (the last may be a punctuation mark) to the next line (*en-gine* and *weak-en;*, but not *a-part* or *shad-y*).

PREFERENTIAL RULES

4. Divide compound words either at the hyphen or where the two words join to make a solid compound (*counter-act*, not *coun-teract*).

5. If a one-letter syllable occurs in the middle of a word, divide after it (*popu-late* is preferred to *pop-ulate*). However, if two separately sounded vowels occur together, divide between them (*medi-ation* is preferred to *media-tion*).

6. Divide after, not within, a prefix. Divide before, not within, a suffix (*multi-media* is preferred to *mul-timedia*, and *prob-able* is preferred to *proba-ble*).

7. Avoid dividing elements that are read as units, such as dates (*June 23*), amounts (*$12,000,000* or *$44 million*), titles and names (*Dr. Hammerstrom*), reference numbers (*Chapter 8* or *page 56*), and so on.

8. Avoid dividing (*a*) after more than two consecutive lines have ended with a word division, (*b*) at the end of the first and the last line of a page, and (*c*) a proper noun.

76-H. Select the words that can be divided. Then type them with a hyphen to show where the division should be.

Answers to the practice exercise appear at the bottom of page 116.

76-H. WORD-DIVISION PRACTICE

1. somewhat	**8.** career	**15.** can't	**22.** skipped
2. shouldn't	**9.** UNICEF	**16.** USMC	**23.** journalize
3. ahead	**10.** educate	**17.** stopped	**24.** stipulate
4. subregion	**11.** barnyard	**18.** mustn't	**25.** specialize
5. shipped	**12.** willpower	**19.** borderline	**26.** occupy
6. Dr. Gilby	**13.** posted	**20.** $76 million	**27.** Mankato
7. AICPA	**14.** Chicago	**21.** Jo Renshaw	**28.** May 1

77-A. Repeat 76-A, page 114.

77-A. WARMUP

77-B. PRETEST: KEYBOARD REVIEW

PRETEST. Take a 1-minute timing; compute speed and errors.

```
20      Metals, unless they are specially treated in some way, 12
     will be quickly destroyed by rust.  One excellent method of 24
     treatment is galvanization, the covering of iron with zinc. 36
     |  1  |  2  |  3  |  4  |  5  |  6  |  7  |  8  |  9  | 10  | 11  | 12
```

PRACTICE. If you made no more than 1 error on the Pretest, type each individual line 3 times for speed development. If you made 2 or more errors, type each group of lines (as though it were a paragraph) 3 times for accuracy improvement.

77-C. PRACTICE: M N O P

```
21   M Meg Marie main madam mammal summit memory memento Morocco
22   N Nan Naomi neon inner annual enmity nation neutron Nigeria
23   O Ola Ollie oleo proof hollow sooner oblong noonday Ontario
24   P Pat Peter prop polyp oppose purple papaya perhaps Pacific

25   Pomade is an ointment that was originally made from apples.
26   Mamie was not opposed to the name Paul picked for the pony.
     |  1  |  2  |  3  |  4  |  5  |  6  |  7  |  8  |  9  | 10  | 11  | 12
```

PART 7

SKILL BUILDING · LETTERS AND MEMORANDUMS, RECORDS FORMS, FORMAL REPORTS

OBJECTIVES FOR PART 7

Part 7 is designed to enable you to demonstrate the following abilities:

1. Technical Knowledge. To answer correctly at least 90 percent of the questions on an objective test covering the technical information in Part 7.

2. Production. To format correctly: *(a)* letters and memos, *(b)* tables, *(c)* forms, and *(d)* a bound report including title page, table of contents, and bibliography.

3. Skill Rate. To type at the following speed and accuracy levels by the end of each unit:

Unit	No. of Minutes	Minimum Speed	Maximum Errors
25	5	42	5
26	5	43	5
27	5	44	5
28	5	45	5

4. WORD PROCESSING INFORMATION. To understand how word processing equipment would function if used to format various production assignments.

77-D. PRACTICE: Q R S T

27 Q Quinn quiz quad quaff equal squat aquatic sequence Quebec
28 R Roger rare roar roast prism error arrears referred Russia
29 S Susan sass skis stops ashes messy wassail restless Sicily
30 T Tonto test tart trust stair attic stutter attested Tehran

31 Statistics is a requirement in an aquatic science sequence.
32 The seven quarts of strawberries were not quite thawed out.
    | 1 | 2 | 3 | 4 | 5 | 6 | 7 | 8 | 9 | 10 | 11 | 12

77-E. PRACTICE: U V W X

33 U Ursula urge rough sugar under truth unsure suburb Uruguay
34 V Vivian vote savvy salve vivid every verify evolve Vermont
35 W Walter wave awful macaw threw widow lawyer winnow Windsor
36 X Xavier exit affix taxes axiom waxed sextet except Xanthus

37 Max verified the widow's extremely high suburban-use taxes.
38 Drew Wilcox will have found four or five extra tax savings.
    | 1 | 2 | 3 | 4 | 5 | 6 | 7 | 8 | 9 | 10 | 11 | 12

POSTTEST. Repeat the
Pretest on page 115 and
compare performance.

77-F. POSTTEST: KEYBOARD REVIEW

77-G. Spacing—double.
Take two 5-minute timings.
Between them, practice any
words with which you had
difficulty.

The small numbers above
the copy are speed markers
for a 5-minute timed writing.
The marker you reach in 5
minutes is your speed.
Record your score.

If you cannot be timed,
type two copies of the
selection.

77-G. SKILL MEASUREMENT: 5-MINUTE TIMED WRITING

39
            1   2
    The way that materials are arranged on a typist's desk   12
         3   4
can create an atmosphere where work is produced efficiently   24
     5   6   7
with a minimum of confusion. Or it can create a climate in   36
                            8   9
which chaos threatens with every departure from an ordinary   48
             10
routine.   50
                          11   12
    Typists must give thought to how and when each item on   62
             13   14
the desk is used. A plan should then be made for the exact   74
     15   16   17
placement of supplies. Items that will be used most often,   86
                          18   19
such as stationery, pens, and a stapler, must be set within   98
             20
one's easy reach.   101
                    21   22
    Once the placement judgment is made, the typist should   113
         23   24   25
seize a minute at the start of the day to quickly place all 125
                          26   27
necessary items in the same spot. There they will be handy 137
             28   29
when they are needed. Such planning and the development of 149
     30   31   32
a good work routine help a typist cope very well with other 161
                    33   34
tasks or problems that arise. Time saved is worth money to 173
             35
a company.   175
    | 1 | 2 | 3 | 4 | 5 | 6 | 7 | 8 | 9 | 10 | 11 | 12

Answers to practice 76-H,
page 115:

1. some-what	19. border-line
4. sub-region	23. journal-ize
8. ca-reer	24. stipu-late
10. edu-cate	25. special-ize
11. barn-yard	26. oc-cupy
12. will-power	

TEST 6-D
REPORT 49
CONTRACT

Paper: Workguide 316
Spacing: single
Tab: 10, center

Use date on which contract is typed

Contract for Services) — *Spread-center in all caps*

THIS contract made and concluded this ~~ninth day of~~

~~June, 19--,~~ by and between the Woodward Entertainment Agency,

of 184 Peterson Road, Rochester, (MN), party of the first part,

and Raymond L. Bonura, 16 South Plainfield Avenue, Rochester,

(MN), party of the second part.

Article 1. Services. The said party of the second

part covenants and agrees *to and* with the party of the first part,

to furnish his services entirely to the said party of the

first part as Director of Public Relations for the period of

two (2) ~~2~~ years, or twenty-four (24) calendar months, beginning

date first of next month
~~January 1, 19--,~~ and ending ~~December 31, 19--,~~ *date 2 years later* and the said

party of the second part covenants and agrees to perform faith-

fully all duties incident to such employment.

Article 2. Wages. And the said party of the first

part covenants and agrees to pay the said party of the second

($36,000)
part, for the same, the sum of Thirty-Six Thousand Dollars per

($1,500)
year, as follows: The sum of Fifteen Hundred Dollars on the

15th and 30th of each month throughout the (2) years of this

contract.

IN WITNESS WHEREOF, the parties to this Contract

first
have hereunto set their hands the day and year above written.

Raymond L. Bonura | Agnes P. Woodward, *President*
Woodward Entertainment Agency

Witness to Signature | Witness to Signature

LESSONS 78/79
SKILL DRIVE

Goal: To improve speed/accuracy.

78-A. WARMUP

S 1 James will have to quit playing ball if that haze keeps up.
A 2 Speedy, staccato–like strokes are extra assets to a typist.
N 3 Series scores were: 123–98 Hawks, 75–69 Jets, 94–80 Hawks.
      | 1 | 2 | 3 | 4 | 5 | 6 | 7 | 8 | 9 | 10 | 11 | 12

78-B. PRETEST: KEYBOARD REVIEW

PRETEST. Take a 1-minute timing; compute speed and errors.

4   The weather is a hazy 87 degrees; wind at 5 knots; our12
  yacht, E–Z 1–2–3, nearly becalmed at 6N, 124W in the ocean;24
  barometric pressure reads 29.6 and falling. July 30, 1984.36
      | 1 | 2 | 3 | 4 | 5 | 6 | 7 | 8 | 9 | 10 | 11 | 12

78-C. PRACTICE: Y Z 0 1

PRACTICE. If you made no more than 1 error on the Pretest, type each individual line 3 times for speed development. If you made 2 or more errors, type each group of lines (as though it were a paragraph) 3 times for accuracy improvement.

5 Y Yancy yaw eye yell yowl stay shyly yearly yellow Yokohama
6 Z Zelda zoo adz zone jazz haze azure hazard zigzag Zaragoza
7 0 ;p0 000 0 put, 00 pin, 00 pens, 00 pads, 00 puff, 00 port
8 1 aq1 111 1 add, 11 aim, 11 quip, 11 quit, 11 zero, 11 zone

9 There were 10 zany zealots who yelled 100 times at the zoo.
      | 1 | 2 | 3 | 4 | 5 | 6 | 7 | 8 | 9 | 10 | 11 | 12

WP Many word processors and microcomputers have a separate 10-key number pad to the right of the regular keyboard to allow you to input numbers quickly when you are keyboarding numerical data.

78-D. PRACTICE: 2 3 4 5

10 2 sw2 222 2 sat, 22 saw, 22 wars, 22 webs, 22 soap, 22 woke
11 3 de3 333 3 did, 33 doe, 33 eels, 33 edge, 33 cats, 33 come
12 4 fr4 444 4 fed, 44 fun, 44 road, 44 rude, 44 very, 44 vine
13 5 fr5 555 5 fir, 55 fog, 55 rise, 55 tire, 55 void, 55 boat

14 She found dimes minted in 1923, 1924, 1925, 1943, and 1945.
      | 1 | 2 | 3 | 4 | 5 | 6 | 7 | 8 | 9 | 10 | 11 | 12

78-E. PRACTICE: 6 7 8 9

15 6 jy6 666 6 jam, 66 jet, 66 yelp, 66 yard, 66 main, 66 nest
16 7 ju7 777 7 jot, 77 jut, 77 used, 77 urge, 77 most, 77 melt
17 8 ki8 888 8 kit, 88 key, 88 idle, 88 iron, 88 kind, 88 kick
18 9 lo9 999 9 lot, 99 lad, 99 oral, 99 open, 99 left, 99 loam

19 The 1980 census shows 7,896 as compared with 6,987 in 1970.
      | 1 | 2 | 3 | 4 | 5 | 6 | 7 | 8 | 9 | 10 | 11 | 12

POSTTEST. Repeat the Pretest and compare performance.

78-F. POSTTEST: KEYBOARD REVIEW

Paper: Workguide 315
Line: 70 spaces
Spacing: as shown
Center vertically

Guardabasco Appliances, Inc. *) all caps & center*

Income Statement

For Quarter Ended December 31, 19-- *] Center*

REVENUE *FROM SALES*

Sales	$215,683.26	
Less: Sales Ret. & Allow.	3,846.47	
Net Sales		$211,836.79

COST OF GOODS SOLD (See schedule) .... | • | 114,650.37

ON SALES
GROSS PROFIT .... | | $ 97,186.42

OPERATING Expenses

Salary Expense	$ 42,250.50
Payroll Taxes Expense	2,384.38
Rent Expense	6,000.00
Insurance Expense	874.50
Supplies Expense	267.54
Delivery Expense	1,685.00
Depreciation Expense	975.00
Miscellaneous Expense	237.60
Total Expenses	

Operating

??? *Compute*
??? *these*
??? *totals*

Net Income Before Taxes ....

78-G. SUSTAINED PRACTICE: NUMBERS

78-G. Take a 1-minute timing on the first paragraph to establish your base speed. Then take successive 1-minute timings on the other paragraphs. You must equal or exceed your base speed before moving to the next paragraph.

20   The typing of numbers is a challenge for many typists. 12
Why should this be so? Is three really easier than 3? And 24
is four easier than 4? And the 5 more difficult than five? 36

21   It is true that the finger reaches up to the 3 and the 12
4 and the 5 are longer. The same is also true of the 6 and 24
the 7 and the 8. But what then can a typist do to improve? 36

22   Typists can type the 3, the 4, the 5, the 6, and the 7 12
keys with speed and accuracy. And this is also true of the 24
0 and 1 and 2 and 8 and 9 keys. The answer is in practice. 36
   | 1 | 2 | 3 | 4 | 5 | 6 | 7 | 8 | 9 | 10 | 11 | 12

79-A. WARMUP

79-A. Repeat 78-A, page 117.

79-B. PRETEST: KEYBOARD REVIEW

PRETEST. Take a 1-minute timing; compute speed and errors.

23   The keys for percent %, hyphen -, apostrophe ', under-12
line _, diagonal /, parentheses (), dollar sign $, colon :,24
quotation ", number #, and ampersand & can be learned fast.36
   | 1 | 2 | 3 | 4 | 5 | 6 | 7 | 8 | 9 | 10 | 11 | 12

79-C. PRACTICE: % - " /

PRACTICE. If you made no more than 1 error on the Pretest, type each individual line 3 times for speed development. If you made 2 or more errors, type each group of lines (as though it were a paragraph) 3 times for accuracy improvement.

24 % ft5 ft5% ft%tf f%f ft5% ft%tf f%f 38% 47% 92% 10% and 65%
25 - ;p- ;p-; ;p-p; ;-; ;p-; ;p-p; ;-; half-truth self-assured
26 " ;'; ;'"; ;'"'; ;"; ;'"; ;'"'; ;"; "Slim" "Curly" "Chubby"
27 / ;/; ;//; ;/;/; ;/; ;//; ;/;/; ;/; and/or he/she 5/6 17/32

28 "One-tenth or 1/10 equals 10%; one-half or 1/2 equals 50%."
   | 1 | 2 | 3 | 4 | 5 | 6 | 7 | 8 | 9 | 10 | 11 | 12

79-D. PRACTICE: : $ _ ( )

WP Word processors have an automatic underscore feature that underscores words, phrases, or entire lines as you type them.

29 : ;;; ;::; ;:;:; ;:; ;::; ;:;:; ;:; as follows: as listed:
30 $ fr4 fr4$ fr$rf f$f fr4$ fr$rf f$f $73 $945 $1,802 $62,370
31 _ ;p- ;p-_ ;p_p; ;_; ;p-_ ;p_p; ;_; will not be Jon and Eve
32 () 1; lo9(lo(ol l(1 ;p0) ;p)p; ;); (blue) (68%) (freshman)

33 The new 9:30 a.m. rebates: $500 (autos) and $700 (trucks).
   | 1 | 2 | 3 | 4 | 5 | 6 | 7 | 8 | 9 | 10 | 11 | 12

79-E. PRACTICE: ' # ; &

34 ' ;'; ;''; ;';'; ;'; ;''; ;';'; ;'; I'm it's Dan's doctors'
35 # de3 de3# de#ed d#d de3# de#ed d#d #76 #45 #20 #19 and #38
36 ; ;;; ;';1 ;'"'; ;;; ;';1 ;'"'; ;;; rained; snowed; hailed;
37 & ju7 ju7& ju&uj j&j ju7& ju&uj j&j 23 & 45 & 67 & 89 & 100

38 Carlson & Son won't buy #4; H & N won't buy #5; but I will.
   | 1 | 2 | 3 | 4 | 5 | 6 | 7 | 8 | 9 | 10 | 11 | 12

POSTTEST. Repeat the Pretest and compare performance.

79-F. POSTTEST: KEYBOARD REVIEW

LESSON 150

TEST 6: PROGRESS TEST ON PART 6

TEST 6-A
5-MINUTE TIMED WRITING

Paper: Workguide 313
Line: 60 spaces
Spacing: double
Tab: 5
Start: line 9

```
                      1                               2
     In recent years, there has been a tremendous growth in        12
        3                              4
travel owing to much greater mobility and modern methods of        24
  5                          6                        7
transportation.  People are traveling much more now than in        36
              8                           9
the past.  Business people, for instance, travel many miles        48
       10                        11                      12
a year conducting company business, and even top executives        60
                    13                          14
spend a lot of time out of their offices on frequent trips.        72
                15                            16
     The new mobility has affected the tourist industry, as        84
    17                      18                       19
more and more people have come to realize the joy of travel        96
                  20                        21
for pleasure and as a way to relax.  The charter planes and       108
            22                      23                    24
group fare rates make travel cheaper and easier these days.       120
                          25                    26
For some people, the world of travel is no longer a luxury,       132
                  27                        28
for it has come to be an essential part of their lifestyle.       144
      29                        30                        31
     Students know that they can learn a great deal through       156
           32                         33
travel.  For this reason, many of them travel during summer       168
         34                       35                      36
breaks, either at home or abroad.  Some are lucky enough to       180
                         37                      38
study overseas and may even have the good fortune of living       192
                 39                       40
with a foreign family and, moreover, being able to learn to       204
      41                        42                       43
speak another language.  Living abroad is probably the best       216
                      44                        45
way to learn in depth about other cultures.                       225
|  1  |  2  |  3  |  4  |  5  |  6  |  7  |  8  |  9  |  10  |  11  |  12
```

TEST 6-B
LETTER 55
MODIFIED-BLOCK STYLE

Standard punctuation
Monarch stationery:
    Workguide 314
Tab: center

Send the following letter to Ms. Alicia Martinez / Marketing Manager /   16
F&R Publishing / 57 West River Road / West Haven, CT 06516 / (*Salu-*   27
tation)   31

    Thank you for your recent inquiry concerning the seminar we are   45
hosting for salespeople. The seminar for your region will be held in   59
Boston during the week of June 24. The enclosed brochure contains all   73
the information you will need to register.   82

    I have also enclosed a directory with names and addresses of indi-   96
viduals who have attended these sales seminars in the past. Please feel   111
free to contact any of these people in order to get a firsthand evalu-   125
ation.   126

    If you have any questions about the seminar after you have looked   140
through the brochure, please call me at (401) 555-4269. / (*Closing*) /   156
Gregg Olkowski / Educational Director / (*Initials*?) / (*Enclosures*?)   172

79-G. Spacing—double. Take two 5-minute timings. Between them, practice any words with which you had difficulty. The marker you reach in 5 minutes is your speed. Record your score.

If you cannot be timed, type two copies of the selection.

79-G. SKILL MEASUREMENT: 5-MINUTE TIMED WRITING

39   Communication is a vital element in the conduct of the   12

country's business.   In fact, just about everything that we   24

do involves communication of some type.   32

     Formal communication is transmitted in oral or written   44

form.   Our written communication skills are used less often   56

than our speaking skills and do take longer to learn.   Most   68

oral skills are gained from talking informally, but writing   80

skills come from hard work.   86

     The next skill in this group that we so often take for   98

granted is listening.   In addition to skills in writing and   110

speaking, we must learn to listen to others.   Amazing as it   122

seems, we usually hear only a small part of what others are   134

saying to us.   137

     Speaking and writing skills are gained quite easily by   149

some persons, but the skill of listening is one that all of   161

us must strive to improve.   We can do this by simply paying   173

attention.   175

| 1 | 2 | 3 | 4 | 5 | 6 | 7 | 8 | 9 | 10 | 11 | 12

| Line: 60 spaces   Tab: 5 |
| Spacing: single   Drills: 3X |
| Proofguide: 51–54 |
| Workguide: 155 |
| Tape: 35A and 36A |

LESSONS 80/81
SKILL DRIVE

Goal: To improve speed/accuracy.

80-A. WARMUP

S 1 Chet got in a jam when he put the box of ice on that shelf.
A 2 Gail may not quit if she thinks Vivian will fix the hazard.
N 3 All 9,800 fans arrived at Gates 2, 3, 4, and 7 by 6:15 p.m.
| 1 | 2 | 3 | 4 | 5 | 6 | 7 | 8 | 9 | 10 | 11 | 12

80-B. PRETEST: SELECTIVE PRACTICE

PRETEST. Take a 1-minute timing; compute speed and errors.

4   The sales representative told us that the <u>retail</u> price 12
will be almost double the <u>wholesale</u> price.   Even so, we may 24
want to consider a large increase in our present inventory. 36
| 1 | 2 | 3 | 4 | 5 | 6 | 7 | 8 | 9 | 10 | 11 | 12

REPORTS 47 AND 48
EMPLOYMENT CONTRACT

Paper: plain, vertical ruled
  lines
Copy 1. spacing: single
Copy 2. spacing: double
Tab: 10, center
Proofguide: 111–112

E M P L O Y ~~E R~~ [MENT]   C O N T R A C T ↓3

(by and) THIS CONTRACT, made and concluded this sixteenth day of January, 19--, between the firm of Oxford Textiles, Inc., of 1715 Industrial Parkway East, Baltimore, Maryland, party of the first part, and Raymond G. Bentley, 127 Cooperstown Road, Baltimore, Maryland, part of the second part, ↓3

W i t n e s s e t h) — all caps and center ↓2

ARTICLE 1. The said party (the) of the second part covenants and agrees to and with party of the first part, to furnish his services to the said party of the first part as Product Operations Research ~~Analyst~~ Consultant in the Baltimore plant for four (4) calendar months, beginning September 1, 19-- and ending December 31, 19--; and the said party of the second part covenants and agrees to perform a complete analysis of product operations and prepare a written report with recommendations for improving production efficiency. ↓2 (and oral)

ARTICLE 2. And the said party of the first part covenants and agrees to pay the said party of the second part, for the same, the sum of ~~Eight~~ [Twelve] Thousand Dollars (~~$8,000~~) in four (4) equal installments of ~~Two~~ [Three] Thousand Dollars ($2,000) each, one (1) installment to be paid on the last working day of each month during the stated period of employment. ↓3

IN WITNESS WHEREOF, the parties of this contract have here unto set their hands and seals, the ~~year and day~~ first above written [day and year] ↓3

Party of the First Part: ↓3   Party of the Second Part: ↓3

_____   _____
James C. Hart, President   Raymond G. Bentley
Oxford Textiles, Inc. ↓3

_____   _____
Witness to Signature   Witness to Signature

PRACTICE. If you made no more than 1 error on the Pretest, type the speed drill lines in 80-C 3 times each; otherwise, type the accuracy drill lines in 80-D 3 times each. Type each machine manipulation drill in 80-E 3 times.

80-C. PRACTICE: SPEED

```
5  That is the right way to sit at the desk if you want speed.
6  Both men and women might be there when they raise the flag.
7  Hale and the rich man got a pair of owls for the giant oak.
8  He will make sure that all the men laugh at the right time.
9  She may not wish that they would come over to see the show.
   | 1 | 2 | 3 | 4 | 5 | 6 | 7 | 8 | 9 | 10 | 11 | 12
```

80-D. PRACTICE: ACCURACY

```
10  waste lumpy errors around joining depress dramatic electric
11  facts ninny adjust breath breadth request headline standard
12  rafts nymph amazed colony message mileage affected implicit
13  great hilly acquit eraser counter monitor kindling fraction
14  beast lumpy timely escape diploma nominal metrical moderate
    | 1 | 2 | 3 | 4 | 5 | 6 | 7 | 8 | 9 | 10 | 11 | 12
```

80-E. PRACTICE: MACHINE MANIPULATION

Backspace key

```
15  The titles for her columns are Clipping Coupons and Leaves.
16  Mrs. Barston will not join them for the early tennis match.
17  Dr. Gale wrote two brochures, Office Ethics and New Trends.
18  She has ordered twelve hardcover books and four paperbacks.
19  Steve wanted a red bike, and Jonathan wanted an orange one.
    | 1 | 2 | 3 | 4 | 5 | 6 | 7 | 8 | 9 | 10 | 11 | 12
```

Tabulator key

Set two tab stops 25 and 50 spaces from left margin. Then type each line tabulating across from column to column.

```
20  ash           cherry          poplar
21  aspen         cottonwood      spruce
22  balsam        elm             tamarack
23  birch         maple           walnut
24  cedar         oak             white pine
```

POSTTEST. Repeat the Pretest and compare performance.

80-F. POSTTEST: SELECTIVE PRACTICE

81-A. Repeat 80-A, page 119.

81-A. WARMUP

81-B. PRETEST: SELECTIVE PRACTICE

PRETEST. Take a 1-minute timing; compute speed and errors.

```
25      The EXIT sign should be placed at the south end of the 12
    hall.  The STAIRS sign should be placed on the east side of 24
    the hall, and the ELEVATOR sign should be high on the wall. 36
    | 1 | 2 | 3 | 4 | 5 | 6 | 7 | 8 | 9 | 10 | 11 | 12
```

81-C. PRACTICE: SPEED

PRACTICE. If you made no more than 1 error on the Pretest, type the speed drill lines in 81-C 3 times each; otherwise, type the accuracy drill lines in 81-D 3 times each. Then type each line in 81-E 3 times.

```
26  and for the|if it is to be|will have some|will not be going
27  she may not|he is to do it|wish that they|hope she is there
28  got the new|or it is to be|they said that|they may go where
29  the man had|it is as if he|came with them|that may be right
30  had run the|as if he or we|some were with|find out it might
    | 1 | 2 | 3 | 4 | 5 | 6 | 7 | 8 | 9 | 10 | 11 | 12
```

hand and seal on this (*spell out today's date*) of (*spell out the month*) in the year one thousand nine hundred and (*spell out the year*). ↓4

Start signature line at the center. LS, or *locus sigilli*, means "place of the seal" and is frequently used in legal documents. The following witness block is called the acknowledgment.

_____(LS) ↓3

THE ABOVE INSTRUMENT was subscribed by the said John B. Drew in our presence and acknowledged by him to each of us; and he at the same time declared the above to be his Last Will and Testament; and we, at his request, in his presence and in the presence of each other, have signed our names as witnesses hereto on the date last above written. ↓3

_____ residing at _____

_____ residing at _____ ↓3

_____ residing at _____ ↓3

REPORTS 45 AND 46
PARTNERSHIP AGREEMENT

Paper: plain, vertical ruled lines
Copy 1. spacing: single
Copy 2. spacing: double
Proofguide: 109–112

P A R T N E R S H I P # A G R E E M E N T ↓3

THIS AGREEMENT, made February 15, 19--↓ between Ray G. Piserchia, of 185 Kennedy Boulevard, city of Hastings, county of Barry, state of Michigan, and Paul M. Harris, of 18 West Knox (St), city of Big Rapids, county of Mecosta, state of Michigan, herein referred to as partners.

Wherein It Is Mutually Agreed as Follows: ↓3 — *Center in all caps* ↓3

1. That the partnership name shall be P & H Tires. The partnership shall be conducted for the purpose of selling and installing ~~all types of~~ automobile and truck tires. The principal place of business shall be 151 Grove (St) *Hastings, Michigan*

|10| 2. That the term of this agreement shall be for six (6) years commencing ~~on~~ July 1, 19--, and terminating ~~on~~ June 30, 19--, unless sooner terminated by mutual consent of parties.

3. That each partner shall contribute Fifteen Thousand Dollars ($15,000) on or before July 1, 19--, to be used by the partnership to establish its capitol position.

4. That each partner will share equally (Fiftey Percent, 50%) in net profits and/or net losses of the firm. Profits shall be distributed annually on June 30.

5. That each partner will draw a salary of ~~Three~~ *Four* Thousand Dollars ($3,000) per month, in addition to the distribution of profits and/or losses. ↓3

IN WITNESS WHEREOF, the parties have executed this agreement at Hastings, Michigan, on the date first above written. ↓3

_____
Ray G. Piserchia ↓3

_____
Paul M. Harris ↓2

Signed & delivered in the presence of: ↓3

_____ ↓3

_____

81-D. PRACTICE: ACCURACY

31 treat pupil travel fasten fateful phonics operetta platform
32 waves mummy reflex graded gizzard placate politics readable
33 tests milky weaken grease polygon postage quadrate taxation
34 beast lymph looked hazard quarter sarcasm traverse unkindly
35 water pylon jumped junior seaward weather vegetate windmill
| 1 | 2 | 3 | 4 | 5 | 6 | 7 | 8 | 9 | 10 | 11 | 12

81-E. PRACTICE: MACHINE MANIPULATION

Shift lock 36 They asked him to use REGISTRANTS for the sign by the door.
37 She predicted that WILDCAT would soon become a best seller.
38 COBOL will probably be used as the language in the courses.
39 A MEMBERS ONLY sign made it clear that we were not welcome.
40 My new book will be titled WINTER'S WONDER or COUNTRY SNOW.

Margin release* 41 The conference will be held on October 9 at the Lakeside Inn in Troy.
Use the margin 42 Those who plan to attend know how important it is to keep up to date.
release to 43 The keynote speaker will discuss the latest word processing concepts.
complete each 44 Nine equipment distributors will have their latest models on display.
sentence on the 45 Those who register early will be eligible for the special door prize.
line. | 1 | 2 | 3 | 4 | 5 | 6 | 7 | 8 | 9 | 10 | 11 | 12 | 13 | 14
**POSTTEST. Repeat the
Pretest and compare
performance.**

81-F. POSTTEST: SELECTIVE PRACTICE

81-G. Spacing—double.
**Take a 5-minute timing with
a 5-second rest after each
minute, then a 5-minute
timing without stopping. Try
to type for 5 minutes with 5
or fewer errors. Record your
score.**

81-G. SKILL MEASUREMENT: 5-MINUTE TIMED WRITING

46   It is to be expected that young people look forward to 12
their employment with a positive attitude. They want to do 24
things the right way. 28

A word of caution is in order, however. Not many days 40
ago I met a very fine young woman with a new college degree 52
who had been sadly disappointed. She told me that her work 64
was not quite what she had expected. 71

After a month on the job, she wasn't sure how well she 83
was doing and didn't quite know what her supervisor thought 95
of her job performance. I explained that, if she was truly 107
concerned and upset, she should ask her supervisor just how 119
she really felt. 122

Her supervisor was amazed when the problem was brought 134
to her attention. As there had been no negative criticisms 146
of her work, she had assumed that my acquaintance was aware 158
that she was doing very well. The busy boss apologized; my 170
friend smiled with relief. 175
| 1 | 2 | 3 | 4 | 5 | 6 | 7 | 8 | 9 | 10 | 11 | 12

* **WP** A word processor
automatically advances
to the next line as each line
becomes full, so it is
unnecessary to use a margin
release.

148-C. Spacing—double.
Take two 5-minute timings.
Between them, practice any
words with which you had
difficulty. Record your score.

148-C. SKILL MEASUREMENT: 5-MINUTE TIMED WRITING

During the last decade, flextime has become one of the 12

major trends in employee work patterns. Not a new idea, it 24

began overseas and came to this country in the seventies as 36

an alternative to the fixed workweek. With flexible hours, 48

the working day is divided into two separate types of time, 60

core time and flexible time. During core time, all workers 72

must be present for peak work-load hours; flexible time, on 84

the other hand, is the time that employees choose for their 96

starting and quitting time within limits set by their firm. 108

As a work concept, flextime is part of a fundamentally 120

new set of changed work conditions to better serve employee 132

needs and, as such, is highly regarded by management. Some 144

firms that have switched to flextime notice important gains 156

in productive work hours due to better organization of work 168

and, also, less paid absence and overtime. Workers seem to 180

be more satisfied when they have more freedom to choose the 192

hours that they work. This, of course, results in improved 204

morale and job satisfaction at no extra cost. Based on the 216

preceding facts, flextime may be a good idea. 225

| 1 | 2 | 3 | 4 | 5 | 6 | 7 | 8 | 9 | 10 | 11 | 12

148/149-D. WILL, EMPLOYMENT CONTRACT, AND PARTNERSHIP AGREEMENT

You will have an opportunity to type additional legal papers in these lessons. Your first assignment will be to type a will. Many times a will is typed on a form; however, it can easily be typed on plain paper following the same format (10-space indentions; ruled lines; using all caps, and so on). You will also type two forms of contracts: an employment contract and a partnership agreement. In all three types of jobs you should use a 2-inch top margin and a 1-inch bottom margin. Single-space the will.

REPORT 44
WILL

Paper: plain, vertical ruled lines
Proofguide: 109–110

LAST WILL AND TESTAMENT↓2
OF↓2
JOHN B. DREW↓3

I, John B. Drew, of the City of Marietta, County of Washington, State of Ohio, being of sound and disposing mind and memory, do hereby make, publish, and declare this to be my Last Will and Testament, hereby revoking and canceling all former Wills and Codicils by me at any time made.↓3

FIRST: I hereby direct that all my just debts and funeral expenses be paid and discharged as soon as possible out of my estate by my executrix hereinafter named.

SECOND: I hereby give, devise, and bequeath all my estate and property, real and personal, of whatsoever nature and wheresoever situated, to my beloved wife, Charlotte P. Drew.

THIRD: I hereby appoint my wife, Charlotte P. Drew, as the sole executrix of my estate; and I direct that no bond be required of her in the performance of her duties.↓3

IN WITNESS WHEREOF, I have hereunto set my

<table>
<tr><td>

Line: 60 spaces   Drills: 3X
Spacing: single
Proofguide: 53–56
Workguide: 155–156,
187–188, 191–198
Tape: 37A

</td><td>

LESSONS 82/83
LETTERS

</td></tr>
</table>

Goals: To build skill in tabulating; to format letters in modified-block style.

82-A. WARMUP

S 1   The boy got a jar of iced tea to take to the lake with him.
A 2   Max must have good technique to zip through difficult copy.
N 3   He returned 15 of item number 3862 for a credit of $14,790.
     | 1 | 2 | 3 | 4 | 5 | 6 | 7 | 8 | 9 | 10 | 11 | 12

82-B. **Clear all tabs. Then set four new tab stops every 12 spaces. Type each line, tabulating across from column to column.**

82-B. SKILL DRILL: TABULATOR PRACTICE—ALPHABET

4 paint	boxer	quilt	razor	shelf
5 joist	rivet	union	wheel	yacht
6 Clark	Delta	Mills	Regis	Walsh
7 Akron	Huron	Miami	Salem	Tulsa

82-C. **Spacing—double. Tab—5. Take a 5-minute timing with a 5-second rest after each minute, then a 5-minute timing without stopping. Try to type for 5 minutes with 5 or fewer errors. Record your score.**

PROFESSIONAL HINT
Whenever you can, perform the following special drills before you start a timing:
1. To sharpen your concentration, type a line or two of the Warmup backwards.
2. To increase speed, race through two or three copies of a very easy sentence, such as the first Warmup line.

82-C. SKILL MEASUREMENT: 5-MINUTE TIMED WRITING

8   A real opportunity exists for many persons who live in   12
colder regions of our country. These people are those who,   24
during the warm summer months, can be found playing tennis,   36
swimming at the beach, water skiing, or involved with other   48
warm weather sports. However, many of these persons can be   60
found glued to their television sets during the cold winter   72
days.   73
     The real sports enthusiast realizes, however, that the   85
really great thrills can be found when the snowflakes begin   97
to fall. A novice can soon acquire the needed basic skills   109
for enjoyment of cross-country skiing. Equipment costs are   121
quite low, and there are no additional costs. While skills   133
for downhill skiing are more complex, many believe that the   145
added excitement makes it all worthwhile. As compared with   157
cross-country costs, downhill equipment is quite expensive;   169
and lift tickets can be costly.   175
     | 1 | 2 | 3 | 4 | 5 | 6 | 7 | 8 | 9 | 10 | 11 | 12

82/83-D. **Before typing Letters 22–25, read:**
Reference Section: xi–xii
Workguide: 187–188
Letter 22

82/83-D. BUSINESS LETTERS

Using the visual guide (Workguide page 189, type Letters 22–25 on the Workguide letterheads.

Be sure to address the envelopes on the reverse side of the Workguide letterheads.

NEW BUSINESS ↓2

    Ms. Walters reported on information leared at a state-
wide meeting for affirmative action officers held in March
in Minneapolis. She gave special emphasis on guide lines being
published by the State of Minnesota Bureau of Labor Statistics.

    Dr. Gimbrere and Mr. Mininberg presented a proposal to
change the forms currently being used to report new employees.
Much discussion centered on the question of identifying ethnic
and racial back ground as currently required. Ms. Walters will
prepare a comprehensive report, with Dr. Gimbrere and Ms.
Mininberg assisting her, and report back at the next meeting. ↓2

                          Respectfully submitted, ↓4

                          Carmen Rodriguez
                          Administrative Asst.
                          Affirmative Action Office ↓2

Distribution:
    Affirmative Action Council Members
    Cabinet Officers
    File

| Line: 60 spaces   Tab: 5, center |
| Spacing: single   Drills: 2X |
| Proofguide: 109–112 |
| Workguide: 155–156 |
| Tape: 43B |

LESSONS 148/149
LEGAL PAPERS

Goal: To format a will, an
agreement, and a contract.

148-A. WARMUP

S   1   The butter on the corn on the cob dripped down on her shoe.
A   2   Jacqueline was glad her family took five or six big prizes.
N   3   There were 19,874 beans in one barrel; 20,365 in the other.
        | 1 | 2 | 3 | 4 | 5 | 6 | 7 | 8 | 9 | 10 | 11 | 12

148-B. **Type lines 4–11 twice
each.**

148-B. PRACTICE ON FREQUENT PHRASES

4   you can|you can see|you can tell|you can plan|you can think
5   she will|she will be|she can see|she will call|she will buy
6   he should|he should plan|he will go|he will buy|he will try
7   they are|they will|they can|they should go|they should plan

8   will you|will they|will she|will he|will she go|will he see
9   can you|can you see|can you tell|can you plan|can you think
10   should he|should he plan|will he go|will he buy|will he try
11   are they|will they|can they|should they go|should they plan
        | 1 | 2 | 3 | 4 | 5 | 6 | 7 | 8 | 9 | 10 | 11 | 12

Shown in elite
Line: 5 inches (50 pica/
60 elite)
Tab: center
Paper: Workguide 191–192
Proofguide: 53–54

*Letters 1–21 appear in
Lessons 1–75.

**Business
Services, Inc.**
6803 Rosecroft Rd.
Richmond, VA 23229

January 5, 19--   3
                              ↓ 5

Mechanical Supply Company   12
3418 Oglethorpe Road   16
Charleston, WV 25314   21
                       ↓ 2

When a letter is addressed to   Attention: Mrs. Judith A. Busch   28
a company, an attention line
is often used to direct the   Ladies and Gentlemen: 34
letter to a particular person
or department. The attention   The questions that you posed in your recent letter were   46
line is blocked at the left   excellent. The answers are, I believe, illustrated by this 58
margin a double space   letter and the enclosed manual.   65
below the inside address.
Type it in the style shown.   This is a _modified-block_ letter, the most commonly used   82
                                  letter style. It is permissible to indent the paragraphs,   94
Always respect a woman's   usually for 5 spaces; but it is not unusual to indent 10   106
preference in selecting _Miss_,   or even more spaces.   111
Mrs., or _Ms._ If her preference
is unknown, use the title _Ms._   In this letter style, the date line and the closing lines   123
                                  start at the center of the page. Also, as is shown above,   135
                                  a "company salutation" is used when there is an attention   147
WP Instead of using a   line.   148
        production word count to
measure output, many word   Standard punctuation is used: a colon after the salutation 161
processing centers measure   and a comma after the complimentary closing. Also, the word 173
output by counting the number   _Enclosure_ is typed below the reference initials to serve as 189
of strokes or lines typed.   a reminder to both the sender and the recipient when some-   201
                                  thing is to be enclosed with the letter.   209

                                                    Sincerely,   213
                                                         ↓ 4

                                                    Alyce A. Frazier, Director   223
                                                    Correspondence Department   229

                    eah   231
                    Enclosure   233

Business letter in modified-block style.

<table>
<tr><td>$1,400.00</td><td>May 15, 19--</td></tr>
</table>

```
$1,400.00 _____          _____ May 15, 19--_____
Ninety days----------------------------after date we promise to pay to
the order of Nelson Shrubs, Inc.-----------------------------------
One thousand four hundred and 00/100---------------------Dollars
at Dothan Savings Bank, Dothan, Alabama-----------------------------
  Value received                    GREENFIELD GARDEN CENTER
No. 152  Due August 13, 19--
```

FORMATTING PROMISSORY NOTES. When typing promissory notes:

1. The ruled line should be in the position of the underscore.

2. Begin all lines except the date as close to the start of the ruled line as possible.

3. After the name and the amount, fill in the rest of the line with hyphens.

4. When spelling out amounts of money, capitalize the first word and express cents as a fraction.

FORMS 41 AND 42
PROMISSORY NOTES

Paper: Workguide 309
Proofguide: 107

FORM 41. PROMISSORY NOTE 152. Greenfield Garden Center promises to pay $1,400.00 to the order of Nelson Shrubs, Inc., at the Dothan Savings Bank in Dothan, Alabama, 90 days from today's date.

FORM 42. PROMISSORY NOTE 153. Rockledge Nursery promises to pay $1,800.00 to the order of Nelson Shrubs, Inc., at the Citizens Bank and Trust in Ozark, Alabama, 60 days from today's date.

REPORTS 42 AND 43
MINUTES OF A MEETING
(BOUND)

Paper: plain
Line: 6 inches (60 pica/70 elite)
Tabs: 5, center
Report 42: single spacing
Report 43: double spacing, but single-space the two listings
Caution: bottom margin
Proofguide: 107–110

This format illustrates one arrangement for minutes. It also shows the proper sequence for reporting what transpired.

Top Margin—2 inches

QUARTERLY

MINUTES OF THE ~~MONTHLY~~ MEETING ↓2

Affirmative Action Council ↓2

May 10, 19-- ↓3

ATTENDANCE ↓2

quarterly

The regular ~~monthly~~ meeting of the affirmative action council was held in Room C-315. The meeting started at 2:30 and ended at 3:45 p.m. Ms. Anita Walters, Affirmative Action Director, presided at the meeting. The following ~~persons~~ were ~~there~~:

present ↓2

council members

Mr. R. MacVane	Ms. E. Mininberg
Dr. R. Gimbrere	Mr. R. Davis
Mr. B. McKinley	Ms. J. Armstrongs

alphabetize names ↓3

UNFINISHED Business ↓2

read *approved*

The minutes of the last meeting were ~~approved~~ and ~~read~~. ↓2

to *the*

Ms. Walters presented a report on number of affirmative action reports filed for all levels of employees for the last ~~month~~:

different

quarter

15 jobs filled in entry-level production
12 jobs filled in entry-level administrative support
2 jobs filled in middle-management administration
1 job filled in upper-management administration

gave *s on*

Ms. Walters detailed the profile of the applicant pool and gave a breakdown of the sex and ethnic background of the candidates. ↓3

(Continued on next page.)

LETTER 23
MODIFIED-BLOCK STYLE

Line: 5 inches (50 pica/60 elite)
Tab: center
Paper: Workguide 193–194
Proofguide: 53–54

(*Current date*) / Chavez Machine Company, 13
Inc. / 5600 Skipley Road / Everett, WA 98205 / 21
Attention: Mr. Gregory E. Young / Ladies and 32
Gentlemen: 34

We are happy to report that our plant in 43
Bellevue is again in full production. We know 53
that you were concerned about the delays 61
which may have caused some problems with 69
your production schedule. 75

Ms. Carole J. Bianchi, our new field repre- 84
sentative for your region, will visit you soon to 94
review pending orders for both production 102
materials and new maintenance supplies. She 111
will be able to set up delivery schedules for 121
past orders at that time. 126

Your company is one of our oldest and most 136
valued customers, and we sincerely appre- 144
ciate the patience which you have exhib- 152
ited during these past months. Our intention 161
will be to reward you with the best service 170
possible. 172

Sincerely yours, / William J. Evans / Direc- 187
tor of Marketing / (*Your initials*) 192

LETTER 24
MODIFIED-BLOCK STYLE

Paper: Workguide 195–196
Proofguide: 53–54

(*Current date*) / Olympia Engineering Com- 13
pany / 4700 Pattison Road NE / Olympia, WA 20
98506 / Attention: Ms. J. T. Edwards, Purchas- 30
ing Director / Ladies and Gentlemen: 38

Your inquiry about our new line of tool ac- 48
cessories was received yesterday afternoon. 57
The timing of your letter was excellent since 66
we finalized arrangements for a distributor in 75
Olympia only a week ago. The Farley Sup- 83

ply Company will deliver these items from its 93
local warehouse. 96

While orders ordinarily should be pro- 105
cessed through this office, arrangements have 114
been made so that small batches can be or- 122
dered and delivered on short notice directly 131
from the Farley Supply Company. 138

One of our sales representatives will call on 148
you within the next week. We shall look for- 157
ward to a mutually profitable association with 166
you. 167

Sincerely yours, / William J. Evans / Direc- 182
tor of Marketing / (*Your initials*) 187

LETTER 25
MODIFIED-BLOCK STYLE

Paper: Workguide 197–198
Proofguide: 55–56

(*Current date*) / Miss Carmen Ramos / Pro- 12
duction Vice President / Allison Metal Fabri- 21
cators, Inc. / 7800 Shoreland Drive South / 29
Seattle, WA 98144 / Dear Miss Ramos: 37

Your letter concerning the late shipment of 47
valve assemblies to your plant was received 55
this morning. Be assured that we are very 64
concerned about this matter. Please accept 73
our apologies. 76

Although we do not think that you would 85
want us to make excuses for the delay, we do 94
want to explain what actually happened. 102

Your order was processed on schedule, and 112
the shipment left our plant by truck within two 121
days of receipt of the order. However, the 130
truck had a mechanical breakdown en route. 139
At the time we had no knowledge that this 147
had occurred; we learned later that the truck 156
was in a garage for repairs for over a week. 166

We were greatly disturbed when we 173
learned that the shipment was not trans- 181
ferred and sent directly to your factory. The 191
trucking firm has been notified that such 199
carelessness will not be tolerated. 206

Sincerely yours, / William J. Evans / Direc- 221
tor of Marketing / (*Your initials*) 226

Paper: plain, full sheet
Line: 60 spaces
Spacing: single
Top margin: 2 inches
Tab: 10
Proofguide: 107

GREAT BEND STATE COLLEGE   5
GREAT BEND, KANSAS   16
↓ 2

RESOLUTION TO GRANT EMERITUS STATUS   38
↓ 2

TO DR. MABEL B. JOHNSON   53
↓ 3

WHEREAS: The Kansas Administrative Code provides that the   68
board of trustees upon recommendation of the   78
President may provide Emeritus status for a re-   88
tiring president, dean, or professor should it   98
desire to recognize meritorious work; and   108
performance

WHEREAS: Dr. Mabel B. Johnson will retire from   119
the School of Business and the faculty   128
of Great Bend State College; and   135

WHEREAS: She has given twenty-four years of dedicated ser-   148
vice to the education of the citizens of the   158
state of Kansas as a faculty member at Great   168
Bend State College; and   174

WHEREAS: She has been a business educator for more than   185
41 years and has consistently served the pro-   195
fession with dedication and distinction; and   205

WHEREAS: She served as President of the Kansas   217
Business Education Association in 1961-1962;   227
and, she served as the graduate and   235
research adviser for business education   244
for the past ⑬ years; and, she was   253
recently recognized as the Outstanding   262
Business Education teacher for the   270
Mountain Plains Business Education   278
Association; Therefore be it   285

RESOLVED: That Dr. Mabel B. Johnson be granted Emeritus   299
status as Professor of Business Education and   309
be it further   313

RESOLVED: That Dr. Johnson shall have all the   325
rights, duties, and privileges thereunto   334
appertaining.   338

LESSONS 84/85
LETTERS AND MEMOS

Goals: To build skill in tabulating; to format a formal display letter and interoffice memorandums.

84-A. WARMUP

S 1 Jake may take the cows to the vet when they cut their legs.
A 2 The flowers, quaking aspens, and azure blue sky are extras.
N 3 The odometer read 21,698; we had gone 357 of the 400 miles.
  | 1 | 2 | 3 | 4 | 5 | 6 | 7 | 8 | 9 | 10 | 11 | 12

84-B. Clear all tabs. Then set four new tab stops every 12 spaces. Type each line, tabulating across from column to column.

84-B. SKILL DRIVE: TABULATOR PRACTICE—NUMBERS

4 2,438	7,019	5,860	3,821	4,958
5 6,007	9,884	1,723	8,506	5,307
6 4,218	3,962	7,755	6,093	2,148
7 1,683	4,290	8,577	9,876	5,432

84-C. Spacing—double. Tab—5. Take a 5-minute timing with a 5-second rest after each minute, then a 5-minute timing without stopping. Try to complete the selection with 5 or fewer errors. Record your score.

84-C. SKILL MEASUREMENT: 5-MINUTE TIMED WRITING

8   The freshman year at college is often a young person's 12
first experience with total freedom. He or she anticipates 24
that a flexible schedule will evolve and that there will be 36
no more orders from Mom and Dad. Freedom from the rules of 48
others is eagerly anticipated. One of my friends just told 60
me that he was very eager to leave home. But he soon found 72
that his new-found freedom was not a bed of roses.   82
          Throughout his high school years he had gotten used to 94
squeezing in a few more minutes of sleep each morning while 106
his mother called him repeatedly. He would leap out of bed 118
at the last possible moment, arriving at school just in the 130
nick of time.   133
          He continued to ignore that alarm clock after he moved 145
into the dormitory. Without his mother's daily tugging, he 157
slept through many of his classes. There was no doubt that 169
disaster was around the corner.   175
  | 1 | 2 | 3 | 4 | 5 | 6 | 7 | 8 | 9 | 10 | 11 | 12

84/85-D. FORMAL DISPLAY LETTER AND INTEROFFICE MEMORANDUMS

Study the arrangement of Letter 26 on page 126; then type a copy. Next, study the arrangement of Memorandum 9 on page 127 and type the memo four times as directed.

146/147-D. RESOLUTIONS, PROMISSORY NOTES, AND MINUTES

The documents prepared in this lesson are not generally classified as legal papers, but they often have legal implications. Resolutions are formal statements adopted by a group or organization with regard to an individual or cause. Promissory notes are formal written promises to repay an amount of money borrowed plus interest at an agreed upon future date. Minutes of meetings are kept by most organizations as a summary of the business transacted. Note that legal-looking, stylistic touches are used even though they are not classified as legal papers.

REPORT 40
RESOLUTION

Paper: plain, full sheet
Line: 60 spaces
Spacing: double
Top margin: 2 inches
Paragraph: tab 10
Proofguide: 107

SAMUEL C. BARUSY   3

WHEREAS Samel Barusy is retiring the position of   16

treasurer of the East Bergen Federal Teachers Credit Union   28

after 31 years of faithful service; and   36

        Whereas he has been a dependable, conscien-   46

tious, personable, and competant treasurer during that period   59

of time; and   61

        WHEREAS he played a major role in reorganizing the   75

office staff and space in the new building of EBTFCU and   91

spent and extensive amount of extra time in carrying out   102

his responsibilities; and   at 610 Palisade Avenue   107

        WHEREAS his knowledge of financial matters and   117

his willingness to council members of EBTFCU regarding thier   130

financial matters has been consistently evident during these   142

past 21 years; and   146

        WHEREAS he has been a strong supporter, loyal work-   153

er, and constant friend: Therefore be it   165

        RESOLVED, That the employees, officers, and members   178

of EBTFCU do commend for his extraordinary contribution to   190

EBTFCU,   192

            SAMULEL C. BARUSY   204

LETTER 26
FORMAL LETTER IN
MODIFIED-BLOCK STYLE
WITH INDENTED
PARAGRAPHS

Shown in elite
Line: 5 inches (50 pica/
 60 elite)
Tab: 5, center
Paper: Workguide 199–200
Proofguide: 55–56

ERIE TRUCKING COMPANY
9300 Lakeland Avenue
Cleveland, OH 44107

January 6, 19—— ↓5   3

Dear Mr. Jacobetti: 11

    A copy of proposed Senate Bill 224–84 was recently   25
received in my office. Since you have demonstrated in the   36
past that you are concerned about the economic environment   48
in which business firms operate in your district, I hope   60
that you will work to defeat this bill.   68

    In Cleveland, small trucking firms such as ours depend   82
to a high degree on connecting terminals that are located   93
outside the Greater Cleveland area. If we did not have the   105
flexibility of operating within a 50–mile radius of the   117
city, firms such as ours would be doomed to failure. An   128
analysis of our bills of lading for the past quarter reveals   140
that over 60 percent of our cargo would have been excluded   152
under the provisions of the proposed bill.   161

    The next meeting of the Association of Cleveland   174
Carriers will be held in the Association building at 7 p.m.   186
on January 18, 19——. We would very much like to have you   197
attend this meeting for the purposes of hearing our objections 210
to Senate Bill 224–84. Your influence in Columbus could be   222
very instrumental in bringing about the defeat of this bill.   235

                   Sincerely yours,   241
                       ↓4

No reference initials are used
when an address is typed be-
low the letter.

                   Lena Irani   248
                   President   252
                     ↓3–5

The style of this letter is "for-
mal" or "official" because the
address is typed at the bottom
(as is often done in a letter to
a public dignitary).

The Honorable Paul J. Jacobetti   263
Ohio State Senate   266
State House Building   270
Columbus, OH 43216   274

Formal letter in modified-block style with paragraph indentions.

LESSONS 146/147
LEGAL STYLING

Goal: To format resolutions, promissory notes, and minutes of a meeting.

146-A. WARMUP

S 1 Lee can see the new car when he goes to the city in a week.
A 2 Junior executives requested help for the biweekly magazine.
N 3 There were 24,560 votes for Sims and 19,873 votes for Lake.
| 1 | 2 | 3 | 4 | 5 | 6 | 7 | 8 | 9 | 10 | 11 | 12

146-B. Think while typing the numbers in lines 4–7. Without marking the text, add 10 to any two-digit number and subtract 20 from any three-digit number.

146-B. THINKING WHILE TYPING NUMBERS

4 A total of 82 students from 16 colleges attended the class.
5 The parade had 20 floats, 13 marching bands, and 19 clowns.
6 There were 89 men, 124 women, 55 girls, and 47 boys eating.
7 The plant owned 146 brand-new cars and 137 very old trucks.
| 1 | 2 | 3 | 4 | 5 | 6 | 7 | 8 | 9 | 10 | 11 | 12

146-C. Spacing—double. Take two 5-minute timings. Between them, practice any words with which you had difficulty. Record your score.

146-C. SKILL MEASUREMENT: 5-MINUTE TIMED WRITING

8 Reporting for a new job is like an exciting adventure. 12
Enthusiasm and energy are high, but getting the job is only 24
the first step. It is just as important to be able to keep 36
it. From the beginning, you will be scrutinized carefully. 48
To create a good impression, arrive alert and on time. Pay 60
close attention to how you dress and what you say to people 72
you meet. Learn to remember their names, and when you need 84
to ask questions, use good judgment. Be very observant and 96
listen attentively to all that is said. It might even help 108
to take notes in order to remember all the new information. 120
Some companies have a formal program for orienting new 132
employees, while others are less organized. However, to be 144
a valuable employee, you will want to learn quickly as much 156
as you can. If there is no company manual to read, you can 168
look through the office files for more information. But do 180
keep in mind that your associates must like and accept you, 192
which may require more than technical skills and knowledge. 204
Once you prove that you are a good worker who can get along 216
with others, then you can really get ahead. 225
| 1 | 2 | 3 | 4 | 5 | 6 | 7 | 8 | 9 | 10 | 11 | 12

MEMORANDUM 9*

Shown in elite
Paper: plain, full sheet
Line: 5 inches (50 pica/60 elite)
Tab: 10
Proofguide: 55–56

Either half-size or full-size plain paper may be used for memos. Use a 1-inch top margin on half-size paper and a 2-inch top margin on full-size paper.

NOTE: The heading INTEROFFICE MEMORANDUM is optional.

WP Word processors have a rapid form-fill-in feature that automatically prints each line of the heading for a memo and pauses to allow you to type in the variable information on each line.

*Forms 1–8 appear in Lessons 1–75.

If the writer's initials are included, they are generally typed at center.

↓ 13
INTEROFFICE MEMORANDUM   5
↓ 3

TO: Suzanne Wagner, Controller   14

FROM: Lena Irani, President   22

DATE: January 7, 19—   29

SUBJECT: Senate Bill 224–84   37
↓ 3

As you are aware, the continuing success of our firm is tied   51
directly to the upcoming vote on Senate Bill 224–84. We must   64
give top priority to its defeat.   71

The Association of Cleveland Carriers will give this matter   84
attention at its meeting at 7 p.m. on January 18, 19—, in   95
the Association building. I should like to have you accom-   107
pany me to this meeting so that we can provide convincing   119
evidence that the bill must be defeated. Any suggestions   130
in regard to the proper strategy to be pursued will be greatly   143
appreciated.   146

                    LI   149

ced   151

Interoffice memorandum on plain paper.

MEMORANDUM 10

Paper: plain, full sheet
Proofguide: 55–56

Type another copy of Memorandum 9 above; address this copy to Alfred T. Headley, Treasurer, rather than to Ms. Wagner.

MEMORANDUMS 11 and 12

Paper: Workguide 201, 203
Proofguide: 55–58

Type two more copies of Memorandum 9: one to Ms. Wagner and one to Mr. Headley. Use letterhead stationery instead of plain paper. Omit the heading *INTEROFFICE MEMORANDUM.* Begin typing on line 13.

REPORT 38
POWER OF ATTORNEY

Paper: plain, ruled*
Spacing: double
Start: line 13 (2 inches)
Proofguide: 105–106

*Remember: The double lines should be 1½ inches from the left; the single line ½ inch from the right.

WP Since much of the wording used in legal documents is standard, word processors are especially useful for typing legal forms. Only the variable information has to be keyboarded each time.

↓13

P O W E R   O F   A T T O R N E Y
↓3

10——————KNOW ALL MEN BY THESE PRESENTS that I, JANE P. COLEMAN, of the City of Flemington, County of Hunterdon, State of NJ, do hereby appoint my niece, Justine P. Colman, of this City, County, and State My attorney-in-fact to act in my name, place, and stead as my Agent in the management of real estate tranactions, chattel and goods transactions, banding and securities transactions, and business operating transactions, giving and granting unto my said attorney full power and authority do/to and perform all and every act and thing whatsoever requisite and necesary to be done in the said management as fully, to all intense and purposes, and I might or could do if personally present, with full power of substitution and revocation, hereby ratifying and confirming all that my said attorny of his substite shall lawfully do for shall cause to be done by virtue herof:

IN WITNESS whereof, I have here unto set my hand and seal this twenty-fourth day of April, 19--. ↓3

_____ (L.S.)
↓2

SIGNED and affirmed in the presence of ↓3

_____ and _____

REPORT 39
POWER OF ATTORNEY

Paper: plain, ruled
Spacing: double
Start: line 13 (2 inches)
Proofguide: 105–106

↓13

P O W E R   O F   A T T O R N E Y
↓3

KNOW ALL MEN BY THESE PRESENTS that I, JOSEPH P. SNYDER, of the Town of Sweetwater, County of Dade, State of Florida, do hereby appoint my daughter, Charlotte S. Cailleteau, of the City of Pompano Beach, Country of Broward, State of FL, my attorney-in-fact to act in my place, name, and stead as my agent in the management of real estate transactions, chattel and goods transactions, banking transactions, and business operating transactions, granting unto my said attorney full authority and power _power and authority_ to do and perform all and every act and thing whatsoever requisite and necessary to be done in the said management as fully, to all intents and purposes, as I might or could do if present personally, with full power of substitution and recovation, hereby ratifying and confirming all that my said attorney or his substitution should _shall_ lawfully do or shall cause to be done by virtue hereof.

IN WITNESS WHEREOF, I have hereunto set my hand and seal this thirteenth day of june, 19--. ↓3

_____ (L.S.)
↓2

SIGNED AND affirmed in the presence of ↓3

_____ and _____

LESSONS 86/87
LETTERS WITH TABLES

Goals: To build skill in tabulating; to format letters that contain tables.

86-A. WARMUP

S 1 She might not be at that quake site if there is a hazy sky.
A 2 She will expect to begin work at a modest, entry-level job.
N 3 He moved on May 26, 1984; it cost him $75 for 1,300 pounds.
| 1 | 2 | 3 | 4 | 5 | 6 | 7 | 8 | 9 | 10 | 11 | 12

86-B. Clear all tabs. Then set four new tab stops every 12 spaces from the left margin. Type each line, tabulating across from column to column.

86-B. SKILL DRILL: TABULATOR PRACTICE—ALPHABET AND NUMBERS

4 Grabow	Calvin	Senior	28,392	23,846
5 Fisher	Bagley	Senior	15,073	31,847
6 Quandt	Palmer	Junior	56,900	19,465
7 Kreitz	Baxter	Junior	27,824	61,598

86-C. Spacing—double. Tab—5. Take a 5-minute timing with a 5-second rest after each minute, then a 5-minute timing without stopping. Try to type for 5 minutes with 5 or fewer errors. Record your score.

86-C. SKILL MEASUREMENT: 5-MINUTE TIMED WRITING

8   An auction is an exciting and enjoyable place to spend 12
an afternoon. My favorite type is held at an auction house 24
where a large assortment of items has been accumulated just 36
for the purpose of resale. There is always an awareness of 48
family roots when one is attending the estate sale of some— 60
one who is deceased. One wonders about the people who were 72
the users of the objects. 77

       Wise persons acquaint themselves with the items before 89
the sale begins. A real prize may be overlooked if all one 101
does is look at the items from a distance. A real treasure 113
may await your discovery. The air is electric as those who 125
are "in the know" await the bidding on those items that may 137
be real bargains. The novice probably will not be aware of 149
the keen competition that exists. 156

       If you are interested in collectibles of any kind, you 168
may wish to adopt the auction habit. 175
| 1 | 2 | 3 | 4 | 5 | 6 | 7 | 8 | 9 | 10 | 11 | 12

86/87-D. BUSINESS LETTERS WITH VARIATIONS

As an aid to improving your speed in the typing of letters, produce the four versions of the letter shown on the next page.

6. A continuation page has 9 blank lines at the top (start on line 10). The top margin is deep because legal papers, if bound together, are bound at the top.

7. Signature lines begin at the center. Each name is typed under the signature line.

8. In this style of page numbering, the final number begins 3 lines under the end of the document, not at the foot of the page.

FORM 39
BILL OF SALE

Form: Workguide 305–306
Data: As shown
Proofguide: 105–106

FORM 40
BILL OF SALE

Form: Workguide 307–308
Data: From Report, page 212
Proofguide: 105–106

FORMATTING INSTRUCTIONS

1. Align the insertions with the preprinted words.

2. Treat any blank areas on the form as follows: Fill in any blank spaces within individual lines of the form with hyphens. Fill in any blank areas that occupy several blank lines with two horizontal underscores joined by a solid diagonal line. This is called a *Z rule*.

3. Leave 1 blank space between the preprinted word and the typed insertion.

↓ 10

5. The Seller agrees to transfer to the Buyer a clear title, free from all incumbrances, to the said 1933 Ford Roadster.

IN WITNESS WHEREOF, the parties hereto have signed this agreement the day and year first above written. ↓ 3

_____
Charles J. Sherman ↓ 3

_____
Christopher T. Edsen ↓ 3

Page 2 of 2

T 1100—Bill of Sale, Short Form.   JULIUS BLUMBERG, INC., LAW BLANK PUBLISHERS

Know all Men by these Presents,

That MARILYN C. SHERIDAN, of 151 South Windsor Drive, Christiana, Delaware 19702--

party of the first part, for and in consideration of the sum of Fourteen Thousand Four Hundred Fifty --- Dollars ($ 14,450------) lawful money of the United States, to the party of the first part in hand paid, at or before the ensealing and delivery of these presents, by ROSALIE SANCHEZ, of 19 Pierpont Avenue, New Castle, Delaware 19720,------

party of the second part, the receipt whereof is hereby acknowledged, has bargained and sold, and by these present does grant and convey unto the said party of the second part, the heirs, executors, administrators, successors and assigns thereof. All pottery equipment and materials located in laboratory at 151 South Windsor Drive.---

To Have and to Hold the same unto the said party of the second part, the heirs, executors, administrators, successors and assigns thereof forever. And the party of the first part does covenant and agree to and with the said party of the second part, to Warrant and Defend the sale of the said goods and chattels hereby sold unto the said party of the second part, the heirs, executors, administrators, successors and assigns thereof, against all and every person and persons whomsoever.

Whenever the text hereof requires, the singular number used herein shall include the plural and all genders.

In Witness Whereof: the party of the first part has duly executed this bill of sale on the fifth --------day of April----------19 --.

In Presence of

....(L. S.)

....(L. S.)

....(L. S.)

Forms may be purchased from Julius Blumberg, Inc., New York, New York 10013, or any of its dealers. Reproduction prohibited.

LETTER 27
MODIFIED-BLOCK STYLE
WITH INDENTED
PARAGRAPHS AND
TABLE

Shown in elite
Line: 5 inches (50 pica/
   60 elite)
Tab: 10, center
Paper: Workguide 205–206
Proofguide: 57–58

A subject line is often used
to indicate what the letter is
about. It is blocked at the left
margin a double space
below the salutation. Type it
in the style shown. (The
terms *Re* or *In Re* are often
used in place of the word
Subject.)

Tables in a letter are
commonly centered within
the line of typing with 6
spaces between columns.

Mr. Edward J. Maurier, President	14
Association of Cleveland Carriers	21
1300 Superior Avenue East	26
Cleveland, OH 44114	30

Dear Mr. Maurier: 35

Subject: Senate Bill 224–84   41

      The large attendance at the Association of Cleveland   53
Carriers last evening is a reflection of the concern that most   66
members feel about proposed Senate Bill 224–84. Please accept   78
my sincere appreciation for the role that you played in the   90
adoption of the resolution against passage of the bill. The   102
following names should be added to the list of contact persons   115
for firms as shown: 119

Rose Filizetti	Metropolitan Truck	141
Barbara Jones	Cleveland Van Lines	150
H. P. Kendall	Champion Trucking	159
Alan Sterling	Berger Transit, Inc.	168

      With the support of influential persons like you,   180
I am quite optimistic that the bill will be defeated. Please   193
let me know if there is anything that I can do to help you.   205

Sincerely yours,   211

Lena Irani   219
President   223

ced   224
cc The Honorable Paul J. Jacobetti   231

WP If you had typed Letter 27
on a word processor, the
only part you would need to
retype for Letters 28–29 would
be the changes. The rest of
the letter could be played out
(printed out) automatically
from the system's memory, or
storage area.

ASSIGNMENT	STYLE	SPECIAL INSTRUCTIONS	WORDS
Letter 28 Workguide: 207–208	Modified-block Proofguide: 57–58	Type Letter 27 with no paragraph indentions. Address the letter to the Association of Cleveland Carriers, attention Mr. Edward J. Maurier, President (see page 123). Change to appropriate salutation. Omit subject line.	224
Letter 29 Workguide: 209–210	Modified-block with indented paragraphs Proofguide: 57–58	Type Letter 27 using 5-space paragraph indentions. Use *In Re* rather than *Subject.*	234
Letter 30 Workguide: 211–212	Modified-block with indented paragraphs Proofguide: 57–58	Type Letter 27 using formal display, as on page 126. Omit subject line and *cc* notation.	219

144/145-D. FORMATTING LEGAL DOCUMENTS

Many different forms and documents are typed in a law office. Keep the following points in mind as you type the legal papers in this lesson:

1. Documents are equally legal whether typed on plain paper or on a printed form.

2. Erasures on key details, such as names, amounts, and dates are forbidden in most states (the page must be retyped or be initialed by all signers of the document).

3. Legal documents are often typed on ruled stationery, which is 8½ by 11 inches. Margin stops are set a space or two inside the double rule (1½ inches from the left) and the single rule (½ inch from the right edge).

REPORTS 36 AND 37
CONTRACT OF SALE

Paper: 8½ by 11 (draw margin-guide ruled lines)
Report 36: double spacing on 2 pages
Report 37: single spacing on 1 page
Proofguide: 103–106

FORMATTING INSTRUCTIONS
1. The top margin of the first page should be 2 inches but can be less if the document will fit on one page and is centered on it.
2. The title is spread-centered.
3. Spacing is usually double but can be single.
4. Paragraphs are usually indented 10 spaces but may be indented only 5 spaces.
5. In many states each page of a multipage document is numbered as shown here: expressed cumulatively, centered between rules, 3 lines under the body and at least an inch above the bottom of the page.

↓13

C O N T R A C T   O F   S A L E ↓3

AGREEMENT made this twenty-eighth day of March, 19--, by and between CHARLES J. SHERMAN, residing at 2362 Ramshorn Road, Webster, Massachusetts 01570, hereinafter called the Seller, and CHRISTOPHER T. EDSEN, residing at 726 A. F. Putnam Road, Charlton, Massachusetts 01507, hereinafter called the Buyer.

WITNESSETH that in consideration of the mutual covenants and agreements herein contained, the parties hereby agree as follows:

1. The Seller shall sell and deliver to the Buyer and the Buyer shall buy and accept a restored 1933 Ford Roadster, Serial No. CE76503.

2. The Seller shall deliver the said vehicle to the Buyer at his place of residence on or before the thirtieth day of April, 19--.

3. The Buyer shall pay to the Seller for the said Roadster the total sum of Thirty-one Thousand Five Hundred Dollars ($31,500), payable upon delivery.

4. Said Roadster has been inspected by the Buyer and is purchased "as is." Seller's warranty is limited to the authenticity of the chassis, motor, and body. Buyer agrees that if he accepts the vehicle, such acceptance satisfies all of Seller's obligations with the exception of the aforementioned. ↓3

Page 1 of 2

LESSONS 88/89
RULED TABLES

Goals: To increase basic skill; to build skill in formatting open and ruled tables.

88-A. WARMUP

S 1 An owl and a quail got caught in the bush when they fought.
A 2 Kim and Max served frozen sweets at the July Fourth picnic.
N 3 Troop 457 found 368 soda bottles and cans on May 19 and 20.
| 1 | 2 | 3 | 4 | 5 | 6 | 7 | 8 | 9 | 10 | 11 | 12

88-B. SKILL DRILL: NUMBER AND SYMBOL PRACTICE

4 1 aql 2 sw2 3 de3 4 fr4 5 ft5 6 jy6 7 ju7 8 ki8 9 lo9 0 ;p0
5 1 ala 2 s2s 3 d3d 4 f4f 5 f5f 6 j6j 7 j7j 8 k8k 9 191 0 ;0;
6 ! al! @ s2@ # d3# $ f4$ % f5% ¢ j6¢ & j7& * k8* (19( ) ;0)
7 ! a!a @ s@s # d#d $ f$f % f%f ¢ j¢j & j&j * k*k (1(1) ;);
| 1 | 2 | 3 | 4 | 5 | 6 | 7 | 8 | 9 | 10 | 11 | 12

88-C. Spacing—double. Take a 5-minute timing with a 5-second rest after each minute, then a 5-minute timing without stopping. Try to reach the same point on the second timing with 5 or fewer errors. Record your score.

88-C. SKILL MEASUREMENT: 5-MINUTE TIMED WRITING

8   Have you ever thought about the detailed planning that 12
goes into the design of a simple box that holds the product 24
you select on the retailer's shelf? Have you ever wondered 36
why you picked a certain brand when there were several that 48
were displayed on the shelf? Your decision might have been 60
based on the design of the box rather than quality or a low 72
price tag. 74

     Buyers may make judgments about a product by the shape 86
of its container as well as the use of color, graphics, and 98
a logo. A package can dazzle the customer and persuade one 110
to buy the product. 114

     Other features are considered when designing packaging 126
for merchandise. A container should be easy to handle both 138
for shipping and for customer convenience. It must protect 150
the product inside and must comply with the many government 162
regulations that apply. Packaging is not as simple as some 174
think. 175
| 1 | 2 | 3 | 4 | 5 | 6 | 7 | 8 | 9 | 10 | 11 | 12

<table>
<tr><td>

Line: 60 spaces   Tab: 5, center
Spacing: single   Drills: 2X
Proofguide: 103–106
Workguide: 155–156, 305–308
Tape: 43B

</td></tr>
</table>

LESSONS 144/145
LEGAL PAPERS

Goals: To improve number typing; to format a bill of sale and a power of attorney.

144-A.   WARMUP

S 1 Bill will see their swimming pool when he visits in August.
A 2 Brown jars prevented the mixture from freezing too quickly.
N 3 Marisa's quota was $256,790; Isabella's quota was $184,325.

| 1 | 2 | 3 | 4 | 5 | 6 | 7 | 8 | 9 | 10 | 11 | 12 |

144-B. Type lines 4–7 two times each. Then take two 1-minute timings. Note that the last two digits of each number are a cumulative word count.

144-B.   NUMBER PRACTICE

4 1501 7302 8903 2404 1805 9106 2307 1408 3609 6710 8911 2012
5 7813 6514 3415 3216 9117 1018 5819 3820 5521 9122 4523 8524
6 7925 8026 3327 7428 5529 1930 3231 8032 4733 7234 1835 9036
7 2137 8338 6539 4840 8741 2342 1743 6044 3845 9746 3047 1248

144-C. Spacing—double. Take two 5-minute timings. Between them, practice any words with which you had difficulty. Record your score.

144-C.   SKILL MEASUREMENT: 5-MINUTE TIMED WRITING

8
    Legal documents that may be typed in everyday business 12
include contracts, bills of sale, agreements, and powers of 24
attorney. Printed legal forms are widely used because they 36
save time. All the typist needs to do is just insert a few 48
words and fill in the blank spaces with hyphens. If a form 60
is not available and the document must be wholly typed, the 72
typist can set it up in manuscript format on special paper. 84
Such paper has ruled lines running down both left and right 96
margins which indicate where to set the margin stops. As a 108
rule, all typing must be done between these vertical lines. 120

    Other aspects of legal typing also have a standardized 132
procedure, such as indenting ten spaces for each paragraph, 144
spelling out sums of money in words and figures, and giving 156
a cumulative page count at the bottom of each page. Common 168
also to all legal work is the need for accuracy. Hence the 180
typist must exercise great care in typing and proofreading, 192
and erasing is not permitted on essential words. This task 204
is easier now with the use of word processing equipment for 216
revising and reproducing copy without errors. 225

| 1 | 2 | 3 | 4 | 5 | 6 | 7 | 8 | 9 | 10 | 11 | 12 |

WP Many word processors have a *phrase-library* function that stores words, clauses, or sentences that are used often (for example, some of the wording used in legal documents, or the complimentary closing and typed signature and title in a letter). To type in these phrases, you type only one key and the entire phrase or sentence is automatically inserted into the document at the appropriate point.

88/89-D. OPEN AND RULED TABLES

Type Tables 12–16. Center each table on a full sheet of plain paper.

88/89-D. Before typing Tables 12–16, complete Workguide pages 213–214 and study the information accompanying Tables 12–16.

TABLE 12*
OPEN TABLE

Paper: full sheet
Proofguide: 59

*Tables 1–11 appear in Lessons 1–75.

REVIEW NOTES
1. Key line consists of the longest item in each column plus 6 spaces between columns.
2. Underscore line is full column width.
3. *AVERAGE* or *TOTAL* is typed at the beginning of the column.
4. The $ sign in the bottom line must align with the $ sign above it.
5. The horizontal arrow indicates center of table. For additional review of tabulation, see pages xiii–xiv in the Reference Section.

LINE

1   PAPER PRODUCTION GOALS
2   ↓2
3   March, 19--
4   ↓3

	Inventory	Number of	Price
	Style No.	Reams	per Ream
	370R	1,200,000	$3.60
→	460R	440,000	4.10
	520B	690,000	7.85
	530B	1,080,000	8.10
	540B	320,000	7.35
	550B	790,000	9.20
	680R	1,230,000	6.90
AVERAGE		821,429	$6.73

Key Line: Inventory₁₂₃₄₅₆Number of₁₂₃₄₅₆per Ream

(Lines numbered 1–17)

TABLE 13
RULED TABLE

Paper: full sheet
Proofguide: 59

NOTES
1. Horizontal placement is the same as in an open table.
2. The parts of the table are divided by horizontal rules.
3. A ruled line is preceded and followed by 1 blank line; therefore, single-space before typing it and double-space after typing it.
4. Column headings are not underscored separately.
5. All horizontal rules extend to the edges of the table.

1   PAPER PRODUCTION GOALS
2
3   March, 19--
                           ↓1
4 _____
5   ↓2

	Inventory	Number of	Price
	Style No.	Reams	per Ream

↓1
_____
↓2

	370R	1,200,000	$3.60
→	460R	440,000	4.10
	520B	690,000	7.85
	530B	1,080,000	8.10
	540B	320,000	7.35
	550B	790,000	9.20
	680R	1,230,000	6.90

↓1
_____
↓2

AVERAGE		821,429	$6.73

_____

(Lines numbered 1–20)

TABLE 37
BOXED LEADER TABLE

Center copy with paper
  inserted sideways and
  centered at 66 (elite) or 55
  (pica).
Proofguide: 103

142/143-D. BOXED LEADER TABLE

Type the following table. If necessary, review the instructions for typing boxed tables with braced headings on page 135.

DELUXE OFFICE EQUIPMENT
Comparative Sales Data for Salespersons in Three Divisions

Salesperson/Division	Last Year		This Year	
	Amount	Percent	Amount	Percent
Tia Caputi/Typewriters	$1,450,709	15.1	$ 1,415,810	13.4
Peter Rocco/Typewriters	1,275,403	13.3	1,478,321	14.1
Lorry Taylor/Copiers	1,115,350	11.6	1,451,322	13.8
Ed Wolwowicz/Copiers	1,084,782	11.3	1,243,785	11.8
Carmen Muni/Calculators	985,750	10.3	1,145,750	10.9
Sharon Woll/Calculators	947,843	9.9	927,439	8.8
Bev Bower/Typewriters	918,732	9.6	1,010,578	9.6
Donald Guidi/Copiers	901,421	9.5	878,457	8.4
Art Collins/Typewriters	895,972	9.4	968,321	9.2
TOTALS	$9,575,962	100.0	$10,519,783	100.0

NOTE: Paper turned sideways
is 8½ inches long; 8½ × 6
lines = 51 lines vertically. It
is 11 inches wide, so that 11
× 12 = 132 elite spaces (66
center) or 11 × 10 = 110 pica
spaces (55 center).

TABLE 14
RULED TABLE

Paper: full sheet
Proofguide: 59

REMINDERS
1. **All horizontal lines extend to the edges of the table.**
2. **The $ sign must align at the top and bottom of a column.**
3. **Single-space before a ruled line and double-space after it.**
4. **Use periods across the width of the column to show that there is no entry.**

REGIONAL FIELD MANAGERS

February 1, 19--

Name	City	Salary
Chase, Paul G.	Orlando	$ 28,460
Frazier, Maurice	Mobile	40,900
Johnson, Sandra A.	Biloxi	28,000
McDonald, Janice	Durham	37,600
Moratti, Lori L.	Columbia	29,145
Wilson, Michael	Augusta	33,100
TOTAL	. . . .	$197,205

TABLE 15
RULED TABLE

Paper: full sheet
Proofguide: 59

Arrangement here is alphabetic by city.

PROPOSED SALARY INCREASES

Effective July 1, 19—

City	Name	Increase	New Salary
Augusta	Wilson, Michael	$ 1,324	$ 34,424
Biloxi	Johnson, Sandra A.	2,800	30,800
Columbia	Moratti, Lori L.	1,749	30,894
Durham	McDonald, Janice	4,512	42,112
Mobile	Frazier, Maurice	4,090	44,990
Orlando	Chase, Paul G.	1,708	30,168
TOTAL	. . . .	$16,183	$213,388

TABLE 16
RULED TABLE

Paper: full sheet
Proofguide: 59

Arrangement here is by percentage of increase.

SPECIAL NOTE: Unlike the $ sign, the % sign is shown with every number if the word *percent* does not appear in the column heading.

PROPOSED SALARY RATIOS

Effective July 1, 19—

Name	Old Salary	New Salary	Ratio
McDonald, Janice	$37,600	$ 42,112	112.0%
Frazier, Maurice	40,900	44,990	110.0%
Johnson, Sandra A.	28,000	30,800	110.0%
Chase, Paul G.	28,460	30,168	106.0%
Moratti, Lori L.	29,145	30,894	106.0%
Wilson, Michael	33,100	34,424	104.0%
TOTAL	$197,205	$213,388	108.2%

Line: 60 spaces   Tab: 5, center
Spacing: single   Drills: 2X
Proofguide: 103–104
Workguide: 155–156
Tape: 42B

LESSONS 142/143
REVIEW

Goal: To review boxed tables.

142-A. WARMUP

S 1 Kay and Alan will be happy to see you and Anne at the lake.
A 2 Max and Kay reviewed the subject before giving Paul a quiz.
N 3 Pam's lot was 170 × 245 feet; Tom's lot was 290 × 368 feet.
| 1 | 2 | 3 | 4 | 5 | 6 | 7 | 8 | 9 | 10 | 11 | 12

142-B. Pivot each of the words in lines 4–7 so that the words in the first column end at center and the words in the second column end at the right margin.

142-B. PIVOTING PRACTICE

4   Esther Diaz   Joseph Fiegel
5   Associate Commissioner   Personnel Director
6   Public Works   Fourth Floor
7   Jefferson Township   American Building

142-C. Spacing—double. Take two 5-minute timings. Between them, practice any words with which you had difficulty. Record your score.

142-C. SKILL MEASUREMENT: 5-MINUTE TIMED WRITING

8   Today millions of folks are working part-time, and the 12
numbers are increasing each year. This is due, in part, to 24
the growth of the service sector of our economy, which also 36
requires workers for peak periods, extended business hours, 48
and other special needs. Women comprise most of this labor 60
force, especially married women with children. Also, there 72
are record numbers of young people working today. Not only 84
are more students working now than at any other time in the 96
past quarter century, but they are also working more hours. 108
      Most of the jobs for these people are in food service, 120
retail sales, and office work. Working part-time is a good 132
way to earn extra income and, at the same time, acquire new 144
skills and broaden career horizons. Some students are able 156
to enroll in cooperative work and study programs, for which 168
they can receive school credit for their jobs. To be sure, 180
working part-time is a way to learn more about the world of 192
work and still have time left over for other pursuits. For 204
some people, it may even be a desirable work alternative on 216
a permanent basis. 220
| 1 | 2 | 3 | 4 | 5 | 6 | 7 | 8 | 9 | 10 | 11 | 12

LESSONS 90/91
BOXED TABLES

Goal: To learn how to format boxed tables (including those with braced headings).

90-A. WARMUP

S 1 The girl kept a map of the big lake as an aid for the quiz.
A 2 Jory received an extra cash reward for saving the red mare.
N 3 We will be 125 miles closer to Exit 87 on Route 46 at 9:30.
      | 1 | 2 | 3 | 4 | 5 | 6 | 7 | 8 | 9 | 10 | 11 | 12

90-B. Type the paragraph twice. Then take several 1-minute timings, trying to increase your speed each time. Keep your eyes on the copy.

90-B. SKILL DRILL: NUMBER AND SYMBOL PRACTICE

4 Carns & Hall quoted 100# @ $7.80 and 10# @ 90¢. Their fall 12
catalog* shows an additional 10% discount. What a buy! We 24
need about 3,000 pounds. May we purchase (on open account) 36
at such "once-in-a-lifetime" prices? If so, call 555-2466. 48
   | 1 | 2 | 3 | 4 | 5 | 6 | 7 | 8 | 9 | 10 | 11 | 12

90-C. Spacing—double. Take a 5-minute timing with a 5-second rest after each minute, then a 5-minute timing without stopping. Try to reach the same point on the second timing with 5 or fewer errors. Record your score.

90-C. SKILL MEASUREMENT: 5-MINUTE TIMED WRITING

5   Persons in the sales field must have a total knowledge 12
of the product they are trying to market. They must have a 24
systematic plan that will enable them to sell their product 36
even though the competition is keen. The same is true when 48
one begins to search for a new job. A job seeker must have 60
a plan of action because he or she is really setting out to 72
sell himself or herself in the labor market. 81
         An excellent personal data sheet is a must. There are 93
an amazing number of my acquaintances who have given super- 105
ficial attention to this important item. While there tends 117
to be a set of standard information on a data sheet, almost 129
any data of an informative nature may be included. It must 141
be neatly typed or it may be printed in a professional man- 153
ner. The wise job seeker will want to devise an impressive 165
data sheet as a part of his or her marketing plan. 175
   | 1 | 2 | 3 | 4 | 5 | 6 | 7 | 8 | 9 | 10 | 11 | 12

90/91-D. BOXED TABLES

Study the information about "boxed" style tables on pages 134–135 and center each table on a full sheet of plain paper.

NOTES ON TYPING TWO-PAGE TABLES

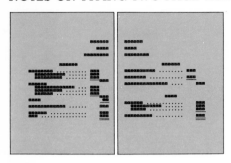

1. Two-page tables are usually planned so that the two pages may be taped in adjacent positions.

2. Divide the data into equal or logical halves.

3. Use the same top margin on both pages. Check the vertical spacing of each half, adding or deleting blank lines to make both halves end evenly.

4. Divide the heading lines to embrace both pages. The section on the first page is pivoted from the right margin; the section on the second page begins with the left margin.

5. Use the same line length on each half; if necessary, spread the data to fill the line. The display on each page *may* be centered horizontally, but the total display will look better if the margins are narrower on the sides where the pages will adjoin.

6. Tape the pages together on the *back* side, fastening them with two or three 1-inch strips of tape.

TABLE 36
BALANCE SHEET
(PAGE 2 OF 2 ADJACENT PAGES)

Paper: full sheet
Line: 70, with ½ inch left margin
Leaders: open
Proofguide: 103

LINE		
13	F I X T U R E S , I N C .	
14		
15	S H E E T	
16		
17	19----	
18		
19		
20	L I A B I L I T I E S	
21		
22	Current Liabilities:	
23	Accounts Payable . . . . $ 6,685.29	
24	Notes Payable 2,778.50	
25	Interest Payable 847.50	
26	Employee State Income Taxes Payable 856.42	
27	Employee Federal Income Taxes Payable 3,927.62	
28	Federal Unemployment Taxes Payable 134.69	
29	State Unemployment Taxes Payable 452.34	
30	FICA Taxes Payable 1,243.20	
31	Total Current Liabilities	$ 16,925.56
32	Long Term Liabilities:	
33	Mortgage Payable	74,837.60
34		
35	Total Liabilities	$ 91,763.16
36		
37		
38	O W N E R ' S E Q U I T Y	
39		
40	Raymond A. Bentley, Capital	128,729.05
41		
42	Total Liabilities and Owner's Equity	$220,492.21

PRODUCTION LABOR HOURS

Presque Isle Plant

(Last Half of 19--)

Month	Total Hours	Overtime Hours	Overtime Proportion
July	16,042	1,577	9.83%
August	18,782	1,324	7.05%
September	17,770	1,410	7.93%
October	15,705	948	6.04%
November	15,755	776	4.93%
December	14,869	657	4.42%

BOXED TABLES

In addition to the horizontal lines of a ruled table, a *boxed* table also has vertical ruled lines to separate the columns. Type the table as you would a ruled table, including the horizontal ruled lines. After proofreading carefully, draw in the vertical lines: (1) Rest a black pen or pencil on the card holder of the typewriter and turn the platen knob; or (2) remove the paper from the machine and draw in the vertical lines with a black pen or pencil and a ruler. The lines divide the headings and columns but do not close in the sides of the table.

PRODUCTION LABOR HOURS

Presque Isle Plant

(Last Half of 19--) ↓1

Month	Total Hours	Overtime Hours	Overtime Proportion ↓2 ↓1
July	16,042	1,577	9.83% ↓2
August	18,782	1,324	7.05%
September	17,770	1,410	7.93%
October	15,705	948	6.04%
November	15,755	776	4.93%
December	14,869	657	4.42%
			↓1

NOTES ON TYPING SPACED LEADERS

Spaced leaders (alternate periods and spaces) are slower to type than *close* leaders (page 204) but look better when a table includes many blank lines.

Begin the first leader line with 1 or 2 spaces (note below the 2 spaces between *Cash* and the first period). Note whether the periods fall in the odd- or even-number spaces on the scale; use this information when you start each subsequent leader line. You will often have to space twice at the start of a leader (see the 2 spaces after *Notes Receivable*) to enable you to keep all the periods aligned.

TABLE 35
BALANCE SHEET
(PAGE 1 OF 2 ADJACENT PAGES)

Paper: full sheet
Line: 70, with ½ inch right margin
Leaders: open
Proofguide: 103

Some word processors have a right-scroll feature that makes it possible to type documents wider than the display screen. For example, if the screen has room to display only 80 characters and your line is 140 characters long, the screen will shift to the right as soon as you have typed the 80th character, thus providing blank space for the remaining 60 characters. Although the entire 140-space line is not displayed on your screen at one time, it will print out correctly on a large sheet of paper.

```
                                          LINE
  B E N T L E Y   L I G H T I N G          13
                                           14
                              B A L A N C E 15
                                           16
                              May 31,       17
                                           18
                                           19
                 A S S E T S                20
                                           21
                                           22
Current Assets:
  Cash . . . . . . . . . . . . . . . . . $16,342.78   23
  Accounts Receivable (Less Allowance              24
    for Bad Debts) . . . . . . . . . . .   5,675.25   25
  Notes Receivable  . . . . . . . . . . .  3,400.75   26
  Merchandise Inventory . . . . . . . . . 36,835.68   27
  Office Supplies . . . . . . . . . . . .  1,762.75   28
  Prepaid Advertising . . . . . . . . . .    102.50   29
  Prepaid Insurance . . . . . . . . . . .    942.00   30
    Total Current Assets . . . . . . . .           $ 65,061.71   31
Fixed Assets:                                       32
  Factory Equipment (Less Accumulated              33
    Depreciation)  . . . . . . . . . . . $31,430.00   34
  Office Equipment (Less Accumulated               35
    Depreciation)  . . . . . . . . . . . 12,875.50   36
  Building (Less Accumulated                       37
    Depreciation)  . . . . . . . . . . . 84,350.00   38
  Land . . . . . . . . . . . . . . . . . 26,775.00   39
    Total Fixed Assets . . . . . . . . . .          155,430.50   40
                                                    41
    Total Assets . . . . . . . . . . .             $220,492.21   42
```

BOXED TABLES WITH BRACED HEADINGS

In addition to the regular column headings, it may be desirable at times to use an additional heading which relates to two or more columns. This is called a *braced heading*, and it should be typed so that it is centered over the columns to which it applies. For example, in Table 19 below, the heading *Academic Level* applies to both the *High School* and the *College* columns.

Detailed instructions for typing a table with a braced heading follow:

1. Determine the vertical placement and type the title. (Table 19 occupies 18 lines of space.)

2. Determine the horizontal placement and set the left margin and the two tabs for the second and third columns.

3. Type the first horizontal rule; then go down 5 lines (thus leaving space for the braced heading) and type the column headings.

4. Roll the paper back 3 lines so that the braced heading *Academic Level* will be a triple space above the column headings.

5. To center *Academic Level* (14) over *High School* + 6 + *College* (24), indent *Academic Level* 5 spaces from the start of *High School*: 24 − 14 = 10; 10 ÷ 2 = 5.

TABLE 19
BOXED TABLE WITH BRACED HEADING

Paper: full sheet
Proofguide: 61

NOTE: Use of a braced heading *requires* that a table be typed in boxed style.

EMPLOYEE EDUCATION ↓1

↓5 Department	Academic Level ↓2	
	High School	College ↓1
		↓2
Finance	8	13
Marketing	10	17
Office Services	6	15
Personnel	4	2
Production	149	22 ↓1
		↓2
TOTAL	177	69 ↓1

TABLE 20
BOXED TABLE WITH BRACED HEADING

Paper: full sheet
Proofguide: 61

NOTE: If a table has a number, it is centered a double space above the title and typed in uppercase and lowercase letters.

Table 1-7

PRODUCTION SUMMARY

Model Series	Shift		
	First	Second	Third
100	2,040	1,780	1,470
200	1,359	1,168	986
300	1,063	863	529
400	859	745	485
500	267	235	169
TOTAL	5,588	4,791	3,639

140/141-D. FINANCIAL STATEMENTS

TABLE 34
BALANCE SHEET
(WITH LEADERS)

Paper: full sheet
Line: 70 spaces
Proofguide: 101

Spread-center the section headings.

Pivot from the right margin to find the point at which to set tabs for the money columns.

To keep your place when typing a financial statement, put a ruler or card under the line being typed and keep moving it as you go down the page.

WP Some word processors have a calculator function that automatically provides totals and subtotals as you type in the number columns— an especially useful feature for preparing financial statements.

BENTLEY LIGHTING FIXTURES, INC.   ↓ 2

BALANCE SHEET   ↓ 2

May 31, 19--   ↓ 2
↓ 3

A S S E T S   ↓ 2

Current Assets:
    Cash $16,342.78
    Accounts Receivable (Less Allowance
      for Bad Debts) 5,675.25
    Notes Receivable 3,400.75
    Merchandise Inventory 36,835.68
    Office Supplies 1,762.75
    Prepaid Advertising 102.50
    Prepaid Insurance 942.00
      Total Current Assets .... $ 65,061.71
Fixed Assets:
    Factory Equipment (Less Accumulated
      Depreciation) $31,430.00
    Office Equipment (Less Accumulated
      Depreciation) 12,875.50
    Building (Less Accumulated
      Depreciation) 84,350.00
    Land 26,775.00
      Total Fixed Assets 155,430.50
        Total Assets .... $220,492.21   ↓ 2
↓ 3

L I A B I L I T I E S   ↓ 2

Current Liabilities:
    Accounts Payable .... $ 6,685.29
    Notes Payable 2,778.50
    Interest Payable 847.50
    Employee State Income Taxes Payable 856.42
    Employee Federal Income Taxes Payable 3,927.62
    Federal Unemployment Taxes Payable 134.69
    State Unemployment Taxes Payable 452.34
    FICA Taxes Payable 1,243.20
      Total Current Liabilities .... $ 16,925.56
Long Term Liabilities:
    Mortgage Payable 74,837.60
      Total Liabilities .... $ 91,763.16   ↓ 2
↓ 3

O W N E R ' S   E Q U I T Y   ↓ 2

Raymond A. Bentley, Capital 128,729.05

    Total Liabilities and Owner's Equity ...... $220,492.21   ↓ 2

LESSONS 92/93
TABLE REVIEW

Goals: To increase basic skill; to build skill in formatting open, ruled, and boxed tables.

92-A. WARMUP

S 1 He will jump in the lake if he hears the buzz of a big bee.
A 2 The fox scared the pony, and she quickly jumped into a van.
N 3 Agent 097 sat in Seat 15E when Flight 134 left at 6:28 a.m.
| 1 | 2 | 3 | 4 | 5 | 6 | 7 | 8 | 9 | 10 | 11 | 12

92-B. Type the paragraph twice. Then take several 1-minute timings, trying to increase your speed each time. Keep your eyes on the copy.

92-B. SKILL DRILL: NUMBER AND SYMBOL PRACTICE

4 All #3 items which are marked at $1.26 (regular price) will 12
be sold at 89¢. The larger items marked "4 @ $4" remain at 24
that price. The B&J Outlet Shop will buy 75% of the unsold 36
stock at 1/3 off the sale prices.* We'll soon be sold out! 48
| 1 | 2 | 3 | 4 | 5 | 6 | 7 | 8 | 9 | 10 | 11 | 12

92-C. Spacing—double. Take a 5-minute timing with a 5-second rest after each minute, then a 5-minute timing without stopping. Try to reach the same point on the second timing with 5 or fewer errors. Record your score.

92-C. SKILL MEASUREMENT: 5-MINUTE TIMED WRITING

5   The style for a typed table is often determined by the 12
nature of the information or the occasion for its use. The 24
typist must know that tables can be set up in the different 36
styles shown by the three models that follow. 45
     First of all, a table can be set up in the open style, 57
which uses ruled lines only for setting off column headings 69
and summary lines with underscores. This style is used for 81
short tables and those in letters. 88
     Secondly, a table can be arranged in the ruled form, a 100
unique pattern that uses horizontal lines of underscores to 112
set off the main parts of the table. The style is normally 124
used for financial statements and tables with many columns. 136
     Thirdly, the boxed display is judged as being the best 148
for very complicated tables. In this form the columns, the 160
headings, and the footings are boxed in with horizontal and 172
vertical lines. 175
| 1 | 2 | 3 | 4 | 5 | 6 | 7 | 8 | 9 | 10 | 11 | 12

92/93-D. REVIEW OF TABLE STYLES

Center the tables displayed on the following page as directed. Leave 6 spaces between columns.

LESSONS 140/141
FINANCIAL STATEMENTS

Goal: To format balance sheets.

140-A.   WARMUP

S 1 The student took his problem to the new Board of Directors.
A 2 I quickly explained that few big jobs involve many hazards.
N 3 The bid for $147,380 was $2,695 less than the bid by Kay's.
| 1 | 2 | 3 | 4 | 5 | 6 | 7 | 8 | 9 | 10 | 11 | 12

140-B. Type paragraph 4 twice. Double each number that appears in the paragraph—enrollment numbers, as well as classroom numbers.

140-B.   THINKING WHILE TYPING NUMBERS

4   There were 7 boys and 5 girls in classroom 21 and 6 boys and 6 girls in classroom 23. There were 240 students in all 10 classrooms in the building. An enrollment of 180 students was expected next year, with 9 students per room.

140-C. Spacing—double. Take two 5-minute timings. Between them, practice any words with which you had difficulty. Record your score.

140-C.   SKILL MEASUREMENT: 5-MINUTE TIMED WRITING

5   Financial statements are the basis of major management 12
decisions. There are two types of statements that are used 24
quite a bit in business. One is the income statement, also 36
called a profit and loss statement, which summarizes all of 48
the sales and expenses of a business over a period of time. 60
The other one is the balance sheet, listing all the assets, 72
the liabilities, and the equity for a firm on a given date, 84
such as at the end of a month, a quarter, or a year. It is 96
getting much easier for many firms to get this type of data 108
at a much faster rate due to the use of desk-top computers. 120
     In business, these statements need to be typed so they 132
can be easily read. This does not take much time if a firm 144
uses the same format year after year. Usually, there is an 156
explanation (stub) on the left and several money columns on 168
the right. Empty spaces after the stub may be connected by 180
leaders which guide the eye across the gap. All the typist 192
needs to do is to follow company practice as to style. One 204
very important factor, however, is proofreading, especially 216
when typing numbers. 220
| 1 | 2 | 3 | 4 | 5 | 6 | 7 | 8 | 9 | 10 | 11 | 12

TABLE 21
OPEN TABLE

Paper: full sheet
Special: insert tomorrow's
date as a subtitle line
Proofguide: 63

DRIVER ASSIGNMENTS

Name	Truck Number	Route Number
Elmhurst, Donald F.	34	2
Jones, Dorothy J.	52	1
Mowafy, Mokhlis Y.	17	6
Seethoff, Sophie	68	5
Komoto, Karen	10	4
Vinocur, Abraham	49	3

TABLE 22
RULED TABLE

Paper: full sheet
Proofguide: 63

JANUARY
~~DECEMBER~~ FUEL CONSUMPTION

Truck Number	Miles Driven	Gallons of Fuel	Miles per Gallon
10	3,780	548	6.9
~~27~~ 17	4,261	~~548~~ 584	7.3
34	2,955	4~~8~~69	6.~~0~~3
49	5,204	897	5.8
~~49~~ 52	4,00~~0~~6	358	11.2
#68	4,137	398	10.4
AVERAGE	4,057	542	8.0

TABLE 23
BOXED TABLE WITH BRACED HEADINGS

Paper: full sheet
Special: double-space the
column entries
Proofguide: 63

NOTE: The percent sign may
be omitted after each
number if the column
heading makes it perfectly
clear that the numbers in a
column represent
percentages.

TABLE 24
BOXED TABLE

Paper: full sheet
Special: use Table 23 content
but omit braced headings
and percent columns; add
a total column (you
compute the totals).
Column headings will be
*Route Number, City
Deliveries, Rural
Deliveries,* and *Total.*
Proofguide: 63

JANUARY
~~DECEMBER~~ DELIVERIES

Route Number	City ~~Route~~ Deliveries		Rural Deliveries	
	Number	Percent	Number	Percent
# 1	598	23.5	182	21.1
2	516 ~~500~~	20.2	~~132~~ 116	13.5
3	394	15.5	97	11.3
4	381	14.9	152	17.~~8~~6
5	319	12.5	153	17.~~8~~7
# 6	342	13.4	162	18.8
Total	2,550 ~~2,534~~	100.0	862 ~~878~~	100.0

TABLES 30 AND 31
BANK RECONCILIATION STATEMENTS (WITH LEADERS)

Paper: full sheet
Table 30: single spacing on 60-space line
Table 31: double spacing on 70-space line
Proofguide: 99–101

PIVOTING. **To spread a statement to fill an assigned line length, backspace from the right margin (pivot) to find the start of the money columns. The explanation (stub) column begins at the left margin.**

LEADERS. **Type a row of periods between the first and second columns, being sure to leave 1 space before and after the row of periods.**

AMERICAN WORLDWIDE TRAVEL ↓2
BANK RECONCILIATION STATEMENT ↓2
Month Ended June 30, 19-- ↓3

Bank Statement Balance, June 30			$16,843.26
Add: Deposit made on June 29	$583.17		
Deposit made on June 30	379.13		962.30
			$17,805.56
Subtract: Outstanding Checks			
517	$535.28		
545	18.75		
572	401.11		955.14
Adjusted Bank Statement Balance			$16,850.42
			↓3
Checkbook Balance, June 30			$15,769.17
Add: Note Receivable Collection	$436.00		
Supercheck Advance	700.00		1,136.00
			$16,905.17
Subtract: Error on Check 536	$ 41.25		
Check Printing Charge	13.50		54.75
Adjusted Checkbook Balance			$16,850.42

TABLES 32 AND 33
INCOME STATEMENTS (WITH LEADERS)

Paper: full sheet
Table 32 (May): single spacing on 60-space line
Table 33 (June): double spacing on 65-space line
Proofguide: 101

Indentions in financial statements should be in uniform steps of 2, 3, or 5 spaces.

PEREZ INTERIOR DESIGN CENTER ↓2
INCOME STATEMENT ↓2
For the Month Ended May 31, 19-- ↓3 *Information for June 30, 19--*

REVENUE FROM SALES			
Sales	$24,685.17		*$22,457.25*
Less: Sales Discount	1,734.26		*1,536.60*
Net Sales		$22,950.91	*$20,920.65*
COST OF GOODS SOLD (See schedule)		6,590.18	*6,380.70*
GROSS PROFIT ON SALES		$16,360.73	*$14,539.95*
		↓3	
OPERATING EXPENSES			
Insurance Expense	$ 435.75		*$ 398.80*
Payroll Taxes Expense	847.32		*873.45*
Rent Expense	1,200.00		*1,200.00*
Salaries Expense	6,841.40		*6,962.95*
Supplies Expense	273.65		*269.43*
Total Expenses		9,598.12	*9,704.63*
NET INCOME BEFORE TAXES		$ 6,762.61	*$4,835.32*

Line: 60 spaces   Tab: 5
Spacing: single   Drills: 3X
Proofguide: 63–66
Workguide: 155–156, 215–219
Tape: 39A

LESSONS 94/95
BUSINESS REPORTS AND NEWS RELEASES

Goal: To build skill in formatting business reports and news releases.

94-A. WARMUP

S 1 Ken froze as he jogged the five or six miles to the square.
A 2 Jo's raft was swept eastward out of the bay by the current.
N 3 Our May 29 meeting is at 4:30 instead of 6:15 in Room P-87.
| 1 | 2 | 3 | 4 | 5 | 6 | 7 | 8 | 9 | 10 | 11 | 12

94-B. SKILL DRILL: INFREQUENT LETTER PRACTICE

J 4 The just judge joked with the jury about a jealous justice.
5 Jill Jenkins adjusted her jogging jacket and jumped across.
K 6 The wicked knight skinned his knuckles and knees on a rock.
7 Kaye Kane packed stacks of bricks in the back of the truck.
| 1 | 2 | 3 | 4 | 5 | 6 | 7 | 8 | 9 | 10 | 11 | 12

94-C. SKILL MEASUREMENT: 5-MINUTE TIMED WRITING

94-C. Spacing—double. Take a 5-minute timing with a 5-second rest after each minute, then a 5-minute timing without stopping. Try to reach the same point on the second timing with 5 or fewer errors. Record your score.

8   It is becoming much more difficult to give examples of 12
jobs that are strictly for men or strictly for women. Old- 24
fashioned stereotypes are fast becoming things of the past. 36
Female doctors and male nurses no longer receive the stares 48
of amazement that were common a few short years ago. There 60
are many men who perform in secretarial positions and women 72
who are machinists. Now, when making their career choices, 84
students do not have to let their sex determine the options 96
that are available. 100

It would be wonderful if we could say today that there 112
is complete equity in the hiring practices for both men and 124
women. But while there are severe problems to be overcome, 136
great progress has been made. So, if you are a young woman 148
who wants to climb telephone poles, go ahead. The same can 160
be said to the young man who would like to become a kinder- 172
garten teacher. 175
| 1 | 2 | 3 | 4 | 5 | 6 | 7 | 8 | 9 | 10 | 11 | 12

138/139-D. BANK RECONCILIATION STATEMENTS AND INCOME STATEMENTS

The four statements on pages 203–204 should be typed twice each. Read the instructions in the left panel before doing each assignment.

TABLES 26 AND 27
BANK RECONCILIATION STATEMENTS
(WITHOUT LEADERS)

Paper: full sheet
Table 26: single spacing
Table 27: double spacing
Allow 8 spaces between the stub (explanations) column and the first money column and 2 spaces between the money columns.
Proofguide: 99

To produce double lines, underscore the column width. Then press the variable spacer while turning the cylinder slightly. Repeat the underscore.

BARNES TRAVEL, INC.
↓2
BANK RECONCILIATION STATEMENT
↓2
Month Ended June 30, 19--
↓3

Bank Statement Balance, June 30		$7,344.50
Add: Deposit made on June 29	$378.40	
Deposit made on June 30	724.30	1,102.70
		$8,447.20
Subtract: Outstanding Checks:		
884	$450.00	
888	351.15	
920	72.80	873.95
Adjusted Bank Statement Balance		$7,573.25
		↓3
Checkbook Balance, June 30		$7,208.40
Add: Supercheck Advance		400.00
		$7,608.40
Subtract: Error on Check 893		35.15
Adjusted Checkbook Balance		$7,573.25

TABLE 28
INCOME STATEMENT (MAY)
(WITHOUT LEADERS)

Paper: full sheet
Spacing: single
8 spaces between stub and money column
2 spaces between money columns
Proofguide: 99

TABLE 29
INCOME STATEMENT (JUNE)
(WITHOUT LEADERS)

Paper: full sheet
Spacing: single
10 spaces between stub and money column
2 spaces between money columns
Proofguide: 99

ALONSO PET SUPPLIES
↓2
INCOME STATEMENT
↓2
For the Month Ended May 31, 19--
↓3

Information for June 30, 19--

SALES		$24,832.57	$27,584.24
COST OF GOODS SOLD (See schedule)		8,210.31	9,134.60
GROSS PROFIT ON SALES		$16,622.26	$18,449.64
		↓3	
OPERATING EXPENSES			
Delivery Expense	$ 437.28		$ 512.50
Depreciation Expense	987.25		1,011.41
Insurance Expense	362.42		387.80
Miscellaneous Expense	86.80		76.38
Payroll Taxes Expense	187.75		210.35
Salaries Expense	5,624.50		6,347.75
Supplies Expense	254.40		237.86
Total Expenses		7,940.40	8,784.05
NET INCOME BEFORE TAXES		$ 8,681.86	$9,665.59

94/95-D. BUSINESS REPORTS AND NEWS RELEASES

Unless you are otherwise directed, each of the business reports and news releases that follow is to be typed on a full sheet of plain typing paper. Before typing Reports 16–19, complete Workguide pages 215–216.

REPORT 16*
UNBOUND BUSINESS REPORT

Paper: plain
Line: 6 inches (60 pica/ 70 elite)
Spacing: double
Tab: 5, center
Visual guide: Workguide 217
Proofguide: 63–64

*Reports 1–15 appear in Lessons 1–75.

REPORT 17
BOUND BUSINESS REPORT

Retype Report 16 as a bound report.
Paper: plain
Line: 6 inches (60 pica/ 70 elite)
Spacing: double
Tab: 5, center
Visual guide: Workguide 218
Proofguide: 65–66

NOTE: To provide a wider left margin in a bound report: (1) Use the visual guide on Workguide page 218 or (2) move the paper guide 3 spaces to the left before inserting your paper in the machine.

Displayed paragraphs are indented 5 spaces on each side.

↓13
WAREHOUSE RENTAL GUIDELINES ↓2   6
Effective March 1, 19— ↓3   20

All management personnel have become   30
aware in recent months that empty and   38
underutilized warehouse facilities have become   47
a real problem. Accordingly, Mr. Howard C. Miller,   57
Vice President for Production, has issued the   67
following policy statement for implementation   76
on March 1, 19—:   80

5   Plant managers may enter into rental   92
contracts for storage facilities for periods   102
not to exceed ninety (90) days. If a   110
longer period of time is desired, the   119
request, along with all supportive   127
SS   documents, shall be filed with my office   136
at least sixty (60) days prior to contract   146
agreement.   151

It has been recognized that a standard   161
requisition form will be desired so that Mr.   171
Miller receives basically the same information   180
from each plant manager. The four attached   189
forms have been prepared for this purpose.   198
Draft requests on these forms may be   205
submitted to the Budget Office for review.   214

Your continued cooperation in working   223
together to reduce costs is greatly appreciated.   232

<table>
<tr><td>

Line: 60 spaces   Drills: 2X
Spacing: single
Proofguide: 99–101
Workguide: 155–156
Tape: 42B

</td><td>

LESSONS 138/139
FINANCIAL STATEMENTS

</td></tr>
</table>

Goal: To format bank reconciliations and income statements.

138-A.   WARMUP

S   1   Pamela will go shopping at the downtown store to buy a pen.
A   2   A wave of six big jet planes quickly zoomed by the freeway.
N   3   We had 14,983 fans at today's game; 20,657 at last night's.
        | 1 | 2 | 3 | 4 | 5 | 6 | 7 | 8 | 9 | 10 | 11 | 12

138-B. Clear your machine of all tabs. Then set four tab stops—one every 14th space from the left margin. Type lines 4–7, using the tab key to go across from column to column.

138-B.   TABULATOR PRACTICE—NUMBERS

4	171	292	383	464	595
5	626	737	828	909	010
6	387	910	521	745	973
7	517	620	864	389	402

138-C. Spacing—double. Tab—5. Take two 5-minute timings. Between them, practice any words with which you had difficulty. Record your score.

138-C.   SKILL MEASUREMENT: 5-MINUTE TIMED WRITING

8   People who can set goals and objectives for themselves   12
have taken an important step toward success in life. These   24
people have often given a great deal of thought about their   36
future and have a clear objective of where they want to go.   48
In other words, they have set an ultimate goal which may be   60
achieved by a series of shorter goals. After the direction   72
has been established, there may be different routes to such   84
goals, and obstacles may appear along the way. However, in   96
order to cut a clear path, the wise person will plan ahead.   108
      After setting goals, it is important to analyze how to   120
reach them. Naturally, because we are living in a changing   132
world, we will need to be flexible in pursuing these goals.   144
If we can anticipate for the future, we can be prepared for   156
change and not squander our time in useless activities. To   168
help control chance, we should develop a positive attitude,   180
get a good education, and meet people who can help us along   192
the way. In the final analysis, success requires more than   204
luck; there is usually a long trail of careful planning and   216
hard work behind it.   220
        | 1 | 2 | 3 | 4 | 5 | 6 | 7 | 8 | 9 | 10 | 11 | 12

FORMATTING A NEWS RELEASE

A news release can be typed on a printed form or on plain paper. To format a news release:

1. Use a 6-inch line (60 pica/70 elite).

2. Double-space the body and indent paragraphs 5 spaces.

3. On a printed form, align the heading information with the guide word. On plain paper, begin the heading on line 7, aligned at the center tab stop.

4. Center the title of the news release in all-capital letters.

5. Leave 2 blank lines above and below the title.

6. Type a date line: city, abbreviated date, and a dash before the first sentence. Include the state only if the city is not well-known or can be confused with a city in another state or country.

REPORT 18
NEWS RELEASE

Paper: Workguide 219
Line: 6 inches
(60 pica/70 elite)
Spacing: double
Tab: 5, center
Proofguide: 65–66

REPORT 19
NEWS RELEASE

Retype Report 18 on plain
paper.
Line: 6 inches
(60 pica/70 elite)
Spacing: double
Tab: 5, center
Proofguide: 65–66

From the left margin, spread *NEWS RELEASE*: Leave 1 space between letters and 3 spaces between words. Begin *From Ernest M. Ruman* at center.

WP To correct an error when typing on a word processor, position the backspace key or the cursor (similar to the print-point indicator on your typewriter) over the incorrect character on the screen and simply type the correct character over it. The correct letter replaces the incorrect one. This correction procedure is called a *backspace strikeover*.

↓ 7

N E W S   R E L E A S E   From Ernest M. Ruman   4
Regional Manager   12
Department of Parks and Recreation   23
4201 Flagg Road   30
Binghamton, NY 13904 ↓ 2   38

Release February 16, 19--   45
↓ 3

ADDITIONAL CAMPSITES PLANNED   64
↓ 3

N.Y.
BINGHAMTON, ∧ Feb. 10--"Heavy usage of ~~area~~ *local* campgrounds   80

additional
has resulted in the need for ~~more~~ campsites,") states Ernest   93

M. Ruman, regional manager for the Department of parks and   105
explained further s

Recreation. He ~~continued,~~ "Expantion plans are being developed   119

for each existing campground."   125

the amount of
In addition to an inœease in lie̶sure time for most people,   142

a second reason for expantion is that people who live int the   154
a

region have eliminated vacation trips to distent points be-   166
fuel
cause of high ∧ costs.   171

sites
"While there is a need for these new ~~sights~~ during the   183
a
coming summer tourist season, construction ~~time~~ will ~~require~~ *necessitate*   195
both
a one-year delay," Ruman stated. the majority of ∧ skilled   208
#

and unskilled workesr will be employed from local ∧ areas.   219

becoming a member of the Association. If your organization is planning 167
to sponsor any seminars or workshops in Colorado in the next six 180
months, I would like very much to have that information too. (*Closing* 193
as in Letter 51?) 205

**LETTER 53
MODIFIED-BLOCK STYLE
TWO-PAGE LETTER**

Standard Punctuation
Deep letterhead: Workguide
  301–302
Proofguide: 97–98

Mr. Alan Templeton, Secretary / Thomas 15
Giordano Contracting, Inc. / 15 Upton Drive / 24
Jesup, GA 31545 (*Salutation*) / Subject: Land 34
Development in Savannah 39

Thank you for spending the entire day with 48
me last Tuesday in Savannah. It was good 57
to see you again and to learn of the interest 66
of your firm in developing the land available 75
in Savannah. I would like to summarize a 83
number of the items that we discussed dur- 92
ing our meetings. 96

As I indicated to you, we have a total of 16 106
acres available in the one parcel on Tunni- 114
son Road and about 21 acres in the parcel off 123
Fremont Street. The asking price for the 16 132
acres is $320,000 and the asking price for the 142
other parcel is $441,000. The sellers of both 151
parcels have been quite firm about these 159
asking prices; however, I would be willing to 169
approach them with any offer you might wish 177
to make. 179

The site on Tunnison Road is zoned for resi- 189
dential development, and the minimum 197
acreage size for single-family dwellings is ⅓ 206
acre. This means that this site could be de- 215
veloped with approximately 48 homes. 223
Homes in that area are currently being re- 231
sold at a median price of $94,000. As you 240
know, this land is currently undeveloped. 248
Improvements needed include streets, sew- 257
ers, and underground utilities. From discus- 266
sions I have had with members of the staff of 275
the Building Department, I do not foresee any 284
problems in obtaining approval for re- 292
quested improvements. In addition, I do not 301
anticipate any major difficulty in obtaining 310
approval of a building proposal for one- 318
family homes. 321

The site off Fremont Street is also zoned for 346
residential development; however, a vari- 354
ance is being considered to increase density 363
per acre, which would permit the building of 372
townhouses on this site. Of course, this would 382
increase the number of units that could be 391
built on this site and thus increase the in- 399
come potential for the contractor. Again, al- 409
though this site is undeveloped at this time, 418
applications for improvements or for build- 426
ing are not likely to meet with any difficulty. 436

I would like to thank you again for visiting 446
me last Tuesday. I hope that the information 455
I have given you in this letter will be useful to 465
you. If you need any additional data, please 475
contact me or our president, Mr. Charles 483
Stempler. (*Closing?*) Thomas Gannon / Vice 498
President / mdp / cc Mr. Stempler 505

**LETTER 54
MODIFIED-BLOCK STYLE
WITH INDENTED
PARAGRAPHS**

Standard punctuation
Monarch stationery:
  Workguide 303–304
Proofguide: 97–98

Dr. Phyllis Langley / 501 Valley View Drive / 16
Waycross, GA 31501 (*Salutation*) 25

This will confirm our telephone conversa- 35
tion earlier this morning regarding a poten- 43
tial site for a new office for your dental prac- 53
tice here in Savannah. 58

I will plan to see you at my office at 10:30 69
a.m. on Thursday, June 4, so that I can show 78
you several locations in Savannah that are 86
currently on the market for lease or rent. 95
These sites are all zoned for business and 104
professional use; therefore, you would have 113
no difficulty in getting the necessary ap- 121
proval or permit for your dental office. 129

Enclosed you will find a number of listings 140
in which you might be interested. Please look 150
them over prior to our meeting so that we 158
can visit those you consider most desirable. I 168
am looking forward to your visit on June 4. 177
(*Same closing as previous letter*) (*Enclo-* 194
sure?) 197

MAGAZINE ARTICLES AND BOOK MANUSCRIPTS

Line: 60 spaces	Tab: 5
Spacing: single	Drills: 3X
Proofguide: 65–66	
Workguide: 155–156	
Tape: 39A	

Goal: To build skill in formatting a magazine article and a book manuscript page.

96-A. WARMUP

S 1 The five pairs of ducks may turn at the end of the big bus.
A 2 We acquired the exquisite prize jewels at an amazing price.
N 3 Her 1984 Louisiana license plates were GLF 532 and GLF 706.
| 1 | 2 | 3 | 4 | 5 | 6 | 7 | 8 | 9 | 10 | 11 | 12

96-B. SKILL DRILL: INFREQUENT LETTER PRACTICE

Q 4 Quincy frequently quoted a quaint queen's quip about quail.
5 Quentin Quamm was quite quiet but quickly requested equity.
X 6 The six extra exits are next to the exquisite wax exhibits.
7 Rex Truex got excited as he expertly fixed those six taxis.
| 1 | 2 | 3 | 4 | 5 | 6 | 7 | 8 | 9 | 10 | 11 | 12

96-C. SKILL MEASUREMENT: 5-MINUTE TIMED WRITING

96-C. Spacing—double. Take a 5-minute timing with a 5-second rest after each minute, then a 5-minute timing without stopping. Try to reach the same point on the second timing with 5 or fewer errors. Record your score.

8   It is common for high school students to believe their 12
friends are so special that neither time, distance, nor the 24
responsibilities of adulthood will keep them apart. Sooner 36
or later, however, there is the realization that nothing is 48
forever. Sad as it seems, the old friendships are commonly 60
replaced with new ones when one leaves the old hometown for 72
a new job or to attend college. 78
    Yet, if two people sincerely value these earlier ties, 90
those bonds can be maintained with the required effort. It 102
is no exaggeration to say that two old friends will be like 114
strangers if they do not make a real effort to communicate. 126
But the cost of a stamp is not great, and the long-distance 138
phone rates are quite low during the late evening and week- 150
end hours. So, you and your pals must put forth the effort 162
to maintain contact or suffer the loss of beautiful friend- 174
ships. 175
| 1 | 2 | 3 | 4 | 5 | 6 | 7 | 8 | 9 | 10 | 11 | 12

96/97-D. MAGAZINE ARTICLES AND BOOK MANUSCRIPTS

The magazine article and the book manuscript are to be typed on full sheets of plain typing paper.

136/137-D. LETTER TECHNICALITIES

Study the information about letter salutations, closings, and paragraphing that follows. Then, before typing Letters 51–54 on this page and the next page, complete Workguide pages 293–294.

LETTER SALUTATIONS

1. Use the last name of the addressee if it is known, preceded by *Dear* and a title, thus:

Dear Mrs. Hall: Dear Ms. Podgorski:
Dear Mr. Kapusinski: Dear Dr. Sanz:

2. If a letter is addressed to a department or a firm instead of to a person by name or title, or if there is an attention line, use *Ladies and Gentlemen:* (unless *Ladies:* or *Gentlemen:* alone would be more appropriate).

3. If a letter is addressed to a person by title (such as, *Department Head*), use *Dear Sir:* or *Dear Madam:* if appropriate; otherwise, use *Dear Madam or Sir:*.

4. Use a first name (*Dear Susan:*) only if it is dictated or was used in previous letters.

5. Plural salutations are quite acceptable:

Dear Mr. and Mrs. Rothenberg:
Dear Messrs. Schwinge and Jackson:
Dear Ms. Bradley and Mr. Collins:

6. All titles other than *Mr., Ms., Mrs., Messrs.,* and *Dr.* should be written out—that is, spelled in full: *Dear President Wong:*.

LETTER COMPLIMENTARY CLOSINGS

7. The word *very* is used to make the tone of a letter more formal. *Very sincerely yours,* is more formal than *Sincerely yours,*.

8. Use a "truly" closing—for example, *Very truly yours* and *Yours very truly*—whenever (*a*) a letter is formal or (*b*) there is no personal name used in the salutation.

9. Use a *cordially* or *sincerely* closing if the letter is casual, friendly, or sales-slanted AND the addressee is named in the salutation.

10. Use a *respectfully* closing in a letter to anyone to whom great respect is due, such as a religious dignitary, a public official, or an elderly person.

11. Use an informal closing (such as *See you soon!*) only when it is specifically dictated.

12. In case of doubt, use a "truly" closing.

LETTER PARAGRAPHING

13. Most letters should have at least two paragraphs, preferably three.

14. Paragraphs should reflect the parts of the body of a letter—opening, message, and closing.

LETTER 51
BLOCK STYLE

Open punctuation
Baronial stationery:
   Workguide 297–298
Proofguide: 97–98

Provide salutation, complimentary closing, and paragraphs.

Send this letter to Mr. Joseph P. Clarke, Treasurer / Lexington Paper Company / 171 Diamond Spring Road / Pueblo, CO 81003. (*Salutation?*) 16 / 30
Thank you for your recent letter concerning our pension plan program. Let me answer your two questions as briefly as possible. 44 / 57
1. We provide seminars and workshops for any number of persons from one business firm or for groups from several different firms. 2. We 72 / 90
have approval from the state of Colorado to offer our various services to business firms in Colorado. I would be happy to meet with you and 105 / 120
discuss our services in further detail at your convenience. Please call me at 555-1751 to arrange for an appointment. (*Closing?*) David A. 135 / 152
Graf / Investment Counselor / bjm 158

LETTER 52
BLOCK STYLE

Open punctuation
Standard stationery:
   Workguide 299–300
Proofguide: 97–98

Provide salutation, complimentary closing, and paragraphs.

This letter will be sent to Association for Investment Services / 1650 M Street, N.W. / Washington, DC 20036 / Attention: Ms. Janice Parker / 15 / 29
(*Salutation?*) 34
I have just read about the conference for individuals involved in investment counseling to be held in August in New Orleans, Louisiana. 49 / 63
I saw the information in my monthly copy of <u>Investment News</u>. Please send me an application form to attend this conference. The topics listed 84 / 98
in the notice are of special interest to me since I am newly employed by Ram Investment Services and have just recently returned to em- 112 / 125
ployment as an investment counselor. In addition to the application form for the conference, please send me an application form for 140 / 153

Paper: plain
Carbon copies: 1
Line: 40 spaces
Spacing: double
Tab: 3, center
Proofguide: 65–66

WP On a word processor you would make additional copies by (1) inserting a carbon pack into the printer (the piece of equipment that actually types out what you have entered on the word processor) or (2) having the system print out as many copies of the document as you need.

↓ 13

GET YOUR ARTICLE PUBLISHED!   6
↓ 2
By June A. Williams ↓ 2   10
↓ 3
(44 Lines of 40 Spaces)   24

THE APPEARANCE of a typed manuscript can   34
help or hinder the publication of a maga-   42
zine article. Editors are busy people   50
who receive many manuscripts, far more   58

(Continue in column one below.)

than they can read or publish. It is natural for   68
editors to be impressed with articles that are   77
arranged the way professional writers and   86
editors do it.   89

There lies the secret of getting your maga-   98
zine article in print: Convince the editor that   108
the article was written by a professional for   117
the particular magazine that the editor   125
manages. ↓ 2   127

↓ 2   128

IT IS NOT enough to tell the editor that such   137
is the case. The typist must prove the point by   147
the form of the manuscript. It must look   156
professional. My advice is as follows: 164

1. Use standard typing paper.   172

2. Use the same length of line as that used   197
in the columns of the magazine. After typing   206
10 lines from a copy of the magazine, deter-   215
mine the average line length—and use it. Do   224
not exceed that line length by more than 2   233
spaces on any one line.   237

3. Indicate how many lines your manu-   246
script will fill in the magazine.   253

4. Double-space the manuscript. If it is di-   263
vided into sections, as this one is, type a   272
number sign in the middle of the blank space   280
to indicate "insert 1 blank line." It counts as a   289
whole line.   292

5. Precede the page number on every   300
page by the author's name.   306

6. Follow the magazine's own distinctive   315
style. If it uses side headings, use them—   324
whatever it does, so should you.   331

332

MY, WHAT a lot of trouble! Yes, but it is not as   342
much trouble as writing an article only to   350
have it rejected because it did not look   358
professional—did not seem to belong in the   367
magazine.   369

(END)   372

Williams / 2

After typing 10 lines from a copy of the
magazine, determine the average line

not look professional--did not seem to
belong in the magazine.
(END)

CONTINUATION PAGES OF A MAGAZINE MANUSCRIPT
   1. Use the same line length as on page 1.
   2. Type the heading (author's last name, a diagonal, and the page number) on line 7 at the right margin.
   3. Triple-space before beginning to type the text.

| Line: 60 spaces   Tab: 5, center |
| Spacing: single   Drills: 2X |
| Proofguide: 97–98 |
| Workguide: 155–156, 297–304 |
| Tape: 41B |

LESSONS 136/137
CORRESPONDENCE REVIEW

Goals: To learn letter technicalities; to format letters on various sizes of stationery.

136-A. WARMUP

S 1 The man took eighty bushels of beets to the downtown store.
A 2 Jan very quickly froze both mixtures in the deep brown jug.
N 3 A final sale will be held on June 17–26, from 9:30 to 8:45.
  | 1 | 2 | 3 | 4 | 5 | 6 | 7 | 8 | 9 | 10 | 11 | 12

136-B. **Type paragraph 4, selecting the correct word as you type.**

136-B. WORD SELECTION

4   The (principle/principal) planned a meeting in order to (accept/except) the (advice/advise) of the teachers. He hoped that the (hole/whole) group that (adapted/adopted) the (calendar/calender) would be vocal in (their/there) support at the meeting. He wanted (to/too) keep (piece/peace) among the entire group as they discussed (weather/whether) the winter (break/brake) should be continued during February or omitted (all together/altogether).

136-C. **Spacing—double. Take two 5-minute timings. Between them, practice any words with which you had difficulty. Record your score.**

136-C. SKILL MEASUREMENT: 5-MINUTE TIMED WRITING

5   The importance of knowing how to use reference sources 12
cannot be stressed enough. There may be times when we need 24
to verify facts or look up the answers to various problems, 36
and knowing where to look will help us be more accurate and 48
productive. Rather than guessing or wasting time, we could 60
discover the right answer quickly in a book. Knowing which 72
sources to rely on is an important skill to have because we 84
are living in an age of information. Indeed, knowing where 96
to locate facts may be even more useful than knowing facts. 108
    Using reference materials is an essential skill in the 120
modern office. Everyone should know how to read an airline 132
flight schedule, and each work station should have at least 144
a dictionary and a reference book. There are handbooks for 156
office workers which cover many subjects, such as the basic 168
rules of grammar, spelling, and even word division. It can 180
be extremely helpful to every office worker to know that it 192
is possible to find specialized reference books for various 204
fields of endeavor in which one might find employment. 215
  | 1 | 2 | 3 | 4 | 5 | 6 | 7 | 8 | 9 | 10 | 11 | 12

REPORT 21
BOOK MANUSCRIPT

NOTES ABOUT BOOK MANUSCRIPTS

Shown in elite
Paper: plain
Carbon copies: 1
Line: 6 inches
(60 pica/70 elite)
Spacing: double
Tab: 5
Top: 2″ on page 1, 1″
on page 2
Proofguide: 65–66

1. They are typed in standard "bound report" form.

2. Listings (other than numbered paragraphs) are single-spaced and indented 5 spaces.

3. The title of the book or chapter is identified in a condensed "running head" of two or three words typed in all caps at the left margin, on a line with the page number.

NOTE: For this job use the visual guide for bound reports on Workguide page 218.

CORRESPONDENCE MANUAL   Page 23 ↓3   9

will know *immediately* ~~right away~~ where to resume transcribing or writing during the   26

day or at the *beginning* ~~start~~ of the next day. ↓3   34

Carbon Copies   44

Carbon Copies may be prepared in *a number of* ~~several~~ ways. *One* ~~You~~ may use manifold   60

paper, onion skin paper, copy letterhead, or preassembled carbon packs.   74

Often an office will use *paper of* different colors to speed the routing of copies.   91

The first step in typing carbon copies is to determine the number of   106

copies *required* ~~needed~~ and the appropriate weight and finish for the carbon paper.   121

Here is a simple guide that can be used in deciding on the weight and   135

finish of the carbon ~~paper~~:   141

SS {
1. For 1 to 4 copies, standard weight, hard finish.   155

2. For 5 to 8 copies, medium weight, *medium* finish.   167

3. For 9 or more copies, light weight, soft finish.   178
}

When *assembling* ~~putting~~ the carbon packs ~~together~~:   188

1. use carbon paper that has the corners cut off (about 3/4 inch   202

down each side). The empty corners ~~will~~ *are a* help ~~you~~ in removing carbons   216

from carbon packs. *Pinch* ~~Grasp~~ the corner (any corner) of the pack and   229

shake it; the carbons will slide out.   237

2. place the glossy side of the carbon against the paper on which   251

the copy is to be made.   256

3. make sure that a sheet of ~~carbon~~ paper is placed on top of each   271

sheet of typing paper *other than* ~~except~~ the top sheet.   281

4. If you have difficulty getting the pack into the machine, depress the   297

Paper Release momentarily. That lets the pack get started.   308

Draft of a book manuscript.

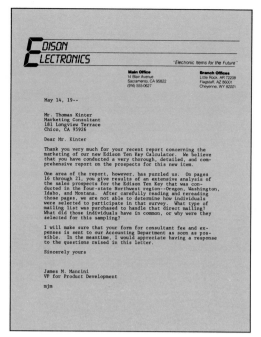

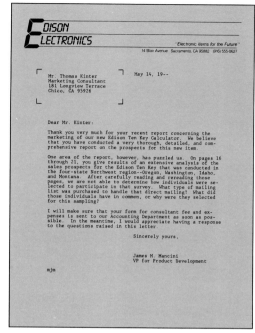

Deep-letterhead standard stationery is 8½ by 11 inches (metric A4: 210 × 297 mm) with a letterhead more than 12 lines deep. Use a 5-inch (50 pica/60 elite) line or a 6-inch (60 pica/70 elite) line. Date goes 3 lines below letterhead. Address begins 3 lines below date. Shown in block style, with open punctuation.

Window-address stationery is for use with a window envelope. Center address in cornered area. Date goes on line 15 and salutation on line 25 (as though address were in normal position).

Special Directions: Type the following letter two times—once on each of the special types of stationery illustrated above—deep-letterhead and window-address.

LETTER 49
BLOCKED STYLE
DEEP LETTERHEAD LETTER

Open punctuation
Workguide: 291–292
Proofguide: 95–96

LETTER 50
MODIFIED-BLOCK STYLE
WINDOW-ADDRESS LETTER

Standard punctuation
Workguide: 293–294
Proofguide: 95–96

January 18, 19— / Ms. Frances Delgado, Vice President / Midwest   16
Association of Personnel Directors / 541 Continental Street / Daven-   29
port, IA 52809 / Dear Ms. Delgado: 37

Ms. Monteyne has indicated to me that you will be responsible   50
for making arrangements for the meal functions that will be nec-   63
essary during your convention on October 14–17, 19—.   74

Enclosed you will find a brochure that describes the different   88
plans that we have for serving luncheons. A second brochure has   101
information concerning our banquet menus and prices. The third   113
brochure contains miscellaneous information concerning proce-   125
dures and costs for serving coffee and danish.   134

Please call Ms. Claudia Stanko at 555-6964 when you wish to   147
begin making plans for the various meal functions at your con-   160
vention. She will be happy to work with you and will be able to   173
answer any questions that you have.   180

Sincerely yours, / Arthur H. Bolton / Director of Sales / djb   196

LESSONS 98/99
REVIEW

Goal: To improve the formatting techniques introduced in Part 4.

98-A. WARMUP

S   1   She may not see the men in the town if they both go by bus.
A   2   Kyle quivered with excitement as the boys jumped the blaze.
N   3   Models 472, 583, and 690 will not be arriving until June 1.
     | 1 | 2 | 3 | 4 | 5 | 6 | 7 | 8 | 9 | 10 | 11 | 12

98-B. SKILL DRILL: INFREQUENT LETTER PRACTICE

Y   4   You and your young friend may buy a yellow yacht in a year.
    5   Bobby Yoder yearns for the day they say his story may play.
Z   6   I was amazed at the size of a dozen lazy zebras at the zoo.
    7   Liza Zimmerman seized the prize of one dozen frozen pizzas.
     | 1 | 2 | 3 | 4 | 5 | 6 | 7 | 8 | 9 | 10 | 11 | 12

98-C. SKILL MEASUREMENT: 5-MINUTE TIMED WRITING

98-C. Spacing—double. Take a 5-minute timing with a 5-second rest after each minute, then a 5-minute timing without stopping. Try to reach the same point on the second timing with 5 or fewer errors. Record your score.

8   There is agreement among high school business teachers   12
that all students should acquire typing skills prior to the   24
time of graduation. Even those who don't type at work will   36
be thankful for their personal—use skills. The evidence is   48
there to show, however, that there are just too many adults   60
who cannot type.   63
      Though they have no need to become expert typists, the   75
managers of today's business firms do have a need for touch   87
keyboarding skills as they sit at their computer terminals.   99
Many have been amazed at how quickly they have gained touch   111
keyboarding skills with the aid of a book designed specifi—   123
cally for this purpose. Without spending drill time on the   135
development of typing production skills, they achieve basic   147
keyboarding speeds of thirty words a minute in a very short   159
period of time. Evening adult programs and college courses   171
serve this real need.   175
     | 1 | 2 | 3 | 4 | 5 | 6 | 7 | 8 | 9 | 10 | 11 | 12

98/99-D. REVIEW OF PART FOUR PRODUCTION WORK

The production work that follows provides an opportunity to review the formatting techniques that you learned in the previous lessons.

134/135-D. LETTERS ON SPECIAL STATIONERY

Although standard-size stationery (8½ by 11) is most commonly used for business correspondence, other sizes and styles are also popular. Study the illustrations below and on the next page and then type Letters 46–50.

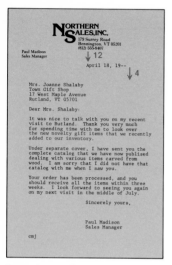

Baronial stationery—5½ by 8½ inches (metric A5: 148 × 210 mm)—accommodates up to 125 words on a 4-inch (40 pica/ 50 elite) line. Longer letters require a second page. Date goes on line 12. Address begins 4 lines below.

Monarch stationery—7¼ by 10½ inches (about 181 × 263 mm)—accommodates up to 250 words on a 5-inch (50 pica/60 elite) line. Date goes on line 14; address begins 5 lines below.

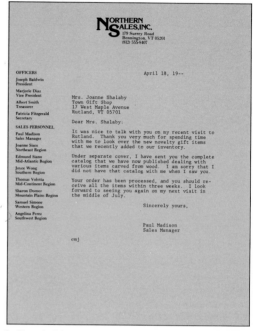

Left-weighted standard stationery is 8½ by 11 inches (metric A4: 210 × 297 mm). Center is moved ½ inch (5 pica/6 elite spaces) to the right, but otherwise placement is standard with either a 5-inch (50 pica/60 elite) line or a 6-inch (60 pica/70 elite) line.

LETTERS 46–48
MODIFIED-BLOCK STYLE

Standard punctuation
Paper: Workguide 285–290
Proofguide: 95–96

WP Using a word processor to type the letters in this unit on stationery of different sizes, you would simply change the margin settings and play out all three letters; you do not have to retype.

Special Directions: Type the following letter three times—once on each of the special types of stationery illustrated above—baronial, monarch, and left-weighted.

January 18, 19— / Mr. Andrew Nicholson, Treasurer / Midwest Association of Personnel Directors / 341 Oak Avenue / Columbia, MO 65201 / Dear Mr. Nicholson:	15 / 27 / 33
Ms. Monteyne indicated that you will be responsible for making all room assignments for the meetings to be held during your convention from October 14–17, 19—.	47 / 60 / 67
Enclosed you will find a map showing all the meeting room space available at Green Hills. Notice that the ballroom can be divided into three separate rooms if necessary. The following meeting rooms are located on the same level as the ballroom: Emporia, Hutchinson, Kansas City, Lawrence, and Wichita.	80 / 93 / 106 / 118 / 130
Please call Ms. Char Eckels at 555-7243 when you are ready to determine the meeting room assignments. She will be happy to work with you and answer any questions you might have.	143 / 156 / 167
Sincerely yours, / Arthur H. Bolton / Director of Sales / djb	186

LETTER 31
MODIFIED-BLOCK STYLE

Line: 5 inches
  (50 pica/60 elite)
Tab: center
Paper: Workguide 221–222
Proofguide: 67–68

(*Current date*) / Schafer-Stiles, Inc. / 7802 28th Avenue South / Ithaca, NY 14850 / Ladies and Gentlemen: / Subject: Instructions for Shipping   18 / 34

Your order of January 27, 19—, has been received. There may be a delay in shipment, however, because no directions for shipment were indicated on the order. Please provide instructions as soon as possible.   48 / 61 / 75 / 76

As this is an initial order from your firm, we are eager to demonstrate to you that the Elmira Manufacturing Company can be depended on for the kind of efficient delivery service to which you are entitled. Most firms in your city request that we ship orders through the Simonson Trucking Company. Some companies use their own trucks, and others request that we send merchandise by railroad freight.   90 / 102 / 116 / 131 / 144 / 158

Thank you for your order; we shall look forward to a long association with your firm. Your order will be on its way to you within 24 hours after you provide directions for shipment.   172 / 187 / 195

Sincerely yours, / Sam G. Kim / Director of Transportation / (*Your initials*)   213 / 215

REPORT 22
BOUND BOOK MANUSCRIPT WITH BOXED TABLE

Paper: plain
Line: 6 inches
  (60 pica/70 elite)
Spacing: double
Tab: 5, center
Proofguide: 67–68

MARKETING TRENDS   Page 37

Many *marketing* executives have learned *through* tr/a/ll and error that *not* all products cannot be promoted in the same manner through the same media. Surprisingly, this is true for those products that v/a/ry only with respect to size or capacity: 4 firms provided the sales data below (the product line is not revealed). *shown*

Table 1-10

REPORT 23
MAGAZINE ARTICLE

Paper: plain
Line: 50 spaces
Spacing: double
Tab: 3, center
Proofguide: 67–68

Use *WATCH THOSE PROMOTION DOLLARS* as a title. The article is written by Marilyn A. Holland. Omit the line that shows the table number.

TYPE A AND TYPE B SALES COMPARISIONS

Company	Type A Units		Type B Units	
	1983	1984	1983	1984
A	942	963	640	617
B	761	773	692	638
C	538	540	352	294
D	508	518	378	340

+ # (*adjusted for inflation*)

Total advertising dollars and the distribution of those dollars *were* was held quite *consistent* constant during each of the 2 years. But there was a *constant* reduction in the number of type A/B units sold by all 4 companies during during the second year. This is true even though type A/B sales remained high through/out the *entire* industry.

Line: 60 spaces   Tab: 5, center
Spacing: single   Drills: 2X
Proofguide: 95–96
Workguide: 155–156, 285–294
Tape: 41B

LESSONS 134/135
SPECIAL STATIONERY

Goal: To format letters on various sizes of stationery.

134-A. WARMUP

S 1 Sally has goals at school that will make her wish for more.
A 2 Paul reviewed the subject before giving Max and Kay a quiz.
N 3 When Barbara adds 51, 47, 23, 60, and 89, she will get 270.
   | 1 | 2 | 3 | 4 | 5 | 6 | 7 | 8 | 9 | 10 | 11 | 12

134-B. Take three 1-minute timings on paragraph 4 and determine speed and accuracy when typing numbers and symbols.

134-B. SYMBOL PRACTICE

4 Employee business expenses* include: (1) travel; (2) food; 12
and (3) lodgings. Thomas & Haller had 24,400 miles @ 20.5¢ 24
per mile (up from 19.5¢). This was $5,002, which was $452, 36
or 9.9%, over last year's sum. "Form #2106" was submitted. 48
   | 1 | 2 | 3 | 4 | 5 | 6 | 7 | 8 | 9 | 10 | 11 | 12

134-C. Spacing—double. Take two 5-minute timings. Between them, practice any word with which you had difficulty. Record your score.

134-C. SKILL MEASUREMENT: 5-MINUTE TIMED WRITING

5   In the past thirty years, styles of office layout have 12
changed a great deal. For example, the modern office is an 24
open office, also known as a landscaped office. Unlike the 36
traditional office, which uses walls and doors to divide up 48
space, the open office has no fixed walls. In their place, 60
we may find partitions that mark off work areas. They seem 72
to be preferred since they are easily moved. Employees are 84
placed according to the work flow, and the desk is known as 96
a work station. For privacy, acoustic screens can be used. 108
      The open office may be more efficient. Workers can be 120
grouped in clusters for a specific job, at the end of which 132
time the work area can be rearranged very quickly. Without 144
walls to tear down, changes can be made over a weekend. In 156
addition, space is very expensive, and the open office uses 168
less space. Critics complain that the open office is noisy 180
and looks like a maze. Top executives will continue to use 192
their own private offices, but for most office workers, the 204
trend appears to be toward the open plan in the future. 215
   | 1 | 2 | 3 | 4 | 5 | 6 | 7 | 8 | 9 | 10 | 11 | 12

LESSON 100

TEST 4: PROGRESS TEST ON PART 4

TEST 4-A
5-MINUTE TIMED WRITING

Line: 60 spaces
Spacing: double
Tab: 5
Paper: Workguide 225

Each of us holds fond memories of our favorite holiday   12
activities. While many of these are of a religious nature,   24
most of them are centered in the family. And over a period   36
of time they merge to become the traditions of a particular   48
family unit. Some of these customs are acquired by most of   60
the people in particular geographic areas and contribute to   72
the culture of the group. Dozens of major cultural activi-   84
ties add to the excitement of both children and adults.   95

Some of these customs have evolved with no real effort   107
or knowledge on the part of those who are involved. But it   119
must be acknowledged that there are those who are very much   131
concerned with the heritage of our people. There can be no   143
doubt that it is through the efforts of such people that we   155
enjoy some of the rich moments of our lives. Will you want   167
to be included in that list of people?   175

| 1 | 2 | 3 | 4 | 5 | 6 | 7 | 8 | 9 | 10 | 11 | 12 |

TEST 4-B
LETTER 32
MODIFIED-BLOCK LETTER
WITH INDENTED
PARAGRAPHS

Line: 5 inches
 (50 pica/60 elite)
Tab: 5, center
Paper: Workguide 226

(*Current date*) / Mr. Donald E. Zimmerman / 1442 University Avenue /   17
Mt. Pleasant, MI 48858 / Dear Mr. Zimmerman: 27

It was a pleasure for us to meet with you and your group last week.   43
You should be aware, however, that a final decision relative to our   59
diversification plans has not yet been made by our Board of Direc-   70
tors. They have agreed to place the item on the agenda for their   83
meeting next week.   87

If a decision is made to open a new plant in your area, you can be   102
sure that Mt. Pleasant will be included among those cities to be con-   116
sidered. The cultural opportunities afforded by your city would be of   130
real interest to a site-selection committee.   139

While it would be inappropriate for me to predict a positive deci-   154
sion by our Board, it may be advantageous for you to begin compil-   167
ing a document for review by a site-selection committee. Three pri-   181
mary concerns will be the availability of raw materials, transportation   195
facilities, and a qualified labor supply.   204

Thanks for your continued interest.   213

Sincerely yours, / Richard A. Kocar / President / (*Your initials*)   233

LETTER 45
**MODIFIED-BLOCK STYLE
TWO-PAGE LETTER**

Page 2: Style B
Workguide: 283–284
Proofguide: 93–94

SECOND PAGE. **Heading on
line 7, across the page.**

WP Word processors have an
automatic page-break
feature that will end one page
at the appropriate point to
provide the correct bottom
margin and then automatically
space down to begin typing on
the next page, leaving the
correct top margin.

January 16, 19— / Ms. Sharon Monteyne, President / Midwest Association of Personnel Directors / 210 Jackson Avenue / Pekin, IL 61554 / Dear Ms. Monteyne:

It was a pleasure to meet with you and the members of your executive board who were responsible for making a site selection for your convention in 19—. I am delighted that your committee has selected our facilities for its meeting during October 14–17, 19—.

Let me take this opportunity to clarify a number of points that we talked about concerning your convention. I should also like to give you the names of the individuals who will be responsible for handling various aspects of your convention so that you or your executive board members may be directly in touch with them if a question should arise. Of course, I can always be called regarding any questions.

I should like to review the policy concerning complimentary rooms. We will give you 10 complimentary rooms, plus one additional room for every 50 rooms that are reserved by someone from your group. The determination of the number of complimentary rooms will be made on the Monday prior to the beginning of your convention. Consequently, I am sure that you will want to encourage your members to register early.

Green Hills will also provide 10 complimentary rooms for August 14–16, 19—, so that your executive board members can meet here as they make final plans for the convention. Please send a list of room assignments by August 10 in order that registration can proceed quickly on August 14.

The following table gives you the names and telephone numbers of the individuals who will be responsible for the various functions and activities of your convention. Please feel free to give these names and numbers to any of your board members who might need to contact someone regarding a specific request.

Person	Responsibility	Telephone
Char Eckels	Meeting Rooms	555-7243
Claudia Stanko	Meal Functions	555-6964
John Madison	Exhibits	555-6892
Paul Janowski	AV Materials	555-5207
Robert Eng	Transportation	555-7109
Ludevina Marinelli	Registration	555-1957

WP The word *convention*
occurs 8 times in Letter
45. Suppose you had misspelled
it *convension* all 8 times. Some
word processors have a search-
and-replace function that will
search for all occurrences of an
incorrect word or phrase and
replace it with the correct word
or phrase.

Again, I am delighted that your group has chosen to hold their convention at Green Hills. I will send you copies of the signed contracts as soon as they are prepared. In the meantime, I will contact your two convention directors regarding meeting rooms and meal functions.

Sincerely yours, / Arthur H. Bolton / Director of Sales / djb

TEST 4-C
TABLE 25
RULED TABLE

Tab: center
Paper: Workguide 227

CENTRAL WAREHOUSE NEEDS
(*Current date*)

Building	Cubic Feet Available	Current Needs	Shortage
Carey	380,000	450,000	70,000
Gries	300,000	400,000	100,000
Hunt	200,000	260,000	60,000
Magers	450,000	500,000	50,000
Spooner	390,000	400,000	10,000
TOTAL	1,720,000	2,010,000	290,000

TEST 4-D
REPORT 24
NEWS RELEASE

Line: 6 inches
  (60 pica/70 elite)
Spacing: double
Tab: 5, center
Paper: Workguide 228

N E W S   R E L E A S E

From Laura R. Paupore   4
Facilities Coordinator   13
Revena Avenue Medical–Dental Center   24
5200 Revena Avenue   32
Riverside, CA 92505   40

Release February 16, 19––   47

MEDICAL–DENTAL CENTER TO EXPAND   68

Riverside, CA, Feb. 16––Mrs. Laura R. Paupore, Facilities Coordinator, has   86
announced expansion plans for the Revena Avenue Medical–Dental Center.   101
"Earlier expectations were that the present buildings would be adequate   116
until 1995. However, the area's population growth has been much   129
greater than earlier predictions indicated," Mrs. Paupore stated. The   144
existing buildings were built in 1980 to house 80 physicians and 20 den-   158
tists, along with the necessary laboratories and support facilities.   173

"The original planners for the site showed a good deal of foresight as   188
~~the acreage is~~
the acreage is sufficient for an extensive expansion project," Mrs.   202

paupore continued. Tentative plans call for the addition of a new west   217

wing on the Wright Building and a new building directly east of the   231
Harris
~~Sabin~~ Building. The ~~present~~ existing facilities are adequate for the center's 246

dental needs, and the 60 new offices will be designed for use by new   260

physicians who possess ~~degrees~~ expertise in various areas of specialization. 274

LESSON 100   147

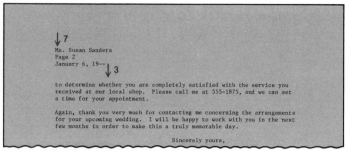

Ms. Susan Sanders
Page 2
January 6, 19—

to determine whether you are completely satisfied with the service you
received at our local shop. Please call me at 555-1875, and we can set
a time for your appointment.

Again, thank you very much for contacting me concerning the arrangements
for your upcoming wedding. I will be happy to work with you in the next
few months in order to make this a truly memorable day.

Sincerely yours,

Page 2 heading: Style A

Ms. Susan Sanders   Page 2   January 6, 19—

to determine whether you are completely satisfied with the service you
received at our local shop. Please call me at 555-1875, and we can set
a time for your appointment.

Again, thank you very much for contacting me concerning the arrangements
for your upcoming wedding. I will be happy to work with you in the next
few months in order to make this a truly memorable day.

Sincerely yours,

Page 2 heading: Style B

LETTER 44
MODIFIED-BLOCK STYLE
TWO-PAGE LETTER

Page 2: Style A
Workguide: 281–282
Proofguide: 93–94

January 6, 19— / Mr. Rodney C. Carter, Pres- 13
ident / Kansas Certified Managers Associa- 21
tion / 156 Westwood Street / Russell, KS 67665 / 29
Dear Mr. Carter: 34

Thank you for your recent inquiry about the 44
availability of our facilities for your Kansas 53
Certified Managers Association Convention 61
during October 6–8, 19—. I am happy to 70
supply you with answers to your five ques- 78
tions. 80

1. Availability. As of this date, we do not 95
have any bookings for those three days in 105
October. If you wish to place a hold on our 114
facilities, it will be necessary for you or your 124
representative to meet with me as soon as 133
possible so that tentative plans can be dis- 142
cussed and a nonbinding contract issued. I 151
would encourage you to arrange for this 160
appointment as soon as possible since it 168
would be to your advantage to have a non- 177
binding contract to hold the facility for a short 187
time. 189

2. Meeting Room Facilities. There is no 208
problem for us to assign you the number of 218
meeting rooms that you indicate you would 226
need. Enclosed is a brochure which has all 236
the meeting rooms identified. You can see 245
that our large convention ballroom can be 254
subdivided into three meeting rooms. In ad- 263
dition, we have five meeting rooms on the 272
same level as the ballroom. If necessary, we 282
can provide meeting rooms (which are 290
smaller in size) on a lower level of our facil- 299
ity. We also have any type of audiovisual aid 310

that you might require in these meeting 318
rooms. 319

3. Sleeping Accommodations. We have a 339
total of 350 rooms affiliated with our conven- 349
tion center. We could easily set aside 300 of 358
these rooms for the participants at your con- 368
vention. This means that we should have no 377
difficulty in accommodating the 500 people 386
you might expect at your convention. We can 395
discuss the rate that would be charged for 418
rooms at the time that you or your repre- 426
sentative visits me. At that same time, I can 437
explain how we could provide you with a 445
reservation form that your members would 454
use in making reservations with us. 461

4. Meal Functions. We would have no dif- 477
ficulty in handling the various meal func- 487
tions that you described in your letter. Our 496
facility is equipped to handle meal functions 506
that have as many as 800 people. Ms. 514
Claudia Stanko, meal functions director, 523
would be able to give you menus, costs, etc., 532
when you visit me. 537

5. Exhibit Space. We would have no diffi- 553
culty providing you with the exhibit space 562
you would require. We have had groups uti- 571
lize the spacious hall space outside the con- 581
vention ballroom, or we could easily ar- 589
range to set up some of the meeting rooms 598
that would not be needed for meetings as 607
exhibit areas. 610

Again, I thank you for your inquiry. I will 620
look forward to meeting with you or your 628
representative and discussing how we might 636
serve your needs. 640

Sincerely yours, / Arthur H. Bolton / Direc- 658
tor of Sales / djb / Enclosure 664

PART 5

SKILL BUILDING ■ LETTER STYLES, BILLING AND PAYROLL FORMS, REPORT DISPLAYS

OBJECTIVES FOR PART 5

Part 5 is designed to enable you to demonstrate the following abilities when you take the test in Lesson 125:

1. Technical Knowledge. To answer correctly at least 90 percent of the questions on an objective test covering the technical information presented in Part 5.

2. Production. To format correctly from unarranged or rough-draft copy: (a) standard business letters with special features, (b) various letter styles, (c) payroll forms, (d) billing forms, and (e) a report with footnotes.

3. Skill Rate. To type at the following speed and accuracy levels by the end of each unit:

Unit	No. of Minutes	Minimum Speed	Maximum Errors
17	5	37	5
18	5	38	5
19	5	39	5
20	5	40	5

4. Word Processing Information. To understand how word processing equipment would function if used to format various production assignments.

Line: 60 spaces   Tab: 5, center
Spacing: single   Drills: 2X
Proofguide: 93–94
Workguide: 155–156, 281–284
Tape: 41B

LESSONS 132/133
TWO-PAGE LETTERS

Goal: To format two-page letters with different second-page headings.

132-A.   WARMUP

S 1 Sue will soon handle the problems of her downtown neighbor.
A 2 Vic quickly mixed frozen strawberries into the grape juice.
N 3 Invoice #12–478 was debited for $569.30 instead of $596.30.
    | 1 | 2 | 3 | 4 | 5 | 6 | 7 | 8 | 9 | 10 | 11 | 12

132-B. Spacing—double. Take two 5-minute timings. Between them, practice any words with which you had difficulty. Record your score.

132-B.   SKILL MEASUREMENT: 5-MINUTE TIMED WRITING

4 Dictation is the oral expression of ideas. It is also 12
the fastest means of word origination, whether one dictates 24
to a secretary who can take shorthand or to a machine. For 36
this reason, it is a skill that is very useful in business. 48
Dictation saves more time than writing out the same message 60
in longhand. Moreover, the cost of correspondence has gone 72
up a great deal in recent years because the labor needed to 84
produce it is so very expensive. To reduce costs, business 96
wants its managers to dictate, and not write out, messages. 108

Proper dictation techniques begin before a single word 120
is spoken. First, start by being organized. Jot down some 132
notes or points in outline sequence. Next, dictate special 144
instructions in advance. Indicate if the message will be a 156
letter, memo, or report. State if it will be final copy or 168
rough–draft form. Speak in a clear voice, spelling unusual 180
words or names. Point out paragraphs and, at the end, give 192
closing instructions as well. Learn to dictate efficiently 204
and always follow these basic rules of good dictation. 215
    | 1 | 2 | 3 | 4 | 5 | 6 | 7 | 8 | 9 | 10 | 11 | 12

132/133-C.   TWO-PAGE LETTERS

Long business letters often require more than one page. Follow these guidelines when typing a two-page letter:

1. Line length: 6 inches (60 pica/70 elite).
2. Date: on line 15 or 3 lines below the letterhead, whichever is lower.
3. Bottom margin: at least 1 inch (6 lines).
4. Paper: page 1, letterhead; page 2, plain.
5. Page 2 heading: name of addressee, page number, and date typed on line 7 or blocked at the left margin.

NOTE: Page 2 must contain at least 3 lines of the body of the letter.

Line: 60 spaces Tab: 5
Spacing: single Drills: 3X
Proofguide: 67–70
Workguide: 155
Tape: 40A and 41A

LESSONS 101/102
SKILL DRIVE

Goal: To improve speed/accuracy.

101-A. WARMUP

S 1 The girl may make a formal gown of fur to go with her hair.
A 2 Jack bought five exquisite bronze bowls at Pam's yard sale.
N 3 Mrs. Benson's $350 raise was not effective until 7/26/1984.
| 1 | 2 | 3 | 4 | 5 | 6 | 7 | 8 | 9 | 10 | 11 | 12

101-B. PRETEST: VERTICAL REACHES

PRETEST. **Take a 1-minute timing; compute speed and errors.**

4   While aboard that ship, Vance was even able to examine 12
the actual knife without having anyone notice him. He used 24
the vacant raft for sneaking away and then sent us a cable. 36
Next he went back to search each room for further evidence. 48
| 1 | 2 | 3 | 4 | 5 | 6 | 7 | 8 | 9 | 10 | 11 | 12

101-C. PRACTICE: UP REACHES

PRACTICE. **If you made no more than 1 error on the Pretest, type each line (e.g., lines 5–9) 3 times for speed development. If you made 2 or more errors, type each group of 4 lines (e.g., lines 5–8), as though it were a paragraph, 3 times for accuracy improvement; then type the sentence (e.g., line 9) 3 times.**

5 aw awhile brawls straws awards outlaw fawns awful away draw
6 se sealed absent search abused accuse sedan based sell used
7 rd orders ordeal garden border absurd horde tardy word card
8 ki kicked kidnap asking skimpy napkin skied skill kind skid

9 The outlaw ordered the skinny kid away from the used sedan.
| 1 | 2 | 3 | 4 | 5 | 6 | 7 | 8 | 9 | 10 | 11 | 12

101-D. PRACTICE: DOWN REACHES

10 ac accept backed actual factor tracks ached beach each back
11 kn knives kneads knotty knocks kneels knows known knee knew
12 ab aboard fabled abroad tabled liable cable about able tabs
13 va vacant valley avails invade canvas vague rival vary oval

14 Mr. Abbott knew about a vacant beach in back of the valley.
| 1 | 2 | 3 | 4 | 5 | 6 | 7 | 8 | 9 | 10 | 11 | 12

101-E. PRACTICE: JUMP REACHES

15 ve velvet avenue invest proved active event above even have
16 ex exceed flexed convex vexing reflex annex exact next exit
17 no noises domino enough donors cannot piano novel none snow
18 ce celery oceans census decent advice cents scene cell iced

19 The next events concerned the scene above that noisy annex.
| 1 | 2 | 3 | 4 | 5 | 6 | 7 | 8 | 9 | 10 | 11 | 12

POSTTEST. **Repeat the Pretest and compare performance.**

101-F. POSTTEST: VERTICAL REACHES

131-C. PRACTICE: ALTERNATE HANDS

18 clan borne pair handle usual sign turkeys dials auburn half
19 fish title rock eighty sight pays element proxy thrown lane
20 worn visit kept signal blame dock suspend field enamel busy
21 bush civic maid theory panel held bicycle towns island cork

131-D. PRACTICE: ONE HAND

22 defeated pumpkin dessert nylon breeze join award pin effect
23 freezers opinion greater milky refers upon extra mop garage
24 cassette million cartage phony arrest lion brave you begged
25 reassess minimum fastest loony grease only scars inn facets

131-E. PRACTICE: BOTH HANDS

26 bedroom injured session omitted creation hundreds stateroom
27 station honored stadium imports ceremony numbered homestead
28 fashion mounted freshly opposed steadily populace onlookers
29 frankly holders longest impress fraction nominate populated

131-F. POSTTEST: ALTERNATE- AND ONE-HAND REACHES

131-G. SKILL MEASUREMENT: 5-MINUTE TIMED WRITING

131-G. Spacing—double. Take two 5-minute timings. Between them, practice any words with which you had difficulty. Record your score.

```
30       More people are traveling today, but the energy crisis  12
     is forcing a change in their basic travel patterns.  People  24
     will still depend on their automobiles, but there will be a  36
     shift to other modes of travel as fuel prices climb higher.  48
     For long journeys, it may be cheaper to fly than drive, and  60
     experts predict a surge in air travel.  Major airlines will  72
     use bigger planes, regional and commuter airlines will have  84
     frequent service, and business will rely on company planes.  96
         Buses and trains will be more popular for short trips. 108
     Pressed to economize, workers will look for alternatives to 120
     the daily auto commute.  Companies will aid their employees 132
     to form car or van pools.  Cities will try to improve their 144
     traffic flow by providing special lanes for buses and heavy 156
     trucks.  Cars will be smaller, lighter, and designed to use 168
     less fuel.  Though people will not give up their cars, they 180
     will be driving them a lot less.  Possible energy shortages 192
     and the rising cost of operating and maintaining a car have 204
     sparked conservation measures.                              210
```
     | 1 | 2 | 3 | 4 | 5 | 6 | 7 | 8 | 9 | 10 | 11 | 12

101-G. Take a 1-minute
timing on the first paragraph
to establish your base speed.
Then take successive
1-minute timings on the
other paragraphs. You must
equal or exceed your base
speed before moving to the
next paragraph.

Information that is sent to
a word processing
department for processing is
called *Input*. Examples of input
are longhand, shorthand, and
machine dictation. As
illustrated in 101-G, changes
(called revisions) are often
made in a document once it is
typed. Since the original
document is stored on a tape or
disk in the word processor, only
the changed material must be
retyped.

101-G. SUSTAINED PRACTICE: COPY FORMAT

20   Every fall the television networks introduce their new 12
shows for the year, and each winter many of these new shows 24
are canceled because of poor ratings. Although ratings de- 36
termine what we watch, few people understand how they work. 48

21   Ratings tell the stations how many people are watching 12
every show. The size of the shows audience indicates what 24
the network will charge a commercial company for time. The 36
prestige of each network is affected also by these ratings. 48

22 Each year a large sample of typical television viewers from 12
around the country agree to have a special device hooked up 24
to their television sets these devices keep track of what 36
times each set is turned on and what show is being watched. 48

23   The rating companies are thus able to tell the network 12
how many television sets were tuned into any program. But 24
what they can't tell is how many of these viewers are watch- 36
ing a show and how many are sitting there fast asleep. 48
| 1 | 2 | 3 | 4 | 5 | 6 | 7 | 8 | 9 | 10 | 11 | 12

102-A. Repeat 101-A, page 149.

102-A. WARMUP

102-B. PRETEST: DISCRIMINATION PRACTICE

24   The three men boiled the oysters in olive oil and then 12
took them ashore in a straw basket. They built a huge fire 24
in the sand and spent one quiet and relaxful day basking in 36
the autumn sun. After dinner they returned to their yacht. 48
| 1 | 2 | 3 | 4 | 5 | 6 | 7 | 8 | 9 | 10 | 11 | 12

PRETEST. Take a 1-minute
timing; compute speed and
errors.

These drills help you to type
correctly those keys which
are most commonly
confused. For example, R
and T, A and S, M and N.

PRACTICE. If you made no
more than 1 error on the
Pretest, type each line 3
times. If you made 2 or more
errors, type each group of 4
lines (as though it were a
paragraph) 3 times; then
type the sentence 3 times.

102-C. PRACTICE: LEFT HAND

25 rtr artist track carton straw charts train escort port trap
26 asa ashore sadly aspect usage basket salad chased asks sand
27 sds sadden midst sudden binds inside bonds biased beds suds
28 rer really erred rebate berry reflex after secure read rear

29 The really sad artist read a used book about the sand trap.
| 1 | 2 | 3 | 4 | 5 | 6 | 7 | 8 | 9 | 10 | 11 | 12

102-D. PRACTICE: RIGHT HAND

30 mnm autumn enemy manage names minute venom margin mane hymn
31 oio boiled irons joined onion poised union adjoin oils soil
32 olo olives lobby boldly along colony allow cooler solo polo
33 iui helium suits podium build tedium quiet medium quit quid

34 Our guides managed to bring olive oil into the quiet lobby.
| 1 | 2 | 3 | 4 | 5 | 6 | 7 | 8 | 9 | 10 | 11 | 12

Line: 60 spaces   Tab: 5
Spacing: single   Drills: 3X
Proofguide: 91–93
Workguide: 155
Tape: 39B and 40B

LESSONS 130/131
SKILL DRIVE

Goal: To improve speed/
accuracy.

130-A. WARMUP

S   1   The chairman owns eight maps for the downtown city streets.
A   2   Kay reviewed the subject before giving Max and Paul a quiz.
N   3   Invoice #12–360 totaled $948.75 and was now six weeks late.
    | 1 | 2 | 3 | 4 | 5 | 6 | 7 | 8 | 9 | 10 | 11 | 12

130-B. PRETEST: CLOSE REACHES

PRETEST. **Take a 1-minute timing; compute speed and errors.**

4   The annual dinner meeting for the patrons of the small 12
poetry group began. A joint resolution was made. After it 24
was debated, however, it did not receive great support. In 36
a sample vote, it passed anyhow by a small number of votes. 48
    | 1 | 2 | 3 | 4 | 5 | 6 | 7 | 8 | 9 | 10 | 11 | 12

130-C. PRACTICE: ADJACENT KEYS

PRACTICE. **If you made no more than 1 error on the Pretest, type each line 3 times. If you made 2 or more errors, type each group of 4 lines (as though it were a paragraph) 3 times.**

5   tr troops strict patron pastry tried stray entry strut trip
6   sa sample usable resale jigsaw salty essay savor psalm safe
7   po poetry spoken export coupon point vapor sport poker upon
8   oi oiling voided anoint devoid soils stoic joint broil coin

130-D. PRACTICE: CONSECUTIVE STROKES

9   ft lifted thrift drafty adrift after often lifts swift soft
10   my myopic whammy myself gloomy foamy myrrh seamy enemy myth
11   ny anyhow canyon colony felony nylon vinyl agony phony tiny
12   lo locker floral melody hollow local blond color hello solo

130-E. PRACTICE: DOUBLE LETTERS

13   ee weeds greed eerily deemed exceed succeed meeting screens
14   ll hilly small bullet allows teller follows fullest ballots
15   nn penny annul annual dinner tennis annoyed funnies manners
16   pp happy upper oppose copper choppy appears support happens

POSTTEST. **Repeat the Pretest and compare performance.**

130-F. POSTTEST: CLOSE REACHES

131-A. **Repeat 130-A above.**

131-A. WARMUP

131-B. PRETEST: ALTERNATE- AND ONE-HAND REACHES

PRETEST. **Take a 1-minute timing; compute speed and errors.**

17   The outcome of the proxy vote was evaluated; one major 12
element that was most unusual was the great number of phony 24
votes. Based only upon that finding, a panel of judges was 36
easily led to form an opinion of illegality for their firm. 48
    | 1 | 2 | 3 | 4 | 5 | 6 | 7 | 8 | 9 | 10 | 11 | 12

102-E. PRACTICE: BOTH HANDS

35 eie eighth field beiges piece height untie deceit diet veil
36 ghg ghosts hinge higher thing mighty hangs enough sigh huge
37 yty yachts types myrtle dirty oyster witty typist myth tiny
38 sks sketch kicks skinny backs frisky looks gasket risk inks

39 The skinny dieter bought eighty huge oysters for the party.
| 1 | 2 | 3 | 4 | 5 | 6 | 7 | 8 | 9 | 10 | 11 | 12

POSTTEST. Repeat the Pretest and compare performance.

102-F. POSTTEST: DISCRIMINATION PRACTICE

102-G. Spacing—double. Take two 5-minute timings. Between them, practice any words with which you had difficulty. Record your score.
   If you cannot be timed, type two copies of 102-G.

102-G. SKILL MEASUREMENT: 5-MINUTE TIMED WRITING

40   Carbon paper is not the magic thing it was before some   12
inventor came up with copying machines, but carbon paper is   24
extremely valuable just the same. You need only to work in   36
an office where the copier breaks down to discover how very   48
important carbon paper is and why you should know about it.   60
      A carbon paper is a sheet of thin, strong paper coated   72
on one side with a solution of ink and wax. The quality of   84
the copy depends upon the quality of the paper and coating.   96
      The thickness, or weight, of the paper used in carbons   108
is one factor to analyze. The thinner a sheet is, the more   120
copies you can make at one typing, but the sooner the sheet   132
wears out. Most people prefer a six-pound carbon, which is   144
the standard carbon used to make from four to seven copies.   156
For fewer copies, you should use heavier carbon paper. For   168
more copies, use the lighter carbon paper. Select whatever   180
weight suits your needs.   185
| 1 | 2 | 3 | 4 | 5 | 6 | 7 | 8 | 9 | 10 | 11 | 12

Line: 60 spaces   Tab: 5
Spacing: single   Drills: 3X
Proofguide: 69–71
Workguide: 155
Tape: 42A and 43A

LESSONS 103/104
SKILL DRIVE

Goal: To improve speed/ accuracy.

103-A. WARMUP

S 1 Mr. Richfield is such a busy man he may not go to the game.
A 2 Felix might hit your jackpot even with the bad quiz answer.
N 3 Read pages 486–537 in Chapter 20 of your text for April 19.
| 1 | 2 | 3 | 4 | 5 | 6 | 7 | 8 | 9 | 10 | 11 | 12

129-D. PRACTICE: WORD ENDINGS

27 ing doing making paying racing getting sending speaking ing
28 ion onion fusion lotion option section mention deletion ion
29 ble noble bubble tumble wobble capable likable portable ble
30 ful awful joyful woeful armful tactful careful faithful ful

31 Careful options in trading are receiving capable attention.
| 1 | 2 | 3 | 4 | 5 | 6 | 7 | 8 | 9 | 10 | 11 | 12

129-E. PRACTICE: OTHER COMBINATIONS

32 gl gloves uglier angles beagle gloom glory eagle gland ugly
33 er erupts derail energy voters error merge every buyer here
34 ea eating beacon breaks appeal ready steam eager cheat lead
35 br bright fabric hybrid brutal bribe zebra broom cobra brag

36 Every global appeal for mergers brought eruptions of anger.
| 1 | 2 | 3 | 4 | 5 | 6 | 7 | 8 | 9 | 10 | 11 | 12

POSTTEST. Repeat the Pretest on page 189 and compare performance.

129-F. POSTTEST: COMMON LETTER COMBINATIONS

129-G. Spacing—double. Take two 5-minute timings. Between them, practice any words with which you had difficulty. Record your score.

129-G. SKILL MEASUREMENT: 5-MINUTE TIMED WRITING

37   This nation has a most remarkable system of education, 12
and it is a great success for the rest of the world to see. 24
We have a good record among the nations of the world in our 36
rate of literacy and number of pupils in school. More than 48
we realize, our schools have tended to equalize and unite a 60
diverse blend of people. Students of different backgrounds 72
have come to know each other in the schools. Education has 84
been the major pathway for advancement and success in life. 96
     This is still true today, and we see more students who 108
are completing more years of school than ever before; since 120
the turn of the century, the number of them completing high 132
school or college has risen sharply. In addition, students 144
are staying in school longer, starting out with a preschool 156
program and continuing, perhaps, for life. This is due, in 168
part, to technology and fast growth, which are causing more 180
adults to return to school for training or retraining. Now 192
that we can mix work and education, we are truly becoming a 204
nation of lifelong learners. 210
| 1 | 2 | 3 | 4 | 5 | 6 | 7 | 8 | 9 | 10 | 11 | 12

103-B. PRETEST: HORIZONTAL REACHES

PRETEST. Take a 1-minute timing; compute speed and errors.

4   The copywriter wrote an ad with a layout featuring our 12
coupons for a free cup of our famous garlic dressing. Even 24
though not everyone took advantage of these offers, we were 36
fairly pleased with the amount of traffic the ads produced. 48
| 1 | 2 | 3 | 4 | 5 | 6 | 7 | 8 | 9 | 10 | 11 | 12

103-C. PRACTICE: IN REACHES

PRACTICE. If you made no more than 1 error on the Pretest, type each line 3 times. If you made 2 or more errors, type each group of 4 lines (as though it were a paragraph) 3 times; then type the sentence 3 times.

5   wr writer wrists wracks awry wreath wrings wrongs wry write
6   ou outdid bought coughs ours courts amount trouts out ounce
7   py spying canopy crispy pyre jalopy occupy python spy pylon
8   ad adhere adopts gladly shad trades spread unload sad adult

9   The writer outdid himself by adapting that adult spy novel.
| 1 | 2 | 3 | 4 | 5 | 6 | 7 | 8 | 9 | 10 | 11 | 12

103-D. PRACTICE: OUT REACHES

10   yo yowled yonder anyone your joyous layoff rayons you yolks
11   fa fading fakery favors fare unfair defame faulty fad farms
12   up update upward duplex soup couple groups warmup cup upset
13   ga gallon garlic gather yoga engage cougar slogan gap cigar

14   Does anyone favor updating our famous slogan about garages?
| 1 | 2 | 3 | 4 | 5 | 6 | 7 | 8 | 9 | 10 | 11 | 12

103-E. PRACTICE: IN AND OUT REACHES

15   wrench wreaks wrecks wrap couples coupon hourly loudly noun
16   occupy grumpy swampy copy adjusts adages cadets leaded bade
17   youths beyond canyon yoyo coyotes fabric facing safari fade
18   upkeep pupils uproar upon upholds gadget gagged gashes gage

19   Beyond that canyon, a young coyote loudly gained attention.
| 1 | 2 | 3 | 4 | 5 | 6 | 7 | 8 | 9 | 10 | 11 | 12

POSTTEST. Repeat the Pretest and compare performance.

103-F. POSTTEST: HORIZONTAL REACHES

103-G. Compare these two paragraphs with the first two paragraphs of 101-G, page 150. Type a list of the words that contain errors, correcting the errors as you type.

WP Word processing supervisors stress the increased importance of first-rate proofreading skills in an automated office.

103-G. PROOFREADING SKILLS

20   Every fall the television networks introduce thier new
shows for the year; and each Winter many of these new shows
are cancelled because of poor ratings. Altough ratings determine what we watch, few people understand how they wrok.

Ratings tell the stations how many people are watching
every show. The size of the shows' audience indicates what
the network will charge a company for commercial time. The
presteige of each net work is also effected by the ratings.

128-G. CENTERING PRACTICE

128-G. Spacing—double. Center this announcement horizontally and vertically on a half sheet. (To review spread centering, see page ix in the Reference Section.) Use the shift lock when typing all capitals.

```
A N N U A L   S K I   T R I P
Sponsored by
W E S T O N   E M P L O Y E E S
Mad River Glen Ski Area
February 22-24, 19--
TOTAL COST:  $115
```

128-H. CAPITALIZATION SKILLS

128-H. Review the capitalization rules on page 186. Then type the two paragraphs, capitalizing where necessary.

20 we left for our annual vacation trip on august 17. we 12
were heading south since we wanted to visit disney world in 24
orlando, florida. when we left our house on warwick street 36
in medford, massachusetts, we went south through boston and 48
new york city. after traveling on the new jersey turnpike, 60
we finally spent our first night in philadelphia. the next 72
day we spent time at independence hall and the liberty bell 84
before heading for norfolk, virginia, for our second night. 96

the next day was to be our longest driving day. about 108
six in the morning we left for savannah, georgia, and drove 120
all day to reach our motel. we spent the next day visiting 132
savannah, a truly beautiful and historic city of the south. 144
our last stop the following afternoon was orlando, florida. 156

| 1 | 2 | 3 | 4 | 5 | 6 | 7 | 8 | 9 | 10 | 11 | 12

129-A. WARMUP

129-A. Repeat 128-A, page 188.

129-B. PRETEST: COMMON LETTER COMBINATIONS

PRETEST. Take a 1-minute timing; compute speed and errors.

21 Energy has been a gloomy concern for all of us. There 12
have been careful, constant appeals to save energy. We are 24
capable of performing in better fashion, and our effort can 36
bring us a joyful solution and comfort if we do not forget. 48

| 1 | 2 | 3 | 4 | 5 | 6 | 7 | 8 | 9 | 10 | 11 | 12

129-C. PRACTICE: WORD BEGINNINGS

PRACTICE. If you made no more than 1 error on the Pretest, type each line 3 times. If you made 2 or more errors, type each group of 4 lines (as though it were a paragraph) 3 times; then type the sentence 3 times.

22 for forge forms forbid forced forgot former forbear foreign
23 con coned conks contra concur consul convex conceal concept
24 per peril perch perish pertly permit period percent perform
25 com combo comet combat comply comedy coming comfort comical

26 Compliance in a foreign trade concept is in complete peril.

| 1 | 2 | 3 | 4 | 5 | 6 | 7 | 8 | 9 | 10 | 11 | 12

103-H. SPELLING SKILLS

103-H. Type each line of these spelling demons twice, paying close attention to the spelling. Then, if time permits, have someone dictate a list of these words for you to type without looking at your text.

21 business sincerely believe contract advise original medical
22 aluminum available already envelope cannot pleasure receipt
23 complete committee current industry accept purchase whether
24 interest necessary forward personal annual recently premium
25 material attention address schedule either separate receive

26 cordially assistance statement coverage college opportunity
27 education experience agreement employee notices convenience
28 equipment facilities customers planning various immediately
29 personnel management financial shipment writing development
30 reference individual operation brochure budgets advertising

104-A. Repeat 103-A, page 151.

104-A. WARMUP

104-B. PRETEST: COMMON LETTER COMBINATIONS

PRETEST. Take a 1-minute timing; compute speed and errors.

31   I used to listen to the long debate on the urgent need 12
to increase income by reducing many benefits for social se- 24
curity recipients, but I finally realized that this was the 36
wrong stand to take for the best results for all concerned. 48
| 1 | 2 | 3 | 4 | 5 | 6 | 7 | 8 | 9 | 10 | 11 | 12

104-C. PRACTICE: WORD BEGINNINGS

PRACTICE. If you made no more than 1 error on the Pretest, type each line 3 times. If you made 2 or more errors, type each group of 4 lines (as though it were a paragraph) 3 times; then type the sentence 3 times.

32 in income incurs insert inch influx injury infant ink index
33 re recent really resume rent rebate redeem review red relax
34 be before beside behind best beyond beauty behave bed befit
35 de debate decide deaths deny decays depend desire den debit

36 I remember an influx of beautiful plants in recent decades.
| 1 | 2 | 3 | 4 | 5 | 6 | 7 | 8 | 9 | 10 | 11 | 12

104-D. PRACTICE: WORD ENDINGS

37 ly busily gladly comply rely poorly rarely yearly ably only
38 ed erased rested amazed need bribed failed valued aged used
39 nt decent parent amount sent recent intent urgent cent want
40 al denial animal manual real dismal social postal deal oral

41 I want and need to comply with those recent annual changes.
| 1 | 2 | 3 | 4 | 5 | 6 | 7 | 8 | 9 | 10 | 11 | 12

104-E. PRACTICE: OTHER LETTER COMBINATIONS

42 fr friend frowns defray from afraid freely frozen free from
43 th theirs things others then bother breath health that they
44 st stairs stands fasten fast listen almost typist stay stop
45 ng angles engine finger ring lounge belong string long ring

46 The old friend of theirs listened freely to the first song.
| 1 | 2 | 3 | 4 | 5 | 6 | 7 | 8 | 9 | 10 | 11 | 12

POSTTEST. Repeat the Pretest and compare performance.

104-F. POSTTEST: COMMON LETTER COMBINATIONS

LESSONS 128/129
SKILL DRIVE

Goals: To improve speed/
accuracy; to improve
proficiency at capitalization.

128-A. WARMUP

S 1 The antique bicycles will be kept down at the meeting room.
A 2 Jeff quietly moved a dozen boxes last night by power truck.
N 3 Sue's number was (609) 555-2873; Jack's was (201) 555-4634.
    | 1 | 2 | 3 | 4 | 5 | 6 | 7 | 8 | 9 | 10 | 11 | 12

128-B. PRETEST: HORIZONTAL REACHES

PRETEST. Take a 1-minute
timing; compute speed and
errors.

 4   The legislators pursued a tax rebate on the agenda. A 12
large number wanted the higher value, but most of them were 24
searching for almost any action they could easily pass. It 36
was a dandy issue that they enjoyed raising at this moment. 48
    | 1 | 2 | 3 | 4 | 5 | 6 | 7 | 8 | 9 | 10 | 11 | 12

128-C. PRACTICE: IN REACHES

PRACTICE. If you made no
more than 1 error on the
Pretest, type each line 3
times. If you made 2 or more
errors, type each group of 4
lines (as though it were a
paragraph) 3 times; then
type the sentence 3 times.

 5 ar larger scares upward arrear harms start sugar arise yard
 6 oy voyage decoys employ joyful loyal annoy royal enjoy toys
 7 pu pursue spurts deputy campus punch spurt input pulse spun
 8 lu luxury fluent column influx lunge slump value plush plus

 9 Tom enjoyed seeing the value of accounts in arrears plunge.
    | 1 | 2 | 3 | 4 | 5 | 6 | 7 | 8 | 9 | 10 | 11 | 12

128-D. PRACTICE: OUT REACHES

10 ge gentle agenda urgent danger geese agent anger merge page
11 da dashes ordain sandal bridal dandy adapt medal panda soda
12 hi higher shifts uphill within hired ethic thing white whip
13 ra ramble trader parade betray raise track rural zebra trap

14 A higher trading rate and mergers were urgent agenda items.
    | 1 | 2 | 3 | 4 | 5 | 6 | 7 | 8 | 9 | 10 | 11 | 12

128-E. PRACTICE: IN AND OUT REACHES

15 eagerness notary occupy easily affair saying fear pets vain
16 obligated campus almost carbon pasted garden cage late only
17 employees rebate motion upward radial judges your race cabs
18 naturally joyful nicely search traced impact most dart upon

19 Your campus leaders are eagerly searching for college tips.
    | 1 | 2 | 3 | 4 | 5 | 6 | 7 | 8 | 9 | 10 | 11 | 12

POSTTEST. Repeat the
Pretest and compare
performance.

128-F. POSTTEST: HORIZONTAL REACHES

104-G. Spacing—double.
Take two 5-minute timings.
Between them, practice any
words with which you had
difficulty. Record your score.

104-G. SKILL MEASUREMENT: 5-MINUTE TIMED WRITING

47   For sheer excitement, nothing beats being a contestant   12
on a television game show. More of these game shows are on   24
television now than before, so that you have better chances   36
of becoming a game show contestant and winning thousands of   48
dollars in cash and prizes or at least having a lot of fun.   60
     The first decision to make is to determine the sort of   72
show you would like to try. Some shows are purely games of   84
chance, some require quickness of thinking, and some others   96
call for concentration. Another factor to consider is what 108
kind of prizes you prefer. Some shows give cash prizes and   120
others just give gifts. You should remember, however, that   132
you will pay taxes on whatever cash and prizes you receive.   144
     If all this appeals to you, the next time you see your   156
favorite game shows, keep paper and a pencil handy, because   168
most shows announce at the end of each program how to apply   180
to become a contestant.   185
| 1 | 2 | 3 | 4 | 5 | 6 | 7 | 8 | 9 | 10 | 11 | 12

Line: 60 spaces	Tab: 5
Spacing: single	Drills: 3X
Proofguide: 71–72	
Workguide: 155	
Tape: 44A and 31B	

LESSONS 105/106
SKILL DRIVE

Goal: To improve speed/
accuracy.

105-A. WARMUP

S 1 A bushel of corn was thrown to the turkeys by the neighbor.
A 2 Did Weldon give Liz your picturesque jukebox for Christmas?
N 3 Read pages 467–518 carefully for the weekend of June 29–30.
| 1 | 2 | 3 | 4 | 5 | 6 | 7 | 8 | 9 | 10 | 11 | 12

105-B. PRETEST: CLOSE REACHES

PRETEST. Take a 1-minute
timing; compute speed and
errors.

4   We started the old unit on the fourth floor of a glass   12
tower. We swept the litter from the dirty green carpet and   24
painted the wall an olive grey. We had to hurry to open on   36
time. In our haste, we forgot to shop for office supplies.   48
| 1 | 2 | 3 | 4 | 5 | 6 | 7 | 8 | 9 | 10 | 11 | 12

127-D. PRACTICE: RIGHT HAND

34 klk killed sulked anklet sickly kilts links bulky look hulk
35 uyu unduly yogurt uneasy joyful unity yummy usury your ugly
36 pop polish oppose pooped option plops optic pools open prop
37 jhj joshed hijack hashed joking hatch joker hutch hush jest

38 A skilled hijacker is uneasy with ugly options open to him.
| 1 | 2 | 3 | 4 | 5 | 6 | 7 | 8 | 9 | 10 | 11 | 12

127-E. PRACTICE: BOTH HANDS

39 rur rubber usurps rusher untrue ruler urged rural ruby curl
40 bnb bundle nabbed bonnet nobody bunny numbs bound nabs bind
41 eie fliers relies seizes dieted piety heist eight diem lied
42 ghg hoagie afghan fights ghosts sighs rough ought hugs high

43 Nobody tied a high bundle beside a hedge in the rural town.
| 1 | 2 | 3 | 4 | 5 | 6 | 7 | 8 | 9 | 10 | 11 | 12

POSTTEST. Repeat the Pretest on page 186 and compare performance.

127-F. POSTTEST: DISCRIMINATION PRACTICE

127-G. Spacing—double. Take two 5-minute timings. Between them, practice any words with which you had difficulty. Record your score.

127-G. SKILL MEASUREMENT: 5-MINUTE TIMED WRITING

44   In recent years, there has been a steady rise in money 12
spent for leisure activities. This is due, in part, to the 24
shorter workweek, which has increased the time for leisure. 36
Also, more people recognize the need to relax and are ready 48
to spend for what they enjoy. Sports are more popular than 60
ever since everyone wants to stay fit. Favorite activities 72
include tennis, jogging, swimming, skiing, and golfing. In 84
short, there is a sport for every season and for every age. 96
     The leisure market is not confined only to sports. In 108
the home, a great deal is spent on entertainment. For this 120
reason, most homes are equipped with television sets. Some 132
even have swimming pools. Outside the home, people are now 144
going to cultural events, such as the theater or ballet, in 156
record numbers. For travel, package tours are still a good 168
bargain. If present trends continue, leisure spending will 180
double within ten years, and we will need to have many more 192
service workers than we now have in order to handle all the 204
demand for leisure activities.   210
| 1 | 2 | 3 | 4 | 5 | 6 | 7 | 8 | 9 | 10 | 11 | 12

PRACTICE. If you made no more than 1 error on the Pretest, type each line 3 times. If you made 2 or more errors, type each group of 4 lines (as though it were a paragraph) 3 times; then type the sentence 3 times.

105-C. PRACTICE: ADJACENT KEYS

```
 5  rt dirty north court part sport worth apart start sort port
 6  as asset basic haste seas taste lasts ideas visas vast asks
 7  op optic hoped roped stop crops adopt shops droop open drop
 8  we weary wedge weigh owes wells tweed dowel tower week wear

 9  That weary lass tasted a torte at the dirty shop last week.
    |  1  |  2  |  3  |  4  |  5  |  6  |  7  |  8  |  9  |  10  |  11  |  12
```

105-D. PRACTICE: CONSECUTIVE STROKES

```
10  sw swaps sways swift swim swing sweep sword swept swam swab
11  gr grace grain grand grow green grape gripe grown gram grid
12  un under unfit units fund bunch hunch ounce rerun noun stun
13  ol olive stole colds poll color solar cools spool oleo bold

14  The graceful old swans swam under the old gray olive trees.
    |  1  |  2  |  3  |  4  |  5  |  6  |  7  |  8  |  9  |  10  |  11  |  12
```

105-E. PRACTICE: DOUBLE LETTERS

```
15  ss brass fussy messy loss amiss class glass dress boss pass
16  oo books booth looks hood roomy foods blood floor door took
17  tt utter butte motto mutt putty patty attic witty putt watt
18  rr arrow berry carry purr marry burro error worry burr errs

19  My boss carried the book from the attic to the class booth.
    |  1  |  2  |  3  |  4  |  5  |  6  |  7  |  8  |  9  |  10  |  11  |  12
```

POSTTEST. Repeat the Pretest and compare performance.

105-F. POSTTEST: CLOSE REACHES

105-G. Type each line of these spelling demons twice, paying close attention to the spelling.

105-G. SPELLING SKILLS

```
20  their successful certificate corporation distribution basis
21  there throughout appropriate appointment organization quite
22  until commission merchandise outstanding particularly among
```

106-A. Repeat 105-A, page 154.

106-A. WARMUP

106-B. PRETEST: ALTERNATE- AND ONE-HAND WORDS

PRETEST. Take a 1-minute timing; compute speed and errors.

```
23       In our opinion, that handcrafted bicycle from Honolulu 12
    should be regarded as an authentic antique; its age exceeds 24
    a hundred years, and it deserves to be treated well because 36
    it will attract many visitors at our Texas and Ohio plants. 48
    |  1  |  2  |  3  |  4  |  5  |  6  |  7  |  8  |  9  |  10  |  11  |  12
```

PRACTICE. If you made no more than 1 error on the Pretest, type each line 3 times. If you made 2 or more errors, type each group of 4 lines (as though it were a paragraph) 3 times; then type the sentence 3 times.

106-C. PRACTICE: ALTERNATE HANDS

```
24  amend handle element ornament endowment auditor signal half
25  chair thrown problem blandish shamrocks penalty profit form
26  signs height visible turndown amendment suspend visual maps
27  usual island figment clemency authentic dormant emblem snap

28  Did the auditor sign the problem amendment or turn it down?
    |  1  |  2  |  3  |  4  |  5  |  6  |  7  |  8  |  9  |  10  |  11  |  12
```

126-G. Paper: Half sheet (inserted sideways).

126-G. CENTERING PRACTICE

There are two ways to find the horizontal center of special-sized paper or cards or odd-sized paper:

1. Center the paper on the line scale.

2. Insert the paper or card into the machine and add the numbers on the line scale at the left and right edges of the paper. Divide this sum by 2. The result is the horizontal center point for that size of paper or card (for example, $10 + 70 = 80 \div 2 = 40$).

Center the following information:

Your name
Your street address
Your city, state, ZIP
Your school or college
Your academic major or program
Today's date

126-H. Review the five rules of capitalization at the right. Then type lines 20–27, capitalizing where necessary.

126-H. CAPITALIZATION SKILLS

1. Capitalize a proper noun (the name of a particular person, place, or thing): *Ms. Henderson, Cincinnati, Italy, Buick.*

2. Capitalize a common noun when it is part of a proper name: *Bethlehem High School, Museum of Modern Art, Candlestick Park, James Plaza.*

3. Capitalize the first word of a sentence.

4. Capitalize *north, south, east,* and *west* when they refer to definite regions, are part of a proper noun, or are within an address; but *do not* capitalize *north, south, east,* and *west* when they merely indicate direction or general location.

5. Capitalize a noun when it is followed by a number or letter indicating sequence: *Invoice 943, Room 20, Class A.*

20 diane, lynn, and david left for florida on monday, april 3.
21 sue met mr. and mrs. mancini when they flew to los angeles.
22 al liked a trip to the statue of liberty on liberty island.
23 united flight 121 to seattle made a stop at o'hare airport.

24 tom morgan is moving from north carolina to the west coast.
25 the hotel is on south main street, just north of lake road.
26 the town of wayne, new jersey, is just south of pequannock.
27 the bunker hill monument is two miles north of fenway park.

127-A. Repeat 126-A, page 185.

127-A. WARMUP

127-B. PRETEST: DISCRIMINATION PRACTICE

PRETEST. Take a 1-minute timing; compute speed and errors.

28   The police nabbed the grouch behind the hedge beside a 12
pool. They were urged on by an ugly group of eight jokers. 24
The police bound the young man's hands. After the fight, a 36
brave officer went looking near all the edges of that pool. 48
| 1 | 2 | 3 | 4 | 5 | 6 | 7 | 8 | 9 | 10 | 11 | 12

PRACTICE. If you made no more than 1 error on the Pretest, type each line 3 times. If you made 2 or more errors, type each group of 4 lines (as though it were a paragraph) 3 times; then type the sentence 3 times.

127-C. PRACTICE: LEFT HAND

29 vbv viable beaver verbal bovine above bevel brave verb bevy
30 wew weekly sewers weapon eschew wedge jewel weeds sewn went
31 ded deeded ensued decide edited delve edges dried dyed dead
32 fgf figure guffaw forget engulf fight goofs fling gift fang

33 The brave writer forgot that an editor would decide length.
| 1 | 2 | 3 | 4 | 5 | 6 | 7 | 8 | 9 | 10 | 11 | 12

106-D. PRACTICE: ONE HAND

29 union seaweed opinion cassette minikin created kimono exact
30 holly barrage plumply eastward pumpkin greater poplin trade
31 onion terrace homonym carefree killjoy exceeds uphill serve
32 plump scatter million attracts minimum reserve unhook defer

33 The jolly staff served pumpkin breads on the hilly terrace.
| 1 | 2 | 3 | 4 | 5 | 6 | 7 | 8 | 9 | 10 | 11 | 12

106-E. PRACTICE: BOTH HANDS

34 evenly destiny afternoon hundred housed fraction illustrate
35 impact holders impressed impress inject imported recreation
36 number limited unpleased omitted really kilowatt federation
37 united pointed populated session weekly reaction attraction

38 The weekly afternoon session of the federation was opposed.
| 1 | 2 | 3 | 4 | 5 | 6 | 7 | 8 | 9 | 10 | 11 | 12

POSTTEST. Repeat the Pretest on page 155 and compare performance.

106-F. POSTTEST: ALTERNATE- AND ONE-HAND WORDS

106-G. Type each line of these spelling demons twice, paying close attention to the spelling.

106-G. SPELLING SKILLS

39 processing conference procedure submitted decision probably
40 assignment commercial excellent recommend director practice
41 convenient accordance knowledge beginning previous progress

106-H. Spacing—double. Take two 5-minute timings. Between them, practice any words with which you had difficulty. Record your score.

106-H. SKILL MEASUREMENT: 5-MINUTE TIMED WRITING

42
What is it that enables many people to tell whether it 12
will be warm or cold tomorrow? Farmers who are weatherwise 24
take their readings from nature. If you learn what to look 36
for, you can see the local weather changes approaching too. 48
In fair weather, for example, air pressure is high and 60
the air is quite stable and perhaps filled with dust. As a 72
storm approaches and air pressure drops, the air clears and 84
you will see more detail than usual. Thus, when objects on 96
the horizon appear distant or hazy, fair weather is likely. 108
When the weather is crystal clear, rain will probably come. 120
You can also smell changes in the weather; just before 132
rain appears, your sense of smell may seem to improve. An- 144
other indicator of the coming of bad weather is an increase 156
in aches and pain. The lower air pressure before the storm 168
also causes animals to act differently. To be weatherwise, 180
become sensitive to nature. 185
| 1 | 2 | 3 | 4 | 5 | 6 | 7 | 8 | 9 | 10 | 11 | 12

Line: 60 spaces   Tab: 5
Spacing: single   Drills: 3X
Proofguide: 89–90
Workguide: 155
Tape: 35B and 36B

LESSONS 126/127
SKILL DRIVE

Goals: To improve speed/accuracy; to improve proficiency at horizontal centering.

126-A.   WARMUP

S 1 You will see the truck when it turns the curve in the road.
A 2 Dick and Sam have won a prize by fixing the antique jalopy.
N 3 The discount of $143.12 from the $957.60 bill left $814.48.
    | 1 | 2 | 3 | 4 | 5 | 6 | 7 | 8 | 9 | 10 | 11 | 12

126-B.   PRETEST: VERTICAL REACHES

PRETEST. Take a 1-minute timing; compute speed and errors.

4   A resort once went beyond all expectations. It really 12
was a small town, with its own bank, bakery, band, acres of 24
park, and animal farm. It devoted much effort to providing 36
just a casual scene for its clientele at the drop of a hat. 48
    | 1 | 2 | 3 | 4 | 5 | 6 | 7 | 8 | 9 | 10 | 11 | 12

126-C.   PRACTICE: UP REACHES

PRACTICE. If you made no more than 1 error on the Pretest, type each line 3 times. If you made 2 or more errors, type each group of 4 lines (as though it were a paragraph) 3 times; then type the sentence 3 times.

5 at atomic rather flatly rebate repeat attest atom late what
6 dr driver adrift drowsy sundry drying tundra drum draw drug
7 es esteem resort thesis access smiles escape desk ages nest
8 ju jumble adjust junior justly injure jurist jury jump junk

9 The driver escaped injury by jumping rather than attacking.
    | 1 | 2 | 3 | 4 | 5 | 6 | 7 | 8 | 9 | 10 | 11 | 12

126-D.   PRACTICE: DOWN REACHES

10 ca casual scarce scales cattle recall fiscal cash scat call
11 nk unkind donkey blanks anklet tinker chunky wink rank bank
12 ba bakery abates ballot cabana global basket balk tuba band
13 sc scheme escort script ascend fiasco scolds scar disc scab

14 The band recalled a scheme to put scarce cash in that bank.
    | 1 | 2 | 3 | 4 | 5 | 6 | 7 | 8 | 9 | 10 | 11 | 12

126-E.   PRACTICE: JUMP REACHES

15 cr crease scrubs outcry critic script crummy crib acre crop
16 on onward fondly sponge beyond convey longer once long soon
17 ev evades devote clever grieve evenly revert ever bevy even
18 ni nitwit animal denial clinic nibble unison nips snip mini

19 Even the critics were united in fondly revising the script.
    | 1 | 2 | 3 | 4 | 5 | 6 | 7 | 8 | 9 | 10 | 11 | 12

POSTTEST. Repeat the Pretest and compare performance.

126-F.   POSTTEST: VERTICAL REACHES

<table>
<tr><td>Line: 60 spaces   Tab: 5
Spacing: single   Drills: 3X
Proofguide: 71–74
Workguide: 155–156, 229–236
Tape: 32B</td></tr>
</table>

LESSONS 107/108
LETTER STYLES

Goal: To format letters in different styles.

107-A. WARMUP

S 1 Bob owns a pair of ancient bicycles and a giant ivory bowl.
A 2 Vamp, the amazing jockey's deaf horse, was quite excitable.
N 3 I now live at 7598 First Street, Apt. 126, Macon, GA 31204.
    | 1 | 2 | 3 | 4 | 5 | 6 | 7 | 8 | 9 | 10 | 11 | 12

107-B. Set five tab stops, each 11 spaces apart. Then type each drill twice.

107-B. TABULATOR PRACTICE: ALPHABET AND SHIFT KEYS

4 Aaron	Bobby	Cecil	David	Eddie	Fluff
5 Gregg	Heath	Irvin	Jonah	Karen	Lloyd
6 Mamie	Nancy	Orion	Pepys	Queen	Roger
7 Susan	Tulsa	Verna	Wyatt	Xenia	Zenia

107-C. Spacing—double. Take two 5-minute timings. Between them, practice any words with which you had difficulty. Record your score.

107-C. SKILL MEASUREMENT: 5-MINUTE TIMED WRITING

8   Have you ever heard someone complain that products are 12
not made as well today as in years past? The fact is, most 24
products are manufactured better now than in years gone by. 36
     For example, today's cars are vastly superior to those 48
of just a dozen years ago; they run longer and require less 60
maintenance, their bodies rust less, oil changes are needed 72
less often, and the tires last twice as long as previously. 84
     Today's homes are more comfortable to live in, and all 96
the mechanical devices are far better than they were in the 108
past. Even with regard to clothes, the synthetic materials 120
in our clothes make fabrics more convenient to care for and 132
they last much longer than natural fiber. Fabric finishes, 144
such as for permanent press, have relieved the homemaker of 156
hours of ironing and cleaning. So even as the items we buy 168
grow more complex and may cost even more, they last longer, 180
need less service, and are more convenient to use. 190
     | 1 | 2 | 3 | 4 | 5 | 6 | 7 | 8 | 9 | 10 | 11 | 12

PART 6

SKILL BUILDING ■ LETTERS, FINANCIAL TABLES, AND LEGAL PAPERS

OBJECTIVES FOR PART 6

Part 6 is designed to enable you to demonstrate the following abilities when you take the test in Lesson 150:

1. Technical Knowledge. To answer correctly at least 95 percent of the questions on an objective test covering the technical information presented in Lessons 75 through 150.

2. Production. To format correctly from unarranged or rough-draft copy: (a) two-page letters, (b) letters on different sizes of stationery, (c) financial statements, (d) boxed tables, and (e) various legal documents.

3. Skill Rate. To type at the following speed and accuracy levels by the end of each unit:

Unit	No. of Minutes	Minimum Speed	Maximum Errors
21	5	42	5
22	5	43	5
23	5	44	5
24	5	45	5

4. Word Processing Information. To understand how word processing equipment would function if used to format various production assignments.

107/108-D. LETTER STYLES

Study the letter styles below and on the next page; then format Letters 33–36 on Workguide pages 229–236.

Retain these letters to include in the Correspondence Portfolio that you will develop from the assignments in Unit 18.

NOTE: If you spoil a letterhead, make a replacement on plain paper. Center the main information of the letterhead on lines 6, 8, and 10.

ENUMERATION. Begun at left margin; 2 spaces follow number and period; turnover lines are indented 4 spaces.

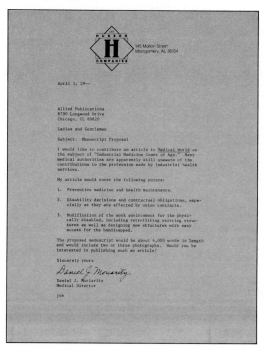

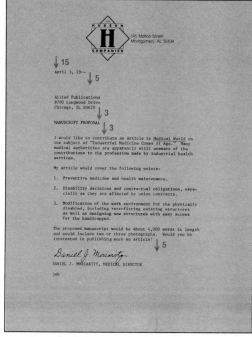

BLOCK STYLE. Date and closing lines begin at left margin.

OPEN PUNCTUATION. No colon after salutation; no comma after complimentary closing.

SUBJECT LINE. Comes after the salutation.

SIMPLIFIED STYLE. Date and closing lines begin at left margin; no salutation or complimentary closing.

SUBJECT LINE. Always included in a simplified-style letter; typed in all caps; preceded and followed by 2 blank lines; the word *Subject* is not typed.

LETTER 33
BLOCK STYLE, OPEN PUNCTUATION

Paper: Workguide 229–230
Proofguide: 73–74

LETTER 34
SIMPLIFIED STYLE*

Paper: Workguide 231–232
Proofguide: 73–74

* Delete the salutation, the word *Subject*, and the complimentary closing when typing this letter in simplified style.

(*Current date*) / Dr. Jean Helmstadter / 125 Washington Street / Montgomery, AL 36104 / Dear Dr. Helmstadter / Subject: Edwin Jones 17 / 31

I am referring to you Mr. Edwin Jones, an employee at The Hudson Companies, who has been complaining of a severe pain in his hip. A copy of Mr. Jones's medical record at our company is enclosed. 45 / 59 / 72

Please note the following items from the patient's medical history: 87

1. Mr. Jones sustained an impacted fracture of his hip when he was a child. 102 / 104

2. This injury has never caused him any work-related problems, but I suspect that arthritis may have developed. 119 / 128

Will you please take the necessary X rays and inform me of your findings. Mr. Jones carries group health insurance with our company; his policy will cover all medical costs associated with your services. 142 / 156 / 170

Sincerely / Daniel J. Moriarity / Medical Director / (*Reference initials*) / Enclosure 185 / 189

Form: Workguide 279

Use the data below to type payroll voucher checks for Carol A. Collins and Robert F. Gwinner.

NO.	NAME	INCOME TAX EXEMP-TION	GROSS PAY		DEDUCTIONS							NET PAY	
					ITW		FICA		GROUP INSURANCE		MISC.		TOTAL		
1	Carol A Collins	4	330	00	67	50	24	75	11	00			103	25	226	75
2	Robert F. Gwinner	1	315	00	63	00	23	62	9	00			95	62	219	38

PAYROLL REGISTER   Week Ending _June 30, 19—_

Spacing: double
Paper: Workguide 280

Type only the first page of this report. You may not need all of the information provided.

Women in Banking: A Perspective
Jane W. Allred

Women have long been highly visible in the American banking industry as clerical workers (Harper, 1983). Only in the past decade, however, have women begun to enter the ranks of bank management in significant numbers.

PROBLEM STATEMENT

This study provides some possible answers to the problem:

Why have women not become bankers in the past, and why are they doing so in increasing numbers today?

PROCEDURES

The methodology employed in this study made extensive use of secondary data from research in the disciplines of sociology (Menosky, 1975; Sluman, 1980) and psychology (Kenard and Snow, 1979; Vanicott, 1960). Primary data from interviews with eight Seattle-area female bankers were used to give added depth to the analysis.

FINDINGS

It was concluded that women have not become bankers in the past largely as a result of discrimination (Vanicott, 1960). This discrimination, however, is of two distinct types.

One type of discrimination against women in banking stems from the societal perception of the occupation of banker as being male-appropriate and, by implication,

7
17
30
41
52
63
68
78
80
91
101
104
114
125
136
148
158
170
171
181
193
205
208
219
231
241

NOTE: An attention line goes before the salutation; a subject line goes after the salutation.

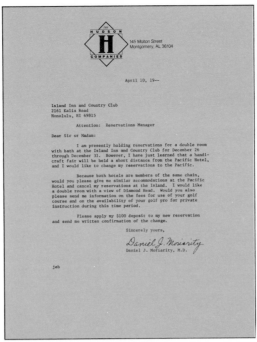

MODIFIED-BLOCK STYLE WITH PARAGRAPH IN-DENTIONS. Shown here with 10-space paragraph indentions (for distinctiveness).

ATTENTION LINE. Typically begins at the left margin; shown here beginning at the paragraph-indention point.

MODIFIED-BLOCK STYLE WITH PARAGRAPH IN-DENTIONS. Shown here double-spaced (to make the short letter cover a full page), with 5-space paragraph indention. Paragraphs must be indented with a double-spaced letter.

FOREIGN ADDRESS. Name of country is typed in all caps on a separate line.

LETTER 35
MODIFIED-BLOCK STYLE

10-space paragraph indentions
Paper: Workguide 233–234
Proofguide: 73–74

(*Current date*) / Health Maintenance Corporation / Rue d'Athenes 17 / 75006 Paris / FRANCE / Attention: Marketing Department / Ladies and Gentlemen:

    The Eastern Industrial Medical Society is holding its annual convention at the Island Inn and Country Club in Honolulu, Hawaii, from December 27 to 30. Approximately 300 professionals in the industrial medical field will be attending the sessions.

    Would your organization be interested in exhibiting your products at this convention? The enclosed brochure provides more complete information about the exhibit requirements. If you would like to participate in the exhibit, complete the enclosed form and return it to me.

    If you plan to participate, the members of our society would be especially interested in having an opportunity to examine firsthand the stress-testing machine that your company introduced last winter.

    Sincerely / Daniel J. Moriarity / Medical Director / (*Reference initials*) / Enclosure

| 18 |
| 33 |
| 36 |
| 51 |
| 64 |
| 79 |
| 88 |
| 104 |
| 117 |
| 131 |
| 146 |
| 162 |
| 175 |
| 189 |
| 212 |
| 214 |

LETTER 36
MODIFIED-BLOCK STYLE

5-space paragraph indentions
Spacing: double
Paper: Workguide 235–236
Proofguide: 73–74

Send this same letter (with the last paragraph deleted) to Mr. Paul Ames, Marketing Director / Scranton Medical Supplies / Norton, MA 02766. Double-space the letter, delete the attention line, and supply an appropriate salutation.

LESSON 125

TEST 5: PROGRESS TEST ON PART 5

TEST 5-A
5-MINUTE TIMED WRITING

Line: 60 spaces
Spacing: double
Tab: 5
Paper: Workguide 277

How are you treated by people? Do you believe you are	12
often used by other people or that others take advantage of	24
you or do not treat you as an equal? If so, you could make	36
life much more enjoyable by knowing how to assert yourself.	48
For example, suppose that you are speaking and someone	60
in the group constantly interrupts you; the normal response	72
of some people would be simply to do nothing. But this may	84
mean that the person will continue to interrupt you, making	96
you feel unimportant. A much more effective response would	108
be to tell the person, in a calm and polite manner, that he	120
or she just interrupted you. Reminding that person of this	132
fact outright is a good teaching device, and if you are po-	144
lite and calm about it, the chances are good that this type	156
of behavior will stop and the person will apologize to you.	168
The purpose of asserting yourself isn't to offend any-	180
one but rather to be treated courteously and to receive the	192
consideration that is due every person.	200

| 1 | 2 | 3 | 4 | 5 | 6 | 7 | 8 | 9 | 10 | 11 | 12 |

TEST 5-B
LETTER 43
MODIFIED-BLOCK STYLE
WITH INDENTED
PARAGRAPHS

Paper: Workguide 278

NOTE: Include necessary notations.

Paul Glencoe, Administrative Manager of DODGE COPPER COMPANY, is sending this letter (dated July 8, 19—) to Ms. Adrienne Snow, Systems Analyst at Chaparral Data Systems Inc., 521 Spruce Street, S.E., Albuquerque, NM 87106. Mr. Glencoe always uses the company name, his name, and his title in the closing lines of a letter.

Dear Ms. Snow: I am enclosing a copy of the payroll register that we	44
are now using in our payroll department. As we discussed, the new	57
data processing system that you are designing for us should allow us	71
to record the same information that we now record manually.	83
We would like to be able to record the deductions only once and	98
then not have to rerecord them unless they change. The order in which	112
the deductions are listed is immaterial. Finally, we would expect the	127
program you design for us to automatically produce the printed payroll	141
checks from the payroll register. Sincerely yours,	154
P.S. I would appreciate having a sample printout of these forms to	190
show at our administrative committee meeting on July 30.	202

LESSONS 109/110
LETTER STYLES

Goal: To format letters in different styles.

109-A. WARMUP

S 1 The auditor panel had the right to risk the firm's profits.
A 2 Zona expected a major earthquake to cause fairly big waves.
N 3 The group will meet from 9:30 to 2:45 on May 17 in Room 68.
| 1 | 2 | 3 | 4 | 5 | 6 | 7 | 8 | 9 | 10 | 11 | 12

109-B. SPACE BAR/SHIFT-KEY PRACTICE

109-B. Take several 1-minute timings, trying to increase your speed each time. Don't let the space bar or the shift key slow you down.

4   If Al gets to go to Del Rio, Lou may go to Elm City to   12
see Max J. May play the part of the man in "The Old Man and   24
the Sea." It is not a new play, but this is the first time   36
that it has been put on here in Elm City; it should be fun.   48
| 1 | 2 | 3 | 4 | 5 | 6 | 7 | 8 | 9 | 10 | 11 | 12

109-C. SKILL MEASUREMENT: 5-MINUTE TIMED WRITING

109-C. Spacing—double. Take two 5-minute timings. Between them, practice any words with which you had difficulty. Record your score.

5   One of the best ways to stretch your dollar is to shop   12
during nonpeak seasons. This just means that you shop when   24
it is to the seller's advantage to sell cheaply. By buying   36
a product at a time when sales are slow, you help a company   48
avoid laying off workers, avoid paying overtime during busy   60
seasons, and minimize the costs of storing its merchandise. 72
To stimulate sales during these nonpeak seasons, firms   84
often hold clearance sales; today, however, firms that once   96
would never mark down their goods have begun discount pric— 108
ing. For example, large utility companies are now offering 120
home owners a cheaper price for electricity when it is used 132
during times of lower demand, such as in the evening hours. 144
The key to buying out of peak season is to inquire how 156
each firm operates and when the demand for the firm's prod— 168
ucts is lowest. Fed by inflation, this method of buying is 180
bound to grow quickly in the next several years.   190
| 1 | 2 | 3 | 4 | 5 | 6 | 7 | 8 | 9 | 10 | 11 | 12

109/110-D. LETTER STYLES

Study the letter styles on the next two pages; then format the four letters on Workguide pages 237–244. As with the previous lesson, retain these letters to include in your Correspondence Portfolio.

REPORT 31
TWO-PAGE REPORT WITH AUTHOR/YEAR CITATIONS
Paper: plain
Proofguide: 87–88

REPORT 32
TWO-PAGE REPORT (WITH ENDNOTES)
Paper: plain
Proofguide: 87–88

REPORT 33
ENDNOTES
Paper: plain
Proofguide: 87–88

REPORT 34
TWO-PAGE REPORT WITH FOOTNOTES
Paper: plain
Proofguide: 87–90

REFERENCE CITATIONS IN A REPORT   6

By Arthur Brownell   17

Whenever you use the words or ideas of an- 28
other person in a report, you must provide the 37
reader with the source of the author's work. 46
Three common methods of doing this are by 55
using (1) author/year citations, (2) endnotes, and 65
(3) footnotes.   68

AUTHOR/YEAR CITATIONS   74

Smith (1982) recommends the use of author/ 83
year citations. In this method, the last name of 93
the author and the year of publication are 102
inserted in parentheses at an appropriate point 111
in the text. However, if the name of the author 121
occurs in the textual discussion, only the year of 131
publication is cited in parentheses. The reader 141
can then easily refer to the bibliography to find 151
the needed reference.   156

ENDNOTES   158

Endnotes may also be used to cite sources 168
(Burns, 1979). For this method, a raised number 177
is typed in the text at the point of reference, and 188
all of the notes are typed together at the end of 198
the report on a separate "NOTES" page. The 207
notes are numbered consecutively throughout 215
the report. Although raised numbers are used 225
in the text, the numbers on the "NOTES" page 235
are typed on the line, followed by a period and 243
two spaces. Use a 2-inch top margin for this page 263
and indent the first line of each note. The lines 273
of each note are single-spaced, with double 282
spacing used between each note.   289

FOOTNOTES   292

Footnotes may also be used for reference 301
sources. For this method a raised number is 310
typed at the appropriate point in the text, just 320
as it is when endnotes are used. However, the 329
actual note is then typed at the bottom of the 338
page, separated from the text by a 2-inch line. 348
Single-space before typing the line and double- 358
space afterwards. The lines of the footnote are 367
single-spaced, with double spacing used be- 376
tween footnotes.   380

The footnote must appear on the same page 389
as the raised number in the text (Rehnquist and 399
Plough, 1980). Begin each footnote at the para- 408
graph indention. Either type the number with a 418
period and 2 spaces, or type a superior number 427
and begin the reference immediately after the 436
number, with no spacing between. On the last 445
page of a report, the footnotes begin immedi- 454
ately after the last line of the text, rather 464
than at the bottom of the page.   470

NOTE: Use the following references in typing the endnotes and footnotes. Don't forget to precede each reference with the appropriate number, typed in correct position. For example, see pages xiv–xv of the Introduction.

Charles R. Smith, "Citation Style for Reference Manuals," <u>Journal of Business Psychology</u>, Vol. 6, No. 2, February 1982, pp. 83–91.

P. J. Burns, <u>Manual of Style</u>, East Publishing Company, Philadelphia, 1979, p. 53.

Haywood Rehnquist and Lana Plough, <u>The Typist's Handbook</u>, Edison, Inc., Boston, 1980, pp. 46–47.

NOTE: It is unlikely that you will ever type letters in more than one or two styles while working for the same firm. The different letter styles that you are learning in this unit will prepare you for typing letters in any office.

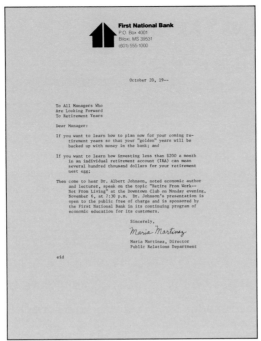

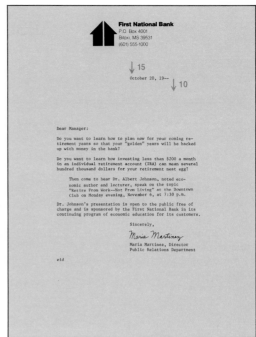

HANGING-INDENTED STYLE. The first line of each paragraph "hangs" in the left margin and all other lines of the body are indented 5 spaces. Note the format of the "inside address" of this form sales letter.

FORM LETTER WITH DISPLAY PARAGRAPH. Modified-block style with display paragraph indented 5 spaces from each margin. Since this is a form letter, the inside address is deleted.

The following letter concerning an upcoming workshop is to be sent to 500 business people in the area. In order to give it a different look, format it first in the hanging-indented style and then in the display-paragraph style (with the third paragraph displayed). Omit the "inside address" in the second version.

LETTER 37
HANGING-INDENTED STYLE

Paper: Workguide 237–238
Proofguide: 73–74

LETTER 38
FORM LETTER WITH DISPLAY PARAGRAPH

Paper: Workguide 239–240
Proofguide: 75–76

(*Current date*) / To All Employees Who / Want to Learn How to / Write	17
Better Letters / Dear Business Writer:	25
When was the last time you received a letter or memorandum that	40
was written so poorly that you could not be sure that you fully understood	56
the message?	59
When was the last time you or your employees received any real	73
instruction in how to write effective letters, memorandums, and business	89
reports?	91
You can increase your communication skills by attending our two-	105
hour workshop on business communications on December 14 at 3 p.m.	120
at the Downtown Club.	124
This workshop is open to the public free of charge and is sponsored	140
by the First National Bank in its continuing program of economic	154
education for its customers.	160
Sincerely, / Maria Martinez, Director / Public Relations Department /	183
(*Reference initials*)	184

LESSONS 123/124
REPORTS

Goal: To format a report using three methods of citation.

123-A. WARMUP

S 1 It is Al's turn to shape the emblem and pay the man for it.
A 2 Liz is brave and quick––a good example to follow on July 4.
N 3 Tickets 19, 20, 37, 84, and 65 were destroyed by Katherine.
| 1 | 2 | 3 | 4 | 5 | 6 | 7 | 8 | 9 | 10 | 11 | 12

123-B. Spacing—double. Take two 5-minute timings. Between them, practice any words with which you had difficulty. Record your score.

123-B. SKILL MEASUREMENT: 5-MINUTE TIMED WRITING

4   Many people miss out on life because of their shyness. 12
People who are shy shrink from human contact, often because 24
they feel unequal to others and are afraid to assume risks. 36
    People are not born shy; shyness comes from unique ex- 48
periences we have in the home, when at school, and with our 60
peers. Research shows that over a fourth of the people who 72
are shy as adults were not shy when they were young; on the 84
other hand, a large number of people who were shy when they 96
were young stop being shy at some point as they grow older. 108
    Shyness is not always a bad trait. It can make people 120
more appealing. Because they are modest and reserved, they 132
contribute by becoming good listeners or by not hogging the 144
spotlight. However, these people find it difficult to meet 156
new people and to make new acquaintances. Shyness prevents 168
them from speaking up and giving their opinions on matters. 180
    Develop self-confidence by emphasizing the positive or 192
by just putting your best foot forward. 200
| 1 | 2 | 3 | 4 | 5 | 6 | 7 | 8 | 9 | 10 | 11 | 12

WP Some word processors have a special feature that enables you to position footnote numbers quickly and correctly and to automatically leave enough space at the bottom of the page for typing the footnotes.

123/124-C. REPORTS IN THREE STYLES

Carefully read the report on page 181, which discusses and illustrates the use of the author/year method of citation. Then type the report in three different formats, first using the author/year method of citation, then using endnotes, and finally using footnotes. After typing the report with endnotes, type the endnotes page.

When typing the second and third reports, delete the references in parentheses and instead type the endnote or footnote numbers in the correct raised position.

Type these reports in unbound format, using double spacing and paragraph indentions. Refer to pages xiv–xv in the reference section of this book for further review of typing reports in different styles.

POSTSCRIPT NOTATION
Typed as the last item in the letter, preceded by 1 blank line. If the paragraphs are indented, indent the first line of the postscript too.

MAILING NOTATION
Shown typed in solid capitals a double space below the date; an alternative position is below the enclosure notation (if used) or below the reference initials.

LONG LETTER IN MODIFIED-BLOCK STYLE. For letters containing more than 225 words in the body (plus any postscript), use a 6-inch line (60 pica/70 elite).

MODIFIED-BLOCK STYLE. Shown here with "military date" (day before month instead of after), enumerated paragraphs, and enumerated enclosures.

LETTER 39
LONG LETTER IN MODIFIED-BLOCK STYLE

Paper: Workguide 241–242
Proofguide: 75–76

LETTER 40

Paper: Workguide 243–244
Proofguide: 75–76

Inside address:
Mr. David S. Yount
31 East 45 Street
Vicksburg, MS 39180

Add:
1. Military-style date.
2. Registered-mail notation.
3. Enumerations for second and third paragraphs.

Delete:
1. Last sentence of the fourth paragraph.
2. Enclosure notation.
3. Postscript notation.

(*Current date*) / Mrs. Leslie Altman / Rural Route 3 / Biloxi, MS 39532 / Dear Mrs. Altman: 18 / 23

I am happy to answer the questions that you asked in your recent letter to Mr. Edward G. Moody, president of First National Bank. 37 / 50

We hold our public forums every month, free of charge to the public. The chosen topics are based upon current interest. For example, a workshop on tax planning was held in February, prior to the tax-filing deadline in April. 65 / 79 / 93 / 97

As mentioned above, the workshops are offered at no cost to the participants. We do this as a public service to the community. First National Bank has always believed that educating the citizens of Biloxi in regard to how to get the most for their money is a part of our obligation as responsible corporate citizens. 111 / 125 / 139 / 152 / 162

We hope that you will take advantage of our workshops in the future. Please select those workshops of most interest to you from the enclosed schedule and then register for those sessions by completing and returning the enclosed registration form. 177 / 191 / 204 / 213

Sincerely yours, / Maria Martinez, Director / Public Relations Department / (*Reference initials*) / Enclosures: / 1. Workshop Schedule / 2. Registration Form / PS: If you would like additional copies of either the schedule or the registration form, please call me. 232 / 242 / 258 / 268 (the, a, an), conjunctions (and, but, or), and prepositions that contain three or fewer letters (in, for, to).

"A Job to Do"

First-Class Mail: A New Beginning

7. Capitalize the first word of each item displayed in an enumerated list.

Please give the following data:
a. Name
b. Address
c. Position

8. Do not capitalize (a) the first word of an indirect quotation, (b) the names of school courses that are not proper nouns, or (c) the names of seasons.

Jim said that he will leave in the fall.

I passed English and home economics.

NUMBER EXPRESSION

1. Spell out numbers 1 through 10 and use figures for numbers above 10.

I worked three days.

Only ten people showed up.

Please make 16 copies.

2. If several numbers both below and above 10 are used in the same sentence, use figures for all numbers.

We need 8 typists and 15 file clerks for the project.

3. When two numbers come together in a sentence and one is a compound modifier, spell out the shorter number and express the longer in figures.

four 8-room homes

350 two-page leaflets

4. Spell out fractions that stand alone and express mixed numbers in figures.

two-thirds of the people

5¾ inch, 6¹⁵⁄₁₆ inch

5. Spell out a number at the beginning of a sentence.

Twenty-one people were present.

Two and one-half inches of snow fell.

6. Use commas to separate thousands, millions, and billions.

4,000

13,842,976

7. Do not use commas in serial numbers, house or street numbers, ZIP Codes, telephone numbers, page numbers, and year dates.

No. 8427, page 1403

8. Use figures in house numbers.

2347 Oak Street, 8 Plaza Drive

9. Spell out numbered streets 1 through 10 and use figures for numbered streets above 10. Omit st, d, or th if a word such as East precedes the street number.

405 Third Avenue, 405 14th Street,

405 East 14 Street

10. Do not use a decimal with even amounts of money.

$458 (Not: $458.00)

11. Use the word cents for amounts under $1.

53 cents (Not: $.68 or 68¢)

12. To express even millions or billions of dollars, use the following style.

$15 million, $18.5 billion

13. Use figures to express time, whether with o'clock or with a.m. and p.m. (which should be typed in small letters without spaces).

10 o'clock, 8:30 a.m.

14. Use st, d, or th only if the day precedes the month.

I started on the 14th of January.

But: I started on January 14.

15. Express percentages in figures and spell out the word percent. (Note: The percent sign (%) may be used when typing tables.

7 percent, 18.5 percent

LESSONS 111/112
CORRESPONDENCE PORTFOLIO

Goal: To format correspondence in different styles.

111-A. WARMUP

S 1 She paid Laurie to fix the ivory box that the visitor made.
A 2 A frozen bird squawked vigorously as Joseph coaxed him out.
N 3 Please order 480 lb of #15 grade @ $17.69 before August 23.
     | 1 | 2 | 3 | 4 | 5 | 6 | 7 | 8 | 9 | 10 | 11 | 12

111-B. Take several 1-minute timings on each line. Stress accuracy rather than speed, and resist the temptation to look at your keys.

111-B. NUMBER/SYMBOL PRACTICE

4 Fox & Day ordered 25# of cheese (mellow) @ $3.19 per pound.
5 On 10/28 he (Bart) paid $97, which is 36% less than I paid.
6 An asterisk (*) showed the loss to be $7,946.50 as of 12/8.
7 The large size (30 oz.) cost 87¢ at the A&P on 46th Street.
   | 1 | 2 | 3 | 4 | 5 | 6 | 7 | 8 | 9 | 10 | 11 | 12

111-C. Spacing—double. Take two 5-minute timings. Between them, practice any words with which you had difficulty. Record your score.

111-C. SKILL MEASUREMENT: 5-MINUTE TIMED WRITING

8   Basketball is now played in almost every nation in the   12
world.   The game began when a young instructor was asked to   24
develop a game for students who were tired of routine exer-   36
cising.   He designed a game involving throwing a large ball   48
through a peach basket that had had the bottom removed; the   60
game became so popular it soon spread throughout the world.   72
        The game sells itself once people realize how fast and   84
exciting it is.   Basic rules are simple, and it is a highly   96
visible sport.   With only five players on the team, you can 108
always follow the action.   The size of a basketball is also 120
a big help.   It is the largest ball used in any team sport. 132
        Basketball is also an inexpensive game to play; it re- 144
quires only a ball and some kind of hoop attached to a tree 156
or a pole.   No costly uniforms and equipment are necessary, 168
the playing area can be modified as desired, and many types 180
of games are played with just one or two players.   190
     | 1 | 2 | 3 | 4 | 5 | 6 | 7 | 8 | 9 | 10 | 11 | 12

111/112-D. CORRESPONDENCE PORTFOLIO

Format Letter 41 and Memorandum 14 on Workguide pages 245–247. Format Memorandum 13 and Report 25 on a full sheet of plain paper. Finally, assemble your jobs in a Correspondence Portfolio.

PROCEDURES MANUAL

Paper: plain
Line: 6 inches (60 pica/70 elite)
Spacing: single
Tab: 4, 9
Proofguide: 85–86

NOTE: Enumerations that contain paragraphs with 4 or more lines may also be typed as indented paragraphs. (Indent the number 5 spaces and start all turnover lines at the left margin.)

↓ 7

↓ 3

not divide the last word on a page. Also leave at least two lines of a paragraph at the bottom of a page and carry at least two lines of a paragraph to the top of the following page. ↓ 3

CAPITALIZATION

↓ 2

1. Capitalize every proper noun and every adjective derived from a proper noun. A proper noun is the official name of a particular person, place, or thing. In general, do not capitalize prepositions (like of) or articles (like the).
the General Electric Company
an American citizen
Thanksgiving Day

2. Capitalize common organizational terms such as advertising department and finance committee only when they are the actual names of units within the writer's own organization and are modified by the word the.
The Software Standards Committee met at noon.
But: Our software standards committee met at noon.

3. Capitalize all official titles when they precede personal names. Do not capitalize official titles when the personal name that follows is in apposition and is set off by commas, when the title follows a personal name, or when the title is used in place of a personal name.
President Gloria Wilson
But: our president, Gloria Wilson,
But: Gloria Wilson, president,

4. Capitalize north, south, and so on, only when they designate definite regions or are an integral part of a proper name.
She lives in the West.
Alex moved to South Dakota.
But: They drove east for two miles.

5. Capitalize a noun followed by a number or letter except for the nouns page, paragraph, or size.
Table 4
Policy C305
page 4

6. In titles of published works and in headings, capitalize (a) the first and last words, (b) the first word following a colon or dash, and (c) all other words except articles

Some word processors have a header/footer function that would automatically print the page heading for the procedures manual in 121/122-D and would automatically number the pages for you. If the page number is typed at the bottom of the page, it is called a footer.

(Continued on next page.)

COMPANY NAME

When a company name is included in the closing lines, type it in all-capital letters a double space below the complimentary closing. Then type the writer's identification on the fourth line below the company name.

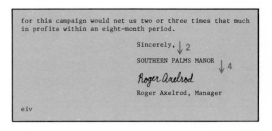

for this campaign would net us two or three times that much in profits within an eight-month period.

Sincerely, ↓2

SOUTHERN PALMS MANOR ↓4

Roger Axelrod

Roger Axelrod, Manager

eiv

LETTER 41
MODIFIED-BLOCK STYLE

Open punctuation
Display paragraph
Company name in closing
Paper: Workguide 245–246
Proofguide: 75–76

(*Current date*) / Mr. Carter L. Frey / Frey Realty Inc. / 19 Bradford Street / Charleston, WV 25301 / Dear Mr. Frey 　19　27

I have now had an opportunity to study carefully the draft of the contract you prepared as the agent for the owners of the property we wish to purchase for the construction of our new West Virginia plant. 　41　55　69

All the sections reflect the conditions we had agreed upon except for Section 3-H on page 3. Please change the wording in that section to read as follows: (*Type the following paragraph in display format.*) 　84　95　102

In the event that the City of Charleston does not rezone the above property to C-4 by December 1 of the year in which the rezoning petition is filed, this contract shall be deemed null and void, and all deposits shall be returned to the William G. Brown Company. 　122　134　149　161

If this change in wording is acceptable to you and to your client, would you please prepare the contract in final form and submit it to us for approval by our board of directors. 　180　193　202

Sincerely yours / WILLIAM G. BROWN COMPANY / Binh G. Nguyen, Controller / (*Reference initials*) 　221　225

Note the various formats for preparing memorandum headings.

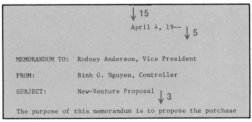

↓13
TO:　Rodney Anderson, Vice President
FROM:　Binh G. Nguyen, Controller
DATE:　April 4, 19--
SUBJECT:　New-Venture Proposal ↓3
The purpose of this memorandum is to propose the purchase or lease of a van to be used as a mobile repair shop for

↓15
April 4, 19-- ↓5
MEMORANDUM TO:　Rodney Anderson, Vice President
FROM:　Binh G. Nguyen, Controller
SUBJECT:　New-Venture Proposal ↓3
The purpose of this memorandum is to propose the purchase

MEMORANDUM 13

Paper: plain
Proofguide: 75–76

An attachment notation is used if the material mentioned is to be physically attached to the memorandum. An enclosure notation is used if the material is enclosed in the same envelope with the memorandum. Type either notation at the left margin a single space below the reference initials.

TO: Janet Claypool, Bethlehem Plant / FROM: Binh G. Nguyen, Controller / DATE: (*Current*) / SUBJECT: Inventory Levels 　19　32

I think that our plan of reducing inventories has outlived its usefulness and that we should increase them by 10 percent, as described in the attached Policy Statement 57. 　49　62　69

I would like to explain my reasons for this decision. The cost of raw materials has increased 13 percent since January. If we had stockpiled inventories, we could have outdistanced all our competitors by offering lower prices. Instead, we have been forced to raise them. 　84　98　112　124

The second reason for my suggestion is the scarcity of raw materials. This situation seems to be getting worse by the hour, and we must buy ahead to assure ourselves of adequate supplies. 　140　154　163

(*Reference initials*) / Attachment 　170

MEMORANDUM 14

Paper: Workguide 247
Proofguide: 77–78

Send the same memorandum, this time on letterhead paper, to Arthur Malandro, Erie Plant.

LESSONS 121/122
PROCEDURES MANUAL

Goals: To increase skills in the use of the shift keys and number keys; to format a procedures manual.

121-A. WARMUP

S 1 My neighbor kept five or six keys for their downtown place.
A 2 The amazing jackals quickly exited from the blue wire cage.
N 3 James moved from 695 East 78 Street to 304 North 12 Avenue.
   | 1 | 2 | 3 | 4 | 5 | 6 | 7 | 8 | 9 | 10 | 11 | 12

121-B. **Type each line 3 times, remembering to keep your eyes on the copy;** *or* **take three 1-minute timings.**

121-B. SHIFT-KEY/NUMBER PRACTICE

4 Mr. Alfred J. Bayless, 1045 Kent Street, Eastview, KY 42732 12
5 Ms. Geneva Jackson, Route 41, Box 389-A, Richland, SC 29675 24
6 Dr. Angela Norris, 98 West Adams, Apt. 12-B, West, IA 52357 36
   | 1 | 2 | 3 | 4 | 5 | 6 | 7 | 8 | 9 | 10 | 11 | 12

121-C. **Spacing—double. Take two 5-minute timings. Between them, practice any words with which you had difficulty. Record your score.**

121-C. SKILL MEASUREMENT: 5-MINUTE TIMED WRITING

7   Many types of office manuals may be used in a business 12
office. For example, all large companies will use a policy 24
manual, which provides a formal record of those policies by 36
which the firm operates. These policies are in the form of 48
rules and regulations the employees are required to follow. 60
         Likewise, an employee manual is often given out to the 72
workers when they start their jobs. This handbook provides 84
such needed data as the working hours, vacations, holidays, 96
and sick leaves, as well as a brief history of the company. 108
         But the manual that you will refer to most often while 120
you are new on the job is the procedures manual. This man- 132
ual gives the firm's guidelines for performing those duties 144
that occur most often, and the steps involved in every task 156
are listed in the most logical order. Each job to be typed 168
is formatted the same way. This not only helps to minimize 180
the amount of time it will take to complete the job but may 192
also enhance the public image of the firm.   200
   | 1 | 2 | 3 | 4 | 5 | 6 | 7 | 8 | 9 | 10 | 11 | 12

121/122-D. PROCEDURES MANUAL

Type Report 30 using single spacing and blocked paragraphs. Leave a 1-inch top margin, number the pages consecu- tively, and pivot the page number from the right margin.

Format the following report single-spaced on a plain sheet of paper. Entitle the report "Correspondence Portfolio" and use your own name in the by-line position.

REPORT 25

Spacing: single
Paragraphs: blocked
Proofguide: 77–78

When reports are single-spaced with blocked paragraphs, double-space between paragraphs.

Side headings are usually typed in all-capital letters, with 2 blank lines above and 1 blank line below.

After you complete this report, assemble the letters and memorandums that you prepared in this unit in the order in which they were typed, place them behind this report, staple the papers in the upper left-hand corner, and turn in your complete project.

The purpose of this report is to discuss various features 31
of formatting correspondence. These features are illustrated 45
in the model letters and memorandums that are a part of this 57
report. 59

Styles 63
Letters are most often typed in modified-block style, 74
with the date and closing lines beginning at the center point 87
and all other lines beginning at the left margin. The para- 99
graphs may either be blocked at the left or indented 5 or more 111
spaces; paragraphs must be indented for short letters that 123
are double-spaced. 127
In the block style, of letter, all lines begin at the left 139
margin. Two other letter styles that are not used as fre- 150
quently are the simplified style and the hanging-indented 162
style. Interoffice memorandums all contain the same informa- 164
tion in the headings, but the position of the information may
vary from firm to firm.

Length 167
Most letters and memorandums contain 225 or fewer words 179
in the body and thus are typed on a line length equal to 50 191
pica spaces or 60 elite spaces. Correspondence that contains 204
more than 225 words uses a longer line length: 60 pica spaces 216
or 70 elite spaces. 220

Features 224
A mailing notation is typed either in all capitals a dou- 236
ble space below the date or in initial capitals on the line 248
below the reference initials or the enclosure notation--if 259
there is one. 262
Attention lines go before the salutation, and subject 274
lines (which use either the word *Subject* or *Re*) go 288
after the salutation. Enumerations begin at the left 299
margin, with each turnover line indented 4 spaces. 309
Display paragraphs are indented 5 spaces from 318
each margin. 321
In the closing lines, a company name is typed 331
in all capitals a double space below the compli- 341
mentary closing, and a postscript notation is typed a 352
double space below the last line of the closing. 362

REPORT 28
MINUTES OF A MEETING

Paper: plain
Line: 6 inches (60 pica/70 elite)
Spacing: single
Tab: 15, center
Proofguide: 83–84

↓13
SOFTWAR~~D~~E STANDARDS COMMITTEE } Double-space   6
Minutes of the Meeting   20
May 19, 19-- ↓3   29

Standards
The Software ∧ Committee held its second meeting   43
of the year on May 19, 19-- ∧ at 10:00 a.m. in   52
the second-floor conference room. Murray   62
Sirkis, chairman, presided.   68

ATTENDANCE   ↓2
Members present were Rhonda Rhodes-Hanna,   81
Put names in   Vera Harper, Elwin Myers, Murray Sirkis, Carl   91
alphabetic order   Lundgren, and Stanford Wayne. *Debra Rojeski*   101
was absent.   105

MINUTES   The minutes of the April 15, 19--, ~~regular~~   115
APPROVED   meeting were read and approved.   125

CHAIR'S   *with*   138
REPORT   Murray Sirkis reported that he had met ∧ the
Vice President for Administration and had re-   149
ceived approval ~~from~~ the committee to visit *for*   159
companies in the Dallas area to observe their   169
automated records-management systems in opera-   179
tion.   182

UNFINISHED   *preliminary*   197
BUSINESS   The ∧ itinerary for company visits was amended
to substitute the Kramer Company for Doctor's   209
Hospital. The itinerary was then unanimously   220
adopted.   223

Lord
Stan ∧ Wayne reported that his sub ∧ committee is   234
working on standardized procedures for evalu-   244
ating and purchasing software for the company, &   254
and will have a report at the next meeting.   264

NEW   It was unanimously agreed to invite a repre-   276
BUSINESS   sentative from the Recordkeepers Group to make   288
a formal presentation of their new Record-   297
master system at the ~~next~~ meeting. Rhonda *June*   307
Rhodes-Hanna will coordinate the visit.   316

ADJOURNMENT   *a.m.*
The meeting was adjourned at 11:30 ∧   328
↓2
Respectfully submitted, ↓4   336

Vera Harper, Secretary   346

REPORT 29
MINUTES IN REPORT FORM

Paper: plain
Line: 70 elite/60 pica
Spacing: double
Tab: center
Proofguide: 83–86

Retype the minutes in report format: Underscore the side headings and type them in capital and lowercase letters. Type the body of the report double-spaced, beginning it at the left margin. Triple-space before and double-space after each side heading.

Type the second-page heading beginning on line 7, single-space, and type a row of underscores. The body of the report continues on the third line below the line of underscores.

Minutes of January 23, 19--   Page 2
_____

and seconded by Elaine Smith, the amendment was defeated. The original

| Line: 60 spaces   Tab: 5 |
| Spacing: single   Drills: 3X |
| Proofguide: 77–79 |
| Workguide: 155–156, 249–257 |
| Tape: 33B |

LESSONS 113/114
BILLING FORMS

Goals: To increase skill in number typing; to format fill-in billing forms.

113-A. WARMUP

S 1 Rush them fifty bushels of corn, but make them sign for it.
A 2 Jo quoted two dozen passages from Val's chemistry textbook.
N 3 Reid was born on July 30, 1958, and died on March 26, 1974.
| 1 | 2 | 3 | 4 | 5 | 6 | 7 | 8 | 9 | 10 | 11 | 12

113-B. Take a 30-second timing on each line, trying to maintain your speed as you move from one line to the next.

113-B. NUMBER PRACTICE

4 1 and 2 and 3 and 4 and 5 and 6 and 7 and 8 and 9 and 10203
5 55 and 56 and 57 and 58 and 59 and 60 and 61 and 62 and 567
6 676 and 677 and 678 and 679 and 680 and 681 and 682 and 683
7 6,028 and 5,684 and 6,091 and 1,456 and 2,687 and 7,153 and
| 1 | 2 | 3 | 4 | 5 | 6 | 7 | 8 | 9 | 10 | 11 | 12

113-C. Spacing—double. Take two 5-minute timings. Between them, practice any words with which you had difficulty. Record your score.

113-C. SKILL MEASUREMENT: 5-MINUTE TIMED WRITING

8 If a large group of people, all of whom spoke a unique 12
language, were suddenly joined together on a desert island, 24
they would still be able to communicate. They could convey 36
their changing moods or needs to one another without words, 48
because people around the world make very similar gestures. 60
For example, the nod of the head up and down, which is 72
always a yes sign, is used everywhere in the world. It has 84
often been observed in people who were born blind and deaf. 96
This finding suggests that nodding may be an innate action. 108
To illustrate that something is acceptable, people may 120
raise their hand and make a circle with the thumb and fore- 132
finger. This signal originates from a similar gesture that 144
people everywhere make when they emphasize some fine point. 156
To say that an idea is precise or exact, you go through the 168
motions of holding something small between the tips of your 180
fingers. Will you make an okay signal after you grade your 192
timed writing? 195
| 1 | 2 | 3 | 4 | 5 | 6 | 7 | 8 | 9 | 10 | 11 | 12

119/120-D. DISPLAY REPORTS

After reading the information in 119-C, page 174, type the following display reports. Pay special attention to the directions in the left panel as you type, but don't lose your place or omit any information.

REPORT 26
MEETING AGENDA

Paper: plain
Line: 6 inches (60 pica/70 elite)
Spacing: single
Tab: 4, center
Top margin: 2 inches
Proofguide: 83–84

WP Word processors have insert (∧) and delete (♂) keys that allow a unit of text (a character, word, paragraph, and so on) to be automatically inserted into or deleted from the existing text.

SOFTWARE STANDARDS COMMITTEE ↓2	6
Meeting agenda ↓2	17
May 19, 19-- ↓3	28
1. Approval of minutes from April 25 Meeting. ↓2	40
2. Report of meeting with vice-president for administration:	55
Murray Sirkis.	59
3. Discussion of preliminary itinerary for Company visits.	73
4. Report from subcommittee on standardizing procedures:	86
Stanford Wayne.	91
5. Vendor presentation of Record Master system. ↓4	103
Murray Sirkis	110
Chairman	114

REPORT 27
ITINERARY

Paper: plain
Line: 6 inches (60 pica/70 elite)
Spacing: single
Tab: 15, center
Top margin: 2 inches
Proofguide: 83–84

NOTE: In order to get the final figure in the 60th space (70th space in elite), pivot (backspace) from the 61st space (71st space in elite).

SOFTWARE STANDARDS COMMITTEE ↓2
Itinerary for company visits ↓2
June 2, 19-- ↓3

9:15–10:15	LONE-STAR INSURANCE COMPANY	Room 44	
	Mr. William Hildebrandt, Manager, will		
	demonstrate their Autoscan system. ↓2		
10:45–11:45	DOCTORS HOSPITAL	Room 48	
	Ms. Alice Bond, records manager, will		
1#	demonstrate their Documentary System.		
12:15– 1:30	LUNCHEON	Bally Room	
2:00– 3:00	DALLAS DEPARTMENT OF REVENUE	Room 46	
	Mr. Peter Polsky, archivist, will dem-		
	onstrate their custom-developed system.		
3:30– 4:30	GREAT WESTERN BANK	Room 49	
	Mrs. Ruth Irving, records manager, will		
	demonstrate their Record-Holder system.		

113/114-D. BILLING FORMS

Study the illustrations on pages 167–168; then type Forms 8–17 on Workguide pages 249–257. Purchasing goods or services is a two-step process in most companies: First, the department needing the goods or services prepares a *purchase requisition* and sends it to the purchasing department. Then the purchasing department prepares an official *purchase order* and sends it to the supplier.

To prepare these fill-in forms:

1. Align the fill-ins in the heading with the guide words.

2. Begin typing the body a double space below the ruled horizontal line. Set tabs as needed.

3. Visually center the information in the number columns.

4. Begin the description 2 spaces after the vertical rule.

5. Single-space each item. Indent turnover lines 3 spaces.

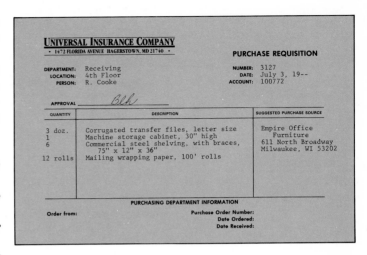

FORMS 8–9*
PURCHASE REQUISITIONS

Forms: Workguide 249
Proofguide: 77

*Forms 1–7 appear in Lessons 1–75.

PURCHASE REQUISITION 3158. On August 3, 19—, R. Marsh, a secretary in the Executive Department on the 17th floor orders these items (charged to Account No. 107826): 48 full-size tubular steel folding chairs, beige; 6 folding tables, 30″ × 72″, black, 3 steel chair caddies, 25-chair capacity; and 1 table caddy, 8-table capacity. She suggests that these items be purchased at Empire Office Furniture, 611 North Broadway, Milwaukee, WI 53202.

PURCHASE REQUISITION 3159. On August 3, 19—, L. Leslie, in the Accounting Department in the basement, requisitions these supplies, which can be purchased at West Coast Distributors, 432 Harbor Drive, Santa Ana, CA 92704: 30 8″ flexible disks, single-side, double density; 6 disk filters, 40 CFM; 8 cartons of line printer paper, green bar, 14⅞″ × 11″; and 20 post binders, 14⅞″ × 11″, for unburst forms, green. Her account number is 100682.

FORMS 10–11
PURCHASE ORDERS

Forms: Workguide 251
Proofguide: 77

PURCHASE ORDER 1062. On August 5, 19—, the Purchasing Department processes Purchase Requisition 3158 and orders the following items from Empire Office Furniture: 48 full-size steel folding chairs, beige (Catalog No. 162-3B) @ $12.95 = $621.60; 6 folding tables, black (No. 152-3B) @ $69.95 = $419.70; 3 steel chair caddies (No. 107-6H) @ $70.95 = $212.85; and 1 table caddy (No. 306-9H) @ $90.95; TOTAL = $1,345.10.

PURCHASE ORDER 1063. On August 5, 19—, the Purchasing Department processes Purchase Requisition 3159 and orders the following items from West Coast Distributors: 3 boxes of 8″ flexible disks, single/double (Catalog No. 886) @ $5.95 = $17.85; 6 disk filters (No. 535) @ $85.00 = $510.00; 8 cartons of line printer paper, green bar (No. 771) @ $51.00 = $408.00; and 2 boxes of post binders, unburst forms, green (No. 102) @ $29.95 = $59.90; TOTAL = $995.75.

<table>
<tr><td>Line: 60 spaces   Tab: 5
Spacing: single   Drills: 3X
Proofguide: 83–86
Workguide: 155–156
Tape: 34B</td></tr>
</table>

LESSONS 119/120

DISPLAY REPORTS

Goal: To use pivoting and leaders when formatting display reports.

119-A. WARMUP

S 1 I may spend eight days down on their turkey farm in August.
A 2 The old, gray boxer won seven unique prizes from lazy Jack.
N 3 Only 5 women and 4 men became 30 years old on May 26, 1978.
   | 1 | 2 | 3 | 4 | 5 | 6 | 7 | 8 | 9 | 10 | 11 | 12

119-B. Read the information in 119-C below; then type the two practice exercises.

WP Many word processors have (a) a right-justified tab feature that automatically pivots the text from the right margin and (b) a leader-tab feature that automatically types rows of periods, stopping at the correct point.

119-C. Spacing—double. Take two 5-minute timings. Between them, practice any words with which you had difficulty. Record your score.

119-B. BACKSPACE PIVOTING

PRACTICE 1. LEADERS

MACHINE ADJUSTMENTS

Chapter	Page
I. Top Margin	1
II. Side Margins	4
III. Bottom Margins	11

PRACTICE 2. SPACED LEADERS

REVISED POLICY MANUAL

Chapter	Page
I	1
II	87
III	123

119-C. SKILL MEASUREMENT: 5-MINUTE TIMED WRITING

4 To pivot a line means to make a line stop at a certain 12
point. For example, in the two practice jobs above, notice 24
that all of the lines end evenly. This gives the typed job 36
quite a professional appearance. To pivot your copy, first 48
move your carrier or carriage one space beyond the point at 60
which you want a line to stop; then backspace once for each 72
letter and space in the line. Now type the line. The last 84
stroke should be at the correct point. 92

Leaders are a row of periods separating items of data. 104
They are used to help guide your eyes horizontally from one 116
column to the next. For example, you often find leaders in 128
tables of contents, as shown above. When the space between 140
the columns is narrow, you may type a solid row of leaders, 152
remembering to leave one space before and one space after a 164
row of periods. However, when the space between columns is 176
wider, you should use spaced leaders, which contain a space 188
between every period. Always align the periods vertically. 200
   | 1 | 2 | 3 | 4 | 5 | 6 | 7 | 8 | 9 | 10 | 11 | 12

The buyer of goods and services prepares the purchase requisition and purchase order. The seller prepares the invoice, credit memorandum (if needed), and statement of account.

An *invoice* (or bill) is an itemized list of the charges for providing the goods or services.

A *credit memorandum* shows the customer the changes in his or her account balance (for example, if the customer returned some of the merchandise).

A *statement of account* is a periodic (usually monthly) summary of all transactions with the customer, showing each charge and credit and the cumulative balance.

FORMS 12–13
INVOICES

Forms: Workguide 253
Proofguide: 77

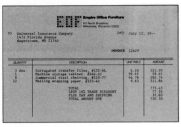

INVOICE 13680. On August 12, Empire Office Furniture invoices Universal Insurance Company, 1472 Florida Avenue, Hagerstown, MD 21740, for its Purchase Order 1062 for the following items: 48 folding chairs, beige, #162-3B, @ $12.95 = $621.60; 6 folding tables, beige, #153-4B, @ $69.95 = $419.70; 3 chair caddies, #107-6H, @ $70.95 = $212.85; and 1 table caddy, #306-9H, @ $90.95; for a total of $1,345.10; less 10% trade discount of $134.51; plus tax and shipping costs of $118.75; total amount due = $1,329.34.

INVOICE 4560. On August 12, West Coast Distributors invoices Universal Insurance Company for its Purchase Order 1063 for the following items, which were shipped by Allied Trucking, Collect: 3 boxes of flexible disks, #886, @ $5.95 = $17.85; 6 disk filters, #535, @ $85.00 = $510.00; 8 cartons of line printer paper, #771, @ $51.00 = $408.00; 2 boxes of post binders, blue, #202, @ $29.95 = $59.90; for a total of $995.75; less 8% trade discount of $79.66; plus tax of $54.97; total amount due = $971.06.

FORMS 14–15
CREDIT MEMORANDUMS

Forms: Workguide 255
Proofguide: 79

CREDIT MEMORANDUM 6612. On October 23, Empire Office Furniture issues a credit memo to Universal to correct an error made on its Invoice 13680. Universal is credited for 6 folding tables, beige (wrong color), #153-4B, @ $69.95 = $419.70; total = $419.70; less a 10% trade discount of $41.97; plus tax of $22.66; for a total amount credited of $400.39.

CREDIT MEMORANDUM 3204. On August 23, West Coast Distributors issues a credit memo to Universal to correct an error made on its Invoice 4560. Universal is credited for 2 boxes of post binders, blue (wrong color), #202, @ $29.95 = $59.90; total = $59.90; less an 8% trade discount of $4.79; plus tax of $3.31; for a total amount credited of $58.42.

FORMS 16–17
STATEMENTS OF ACCOUNT

Forms: Workguide 257
Proofguide: 79

STATEMENT OF ACCOUNT. Empire Office Furniture prepares the monthly summary of its transactions with Universal, dated September 1:
Aug 1: Brought forward; balance of $637.11
Aug 5: Invoice No. 13550 for $457.06 (charge); balance of $1,094.17
Aug 10: Payment on account of $637.11 (credit); balance of $457.06
Aug 12: Invoice No. 13680 for $1,329.34 (charge); balance of $1,786.40
Aug 21: Payment on account of $457.06 (credit); balance of $1,329.34
Aug 28: Invoice No. 13704 for $227.25 (charge); balance of $1,556.59

STATEMENT OF ACCOUNT. West Coast Distributors prepares the monthly summary of its transactions with Universal, dated September 1:
Aug 1: Brought forward; balance of $236.57
Aug 7: Payment on account of $156.95 (credit); balance of $79.62
Aug 12: Invoice 4560 for $971.06 (charge); balance of $1,050.68
Aug 20: Payment on account of $79.62 (credit); balance of $971.06
Aug 23: Credit Memo 3204 for $58.42 (credit); balance of $912.64

LETTER 42
LONG LETTER,
MODIFIED-BLOCK STYLE

Paper: Workguide 267–268
Proofguide: 81–82

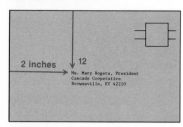

2 inches ↓ 12

Ms. Mary Rogers, President
Cascade Cooperative
Brownsville, KY 42210

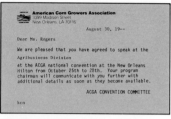

American Corn Growers Association
3399 Madison Street
New Orleans, LA 70116

August 30, 19--

Dear Ms. Rogers

We are pleased that you have agreed to speak at the
Agribusiness Division

at the ACGA national convention at the New Orleans
Hilton from October 25th to 28th. Your program
chairman will communicate with you further with
additional details as soon as they become available.

ACGA CONVENTION COMMITTEE

kcn

CONTENTS
(Check One)

☒ FIRST CLASS
☐ AIRMAIL
☐ THIRD CLASS
(Printed Matter)
☐ BOOKS
☐ LETTER ENCLOSED
☐ SPECIAL FOURTH-
CLASS RATE
(Merchandise)
☐ FILM
☐ LIBRARY RATE

American Corn Growers Association
3399 Madison Street
New Orleans, LA 70116

ACCOUNT NO: 93
FROM: Paul W. Myerson

TO: Ms. Mary Rogers, President
Cascade Cooperative
Brownsville, KY 42210

RETURN POSTAGE GUARANTEED

August 23, 19— / Mr. R. W. White / 4130 Third Avenue, S.W. / Cedar 15
Rapids, IA 52401 / Dear Mr. White: 23

Enclosed are the forms you will need as convention program chair- 37
man for the Agribusiness Division of the American Corn Growers 50
Association. 52

As of this date, we have received applications from only two com- 66
panies that wish to exhibit at your divisional meetings: DeKalb Seed 80
Company (Route 3, DeKalb, IL 60115) and International Farm Equip- 93
ment Inc. (456 Whittier Lane, Clinton, IA 52732). Please send them the 108
enclosed promissory notes to sign in lieu of their making a deposit for 122
their exhibit space. 126

Three people have been asked to speak at your general session 140
meeting: Ms. Mary Rogers (President, Cascade Cooperative, Browns- 153
ville, KY 42210); Professor W. C. Magnusen (College of Agriculture, 166
University of Arizona, Tucson, AZ 85721); and Mr. Thurmond Ashley 180
(Highway 32, Edenton, NC 27932). 186

As soon as you receive confirmations from them, please send them 200
the enclosed postal cards, which give speaker information. When the 214
official convention literature becomes available later this month, you 228
should also send them each a packet (use the enclosed mailing labels). 243
Finally, the three checks are to be presented to the speakers immedi- 256
ately after the conclusion of their program. 265

Sincerely, / Paul W. Myerson / Executive Director / (*Initials*) / Enclosures 285

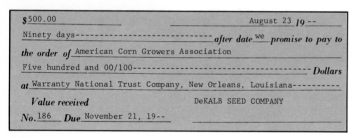

$ 500.00   August 23 19 --

Ninety days----------------------------------*after date* we *promise to pay to*

the order of American Corn Growers Association

Five hundred and 00/100----------------------------- *Dollars*

at Warranty National Trust Company, New Orleans, Louisiana----------

Value received   DeKALB SEED COMPANY

No. 186   *Due* November 21, 19--

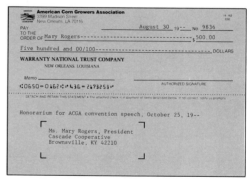

American Corn Growers Association
3399 Madison Street
New Orleans, LA 70116

PAY
TO THE
ORDER OF Mary Rogers   August 30 19-- No. 9836
$500.00

Five hundred and 00/100----------------------------- DOLLARS

WARRANTY NATIONAL TRUST COMPANY
NEW ORLEANS, LOUISIANA

Memo
⑃0650⑃0162⑃436⑃2173253⑃   AUTHORIZED SIGNATURE

DETACH AND RETAIN THIS STATEMENT

Honorarium for ACGA convention speech, October 25, 19--

Ms. Mary Rogers, President
Cascade Cooperative
Brownsville, KY 42210

FORMS 26–27
PROMISSORY NOTES

Forms: Workguide: 269
Proofguide: 81

Prepare 90-day promissory notes (Nos. 186 and 187) for DeKalb Seed Company and International Farm Equipment Inc. in the amount of $500, payable to the American Corn Growers Association at the Warranty National Trust Company of New Orleans, Louisiana. The notes are dated August 23, 19—, and are due November 21, 19—.

FORMS 28–30
POSTAL CARDS

Forms: Workguide 271–272
Proofguide: 81–82

Send form postal cards, dated August 30, 19—, to the three speakers who will be speaking at the Agribusiness Division. Their addresses are given in Letter 42.

FORMS 31–33
MAILING LABELS

Forms: Workguide 269–270
Proofguide: 81

Prepare mailing labels for the three speakers. The packages will be sent by first-class mail from Paul W. Myerson, Account No. 93.

FORMS 34–36
VOUCHER CHECKS

Forms: Workguide 273–274
Proofguide: 83–84

Prepare voucher checks for the three speakers, dated August 30, 19—, for $500 as an honorarium for ACGA convention speech, October 25, 19—.

LESSONS 115/116
PAYROLL FORMS

Goal: To format various payroll forms.

115-A. WARMUP

S 1 Did the eight men buy a bushel of beans for their visitors?
A 2 During the very quick break, we played jazz on the jukebox.
N 3 One individual had 1,032 votes; the others had 947 and 865.
| 1 | 2 | 3 | 4 | 5 | 6 | 7 | 8 | 9 | 10 | 11 | 12

115-B. With a pen and ruler, draw four rectangles about 1 by ½ inch. Then insert the paper into the machine and visually center (both horizontally and vertically) the numbers at the right in the rectangles.

115-B. ALIGNMENT PRACTICE

104.76			
23.58			
86.79			
3,074.72			

115-C. Spacing—double. Take two 5-minute timings. Between them, practice any words with which you had difficulty. Record your score.

115-C. SKILL MEASUREMENT: 5-MINUTE TIMED WRITING

4   At some point in our lives, many of us are required to   12
make a speech, but not many of us do it well; either we get   24
up to talk unprepared, stumbling over words, or we talk too   36
much, boring our audience. We may have a squeaky voice and   48
our choice of words may not be exactly right, but by giving   60
serious thought to planning our speeches, we can do better.   72
        Develop a thorough understanding of the audience so as   84
to talk neither beneath them nor over their heads. If your   96
audience has some common interest that draws them together, 108
then emphasize that interest immediately to gain attention. 120
        Learn what role you are supposed to play; that is, de- 132
termine the objective of the talk. Develop a theme for the 144
speech and begin researching and making notes as necessary. 156
Start by writing key words that will bring entire sentences 168
to mind rather than writing out the complete speech. Prac- 180
tice your speech. And remember: Be sincere, be clear, and 192
then be seated.   195
| 1 | 2 | 3 | 4 | 5 | 6 | 7 | 8 | 9 | 10 | 11 | 12

115/116-D. PAYROLL FORMS

Study the illustrations that follow; then type the payroll forms on Workguide pages 259–265.

LESSONS 117/118
MISCELLANEOUS FORMS

Goal: To format small fill-in forms.

117-A. WARMUP

S 1 Ruth paid them for the eight enamel signs and the six keys.
A 2 Six beef pizzas were driven quickly to Johnny's huge store.
N 3 She read 5 books for a total of 476 pages on June 20, 1983.
| 1 | 2 | 3 | 4 | 5 | 6 | 7 | 8 | 9 | 10 | 11 | 12 |

117-B. First type a list of all the double-letter words in this passage; then take several 1-minute timings on the entire passage.

117-B. PRACTICE: DOUBLE LETTERS

4 Lee and Della are excellent accounting students. They 12
search for all manner of errors in class; in addition, they 24
make good speed in pulling off the answers to difficult and 36
odd problems. They will soon become excellent accountants. 48
| 1 | 2 | 3 | 4 | 5 | 6 | 7 | 8 | 9 | 10 | 11 | 12 |

117-C. Spacing—double. Take two 5-minute timings. Between them, practice any words with which you had difficulty. Record your score.

117-C. SKILL MEASUREMENT: 5-MINUTE TIMED WRITING

5 In former years, farmers harvested their crops of corn 12
manually and picked each ear by hand. Then came mechanical 24
equipment which plucked the ears of corn but still left the 36
kernels on the ears. Today, most large farms use combines, 48
so named because they combine the jobs of plucking the ears 60
of corn as well as stripping the kernels from the corncobs. 72
These giant machines, with cozy air-conditioned cabs, power 84
steering, and a warning light for every possible mechanical 96
hitch, are easier to drive than a car because the cab is so 108
high off the ground and the driver has an excellent view of 120
the path ahead. 123
Because this large equipment is so very expensive, the 135
farmers need to harvest several thousand acres of croplands 147
each year. Often, today's farmer might buy one combine and 159
harvest not only his own crop but those of his neighbors as 171
well. And if all goes well and there are no serious break— 183
downs, the farmers will get all the corn harvested on time. 195
| 1 | 2 | 3 | 4 | 5 | 6 | 7 | 8 | 9 | 10 | 11 | 12 |

117/118-D. MISCELLANEOUS FORMS

The enclosures that accompany Letter 42 provide a good review of typing forms.

FORM 18
PAYROLL REGISTER

Form: Workguide 259
Proofguide: 79

FORMATTING PAYROLL FORMS

1. When typing *between* a series of horizontal lines, center (approximately, by estimating) the typing vertically between the lines.

2. When typing amounts in a column with a vertical rule to separate dollars from cents, adjust the paper so that the decimal (which is *not* typed) would, if typed, fall on the separation rule.

3. When typing *on* a single ruled line,

adjust the paper so that the line is in the underscore position.

4. When typing amounts after a printed $ sign, position the figures so close to the $ sign that no figure could be inserted between the $ and the number.

5. To fill in a blank line so that no one can add information, type hyphens across the empty line.

					PAYROLL REGISTER			Week Ending *February 8, 19—*				
NO.	NAME	INCOME TAX EXEMP- TION	GROSS PAY	DEDUCTIONS								NET PAY
				ITW		FICA		GROUP INSURANCE		MISC.		TOTAL	
1	Albright, Thomas W.	1	248 00	29	80	14	51	2	48	– –	46 79	201 21
2	Chavez, Denise A.	2	382 80	44	30	22	39	3	83	—	70 52	312 28
3	Howell, Robert	4	544 50	62	20	31	85	5	45	37 00	136 50	408 00
4	Manzer, Virginia	2	244 50	15	50	14	30	2	45	6 25	38 50	206 00
5	Morley, Sean A.	3	393 70	38	60	23	03	3	94	—	65 57	328 13
6	Whittaker, Denis	3	495 00	56	90	28	96	4	95	18 75	109 56	385 44
7	Wilmouth, Gregory	1	370 50	58	20	21	67	3	71	—	83 58	286 92
8	Zumach, Cheryl S.	2	425 00	51	60	24	86	4	25	6 25	86 96	338 04

In small companies the permanent payroll register is often a typed copy of a handwritten draft made from employees' time cards and related records.

FORMS 19–20
VOUCHER CHECKS

Forms: Workguide 261
Proofguide: 79

Prepare voucher checks for Denise A. Chavez and Robert Howell above.

A payroll check is usually (as here) a voucher check with a stub that explains the origin of the amount of the check; the information is taken from a payroll register or a similar record.

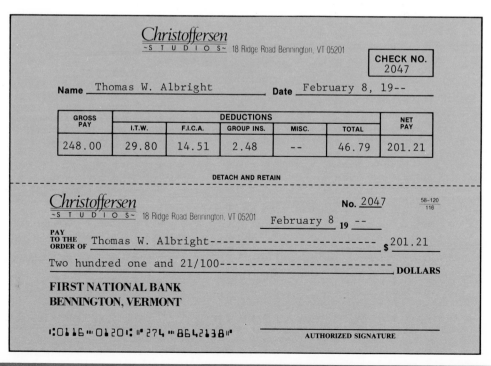

Forms: Workguide 263
Copy 1. Mr. Albright
Copy 2. Ms. Chavez
Proofguide: 79

An earnings record is kept for each employee. It must match corresponding payroll registers and is brought up to date at the end of each payroll period.

EARNINGS RECORD OF _Thomas W. Albright_
NAME

ADDRESS _103 Pin Oak Lane, Apt. 4_ SOCIAL SECURITY NO. _246-72-8480_

Bennington, VT 05201 MARRIED _____ SINGLE _X_

TELEPHONE _603-8925_ NO. INCOME TAX EXEMPTIONS _1_

| DATE PERIOD ENDED | AMOUNT EARNED | DEDUCTIONS | | | | NET PAY |
		I.T.W.	F.I.C.A.	GROUP INS.	MISC.	
1/4	248 00	29 80	14 51	2 48	- -	201 21
1/11	248 00	29 80	14 51	2 48	—	201 21
1/18	248 00	29 80	14 51	2 48	—	201 21
1/25	248 00	29 80	14 51	2 48	—	201 21
2/1	248 00	29 80	14 51	2 48	—	201 21
2/8	248 00	29 80	14 51	2 48	—	201 21

FORM 22. For the same six payroll periods that are in Form 21, prepare the earnings record of Denise A. Chavez, who lives at 109 Elder Drive in Bennington, VT 05201. Her telephone number is 603-3206. Her Social Security number is 236-63-7259. She is married and claims two exemptions. Each line of her record will contain the same information as that on the payroll register on page 170.

Forms: Workguide 265
Copy 1. Mr. Albright
Copy 2. Ms. Chavez
Copy 3. Mr. Howell
Proofguide: 81

The W-2 income tax form is a summary of an employee's earnings record and tax withholdings for the previous calendar year.

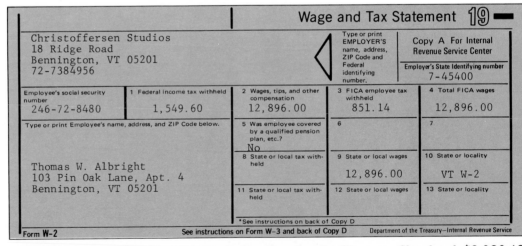

	Wage and Tax Statement 19 ━	
Christoffersen Studios 18 Ridge Road Bennington, VT 05201 72-7384956	Type or print EMPLOYER'S name, address, ZIP Code and Federal identifying number.	Copy A For Internal Revenue Service Center
		Employer's State Identifying number 7-45400

Employee's social security number 246-72-8480	1 Federal income tax withheld 1,549.60	2 Wages, tips, and other compensation 12,896.00	3 FICA employee tax withheld 851.14	4 Total FICA wages 12,896.00
Type or print Employee's name, address, and ZIP Code below.		5 Was employee covered by a qualified pension plan, etc.? No	6	7
Thomas W. Albright 103 Pin Oak Lane, Apt. 4 Bennington, VT 05201		8 State or local tax withheld	9 State or local wages 12,896.00	10 State or locality VT W-2
		11 State or local tax withheld	12 State or local wages	13 State or locality

*See instructions on back of Copy D

Form W-2 See instructions on Form W-3 and back of Copy D Department of the Treasury—Internal Revenue Service

FORM 24. Prepare the W-2 form for Denise A. Chavez. She had $2,303.60 federal income tax withheld; her wages were $19,905.60; her FICA taxes withheld were $1,313.77; her FICA wages (as well as her state wages) were $19,905.60. The other information is the same as that in the W-2 form above.

FORM 25. Prepare the W-2 form for Robert Howell, who lives at 708 Mountain View Lane, Bennington, VT 05201. His Social Security number is 859-54-6430. He had $3,234.40 federal income tax withheld; his wages (in Boxes 2, 4, and 9) were $28,314.00; his FICA taxes withheld were $1,868.77.